Mahāyāna Buddhism

The Library of Religious Beliefs and Practices

Series editors:
John Hinnells and Ninian Smart

This series provides pioneering and scholarly introductions to different religions in a readable form. It is concerned with the beliefs and practices of religions in their social, cultural and historical setting. Authors come from a variety of backgrounds and approach the study of religious beliefs and practices from their different points of view. Some focus mainly on questions of history, teachings, customs and ritual practices. Others consider, within the context of a specific region, the interrelationships between religions; the interaction of religion and the arts; religion and social organisation; the involvement of religion in political affairs; and, for ancient cultures, the interpretation of archaeological evidence. In this way the series brings out the multi-disciplinary nature of the study of religion. It is intended for students of religion, philosophy, social sciences and history, and for the interested lay person.

Other titles in the series include:

Hindus
Their Religious Beliefs and Practices
Julius Lipner

Mahāyāna Buddhism
The Doctrinal Foundations
Paul Williams

Muslims
Their Religious Beliefs and Practices
Andrew Rippin

Religions of Oceania
Tony Swain and Garry Trompf

Theravāda Buddhism
A Social History from Ancient Benares to Modern Colombo
Richard Gombrich

Zoroastrians
Their Religious Beliefs and Practices
Mary Boyce

Mahāyāna Buddhism

The doctrinal foundations

Paul Williams

Lecturer in Indo-Tibetan Studies
University of Bristol

London and New York

First published in 1989
Reprinted 1991, 1993, 1994, 1996, 1998, 1999, 2001 and 2002
by Routledge
11 New Fetter Lane, London EC4P 4EE
29 West 35th Street, New York, NY 10001

Set in Garamond
by Witwell Ltd, Southport
Printed in Great Britain by St Edmundsbury Press Ltd,
Bury St Edmunds, Suffolk

Routledge is an imprint of the Taylor & Francis Group

British Library Cataloguing in Publication Data
A catalogue record for this book is available
from the British Library

Library of Congress Cataloging-in-Publication Data
A catalogue record for this book is available from the Library of Congress

ISBN 0-415-02536-2 (hbk)
ISBN 0-415-02537-0 (pbk)

For all my teachers

Contents

Preface

This book is intended as an introduction to the ideas of Mahāyāna Buddhism, and also to some of the recent scholarly work in the field. It presupposes that the reader already has an idea who the Buddha was, and what his basic teachings were. In writing, I have had in mind university undergraduates and college students, although I hope very much that others will also be able to benefit from what I have written.

In the last twenty-five years there has been an immense increase in research and scholarly publication on all aspects of Mahāyāna Buddhism. The scholarly study of Buddhism is no longer in its infancy, although it seems to me that it has not yet progressed much beyond toddler stage. There are still very many areas in which there is no agreement among scholars, and an understanding of both tenet and meaning in Buddhist thought has not progressed as far as one might like and hope. There are disputes over translation of key terms; the century in which the Buddha died is as yet uncertain. No scholar can claim expertise in all areas of Mahāyāna Buddhism. It may be a platitude, but it is true nevertheless that as research increases so the scholar comes to know more and more about less and less. It is perhaps rash, therefore, to attempt a single volume on Mahāyāna Buddhism. Still, fools rush in! There seems to be a need for such a book, and progress occurs precisely through attempting the rash and modifying the results in the light of informed and constructive criticism. I myself hope to contribute to this criticism in the future. Nevertheless, at the moment, and making allowance for necessary simplification and generalization in a book of this sort, this is how I understand the various aspects of Mahāyāna Buddhism which I have ventured to treat in this volume. A number of interesting areas have had to be omitted, or receive very cursory treatment – most notably, to my mind, Tantric Buddhism and Zen. Tantric Buddhism is complex and obscure, and sufficiently different in origins and sometimes perhaps tenet from other aspects of Mahāyāna Buddhism to require separate treatment. There are many books on Zen. I have given, I believe, the doctrinal basis necessary for understanding Zen as a particular expression of Buddhism. In the last analysis I must bow to restrictions of space.

A number of scholars, as well as my students, have read parts of the manuscript and made helpful comments. It gives me great pleasure to thank Steven Collins, Richard Gombrich, and John Hinnells for their observations and constant encouragement. A special appreciation must go to Lance Cousins, who made extensive and detailed comments on a number of the chapters, drawing in particular on his deep knowledge of the Theravāda tradition. I found these comments very stimulating. I always took them into account, even on the occasions where I ventured to disagree and continue stubbornly on my own way. Thanks also to Sharon and the children for enabling me not just to study the Dharma but also to attempt to put it into practice. And finally, I would like to express my deep respect and appreciation to the Venerable Lharampa Geshe Damchö Yönten for showing me, with patience, gentleness, and sparkling wit, how little I really know!

Unless otherwise noted, all translations are supplied by the author.

CHAPTER ONE

Introduction

BUDDHISM – DOCTRINAL DIVERSITY AND MORAL UNITY

There is a Tibetan saying that just as every valley has its own language so every teacher has his own doctrine. This is an exaggeration on both counts, but it does indicate the diversity to be found within Buddhism and the important role of a teacher in mediating a received tradition and adapting it to the needs, the personal transformation, of the pupil. This diversity prevents, or strongly hinders, generalization about Buddhism as a whole. Nevertheless it is a diversity which Mahāyāna Buddhists have rather gloried in, seen not as a scandal but as something to be proud of, indicating a richness and multifaceted ability to aid the spiritual quest of all sentient, and not just human, beings.

It is important to emphasize this lack of unanimity at the outset. We are dealing with a religion with some two and a half thousand years of doctrinal development in an environment where scholastic precision and subtlety was at a premium. There are no Buddhist popes, no creeds, and, although there were councils in the early years, no attempts to impose uniformity of doctrine over the entire monastic, let alone lay, establishment. Buddhism spread widely across Central, South, South-East, and East Asia. It played an important role in civilizing and spiritualizing nomads and tribesmen, but it also encountered peoples already civilized, most notably those of China, where it interacted with the indigenous civilization, modifying its doctrine and behaviour in the process. Some scholars have seen this looseness and adaptability of its doctrinal base as a major weakness in Buddhism, contributing to its eventual absorption by a triumphant Hinduism in India and tending to syncretism when confronted by indigenous cultures. Etienne Lamotte (1958), in his *Histoire du Bouddhisme indien*, the standard work on pre-Mahāyāna Buddhist history, has bemoaned the way the Buddha left the order without master or hierarchy, and sees this as a major factor contributing to the eventual collapse of unity and the formation of sects. While Buddhists themselves lament the disappearance of the Dharma, the Doctrine, from its homeland, however, they tend to see this as an inevitable occurrence in an epoch when, as the Buddha predicted, spirituality is on the decline. Mahāyānists in particular see adaptation, and perhaps even syncretism, as a virtue in the Dharma, enabling the teachings to be adapted to the needs of hearers, and thereby indicating the wisdom and compassion of the Omniscient Buddha. From earliest times in Buddhism there was a strong tendency to portray the Doctrine not as a series of tenets to be accepted or rejected, but rather as a medicine for curing quite specific spiritual ills. As we shall see, in Mahāyāna Buddhism the emphasis on intention dominated by compassion has often led to a pragmatic view of truth, whereby the value of teachings lies in their spiritual benefit. Great scholar as he was, Monsignor Lamotte's negative assessment of Buddhist diversity reflects perhaps the inherent Western tendency to adopt a view of truth which requires an exclusive correspondence of certain statements with an objective reality. The first lesson for the student of Buddhism is a constant mindfulness and wariness of his or her own cultural presuppositions.

The importance of appreciating doctrinal diversity applies not just to Buddhism as a whole but to the Mahāyāna itself. There is a fallacy which I shall call the 'essentialist fallacy'. This occurs when we take a single name or naming expression and assume that it must refer to one unified phenomenon. This is indeed a fallacy, as a little thought will show, but it is a peculiarly pervasive and deep-rooted fallacy, giving rise to the feeling that because we use the same word so there must be some core, an essence, identified by the relevant definition. Thus the *same thing* is expressed each time the utterance is used. Because the expression 'Mahāyāna' (or its equivalent in the local language) has been used by Buddhists from perhaps as early as the first century BCE to the present day, from India through Tibet, Central Asia, Mongolia, China to Japan, Far East Asia and the Western world, so it must refer to some identifiable characteristics which we can capture in a definition. 'Surely the author must be able to define his subject,' we are thinking, 'otherwise how does he know what he is talking about?'

Buddhist philosophy from its inception embodied a sustained criticism of this essentialist fallacy. As far back as we can trace the teaching of the Buddha we find a penetrating analysis by which unities are dissolved into their constituent parts and true diversity is revealed. An ability to look behind unities and see them as merely words, convenient but misleading linguistic constructs, has always formed an important factor in developing insight meditation, the spiritual cultivation which alone will lead to seeing things the way they really are, the *sine qua non* of *nirvāṇa*, enlightenment, the cessation of moral obscurations and ignorance. The Buddha himself dissolved away the unity we call the human being, or person, into an ever-changing series of physical matter, sensations, conceptions, further mental contents such as volitions and so on, and consciousness. Thus there is dissolved away any real Self, any essence or unchanging referent for the name, the word 'I'. To understand this deeply and directly is to see things the way they really are, the practical repercussion of which is a complete cessation of egoistic grasping, attachment, and self-concern. Thus the forces which lead to continued rebirth come to an end, and thence ends, to quote the scriptures, 'this complete mass of frustration, suffering' (*dukkha*). Such, as far as we can now tell, was the principal religious project of the Buddhist virtuoso monk at the time of the Buddha and in the early centuries after his death. As time went on, so those monks engaged in insight meditation took their analytical knives to the unities into which the human being had been dissolved, extending them to other beings, taking a closer look at the world around them and, as we shall see, in the Mahāyāna one tradition, the Madhyamaka, set out to show that absolutely nothing, no matter how exalted, could resist this penetrating analysis, this analytic dissolution.

So the critique of the essentialist fallacy was always an integral part of Buddhist philosophy and spiritual practice, although not all Buddhist traditions went as far as the Madhyamaka in its application. It would be a good idea, I think, if we too could learn from the Buddhists at this early stage in our study of Mahāyāna to look behind linguistic unities and see them as simply constructions imposed by the use of a single naming expression. Mahāyāna is not, and never was, a single unitary phenomenon. It is not a sect or school, but rather, perhaps a spiritual movement which initially gained its identity not by a definition but by distinguishing itself from alternative spiritual movements or tendencies. Within Mahāyāna as a spiritual movement we find a number of philosophical schools and thinkers who cannot be placed so easily inside identifiable schools. Mahāyāna was, moreover, not a sudden phenomenon with a readily identifiable and unitary geographical or conceptual origin, it was not a planned movement spearheaded by a committee of geniuses (or fanatics). It developed over a number of centuries as an alternative and distinctive view of what Buddhism and the concern of Buddhists should ultimately be, and its growth and development in the early centuries was marked by, and from our perspective is all but identical with, the evolution of a new and distinctive canonical literature, the Mahāyāna *sūtras*. If we look at this enormous literature, claiming a disputed canonical authenticity, what we find in reality is a shifting mass of teachings with little or no central core, many of which are incompatible with each other and within which we can sometimes detect mutual criticism. There is scarcely a unitary phenomenon here, save in its concern to identify itself as Mahāyāna, as a great, superior path to religious fulfilment, distinguished from other religious tendencies which are seen as inferior, small in scope, that is, as Hīnayāna.

What unifying element there is in Buddhism, Mahāyāna and non-Mahāyāna, is provided by the monks and their adherence to the monastic rule. In the centuries after the death of the Buddha there arose a number of schools, often with their own Vinayas, or monastic codes. These do differ, and their differences indicate past schism and form fruitful fields of minute comparison for modern scholars. Theravāda monks in Sri Lanka are forbidden to handle money. In Tibet monks were sometimes quite wealthy. Sri Lankan monks wear orange robes. Tibetan monks wear robes of heavy-duty maroon cloth, while Zen monks in Japan wear black. Heinz Bechert has pointed out that the Buddhist term usually translated as 'schism', *saṃghabheda*, literally 'splitting of the *saṃgha*', the monastic order, 'does not mean a "schism" in the sense known from Christian church history, where it nearly always implies dissensions in the interpretation of dogma. In Buddhist tradition, "splitting of the Sangha" always refers to matters of monastic discipline' (Bechert 1982a: 65). This is important. Schools and traditions might differ on doctrinal matters, and of course doctrinal differences might arise after schism has occurred, which would then differentiate further the groups thus formed. Nevertheless, differences of doctrine as such are a personal matter. In theory a monastery could happily contain monks holding quite different doctrines so long as they *behaved* in the same way – crucially, so long as they adhered to the same monastic code. One of the major non-Mahāyāna philosophical schools, the Sautrāntika, seems to have had no monasteries and no separate monastic code. There were no Sautrāntika monks, although there were monks who held Sautrāntika views.

Although there are a number of different Vinayas the differences, while important to the monks concerned, are nevertheless relatively insignificant. Moreover there is no Mahāyāna Vinaya as such. Mahāyāna Buddhist monks and nuns adhered to Vinaya rules which were formulated by the non-Mahāyāna traditions. In ninth-century Tibet, for example, during the early transmission of Buddhism to Tibet, the king Khri lde gtsug brtan (pronounced: Tri day tsuk ten) decreed that monks should all adhere to the monastic code of a non-Mahāyāna tradition, the Mūlasarvāstivāda. As a result of this only the Mūlasarvāstivāda Vinaya was translated into Tibetan. The only complete Vinaya surviving in the original language is the Pāli Vinaya of the Theravādins, the non-Mahāyāna tradition associated with Sri Lanka and South-East Asia. Other Vinayas are available in Chinese translation, and Chinese monks, almost completely Mahāyāna, generally adhered to the Sarvāstivāda and Dharmaguptaka Vinayas. The Mahāyāna produced texts modifying the spirit of the Vinaya, emphasizing the importance of a compassionate intention even if that might involve breach of the letter of the precept, but there was no significant attempt, indeed no need, to construct and impose a systematic Mahāyāna Vinaya rivalling those of the non-Mahāyāna schools. Mahāyāna was not a rival *school*. It was therefore not, incidentally, a result of schism (*saṃghabheda*). Mahāyāna and non-Mahāyāna monks could live without discord in the same monastery so long as they held the same code, even though we have reason to believe that the non-Mahāyāna monks may have viewed with some scorn the beliefs and private practices of the Mahāyāna monks. It is not surprising that Chinese pilgrims to India, who left detailed accounts of their travels, often found monasteries containing both Mahāyāna and non-Mahāyāna monks. This is not so much Buddhist tolerance as different ideas of what makes for unity and which forms of unity are important. It follows from this that it is possible for members of any Buddhist school, or any Buddhist tradition with a separate Vinaya, also to embrace Mahāyāna. Mahāyāna is held by its adherents to be a higher religious aspiration, the aspiration to full and perfect Buddhahood for the benefit of all sentient beings, and it seems certain that this aspiration as a concern originally took form across the boundaries of a number of pre-Mahāyāna traditions.

That Mahāyāna was embedded in its origins and development in the non-Mahāyāna schools is supported by inscriptional evidence. With the exception of one inscription from perhaps 104 CE (Indian dating is an extremely precarious business), the earliest inscriptions containing recognizably Mahāyāna formulations date from as late as the fourth or fifth centuries CE. Moreover the earlier inscription, on a statue of Buddha Amitābha found recently in North India, while clearly Mahāyāna, also uses formulae characteristic of non-Mahāyāna epigraphy. As far as inscriptional evidence is concerned, Mahāyāna appears to have been an uninfluential minority interest until well into the Common Era, originating firmly within the framework of other monastic traditions thought of as non-Mahāyāna (Schopen 1979; and forthcoming). It seems clear that Mahāyāna was in its origins and for some centuries almost exclusively the concern of a small number of monks and nuns from within the non-Mahāyāna schools, and as such subject to non-Mahāyāna Vinayas. The idea of schism or radical break, and dramatic religious changes, simply fails to cohere with what we now know of Buddhist religious development as it occurred, not in texts but in actual practice.

The moral unity provided by the Vinaya also has its parallel in the code for the laity. There are some differences, but generally speaking all over the Buddhist world someone will be deemed a good Buddhist, a pious lay person, if he or she takes refuge in the Buddha, his Dharma, and the Community (*saṃgha*) – usually or primarily the monastic order, although in Mahāyāna it can also include the wider community of committed practitioners – and tries to adhere firmly and strictly to a renunciation of killing, stealing, sexual immorality, lying, and taking alcohol or mind-disturbing drugs. Thus in spite of the considerable diversity in Buddhism there is a relative unity and stability in the moral code and in particular in the order of monks (and, in Mahāyāna countries, nuns).

THE INDIAN BACKGROUND

Richard Gombrich, in his companion volume to this one on Theravāda Buddhism (1988), has spoken of the councils after the death of the Buddha. Only the first two councils are accepted by all Buddhist traditions, although even here the details of their occurrence differ widely, so much so that it has been suggested that the First Council, supposedly held at Rājagṛha immediately after the death of the Buddha, was in fact not held at all. Traditionally the reason for holding the First Council was a hint of moral laxity (that is, *saṃghabheda*) on the part of at least one monk, combined with the need to establish through recitation the Canon, to be transmitted in immaculate state to succeeding generations. The reciting and authorization by Arhats, those who had achieved sainthood, of the texts of the Canon was the most important event of the First Council as far as Buddhist tradition is concerned. Indeed the event of the council was so important for succeeding generations that there is a Mahāyāna tradition which maintains that contemporaneous with the First Council which established the non-Mahāyāna canon there was another council of Bodhisattvas, those beings who have vowed to become perfect Buddhas, superior to the Arhats. At this contemporaneous council the Bodhisattvas recited and authorized the collection of Mahāyāna *sūtras*. Thus the Mahāyāna *sūtras*, of debated authenticity, were given the prestige of antiquity and a respectable *imprimatur*.

Nevertheless, with all due respect to Buddhist tradition, it really would be quite wrong to think that the Canon was settled and closed at this early date. There are works contained in the Theravāda canon, for example, which date from many years after the death of the Buddha. In time different sects produced different canons, each claiming to be the one recited at the First Council. Perhaps it is not surprising, therefore, that over a period of centuries there arose new texts also claiming to be the authentic word of the Buddha. One school, the Sarvāstivāda (Vaibhāṣika) complained, with reference to the three-fold division of the Canon, 'After the Nirvāṇa of the Buddha in the Sūtras, false Sūtras were placed; in the Vinaya, false Vinayas were placed; in the Abhidharma, false Abhidharmas were placed' (Lamotte 1983–4: 9); and a later text: 'What can we do about it? The Master has entered Nirvāṇa, the Saddharma [True Doctrine] no longer has a leader. Many sects have formed which debase the meaning and the letter as they fancy' (ibid.). Be that as it may, there is significant legendary evidence of dissension even at the time of the First Council. A monk named Purāṇa is reported to have commented that 'the Doctrine and the Discipline have been well chanted by the Elders; nevertheless, I maintain that I retain the Doctrine in my memory just as I heard it, just as I obtained it from the very lips of the Blessed One' (ibid.).

It is important in looking at the development of Buddhism in India between the death of the Buddha and the rise of Mahāyāna to remember that we are dealing with centuries of doctrinal change combined with geographic dispersal over a subcontinent. It is easy to forget that while we can write in a few words about changes which took, say, two hundred years, this is nevertheless to render artificially definite what was in reality a gradual shift not experienced, not lived through, by any one person. A series of gradual, almost imperceptible changes, from the perspective of the scholar who stands back and observes centuries in one glance, can indicate a massive change which no monk or lay person ever actually experienced. As with a painting by Seurat, for example, the picture is only visible from a distance. At the level of the canvas itself there is simply no picture at all. So too with changes in space. Buddhism probably spread within India and into Central Asia along trade routes, particularly the rivers, and the monks, who were by nature semi-nomadic, were natural missionaries. Nevertheless, India is a subcontinent with considerable regional, cultural, and geographic variation. In the days before fast public transport and telephones the spread of ideas was slow and ideas would necessarily undergo changes to suit local conditions and interests. It is quite wrong to think of Buddhism as an identifiable and homogeneous doctrine superimposed upon an identifiable and homogeneous 'Indian people'. Time and space led to change and adaptation (without necessarily changing the fundamental moral and soteriological concerns). Moreover, in India after the time of the Buddha variations of time and space were compounded with considerable forces of political and social change. During the period from the death of the Buddha to an identifiable Mahāyāna we find, first of all, the breakdown of old monarchies and republics under forces of political unity and centralization, issuing in the first great national empire of Ancient India, that of the Mauryas. With unification and strong central control, national and international trade and travel, society and ideologies invariably changed.

Richard Gombrich has devoted some space to discussing the importance for Buddhism of the great Buddhist Mauryan emperor Aśoka (Asoka in Pāli). Aśoka seems to have extended the Buddhist cult of relic worship (contained in *stūpas*, relic mounds), perhaps as a unifying factor for his fundamentally disunited empire, and to have encouraged Buddhist missionary activity. More importantly, he provided a favourable climate for the acceptance of Buddhist ideas, and generated among Buddhist monks certain expectations of patronage and influence on the machinery of political decision making. The historian A. L. Basham has argued convincingly in a recent paper that prior to Aśoka Buddhism was a relatively minor factor in the religious life of India (Basham 1982: 140). Indeed one suspects that the impact of the Buddha in his own day was relatively limited. He is portrayed as an intimate of kings and nobles, and yet the friendship of the Buddha did not prevent the deposing by the crown prince of the king of the imperial power of Magadha, Kingra. Bimbisāra. According to the legends, this ungrateful son, Ajātaśatru, even conspired with the Buddha's erring cousin Devadatta to kill the Buddha himself, a story of jealousy and enmity which suggests that the Buddha's charisma was not such as to banish all evil thoughts from the mind! According to Basham, archaeological evidence for Buddhism between the death of the Buddha and Aśoka is scanty; after the time of Aśoka it is abundant. Unfortunately, however, the sequence of events in these centuries is extremely complex and obscure. It is often held by scholars that the Buddha died sometime around 480 BCE. Aśoka died in about 232 BCE. This date for the death of the Buddha is based on what is known as the 'corrected Ceylonese chronology' (see Bechert 1982b: 30). This chronology has recently been strongly criticized, however, by Heinz Bechert. Bechert favours the shorter 'Indian chronology'. What this amounts to is that in common with certain earlier scholars Bechert advocates placing the death of the Buddha more than a century later than is usual, at roughly 370–368 BCE. There is much to favour this later date, which would give just one hundred years between the death of the Buddha and the reign of Aśoka and would increase the value of the relatively abundant Aśokan and post-Aśokan materials in understanding early Buddhism. Aśoka himself advised monks on their reading matter and, according to tradition, purified the monastic order by expelling erring monks. This established a tradition of close contact between the monastic order and the secular arm which was not always to have favourable results, but for our purposes what is significant is the phenomenon of extensive lay patronage, with monks and laity drawing closer together. As we shall see, while I do not hold to the theory that Mahāyāna Buddhism arose under direct lay influence and involvement, nevertheless it is in the close relationship between monks and lay patrons, and the concern of certain monks with the spiritual welfare of as wide a social group as possible, that we can trace formative elements of the Mahāyāna. It is from the time of Aśoka that the forces issuing in the Mahāyāna, forces for an alternative conception of the spiritual path and goal, begin to crystallize.

Etienne Lamotte has commented that if the Mauryan period, and particularly that of Aśoka, marks the golden age of Buddhism, the two final centuries of the ancient era constitute a period of crisis (Lamotte 1958: 385). The Mauryan empire fell within fifty years of the death of Aśoka, seized by a Brahmin general, Puṣyamitra Śuṅga. There is a tradition that this general inaugurated a persecution of Buddhism, and it is from this time that it is possible to detect the growth of classical devotional Hindu theism. Nevertheless Buddhist missionary activity continued, and the Suṅga period (second century BCE) also inaugurated the flowering of early Buddhist sculpture. With the decline of the Suṅgas, North Indian history is dominated by invasions from Central Asia – by Greeks, Scyths (known as the Sakas in India), and the Yüeh-chih. These Yüeh-chih were known in India as the Kuṣāṇas, and their Indian empire was part of an extensive empire in Central Asia. The Kuṣāṇa king Kaniṣka (*c.* 78 CE, or possibly *c.* 144 CE) is said to have been an important patron of Buddhism, and in terms of patronage the age of invasions was significant for Buddhists, since the foreign invaders were among the most enthusiastic supporters of Buddhism. This was no doubt partly due to the willingness of monks to recognize kings as Bodhisattvas, or Universal Emperors (*cakravartin*), and also the fact that Buddhism is more readily able to accept foreigners than is orthodox Brahminism, for which a foreigner is automatically an outcaste.

There is some reason to think that these foreign invasions may have engendered a sense of crisis in both orthodox and heterodox Indian traditions. According to Basham (1981: 46–7):

> The well known *Mārkaṇḍeya Parvan*, interpolated into the *Mahābhārata*, gives us an idea of how the time appeared to some at least of the orthodox brahmins. In the form of a prophecy, ... we are told of impure barbarians overrunning the holy land of Bhāratavarṣa [India], slaughtering and looting, bringing in their wake insecurity of life and property, banditry, and the disintegration of the norms of family life. In these circumstances the sacrifices and rituals of orthodoxy are neglected, and the only religions to flourish are those of the heretics, who teach people to worship mounds (*eḍūka*) containing dead men's bones – a clear reference to the Buddhists.

Nevertheless, in Buddhism too invasion by foreigners seems to have been associated with legends and traditions of the final disappearance of the Buddha's teaching. There was a widely held view, found in the Canon, that the Buddhist Doctrine would last for only 500 years. It would have lasted for 1,000 years had it not been for the decision to admit women into the order! After these 500 years the Dharma would not completely disappear. There would remain a 'counterfeit Dharma' followed by the Final Dharma. But eventually the Dharma would be completely lost – until its rediscovery by a future Buddha. Not all sources are agreed on the figures of this eventual decline (see Lamotte 1958: 210 ff.). There is not infrequently a tendency to prolong each period. Nevertheless, an awareness of living in the 'last days', an era when things are on the decline, or are not what they were, 'life under siege', is common in early Mahāyāna sources, and it is possible that Mahāyānists saw their own practices and beliefs in this context as bulwarks against moral and spiritual decline.

FACTORS WHICH TENDED TO PROMOTE CHANGE

I have argued that for Buddhism doctrinal differences are not a serious matter in the way they are for religions where salvation is based primarily on faith. Schism, however, is classed as one of the most serious monastic offences, and we have also seen that the appearance after the death of the Buddha of *sūtras* deemed spurious was a source of concern to each school which considered its own canon to be the sole complete and authentic testimony of the teaching of the Master. As far as we can tell from accounts of the last days of the Buddha, the Lord was at some pains to make sure that his followers were united as a monastic body, and also united on, and fully understood, those practices which would lead to *nirvāṇa*, to Arhatship. He nevertheless refused to appoint a successor, but seems to have favoured a relative freedom for each disciple to go his or her way within the framework of Dharma thus laid down. He does not seem to have thought of his teaching as a massive and monolithic dogmatic structure. According to the account of the Buddha's last days contained in the Sarvāstivāda *Mahāparinirvāṇa Sūtra* the Lord gently told his attendant, Ananda

> From the beginning, Ananda, I have taught you that whatever things are delightful and desirable, joyful and pleasing, these are subject to separation and destruction, to disintegration and dissociation. So Ananda, whether now or after my decease, whoever you are, you must remain as islands to yourselves, as defences to yourselves with the *Dharma* as your island and the *Dharma* as your defence, remaining unconcerned with other islands and other defences. If you ask the reason for this, then know that whether now or after my decease, whoever remain an island to themselves, as defences to themselves, with the *Dharma* as their island and the *Dharma* as their defence, not concerning themselves with other islands and other defences, such ones are the foremost of my questing disciples.
>
> (Trans. in Snellgrove 1973: 401–2)

It seems clear to me that the Buddha would not have been averse to later doctrinal innovation if it occurred within the fundamental structure of the Dharma, that is, if it was of spiritual benefit on the path to *nirvāṇa*. Of course, the absence of a hierarchical system with a leader at the top to whom all disputes could be referred tended to promote the possibility of doctrinal divergence as each person or group 'remained an island to itself'. In particular, much of the Master's teaching was unsystematized and perhaps sometimes ambiguous – or, from a point of view favourable to innovation, flexible and open. From the perspective of later doctrinal concerns it was not always clear whether the Buddha had been talking in colloquial terms or within the framework of literal philosophical truth. For example, the school (or schools) known as the Vātsīputrīya-Sammatīya taught the existence of a *pudgala*, a person, which appeared to its opponents to play a number of the roles given to a Soul or Self. In defence of this teaching the Vāstīputrīya-Sammatīya quoted a *sūtra* in which the Buddha maintained that the five psycho-physical constituents (*skandhas*) which make up the human being are a burden, and the bearing (or 'bearer'; see Collins 1982: 164–5) of the burden is the person (*pudgala*) with this or that name. The person must therefore be an entity in addition to the psycho-physical constituents which other Buddhists accepted as the true analysis of the human being. Opponents objected that the Buddha was not speaking here literally but loosely. The so-called 'person' is not an ultimate reality but just a verbal object, a concept superimposed upon the psycho-physical constituents in the same way that the concept 'table' is superimposed upon the table's parts. The need to elucidate and systematize, to list the phenomena which do indeed really exist and distinguish them from the conceptual constructions of our everyday life, eventually issued among the pre-Mahāyāna schools in the great lists of the Abhidharma. It is important to remember, however, that all the schools of pre-Mahāyāna Buddhism considered their teachings and traditions to be perfectly orthodox. They each tended to highlight passages of their canon which supported their own views while ignoring or reinterpreting passages which might be taken to support other schools.

Let us note now some institutional factors in early Buddhism, in addition to the absence of one supreme head, which may have promoted the development of rival traditions of interpretation and practice, and eventually rival schools (see here, in particular, Dutt 1970: 42–50).

First, there was the division of monks into bodies, each concerned with the recitation and preservation of particular sections of the scriptures. We know that from an early time there were specialists in the *sūtras*, and specialists in the Vinaya. With time the *sūtra* specialists, for example, also tended to divide into groups specializing in particular sections of the *sūtra* canon. With the rise of the Abhidharma as a systematic analysis of the totality into its ultimate constituents there undoubtedly followed groups of monks specializing in philosophical analysis, fragmentation of the everyday world into its ultimately or finally real elements. It is quite possible that the Sautrāntika tradition, which rejected the Abhidharma and subjected it to trenchant criticism, favouring the *sūtras*, was composed of *sūtra* specialists and its opposition to the Abhidharma reflected such opposition between rival groups of scriptural recitation and exegesis.

Second, there was the grouping of monks around noted teachers, who were themselves specialists in particular branches of the teaching. The names of a number of the early schools appear to be derivatives from personal names – Dharmaguptakas from a teacher named Dharmagupta, the Vātsīputrīyas from Vātsīputra, and so on. We hear in the Canon of personal disciples of the Buddha who were noted for their attainments in particular branches of the Doctrine. Thus we find reference to Śāriputra as the great philosophical analyst, and Upāli as a specialist in the Vinaya.

Third, we should note that initially there appears to have been a relative flexibility in the rules of discipline. According to Nalinaksha Dutt, the monastic rules were defined but not codified at the time of the Buddha, and there is evidence that the Buddha himself was willing to adapt the rules to fit in with particular personal or group circumstances. Adaptation was possible to suit particular local conditions and it appears that a well-controlled monk could be permitted greater freedom than his ill-disciplined brethren. We know also that the Buddha permitted greater austerity in some cases, but resisted attempts to persuade him to require austerities of all monks.

Finally, it has been suggested that the Buddha's preference for preserving and teaching the Dharma in local languages rather than the pan-Indian Sanskrit may have led to misunderstanding and differences between traditions. In some cases, such undoubtedly happened, but it is doubtful to my mind whether this could have been a major factor in promoting the growth of different schools.

ABHIDHARMA

Perhaps the most interesting doctrinal developments among the early non-Mahāyāna schools were the growth of the Abhidharma on the one hand and the 'supramundane' (*lokottaravāda*) teachings on the other.

Early Mahāyāna *sūtras*, particularly those of the *Perfection of Wisdom* (*Prajñāpāramitā*), show in general a certain animosity towards the Abhidharma, while it is possible to detect in the Mahāsaṃghika supramundane doctrines the crystallization of ideas which, in a developed and systematized form, are often thought of as characteristically Mahāyāna. In spite of this, however, it would be wrong, I think, to portray the Mahāyāna as originating or occurring exclusively, or even mainly, within the Mahāsaṃghika group of schools, perhaps in some sort of rivalry with those schools associated with the Abhidharma. We have already seen that Mahāyāna did not originate on a sectarian basis, and we have no historical evidence to identify the Mahāyāna as a whole with one particular group of pre-Mahāyāna schools.

The Abhidharma itself is not a school but a body of literature. Not all the non-Mahāyāna schools had Abhidharmas, but those that did, most notably the Sarvāstivāda (Vaibhāṣika) and the Theravāda, gave their Abhidharmas canonical status alongside the *sūtras* and the Vinaya, the three together forming the Tripiṭaka, the Three Baskets, the Buddhist canonical corpus. This Abhidharma literature seems to have grown out of lists of technical concepts which were drawn up very early in the history of Buddhism, perhaps as mnemonic devices which provided the framework for teaching, systematic exegesis through discussion, and also equally systematic meditation. The Abhidharmas we have now appear to be a product of the period between Aśoka (third century BCE) and Kaniṣka (first or second century CE), although the taxonomic tendencies of the Abhidharma can be found in the *sūtras* and were common to pre-Mahāyāna Buddhism.

All Buddhist traditions accepted an analysis of the human being into the five psycho-physical constituents. As we have seen, there is no independent being, he or she is really made up out of an ever-changing series of physical matter, sensations, conceptions, volitions and so on, and consciousness. Implicit in this very old analysis, therefore, is a distinction between what appears to be true and what is really the case. Eventually, in the Abhidharma traditions, this issues in a distinction between conventional (*saṃvṛti*) and ultimate (*paramārtha*) truth (or reality – *satya*). The conventional reality is the world in which we live. Ultimate realities are the elements which *really* compose the world of our experience. The main concern of the Abhidharma, at least as it was systematized by Buddhist scholars, is the analysis of the totality, of all that is, into the building blocks which, through different combinations, we construct into our lived world. The name given to these building blocks, which are said to be ultimate realities in the sense that they cannot be reduced further to other constituents, is *dharmas* (*dhammas* in Pāli; not to be confused with Dharma, meaning the Doctrine). In the Theravāda there are eighty-two such constituents. Eighty-one are said to be conditioned, and one, *nirvāṇa* (Pāli: *nibbāna*), is unconditioned. In the Sarvāstivāda there are seventy-five, seventy-two conditioned and three unconditioned. Conditioned constituents arise and cease in a continuous stream. They are the results of causes, exist for a very short time indeed, and yet, unlike the objects of our everyday world, which have merely conventional or conceptual existence, all *dharmas* in some fundamental sense really exist. According to the Sarvāstivāda they are substances (*dravyas*); each one inherently and uniquely exists; it alone, in the technical terminology of the Abhidharma, 'bears its own essence' (*sasvabhāva*: see Williams 1981).[1]

The Theravāda Abhidhamma divides its list of constituents into:

(i) Physical constituents – twenty-eight *dhammas*, including the four gross elements of earth, water, fire, and air, and agility, elasticity, malleability, material food and so on;

(ii) Mental constituents – fifty-two *dhammas*, twenty-five morally good, including non-greed, non-hatred, and non-delusion (the opposites of the three root poisons), faith, mindfulness, compassion; fourteen morally bad, including wrong views; and thirteen morally neutral, which gain moral colouring depending on the *dhammas* to which they are conjoined. The first seven of these thirteen are common to all mental acts: contact, sensation, conception (these are the second and third *skandhas* (*khandha* in Pāli)), will or volition, mental life, concentration, and attention.

(iii) Consciousness, the last conditioned constituent, which like all other conditioned *dhammas* arises, remains for a split second, and ceases, to be replaced by another constituent of the same type.

A monk developing insight meditation, wishing to see things the way they really are, develops the ability constantly to analyse his experiences into their constituents. He is said to dwell peacefully, observing the rising and falling of *dharmas*, thereby dissolving the objects of his attachment and cutting at the root of desire. Thus by learning to see things the way they really are he brings his ignorance to an end. With the cessation of ignorance, craving ceases and the meditator attains *nirvāṇa* and becomes a saint, an Arhat.

Not all of the early non-Mahāyāna schools accepted the Abhidharma analysis of the world. The Sautrāntikas appear to have rejected the Abhidharma Piṭaka *in toto*. It is sometimes thought that one of the characteristics of early Mahāyāna was a teaching of the emptiness of *dharmas* (*dharmaśūnyatā*) – a teaching that these constituents, too, lack inherent existence, are not ultimate realities, in the same way as our everyday world is not an ultimate reality for the Abhidharma. As a characteristic of early Mahāyāna this is false. Such a teaching can be found already in a canonical text of the Pūrvaśailas, one of the non-Mahāyāna subschools of the Mahāsaṃghikas. There is a *sūtra* called the *Lokānuvartana Sūtra*, described in the Chinese and Tibetan canons as a Mahāyāna *sūtra*. However, this very same *sūtra* seems to be quoted by the Madhyamaka commentator Candrakīrti (seventh century CE) as a canonical *sūtra* of the Pūrvaśailas (see Harrison 1982: 225–7). The *Lokānuvartana Sūtra* teaches both the doctrine of a supramundane Buddha and the absence of ultimate, inherent existence in all things, including *dharmas*. Thus not only is the emptiness of *dharmas* found in a non-Mahāyāna text (the same is also found in the non-Mahāyāna *Satyasiddhi Śāstra* of Harivarman), but this *sūtra* was later accepted into the Mahāyāna. This was certainly not the only time that non-Mahāyāna *sūtras* were subsequently to be taken as Mahāyāna.[2]

MAHĀSAMGHIKAS AND THE LOKOTTARAVĀDA

According to the Ceylonese chronology, about a century or so after the death of the Buddha a Second Council took place at Vaiśalī which, if we can follow Theravāda accounts, led to a schism between the Sthaviravādins, using this term to include the sects which later rose from them, such as the Sarvāstivāda, and the Mahāsaṃghikas. The expression 'Sthaviravāda' means Doctrine of the Elders, and it is this tradition with which the Theravāda identifies itself. For Heinz Bechert's shorter chronology the Vaiśalī council should occur during the reign of Aśoka, were he to accept the traditional view of one hundred years between the death of the Buddha and the calling of the council. However, Bechert calculates the Vaiśalī council at forty to fifty years after the death of the Buddha, which would place it perhaps at 330 or 320 BCE.

The Theravāda tradition leads us to believe that the schism occurred over a number of points of discipline in which the monks who were later to become the Mahāsaṃghikas were relaxing the Vinaya rules. They were accused of handling money donated by laymen, for example, which may reflect an adaptation of the Vinaya to the growing town-based mercantile economy of North India.[3] A council was convened, the 'lax' monks were defeated but they remained stubborn and sometime later convened their own council, breaking away from the orthodox body. They are said to have then altered the Canon and added new scriptures. This explanation is clearly one of schism, of *saṃghabheda*, but it does not fit with another well-attested tradition found in non-Theravāda sources which attributes the breach to the so-called 'Five Points of Mahādeva'. According to this tradition a council was held some decades after the Vaiśalī council, this time at Pāṭaliputra. The five points were debated at the council and were accepted by the majority, hence the name 'Mahāsaṃghikas', those who adhere to the Great Saṃgha, that is, the majority. The monks who refused to accept the majority decision subsequently named themselves Sthaviravādins. Since the five points of Mahādeva concern doctrinal matters there was not at this time technically a schism. Nevertheless, it is clear that where doctrines differ so differences in monastic practice may well follow, and such seems eventually to have happened in this case.

Mahādeva's five points mainly concern the status of the Arhat, the enlightened saint. Mahādeva is said to have taught:

(i) An Arhat is able to be seduced by another. This appears to mean that an Arhat was capable of having erotic dreams.
(ii) An Arhat can be subject to ignorance. This probably does not mean religious ignorance, but rather an Arhat may be ignorant of a person's name, and so on
(iii) An Arhat may have doubt.
(iv) An Arhat may be instructed by another person.
(v) And finally, entry into the Buddhist Way may be accompanied by a sound, such as 'Oh, sorrow'. It is difficult to know now what this last point meant (see Lamotte 1958: 300 ff.).

According to Paramārtha (sixth century CE), who wrote a treatise on the schools, the 'heresy' of Mahādeva lay in wishing to incorporate into the Canon the Mahāyāna *sūtras*, and in attributing to the Arhats imperfections. We know that Mahāsaṃghika *sūtras* were incorporated into the Mahāyāna canon. It is possible that the reverse occurred. At any rate, what is interesting is the way in which Paramārtha connects Mahādeva, and the tendencies contained in Mahādeva's teachings, with support for, and possibly the creation of, Mahāyāna literature. The five points seem to contain an implicit lowering of the status of the Arhat, although A. K. Warder (1970: 216) has pointed out that the views of Mahādeva seem little different from the position on the Arhat found in the Pāli canon. It is possible that in certain circles the Arhat had been exalted in such a way as to abstract him from all possibility of occurrence. Be that as it may, after the breach between the two groups of Sthaviras and Mahāsaṃghikas they gradually began to differ on a number of other matters as well. Among the most important and far-reaching of these differences that arose was the Mahāsaṃghika teaching of the 'supramundane Buddha', an exaltation of the Buddha corresponding with the lowering of the status of the Arhat.

As far as we can tell, in all Buddhist traditions there was a tendency to see the Buddha as more than just a purely human being. He was said to have various miraculous powers and the thirty-two major and eighty minor marks of a superman. At one important point the Buddha denied that he was a man or a god. Rather, he was a Buddha, a fully enlightened one. His skin is described in the *Mahāparinibbāna Sutta*, the Pāli account of the Buddha's last days, as taking on a golden and shining appearance, and in the same text the Buddha explains to Ananda that a Buddha can, if he so wishes, live for an aeon.

We know of the supramundane teachings (*lokottaravāda*) of the Mahāsaṃghikas primarily from a work known as the *Mahāvastu*, which describes itself in the preface as a Vinaya text of the Lokottara branch of the Mahāsaṃghikas. Although there was a subschool of the Mahāsaṃghikas known as the Lokottaravāda, nevertheless some form of supramundane teaching appears to have been common to all Mahāsaṃghika schools, since it is found strongly stated in the Pūrvaśaila *Lokānuvartana Sūtra* as well, and Paul Harrison (1982: 224) has argued that this *sūtra* may indeed be one of the sources for the *Mahāvastu*. It is not clear how early the supramundane doctrine developed, however. It seems probable that, as the Theravāda *Kathāvatthu* suggests, the supramundane teaching was based on a statement in the Canon that although the Buddha was born in the world, and so on, he was not tainted by it. From this it was concluded that the Buddha during his life was in reality completely devoid of the impurities of the mundane world – he was not worldly, but was rather extraordinary, supramundane. During the centuries after the death of the Buddha we find developed an extensive and popular literature consisting of tales recounting the many virtuous deeds of the Buddha in his previous lives as a Bodhisattva, one on the path to Buddhahood. In Buddhist theory the result of good deeds is merit, and since the Buddha had developed such immense stores of merit from his previous lives, so there grew up the idea that the Buddha's birth and life could not really be like that of ordinary humanity. Nevertheless, the Buddha was originally a human being. This is not a case of deification, for gods in Buddhism are as much subject to death, suffering, and rebirth as other unenlightened sentient beings.

So the texts of the supramundane tradition describe the Buddha's birth in a wholly miraculous manner. He is conceived without intercourse, and his birth involves no pain. He emerges from his mother's right side without piercing her body. He is not an illusory being himself, however, but rather all his activities which appear ordinary are illusory. He merely appears to wash, eat, sit in the shade, take medicine, and so on out of conformity with the ways of the world. To quote the *Mahāvastu*:

> The conduct of the Lord is supramundane, his root of goodness is supramundane,
> The walking, standing, sitting and lying down of the Sage are supramundane.
> The Sage's wearing of robes is supramundane; there is no doubt about this.
> The Sugata's eating of food is likewise purely supramundane.
> The Fully Awakened Ones do indeed bathe, but no dirt is seen on them;
> Their forms resemble golden images; this is in conformity with the world.
> They make use of medicine, yet there is no sickness in them.
> The fruit (of the act of giving the medicine) is to accrue to the givers.
> This is in conformity with the world.
> Although able to suppress *karma*, the Victors make a show of *karma*.
> They conceal their sovereign power; this is in conformity with the world.
> They make a show of old age, but there is no old age for them;
> The Victors are endowed with a host of good qualities; this is in conformity with the world.
>
> (Translated in Harrison 1982: 216–18; some material omitted.)

And so on and so on. The Buddha is said to be omniscient, never to sleep but in reality always to be in meditation. Such an exaltation of the Buddha among the Mahāsaṃghikas is one with the denigration (by comparison) of the Arhat. We are not very far here from the Mahāyāna teaching that the Buddha's death was also a mere appearance; in reality he remains out of his compassion, helping suffering humanity. Man's religious goal should be not to become an Arhat but to take the Bodhisattva vows, embarking on the long path to a supreme, totally superior Buddhahood.

THE ORIGINS OF THE MAHĀYĀNA, AND THE LAITY

There is a theory that the origins of the Mahāyāna can be traced to the activities of the laity, a lay revolt against the arrogance and pretensions of the monks. This view was held strongly by the late Etienne Lamotte. In one of his last articles he summed up his views on the origins of the Mahāyāna as follows:

> During the first five centuries of its history, Buddhism progressed considerably; nevertheless, it had to face both external and internal difficulties because of the divergent tendencies which formed at the heart of the community. Some monks questioned the authenticity of the early scriptures and claimed to add new texts to them; others leaned towards a more lax interpretation of the rules governing their life; the scholastic treatises, continuously increasing in number, became more and more discrepant; finally, and above all, the laity, considering the monks' privileges to be excessive, tried to win equal religious rights for themselves.
>
> (Bechert and Gombrich 1984: 90)

The view of the lay origins of the Mahāyāna, that lay people were instrumental in the formation of the Mahāyāna, is also widely held as established fact among contemporary Japanese scholars where, it should be said, their emphasis on lay orders of Bodhisattvas engaged in altruistic activities reflects rather closely the situation, interests, and concerns of much of contemporary Japanese Buddhism. An important and widely accepted case for considerable lay influence on the rise of the Mahāyāna was published in an article by Akira Hirakawa (1963). Hirakawa's main point appears to be that the Mahāyāna grew up among an identifiable order of Bodhisattvas, composed of lay and renunciate members of equal status, centred on the *stūpas*, relic mounds, and relic shrine worship. The *stūpas* were administered by the laity, and as relic mounds were eventually identified with the Buddha himself. Hence the growth of Buddha cults and the importance of the Buddha in the Mahāyāna. According to Hirakawa these *stūpas* were quite separate from, and in certain rivalry with, the monastic orders of the monks. Thus we find the development of an alternative religious tradition centred on Bodhisattvas and Buddhas, showing some hostility to the conduct and aspirations of the monasteries, particularly in respect to the definitely inferior status given to the laity in monastic Buddhism (on the role of the laity in Theravāda, see Gombrich 1988: 118 ff.).

It is impossible to do justice to Hirakawa's long article here. Certainly, many early Mahāyāna *sūtras* show a clear awareness of the superiority of Bodhisattvas and the Bodhisattva path, together with a disparaging attitude to the Hearers (*śrāvakas*), those monks who were following the old path to Arhatship. Moreover, a number of the early Mahāyāna *sūtras* stress the importance of the laity. In the *Vimalakīrtinirdeśa Sūtra* the layman Vimalakīrti is portrayed as an advanced Bodhisattva with a developed understanding of philosophy, admonishing and correcting a number of the Buddha's leading monastic followers. In another *sūtra*, the *Bhadramāyākāravyākaraṇa Sūtra*, it is said that Bodhisattvas are the true renunciates, not those (like monks) who merely renounce the household life; while yet another *sūtra* teaches that Bodhisattvas of correct understanding have no need to renounce the world and become monks. Corresponding to this is the role of interlocutors of the Buddha given to wise lay women and girls, who are finally predicted to obtain perfect Buddhahood in the future. Particularly interesting in this context is the *Aśokadattāvyākaraṇa Sūtra*. Aśokadattā was a 12-year-old princess who refused to stand and make obeisance to the monks when they entered the palace. The monks were followers of an Inferior Vehicle, a Hīnayāna: 'Your Majesty, why should one who follows the path leading to supreme enlightenment, who is like the lion, the king of beasts, salute those who follow the Hīnayāna, who are like jackals?' (trans. in Chang 1983: 116). She explained the supremacy of the Bodhisattvas. Even a novice Bodhisattva exceeds all those on the Arhat path. To mock the monastic teaching of the spiritual inferiority of women, a low, dualistic way of thinking, Aśokadattā turns herself into a man, and then back into a girl again. It is all relative, all in the mind! Her female form, we are told, was taken out of compassion to win (feminists?) over to the Dharma. Of course, to the traditional pre-Mahāyāna monastic way of thinking nothing could be worse, nothing more absurd, than religious instruction of monks by a 12-year-old lay girl!

In spite of these texts, however, and many like them, I remain extremely sceptical of the thesis of the lay origins of the Mahāyāna. Hirakawa's paper relies on too many suppositions to be fully convincing, and Gregory Schopen has argued against Hirakawa that a number of important early Mahāyāna *sūtras* show a distinctly hostile attitude to the *stūpa* cult. Schopen's view, convincingly argued, is that reference to worshipping the texts themselves, an extremely reverential attitude to the Mahāyāna *sūtras*, indicates that early Mahāyāna was centred on a number of book cults, groups of followers who studied and worshipped particular *sūtras*. In the *sūtras* themselves worshipping the text is specifically contrasted with the *stūpa* cult, to the detriment of the latter. Geographically, Schopen argues, early Mahāyāna gravitated towards the place where the book was set up, worshipped with 'incense, flags and bells' – the very same forms of worship usually given to *stūpas*.[4] Many Mahāyāna *sūtras* conclude with the great, immense merits to be obtained from studying, memorizing, or just worshipping even one verse of the *sūtra*. They likewise condemn to hell those who would denigrate the *sūtra*, or the person who preaches the text (*dharmabhāṇaka*), a figure who seems to have played an important institutional role in the origins and spread of the early Mahāyāna. Schopen concludes that,

> since each text placed itself at the centre of its own cult, early Mahāyāna (from a sociological point of view), rather than being an identifiable single group, was in the beginning a loose federation of a number of distinct though related cults, all of the same pattern, but each associated with its specific text.
>
> (Schopen 1975: 181)

It seems unlikely to me that the Mahāyāna was the result of organized and influential activity by lay people. Gregory Schopen's further work on the evidence for Mahāyāna in Indian inscriptions has shown that by far the majority of those associated with making donations and other religious activity towards *stūpas* were monks and nuns, and a large number of these were also learned members of the monastic community rather than their exclusively simpler brethren. Moreover in all inscriptions which are recognizably Mahāyāna in type, over 70 per cent of the donors are monks or nuns, mainly monks. Laymen are very much in the minority (Schopen 1985: 25–6; cf. 1979). Epigraphic evidence shows conclusively that by far the majority of those associated with donor activity from the earliest available inscriptions onwards were monks and nuns, and the proportion of monastic donors increased as time passed. These monks and nuns were not ignorant but often doctrinal specialists. Inscriptional evidence also shows that the cult of images was primarily a monastic concern, and that it was moreover a monastically initiated cult (Schopen 1985: 28–30). Japanese scholars and Etienne Lamote notwithstanding, this should not come as a great surprise. In India generally, religious change was initiated by those who had the time, which is to say, Brahmins and renunciates. We have absolutely no historical evidence of lay people constructing or preaching new *sūtras*, and while we have the names of a number of monks, such as Nāgārjuna (probably second century CE), who advocated the early Mahāyāna – indeed, according to one source Nāgārjuna was accused of actually composing one of the Mahāyāna *sūtras* – nevertheless apart from the mythical lay heroes and heroines of the *sūtras* we have no names of lay people who contributed to the doctrinal origins of the Mahāyāna. The Mahāyāna *sūtras* were clearly the products of monks, albeit monks whose vision of the Dharma embraced the aspirations of the laity, and who used lay figures in the *sūtras* to embody a critique of other monks seen as elitist or perhaps ultra-conservative. I am influenced in this view by a comment made in a different context by J. A. B. van Buitenen. Commenting on the theory that there was a tradition of *kṣatriya* (warrior) philosophy in Ancient India, he observes:

> I do not wish to raise once more the specter of '*kṣatriya* philosophers,' ... for I think it is without substance. What such a *kṣatriya* alignment means is not that there existed independently a strain of *kṣatriya* thought zealously and secretively concealed from brahmins who were hermetically sealed off from it; but that new thought might identify itself as 'new' by calling itself non-brahmin, i.e., not in line with those hidebound orthodox Vedic specialists who could think only old thoughts.
>
> (Buitenen 1981: 12)

It seems to me that there were equally no lay doctrinal traditions in Buddhism at the roots of Mahāyāna. Rather, to adapt the quotation, 'new thought might identify itself as "new" by calling itself non-monastic, i.e. not in line with those hidebound orthodox monks who could think only old thoughts'. My view is supported, I think, by the *Ajitasenavyākaraṇanirdeśa Sūtra*, which we will examine in the next section, and also by a very interesting and early Mahāyāna *sūtra* with the wonderful title of the *Pratyutpannabuddhasaṃmukhāvasthitasamādhi Sūtra* – or *Pratyutpanna Sūtra* for short! This *sūtra* was delivered by the Buddha to a group of Bodhisattvas and monks, but the most important group in the audience was said to be 500 householder Bodhisattvas, led by a certain Bhadrapāla to whom the body of the *sūtra* is addressed. The text describes how, after circulating for a short period, it will be hidden in a cave and rediscovered in the future, during the period of the decay of the Dharma (see Harrison

1978: 57; trans. in Harrison 1979: 86 ff.). The 500 lay Bodhisattvas ask that it should be their future incarnations which will rediscover and propagate the text. Thus far, the *sūtra* appears to teach the lay origins of the work. However, it does not say that the 500 Bodhisattvas will be laymen in their future incarnations. Rather the *sūtra* explains in detail how, in future times, very few people will believe in this *sūtra*. There will be monks who will revile the *sūtra* and laugh at it, saying: 'Such sūtras as these they made themselves, they are poetic inventions; they were not spoken by the Buddha, nor were they authorised ... by the Buddha' (trans. in Harrison 1979: 50). And they will ridicule those few monks who accept the *sūtra*:

> These bhikṣus [monks] are arrogant. ... These bhikṣus are garrulous. ... It is a great wonder indeed that they should give the name of 'sūtra' to that which was not spoken by the Buddha, that which they made themselves and is a poetic invention, that which is a motley of words and syllables. ...
>
> (trans. in Harrison 1979: 52)

Thus the *sūtra* itself describes how one group of monks will accuse another group of monks with having fabricated the *sūtra*. We see how literary sources support the epigraphic evidence that early Mahāyāna was very much a monastic movement with little widespread support. From a non-Mahāyāna perspective the Mahāyāna was simply *absurd*. All of this fits with the accusation of Nāgārjuna, and the association of the Mahādeva with a wish to incorporate the Mahāyāna *sūtras* into the Canon. Both Nāgārjuna and Mahādeva were monks.

One final point. Doctrinal innovation in Buddhism was almost entirely the concern of monks, but it should not be thought that there is a great divide between monks and laity in Buddhism, as has sometimes been the case in the West. It is always possible for a fully ordained monk to return to lay life, or for a lay person to become a monk for a short period. Thus while it is not possible to see the Mahāyāna as an attempt by the laity to obtain equal status with the monks, nevertheless one can see in the Mahāyāna growth of a form of religiosity prepared to give validity and doctrinal orthodoxy to religious practices and concerns, such as *stūpa* worship and devotion, which are seen as inferior, not the concern of monks and, in a sense, not properly 'Buddhist' by certain other rather elitist monks. The growth of the Mahāyāna can perhaps be characterized by what might be called 'doctrinal widening', rendering doctrinally respectable certain activities and beliefs which some monks viewed with disdain, and associated primarily with the ultimately useless activites of lay people.[5] The origins of the Mahāyāna are obscure in the extreme, and it is difficult to give a satisfactory explanation of why this widening happened. But from a doctrinal point of view the key lies in the changing status of the Buddha, and the growth of an idea that the Buddha's death was mere appearance – out of his compassion he remains to help suffering, sentient beings. Sociologically, it may be that the changing status of the Buddha corresponds with the growing socialization of Buddhism, its reabsorption into the society which it had originally renounced and from which it had distanced itself.

Parallel to this reabsorption the monk, or the lay Bodhisattva, lays claim to a pre-eminent position within society, rather than outside it, and the Buddha himself, as the religious hero writ large, becomes a spiritual king, relating to and caring for the world, rather than a being who, after his death, has completely 'gone beyond' the world and its cares.[6] This changing attitude to the Buddha correspondingly turned attention also towards his previous lives as a Bodhisattva (or perhaps it was the other way round). First, if the Buddha is so compassionate then *all* religious practices, if they are of spiritual benefit, become the teaching of the Buddha, regardless of what they are or who is carrying them out. Second, the Buddha as a Bodhisattva was often a lay person, or sometimes even an animal, always out of compassion and acting to develop the path to supreme Buddhahood. As Buddhahood became supreme over Arhatship, so attaining Buddhahood, and therefore becoming a Bodhisattva, became the new religious goal advocated for all Buddhist practitioners. This, if anything, characterizes the Mahāyāna. While the notion of the Bodhisattva as one who is destined to full Buddhahood is common to all Buddhist traditions, to set forth the path of the Bodhisattva as the ultimate aspiration for all seems to be a uniquely Mahāyāna conception. Within this context the lay person, as a Bodhisattva or potential Bodhisattva, gains in importance. Correspondingly, the religious activities held by some to be characteristic of, or of most benefit to, lay people become respectable. We find this growing respectability already in the pre-Mahāyāna tradition. Alone of all the Vinayas the Theravāda Vinaya has no discussion of the construction and cult of the *stūpa* (Bareau 1962: 229). In the *Ekottarāgama*, a canonical collection of the pre-Mahāyāna, we find a *sūtra* in which recollection of the Buddha (*buddhānusmṛti*) can lead to enlightenment (Harrison 1978: 37–8; see Chapter 10 below). The Mahāyāna represents a coming to self-awareness of these currents of thought, and an attempt, through the creation of a new canon and a new religious system, to render these currents doctrinally orthodox and respectable.

MAHĀYĀNA BEFORE 'MAHĀYĀNA' – THE *AJITASENAVYĀKARAṆANIRDEŚA SŪTRA*

The *Ajitasena Sūtra* describes itself as a Mahāyāna *sūtra*, although I suspect that this is another example of a *sūtra* which originally belonged to a pre-Mahāyāna tradition. There appears to be neither a Chinese nor a Tibetan version, and the Sanskrit text (in a rather non-standard Sanskrit) was discovered early in this century inside a mound near Gilgit, which is now in Afghanistan.[7] The mound was perhaps an ancient library, and the texts discovered date from the sixth or seventh centuries CE (see Dutt *et al.* 1939). The *Ajitasena Sūtra*, however, is undoubtedly much earlier in origin, although how early is at the moment uncertain. It has been little studied, is quite short, and does not appear to have been an important Mahāyāna *sūtra*. Nevertheless, for our purposes it is extremely important, since it seems to indicate a stage of proto-Mahāyāna, a stage of Mahāyāna prior to its own self-awareness as 'Mahāyāna', with all the concomitant senses of superiority and contrast with religious practices and beliefs deemed inferior.

The *sūtra* was clearly written by monks and aimed at the laity. Sociologically it occupies the Buddhist world we are familiar with from Theravāda practice. One of the main themes of the *sūtra* is the importance of giving to monks, and the immense results which will follow from this in the future. An old beggar woman attempts suicide because she has nothing to give to the Buddha. She is presented with suitable alms by a god, and the Buddha explains that she had given such gifts to many previous Buddhas in her former lives. Her present poverty, and the poverty of many of her previous incarnations, was the result of a time when she had changed her mind about giving alms to a begging monk. As a result of her present gift she is now predicted to future Buddhahood, that is, she realizes her status as a Bodhisattva, and it is said that she will not be born in the future as either a woman or a pauper.

One of the key figures in the *sūtra* is a monk disciple of the Buddha called Nandimitra, described as a *mahāśrāvaka*, a Great Hearer, who is sent by the Lord to King Ajitasena as a spiritual friend (*kalyāṇamitra*). The main instruction Nandimitra gives to Ajitasena is on the merits of giving to monks, exactly the form of instruction traditionally given by non-Mahāyāna monks to their lay patrons. In the meantime the old beggar woman had died and been reborn as the son of King Ajitasena. Both king and son subsequently wish to renounce the world in the presence of the Buddha and become monks. The prince is ordained first, thus gaining monastic superiority over his father. The *sūtra* continues with verses in which the son praises monkhood and exhorts his father to renounce the world while he has the possibility of doing so in the presence of the Buddha himself. The moment he was ordained the prince is said to have become an Arhat. On becoming an Arhat he sees all the Buddha Fields (*buddhakṣetra*; see Chapter 10 below). These are the realms in which the Buddhas reside and teach. They are not a completely Mahāyāna idea, but the notion of seeing all the Buddha Fields does appear to be Mahāyāna, as are the names of two of the realms, Sukhāvatī and Abhirati, which were mentioned earlier in the *sūtra*.

There is some reason to think that seeing Buddhas and Buddha Fields was a particularly potent impetus to religious practice for Buddhists during the formative period of the Mahāyāna. There is a *sūtra* called the *Pradakṣiṇā Sūtra*, on the merits of worshipping *stūpas*. A version of this *sūtra* has been found written in Khotanese, a Central Asian language, with an epilogue written presumably by the person who had the *sūtra* copied. He describes how, through further endeavour, he would like to be able to see Buddhas everywhere, and how by his merits he hopes to be reborn in the Pure Land, or Buddha Field, of Sukhāvatī, where Amitāyus (=Amitābha) Buddha will foretell for him future Buddhahood (see Bailey 1974: 18). As we shall see, the *pratyutpanna* absorption (*samādhi*), in the *sūtra* of that name, is a meditative practice whereby a Bodhisattva can see with his eyes the Buddhas and receive teachings from them.

So the world of the *Ajitasena Sūtra* presents what appears initially to be a strange mixture of pre-Mahāyāna and Mahāyāna elements. This world is one of monastic supremacy. There is absolutely no antagonism towards the Hearers or the notion of Arhatship. Nevertheless, the Great Hearer Nandimitra is also predicted to full Buddhahood, that is, he too realizes that he is a Bodhisattva. In this respect he is no different from the beggar woman, a lay female, who turns into a prince and then becomes a monk and an Arhat. The *sūtra* describes the miracles of the Buddha, and reciting the name of the Buddha is said to save from suffering and hell. The text ends in the traditional manner of early Mahāyāna *sūtras*. Those who promulgate this *sūtra* will attain Buddhahood, while those who listen to even one verse will become Bodhisattvas. The preachers of the Dharma who recite this *sūtra* will receive favourable rebirths and ultimately become enlightened. Those who condemn the *sūtra* will go to some very nasty hells.

What marks this *sūtra* is the supremacy of Buddhahood and the possibility of anyone, monk or lay, becoming a Bodhisattva. But what distinguishes it from most other early Mahāyāna sutras is the lack of antagonism towards the Hearers, Arhatship, and the monastic tradition. This is a gentle, harmonious *sūtra*. What I want to suggest is that the reason why this *sūtra* is different from other and more familiar early Mahāyāna *sūtras* is that the word 'Mahāyāna' does not occur in it, save in the title given in the colophon. This *sūtra* shows clearly Mahāyāna tendencies, but is conceptually prior to the Mahāyāna's own self-awareness. As Mahāyāna, the Great Vehicle, there is always an immedite contrast with Hīnayāna, the Inferior Vehicle. But initially, as the so-called Mahāyāna began to emerge, there was no sense of opposition to the Hearers as such, only an opposition to those who denied the authority of the relevant *sūtra*.

This lack of opposition to the non-Mahāyāna traditions as such in the very earliest proto-Mahāyāna is borne out by Lewis Lancaster's examination of the earliest Chinese versions of the *Aṣṭasāhasrikā* (8,000 verse) *Perfection of Wisdom Sūtra*, in which he shows that a number of key Mahāyāna concepts are missing from the earliest versions although present in later texts. The world of the earliest *Aṣṭasāhasrikā* text is reasonably close to that of the pre-Mahāyāna traditions. This is exactly what we would expect from the epigraphic evidence. The earliest use of the word 'Mahāyāna' in Indian inscriptions dates from the sixth century CE, although other terms with an exclusive reference to Mahāyāna monks and lay followers had been used from about the fourth century (Schopen 1979). This is a very long time after the earliest Mahāyāna literature, and indicates that while doctrinally there may have been a growing idea of the Mahāyāna as an alternative aspiration and spiritual path from, say, the first century BCE, nevertheless the notion of a clear separate group identity among Mahāyāna followers, represented by their using a separate name for themselves, took centuries to develop. To a monk in the first or second century CE the Mahāyāna as a visible institution was scarcely evident. Doctrinally, on the other hand, as expressed in texts, what marks the Mahāyāna as Mahāyāna is its own self-awareness in spite of its diversity, from which followed opposition and further distinction. The *Ajitasena Sūtra* is a Mahāyāna *sūtra* prior to the concept 'Mahāyāna'. It shows, therefore, the gentle shift of ideas which was already occurring prior to the polarization and unification given by that self-awareness alone.

ON THE ORIGINS AND JUSTIFICATION OF THE MAHĀYĀNA SŪTRAS

Finally, where did these Mahāyāna *sūtras* come from, and what justification could possibly be given by Mahāyānists for their creation? We have already seen that as far as the non-Mahāyāna traditions were concerned the Mahāyāna *sūtras* were not the words of the Buddha but rather the work of poets. In the *Aṣṭasāhasrikā Perfection of Wisdom*, Mahāyānists are warned to be on their guard against this accusation, since it comes from Māra, the Buddhist Tempter (see MacQueen 1981: 304). Nevertheless, we should not think that even for the non-Mahāyāna traditions all the works forming the *sūtra* section of the Canon were considered actually to have been uttered by the Buddha himself. As always with Buddhism, the situation is more complex than that! What was necessary for a text not uttered by the Buddha himself to receive full authority was that the Buddha personally certified the utterance concerned. Graeme MacQueen, in a long and interesting article, speaks of three types of certification recognized among the pre-Mahāyāna traditions: approval after the event, approval before the event, and authorization of persons (MacQueen 1981: 309). Thus the Buddha approves of something someone has preached, or invites a person to preach on his behalf, or a teaching is given by a preacher who has been authorized by the Buddha, in the sense that the preacher has been praised by the Lord for his wisdom and ability. The important point about all of these forms of certification is the requirement of the Buddha's presence in the world. With the death of the Buddha and his immediate disciples, therefore, the Canon in theory becomes closed. It thus follows that the development of the doctrine that the Buddha remains in compassionate contact with the world carried with it the possibility of the creation of a new 'mystically authorized' canon of scriptures.

Most Mahāyānists consider that the Mahāyāna *sūtras* were preached by Śākyamuni Buddha, the 'historical' Buddha, and the *sūtras* themselves almost invariably start with Ananda's phrase 'Thus have I heard at one time', plus the geographical location of the discourse. However, source-critical and historical awareness has made it impossible for the modern scholar to accept this traditional account. Nevertheless, it is not always absurd to suggest that a Mahāyāna *sūtra* or teaching may contain elements of a tradition which goes back to the Buddha himself, which was played down or just possibly excluded from the canonical formulations of the early schools. We have seen that even at the First Council there is evidence of disagreement as regards the details of the Buddha's teaching. Luis Gomez (1976) has detected in one of the earliest sections of the Pāli canon, the *Sutta Nipāta*, teachings close enough to those found in the Mahāyāna Madhyamaka philosophy to justify the name 'Proto-Madhyamaka'. Madhyamaka represents the philosophical systematization and development of the *Prajñāpāramitā* (*Perfection of Wisdom*) *sūtras*, and it is not absurd to see in the *Prajñāpāramitā* a protest against the innovations of the Abhidharma scholars, and perhaps a return to an earlier understanding of the Dharma and the world. More important, however, is a tradition found in the Mahāyāna *sūtras* themselves which would associate the origins of these texts not with the historical Buddha who died, perhaps, in 483 or 370 BCE, but rather with visionary experience and inspiration by one of a number of Buddhas who continue to exist on a higher plane, in their Buddha Fields or Pure Lands (cf. MacQueen 1982: 51 ff.). This teaching, which to my mind provides a convincing basis for understanding the origins of at least some of the Mahāyāna *sūtras*, can be found most vividly stated in the *Pratyutpanna Sūtra*. The central message of this *sūtra* concerns a meditation practice whereby the meditator recollects a Buddha (Amitāyus is particularly mentioned), visualizing him in his Pure Land surrounded by Bodhisattvas and preaching the Doctrine. The practitioner concentrates day and night for some seven days. After this, not surprisingly, perhaps, he sees the Buddha in a vision or in a dream:

> while remaining in this very world-system that bodhisattva sees the Lord, the Tathāgata Amitāyus; and conceiving himself to be in that world-system he also hears the Dharma. Having heard their exposition he accepts, masters and retains those Dharmas. He worships, venerates, honours and reveres the Lord ... Amitāyus. After he has emerged from that *samādhi* [meditative absorption] that bodhisattva also expounds widely to others those Dharmas as he has heard, retained and mastered them.
>
> (Harrison 1978: 43; see Chapter 10 below)

It is possible to question the Buddha while in this absorption, and: 'Further ... undeclared, unobtained words of the Dharma come within the range of hearing of that bodhisattva, and he acquires them; by the power of that *samādhi* that bodhisattva hears those dharmas' (ibid., 54).

We have here, therefore, a theory of the revelatory origin of the Mahāyāna *sūtras*, a theory based on the teaching that the (or 'a') Buddha remains in his Pure Land teaching the Dharma.[8] There is, however, yet another justification for the Mahāyāna *sūtras*, separate but not necessarily contradictory to the theory of revelation, found in a *sūtra* quoted by Śāntideva in his *Śikṣāsamuccaya* (eight century CE):

> Through four factors is an inspired utterance [*pratibhāna* – see MacQueen 1981/1982] the word of the Buddhas. What four? (i) ... the inspired utterance is connected with truth, not untruth; (ii) it is connected with the Dharma, not that which is not the Dharma; (iii) it brings about the renunciation of moral taints [*kleśa*] not their increase; and (iv) it shows the laudable qualities of *nirvāṇa*, not those of the cycle of rebirth [*saṃsāra*].
>
> (Śāntideva 1961: 12)

The *sūtra* explains that if an utterance has these four features then the believing men and women of a good family (an expression used for the hearers of Mahāyāna *sūtras*) will form the conception of 'Buddha' and hear it as the Dharma. Why? 'Whatever is well spoken [*subhāṣita*], all that is the word of the Buddha [*buddhabhāṣita*].'

This apparent openness as to what is to count as the word of the Buddha can be traced in the Pāli canon, for the assertion that what is well spoken is the word of the Buddha is also found in the Pāli *Uttaravipatti Sutta* (cf. Aśoka's 'Whatever is spoken by the Lord Buddha, all that is well said'). However, in the Pāli context the assertion does not seem to have quite the same meaning as it does in the Mahāyāna. MacQueen has pointed out that we have here an obvious ambiguity:

> This can mean that all of the good things in the tradition come from the Buddha, but it can equally well imply that *buddhavacana* [the Buddha's discourse] is being redefined to mean 'whatsoever be well spoken', rather than meaning the actual words of Gautama.
>
> (MacQueen 1981: 314)

Elsewhere in the Pāli canon the Dhamma is characterized as whichever doctrines lead to enlightenment. Of course, to say that whatsoever is well spoken is the word of the Buddha is not to explain exactly what is to count as being well spoken. It is not enough to say that it leads to *nirvāṇa*, since opinions will differ as to which processes and practices will lead thither. Even the standard source among the pre-Mahāyāna traditions on what is to count as an authentic scriptural text, the *Mahāpadeśa Sūtra*, is of little concrete help in the examination of a disputed case. This *sūtra* recommends relying not on the authority of a person, but on checking the new text for coherence with the authentic *sūtra* and Vinaya corpus (according to the Sanskrit versions it should also not contradict the nature of things (*dharmatā*); see Lamotte 1983/4: 9 ff.). However, as we have seen, the Canon was not in a stable state during the centuries after the death of the Buddha, nor was it clear and unambiguous. Nevertheless, for us the important point is that the framework was there, developed and systematized by the early Mahāyāna, for innovation on the basis of spiritual efficacy.

The Mahāyāna took up the Buddha's assertion that the Dharma should guide his followers after his death, and stressed that the Lord had described the Dharma as whatever leads to enlightenment, that is, whatever is spiritually helpful. What is spiritually helpful will vary considerably, depending on person, time, and place. As time, place, and person change, so innovation becomes inevitable. The only problem lies in justifying that innovation. In a sense, for the non-Mahāyāna traditions to argue against the Mahāyāna that it is not the word of the Buddha is to miss the point. The historical Buddha had declined in significance in favour of, first, the principles which he enunciated and which he set forth as their guide after his death, and second, the growing importance of a continuing Buddha on a plane different from and spiritually more refined than this world occupied by Śākyamuni Buddha as a figure in human history. In the light of this second point, to appeal to the historical Buddha is to appeal to that which is in a sense inferior. Indeed in the light of the doctrine of no-Self (*anātman*) the Mahāyānist attitude is that if the other traditions talk of human beings, as was the Buddha, as though they inherently exist or have any ultimate importance, so this itself is an indication of spiritual backwardness.

Let me now summarize briefly the direction of the preceding discussion. From about the first century BCE the changes ocurring within Buddhism seem to have issued in a new literature claiming to be the word of the Buddha himself. This literature is not the product of an organized or unitary movement, and appears to have been produced by monks well within the existing Buddhist traditions. Much of the literature is concerned with the supremacy of the Buddha and his perception of things, and advocates the path of the Bodhisattva, the aspirant to full Buddhahood, as a noble and higher path to be pursued by all who can for the benefit of others. Indeed, concern with the welfare of all beings, not just a specific group, seems to be a characteristic of Mahāyāna Buddhist inscriptions also (Schopen 1985: 42). The monks, nuns, and perhaps a small number of lay practitioners who accepted this new literature formed a series of cults, probably based on different *sūtras* and their attendant practices. It is likely that they had little or no direct and regular connection with each other. In some cases the followers may have felt themselves in direct contact with a Buddha who inspired them in meditation or in dreams. Sometimes they proclaimed the Doctrine itelf, embodied in the text, as the body of the Buddha, his Dharma-body, superior to that found and worshipped in *stūpas*. Our early Mahāyānists may certainly have perceived themselves as a righteous bulwark against moral and spiritual decline. Nevertheless, their public behaviour was not notably different in any fundamental way from that of other monks and nuns. All the evidence suggests that these followers were very much in the minority within Indian Buddhism. As time passed so they identified their aspirations as a 'Mahāyāna', a Superior Way, and the literature begins to show greater animosity towards those who failed to heed the message and still followed the Inferior Way, the Hīnayāna. Even so, it was some centuries before the followers of the Mahāyāna began to identify themselves in everyday life by a different name (*śākyabhikṣu* for a monk; Schopen 1979), and still there is no evidence that in general they radically differed in public behaviour from non-Mahāyāna practitioners.

With this as an introduction, let us now begin to look at the *sūtras* themselves.

PART I

Wisdom

CHAPTER TWO

The *Perfection of Wisdom (Prajñāpāramitā) Sūtrās*

ON THE MAHĀYĀNA *SŪTRAS*

In approaching the Mahāyāna *sūtras* we immediately confront presuppositions concerning the nature of the book which these texts put into question. As we have seen, the *sūtra* is not one object among others, but is rather the body of the Buddha, a focus of celebration and worship on the model of relic worship. The book is not a free-standing, self-explanatory item, but an entity embedded in religious practice, a product of and a guide to spiritual experience. Those of the westernized world expect a book, perhaps, to lead through systematic and clearly defined stages from a beginning through a middle to a conclusion. Reading, we think, is a private, solitary affair, requiring peace, leisure, and silence. But the landscape of the Mahāyāna *sūtras* is quite extraordinary, space and time expand and conflate, connections seem to be missed, we move abruptly from ideas so compressed and arcane as to verge on the meaningless, to page after page of repetition. If we approach books as a consumer, regarding texts as goods to be devoured one after the other from cover to cover, then all too often we find the Mahāyāna *sūtras* boring – about as boring as a board game for which we have only the rules, lacking pieces and the board!

In fact the study of a Buddhist *sūtra* was neither private nor peaceful. Certainly in classical times in India the text would be copied and read, but reading was closer to chanting out loud. Widespread mastery of the art of silent reading is a relatively recent development in world culture. The historian of medieval monasticism Jean Leclerc has observed that

> in the Middle Ages, as in antiquity, they read usually not as today, principally with the eyes, but with the lips, pronouncing what they saw, and with the ears, listening to the words pronounced, hearing what is called the 'voices of the pages'. ... Doctors of ancient times used to recommend reading to their patients as a physical exercise on an equal level with walking, running or ball-playing.
>
> (Leclerc 1961: 34)

Each Buddhist monk would probably own no more than one or two *sūtras*, which would rapidly be learnt by heart, not only through frequent repetition but because memory of the texts was demanded by the scholastic environment. Moreover, since the *sūtras* and their exegetical treatises were also guides to meditation, so, as anyone who has practised knows, meditation cannot be performed effectively through repeated reference to a series of written instructions. Buddhist texts were intended as no more than mnemonic devices, scaffolding, the framework for textual exposition by a teacher in terms of his own experience and also the tradition, the lineage transmission from his teachers, traced back to the Buddha himself, or to *a* Buddha, or to some other form of authorized spiritual revelation. This approach to, and treatment of, the sacred text in Buddhism is not only of historical interest. In traditional Mahāyāna cultures, particularly among the Tibetans, these texts are still used and studied in the age-old way. The scholar who would write a study of Buddhist practice or even doctrine without bearing this in mind is like an art historian who would study architecture by ignoring the building and looking only at the bricks!

The Mahāyāna *sūtras* vary in length from a few words to, say, the *100,000 verse Perfection of Wisdom*. The larger *sūtras* are often very repetitive and although as yet adequate editions of most of the *sūtras* are almost entirely lacking (where the Sanskrit version has survived at all) it is nevertheless possible through careful text-critical scholarship to detect the growth of the *sūtras* over the centuries, although exact details are very much open to dispute (see Conze 1967a). It would be wrong, therefore, to think of the larger *sūtras* as we now have them as necessarily historically unitary phenomena. Because the *sūtras* grew and developed, often over some time, we should likwise not necessarily expect to find one consistent and systematic doctrine throughout a particular *sūtra*. This is not to say, however, that the Buddhist tradition has not been able subsequently to interpret a *sūtra* in a unitary manner.

A feature of the earlier *sūtras* is the phenomenon of laudatory self-reference – the lengthy praise of the *sūtra* itself, the immense merits to be obtained from treating even a verse of it with reverence, and the nasty penalties which will accrue in accordance with *karma* to those who denigrate the scripture. We find similar indications of the historical reception of the early Mahāyāna in a famous passage in the *Saddharmapuṇḍarīka* (*Lotus*) *Sūtra*, where 5,000 of those in the assembly walk out rather than listen to the preaching of the *sūtra*, because of their 'deep and grave roots of sin and overwheening pride, imagining themselves to have attained and to have borne witness to what in fact they had not' (trans. in Hurvitz 1976: 29). Not infrequently, as we have already seen, the *sūtra* itself has one group of monks declaring to another that this *sūtra* is not the word of the Buddha, together with the reply of the *sūtra*'s partisans.

Sometimes stories or sermons which must have originally circulated separately, products, perhaps, of a different intellectual milieu, are inserted into the text. It is occasionally possible to detect short insertions by comparison of the prose and the verse versions of a particular episode, for many of the *sūtras* have both. Generally the verses tend to be the older. The metric form prevents easy tampering, and it is possible sometimes to detect archaic or non-standard linguistic features which indicate, together with other clues, that a number of the early Mahāyāna *sūtras* were not originally in Sanskrit at all, but in a Middle Indic dialect which has been subsequently Sanskritized – not always very well from a classical point of view. Occasionally a number of different *sūtras* have been gathered together and referred to as one conglomerate *sūtra*, as in the case of the *Mahāratnakūṭa Sūtra*, or the *Avataṃsaka Sūtra*. There is evidence, moreover, that the Chinese in particular were so impressed with the Mahāyāna *sūtras* that they created a number of spurious *sūtras*, some of which have been of considerable importance in the development of Chinese Buddhism. The great Japanese Zen Master Dōgen (thirteenth century), in his younger days in China, suspected that the so-called *Śūraṅgama Sūtra* (to be distinguished from the genuine *Śūraṅgamasamādhi Sūtra*), an important *sūtra* in Zen Buddhism, was not an authentic Indian *sūtra*, a point now generally accepted by scholars. How one assesses the Central Asian and Chinese spurious *sūtras* in the light of continuing revelation is open to debate, however. After all, from the point of view of the pre-Mahāyāna tradition *all* the Mahāyāna *sūtras* were spurious!

THE ORIGINS AND DEVELOPMENT OF THE *PRAJÑĀPĀRAMITĀ* LITERATURE

It is not possible at the present stage of our knowledge to make very many certain statements concerning either the origins or the development of the *Prajñāpāramitā* literature. It is widely held that this literature, and possibly Mahāyāna Buddhism itself, originated in Central or Southern India, and this is supported by a comment in the *Aṣṭasāhasrikā Prajñāpāramitā* that after the death of the Buddha the perfection of wisdom will proceed to the south and thence to the east and north (Conze 1973b: 159).[1] Etienne Lamotte has argued, however, for the North-Western and Central Asian (Khotanese) origins of the *Prajñāpāramitā*, and indeed Lamotte is inclined to see some Mediterranean and Greek influences at work in the changes occurring in Buddhism during the period of Mahāyāna emergence (Lamotte 1954: 377 ff.; 1958). Edward Conze has observed that Lamotte's arguments have shown only that the *Perfection of Wisdom* had a great success in the north-west during the Kuṣāṇa period (*c.* first century CE), not that it originated there (Conze 1960: 9 ff.).

Issues of the origins of the *Prajñāpāramitā* and those of the Mahāyāna are closely connected, since at the present stage of our knowledge the earliest Mahāyāna *sūtras* are probably *Prajñāpāramitā sūtras*. The problem is complicated by the fact that archaeological and epigraphic evidence point one way, and textual evidence the other. A. L. Basham has asserted quite categorically that the inscriptional evidence points to a northern origin for Mahāyāna Buddhism. Observing that some scholars trace the origins of the Mahāyāna to the south, he distinguishes between Mahāyāna mythology and its philosophical ideas. These latter could possibly have a southern origin, but phenomena like the belief in heavenly Bodhisattvas are definitely northern (Basham 1981: 37). It may indeed be necessary to distinguish between the philosophical ideas of the *Prajñāpāramitā*, and the mythology of Bodhisattvas, Buddhas, and their activities, although both are blended in the extant *Prajñāpāramitā* literature. It is possible, although purely hypothetical, to see in the emergence of the Mahāyāna as an identifiable entity the commingling of two originally separate strata, say 'philosophical' and 'religious' (these terms are purely shorthand). The extant *Prajñāpāramitā* literature, at least in its earliest form, shows a predominance of the philosophical, while the other wing is represented by the Sukhāvatī *sūtras* and the *Akṣobhyavyūha Sūtra*. It has been suggested that the *Pratyutpanna Sūtra* represents a deliberate attempt to unite these two originally separate traditions (Harrison 1978: 40). It would be possible thus to trace the origins of these two tendencies to different (although not necessarily intrinsically separate) religio-philosophical trends, and therefore perhaps to different geographical areas. Speculation, of course, but one interesting conclusion we could draw from such speculation is that since the name 'Mahāyāna' is attributed to an entity showing a commingling of both streams, so it may be a mistake to look for the geographical origins of the Mahāyāna. We should rather look as far as possible to a number of centres, and trace in literature, archaeology, and epigraphy their contacts and mutual influences.

Edward Conze has distinguished four phases in the development of the *Prajñāpāramitā* literature, stretching over more than a thousand years (Conze 1960: 9 ff.; 1968; 11 ff.). From about 100 BCE to 100 CE we have the elaboration of a basic text. During the following 200 years this basic text was very much expanded, while the subsequent 200 years up to about 500 CE was characterized by the restatement of basic ideas in short *sūtras* on the one hand, and versified summaries on the other. During the final period, from 600–1200 CE, Tantric influences make themselves felt, and we find evidence of magical elements in the *sūtras* and their use. So, for examples of each category we have:

(i) The oldest text, the *Aṣṭasāhasrikā (8,000 verse) Perfection of Wisdom*, together with the *Ratnaguṇasaṃcayagāthā*, which Conze sees as its verse summary.

(ii) The *Śatasāhasrikā (100,000 verse)*, the *Pañcaviṃśatisāhasrikā (25,000 verse)*, and the *Aṣṭadaśasāhasrikā (18,000 verse) Prajñapāramitās.*

(iii) (a) The *Vajracchedikā*: this is the famous *Diamond Sūtra*, the 300 verse *Perfection of Wisdom.*

(b) The *Abhisamayālaṃkāra*, an exegetical work attributed to the 'celestial Bodhisattva' Maitreya. This is said to be the *Perfection of Wisdom* systematized for practice. Tibetans always study the *Prajñāpāramitā* through the medium of this text and its commentaries.

(iv) The *Adhyardhaśatikā (150 verse) Prajñāpāramitā.*

Edward Conze's four phases are widely accepted by scholars, and their broad outline, particularly the expansion of a basic text and its subsequent contraction, had been independently suggested by Ryusho Hikata (1958) in Japan. One should be wary of accepting such schema as definitely established, however. Conze and Hikata disagree on the antiquity of the *Vajracchedikā*, which Japanese scholars generally place much earlier than is usual in the West. Gregory Schopen has now suggested that the *Aṣṭasāhasrikā* may actually contain a reworking of ideas found in the *Vajracchedikā* (Schopen 1975: 153n). No notice has been taken, I think, of the quotations from the *Diamond Sūtra* contained in the *Sūtrasamuccaya*, the attribution of which to Nāgārjuna (*c.* second century CE) has not yet been disproved. The issue must be left open, but at the moment there is reasonable possibility that the *Vajracchedikā* in some form or another dates from a very early phase of *Prajñāpāramitā* literary activity.

Edward Conze has elsewhere distinguished nine stages in the development of *Prajñāpāramitā* thought (Conze 1967b: 123–47): (i) The initial phase represented by the first two chapters of the *Ratnaguṇasaṃcayagāthā*; (ii) chapters 3–28 of the *Aṣṭasāhasrikā*; (iii) incorporation of material from the Abhidharma; (iv)concessions to the Buddhism of Faith; (v) the last third of the *Śatasāhasrikā*; (vi) the short *sūtras*; (vii) Yogācārin (Cittamātra) commentaries; and finally (viii) Tantric and (ix) Ch'an (Zen) uses and commentaries. As with his four phases in the development of the literature, with which this list overlaps, Conze's schema here is reasonable but may have to be amended in the light of further research.[2]

WISDOM (*PRAJÑĀ*) AND ITS PERFECTION

Wisdom is, alas, all too rare; *prajñā* is not. This apparent paradox should make us sensitive to the usual translation of '*prajñā*' by 'wisdom'. *Prajñā* is a mental event, a state of consciousness, normally in the Indo-Tibetan Buddhist context a state of consciousness which results from analysis, investigation. 'Its function', the *Abhidharmasamuccaya* tells us, 'is to exclude doubt.' In this sense some Buddhist texts refer to a worldly or conventional (*saṃvṛti*) *prajñā*, the understanding through investigation of, say, grammar, medicine, or some other mundane skill.[3] These skills may or may not have religious significance, depending on how they are used. Texts also refer to ultimate (*paramārtha*) *prajñā*, the understanding which results from an investigation into the way things really are, what we might call 'metaphysical' understanding, the result of deep and sharp rigorous thought. In this sense there is the *prajñā* not only of Buddhists but also of rival non-Buddhist systems of thought – *prajñā* which apparently excludes doubt but is from a Buddhist point of view the result of a defective analysis. Thus it is possible to speak, as does the Sarvāstivāda-Vaibhāṣita tradition, of false *prajñā* (Jaini 1977). Since the principal concern of Buddhist writing is with the correct understanding of the way things really are, however, by an understandable process of thought '*prajñā*' comes to be used for the correct discernment of the true situation, the ultimate way of things. So, in the non-Mahāyāna *Abhidharmakośa Bhāṣya prajñā* is given simply as the discernment of *dharmas* (*dharmapravicayaḥ*), those ultimates which mark the terminating point of Abhidharma analysis. It will be recalled, however, that in the early Mahāyāna, as well as in some non-Mahāyāna schools, the teaching of *dharmas* as those final realities out of which we construct the world was rejected in favour of a teaching of the emptiness of *dharmas* (*dharmaśūnyatā*). *Dharmas* too lack any fundamental status and are not ultimate realities, *dharmas* too can be analysed away. For these traditions the analysis associated with the Abhidharma had ended too early, and thus such a *prajñā* was a defective *prajñā*, not the perfection of *prajñā*, or no real *prajñā* at all. Now *prajñā* is said to be a state of consciousness which understands emptiness (*śūnyata*), the absence of self or essence even in *dharmas*. Since this *prajñā* is the principal concern of the *Perfection of Wisdom* texts, and since this *prajñā*, this wisdom, appears to have been advocated in certain non-Mahāyāna schools also, it is not surprising that there is a Tibetan tradition of a non-Mahāyāna *Prajñāpāramitā* in a Prakrit, that is, a non-Sanskrit, dialect belonging to the Pūrvaśaila school (Conze 1960: 9).

Wisdom (*prajñā*) in the Indo-Tibetan tradition is primarily an understanding which results from analysis. There is, however, a distinction familiar to philosophers between knowing *that* something is the case – knowing who Archibald is, for example – and knowing by acquaintance – that is, having the dubious pleasure of actually meeting Archibald. In speaking of wisdom as understanding the way things really are there is correspondingly a distinction between knowing intellectually, through deep, even meditative, analysis, the way things must really be, and the 'paranormal' experience of a meditative absorption directed towards the results of such analysis – *dharmas* or emptiness as the case may be. We thus face another understandable shift in the meaning of *prajñā*. *Prajñā* is sometimes a meditative absorption the content of which is the ultimate truth, the way things really are. Thus the *Mahāyānasaṃgraha* can refer to the perfection of wisdom as 'non-conceptual awareness' (*nirvikalpakajñāna*). This is still *prajñā*, wisdom, for it is still a state of consciousness which results from analysis, although the analysis has been refined, as it were, out of existence, it has transcended itself, and the mind is left in one-pointed absorption on the results of analysis (see Chapter 3, pp. 72–4). Note, however, that this *prajñā* is non-conceptual and non-dual, whereas the preceding examples have been conceptual. That there is a gulf between conceptual and non-conceptual appears to have led certain traditions, notably that of some Ch'an (Zen) practitioners in East Asia, to conclude that *prajñā* can in no way result from analysis, but rather is a natural response to *cutting* all analytic and conceptual thought. There are nevertheless Indian bases and precedents for this (Williams 1980: esp. 25–6), although the particular emphasis on anti-intellectualism and cutting conceptual thought in some Chinese traditions may have been the results of unconscious Taoist influence (cf. the *Tao te ching*'s 'The *Tao* that can be spoken of is not the eternal *Tao*').

Thus far '*prajñā*' and its perfection refer to interconnected forms of conceptual and non-conceptual understanding. There is, however, one further slide in meaning to be noted. By a shift understandable in the Indian context of meditation, '*prajñā*/*prajñāpāramitā*' come through non-conceptual and therefore non-dual awareness to equal the content or object of such an ultimate awareness, that is, in this context emptiness itself. Thus the *Ta-chih-tu lun* (*Mahāprajñāpāramitā Śāstra*), an enormous commentary on the *25,000 verse Prajñāpāramitā* attributed probably incorrectly to Nāgārjuna and extant only in Chinese, refers to the perfection of wisdom as the indestructible and imperishable 'real mark of all the *dharmas*'. This is what is really the case, emptiness, the universal absence of any ultimate existence 'whether Buddhas occur or whether they do not occur'.

Ultimate *prajñā* as understood by the Mahāyāna, and *prajñāpāramitā*, the perfection of wisdom, appear to be generally the same. Mahāyāna and non-Mahāyāna sources refer to a number of perfections (*pāramitā*) mastered by the Bodhisattva as he or she follows the long path to perfect Buddhahood. The most frequent list contains six: giving (*dāna*), morality (*śīla*), patience (*kṣānti*), effort (*vīrya*), meditative concentration (*dhyāna*), and wisdom (*prajñā*). The perfection of wisdom is primary; it is said to lead the other perfections as a man with eyes leads the blind (*Madhyamakāvatāra* 6:2), although later writers in particular are sensitive to the suggestion that wisdom is sufficient unto itself and the other perfections are unnecessary. Candrakīrti, in his *Madhyamakāvatāra*, distinguishes between mundane or ordinary perfections, and supramundane perfections (1:16). The difference is that the supramundane perfection of giving, for example, is giving with no conception of the inherent real existence of giver, gift, or receiver, that is, it is giving in the light of perfect *prajñā*. Generally, therefore, the perfection of wisdom is that wisdom which goes beyond the wisdom of the world and that associated by the Mahāyāna particularly with the Abhidharma scholars. It transcends their wisdom both in terms of its more refined analysis, and of the fact that it occurs within the context of the extensive and compassionate Bodhisattva deeds, the aspiration to full Buddhahood for the benefit of all sentient beings.

ABSENCE OF SELF — THE EXTENSIVE PERSPECTIVE

Edward Conze has argued that the earliest *Prajñāpāramitā* is contained in the first two chapters of the *Ratnaguṇasaṃcayagāthā* and the corresponding chapters of the *Aṣṭasāhasrikā*. The *Ratnaguṇasaṃcayagāthā* (*Ratna*) are verses in a non-standard Sanskrit, and there is reason to believe that these verses were originally incorporated into the *Aṣṭasāhasrikā* (*Aṣṭa*) on the model of many other Mahāyāna *sūtras*. Whether Conze is right in maintaining that these sections represent the earliest *Perfection of Wisdom* awaits further research, but they certainly contain the principal features and doctrines of the *Prajñāpāramitā* in a very early and accessible form. The antiquity of the texts is shown, among other reasons, by their immediate need to establish their authority. It is significant that in the *Aṣṭa* the principal speaker, apart from the Buddha, is Subhūti, 'the foremost of those who dwell in Peace', and not Śāriputra, traditionally the disciple most advanced in wisdom, and the patron of the Abhidharma.[4] The wisdom of the *Prajñāpāramitā* is a wisdom which calms all discursive thought and brings true peace. The *sūtra* is quick to point out, however, that all Subhūti teaches, and all that other teachers preach which is in conformity with the truth (i.e. *prajñā*), is in fact the work of the Buddha speaking through them. Indeed the *sūtra* ends with the assertion that 'One should know that those beings are living in the presence of the Tathagata [the Buddha] who will hear this perfection of wisdom, take it up, study, spread, repeat and write it, and who will honour, revere, adore and worship it' (trans. in Conze 1973b: 300; all citations of *Aṣṭa* and *Ratna* are to this translation). As the *Ratna* puts it, 'Their teaching stems but from the might of the Buddhas, and not their own power' (ibid., 9).

The *Perfection of Wisdom* scriptures, as with most Mahāyāna *sūtras*, do not indulge in elaborate philosophical argument. For this we must look to the philosophical schools, particularly in this case the Madhyamaka. The scriptures make assertions which indicate the true way of things and behaviour in the light of that truth. All assertions of the *Prajñāpāramitā* are made from the perspective of perfect wisdom, that is, they occur from the position of a Buddha's perception wherein absolutely nothing has any inherent or ultimate existence, but remains only in terms of conventional truth. All entities are like hallucinatory objects (*Ratna* 1:14). By switching between these two levels, ultimate and conventional, it is possible to generate apparent paradoxes for pedagogic effect, but (*pace* Conze) there are no genuine paradoxes, no real 'speaking in contradictions' in the *Perfection of Wisdom*.

The principal ontological message of the *Prajñāpāramitā* is an extension of the Buddhist teaching of no-Self to equal no essence, and therefore no inherent existence, as applied to all things without exception. This is not some form of Monistic Absolutism, negating in order to uncover a True Ultimate Reality. The ultimate truth is that there is no such thing:

> *Subhuti*: Even Nirvana, I say, is like a magical illusion, is like a dream. How much more so anything else!
> *Gods*: Even Nirvana, Holy Subhuti, you say is like an illusion, is like a dream?
> *Subhuti*: Even if perchance there could be anything more distinguished, of that too I would say that it is like an illusion, like a dream.
>
> (trans. in Conze 1973b: 99)

Who will there be who could possibly grasp such a teaching? The answer is that there is no one around who could grasp it – nor has anything really been taught at all! One should be clear, however, what is being said here. There is a widely held view that the philosophical origins of the Mahāyāna lay in a move from the absence of Self in persons (*pudgalanairātmya*) found in the non-Mahāyāna traditions, to the absence of Self in *dharmas* as well, (*dharmanairātmya* = *dharmaśūnyatā*) found in the Mahāyāna. This is naïve both historically and in terms of the image of its own teaching found in the *Perfection of Wisdom* texts themselves. Historically, it should be clear that the teaching of absence of Self in persons (in opposition to that of *dharmas*) is a feature of certain interpretations of the Abhidharma. The *Perfection of Wisdom* shows a clear opposition to any conception of inherently existing *dharmas*, but this is not the same as an opposition to the non-Mahāyāna traditions as such, since at this time the non-Mahāyāna traditions and the Abhidharma schools which taught inherent existence of *dharmas* were not equivalent. As we have seen, there were non-Mahāyāna traditions which held to a doctrine of absence of Self in *dharmas*. The presence of teachings akin to those of emptiness in the *Sutta Nipāta* of the Pāli canon suggests (speculatively) that those who formulated the *Prajñāpāramitā* may have seen the teaching of mere absence of Self in persons alone as a dangerous innovation. It was certainly possible for Candrakīrti to point to passages (extant in the Pāli canon) of the non-Mahāyāna canon which refer to each of the five psycho-physical constituents (*skandhas*) as being like bubbles, mirages, illusions, and so on (*Madhyamakāvatāra Bhāṣya* on 1:8), a clear indication as far as the Mahāyāna is concerned that the Buddha taught even non-Mahāyānists emptiness, the absence of inherent existence in *dharmas* as well as persons (cf. also *Aṣṭa*, Conze 1973b: 167).

Second, the *Perfection of Wisdom* does not claim that complete emptiness is the doctrine for Mahāyānists in opposition to the non-Mahāyāna teachings concerning *dharmas*. Rather, the *Ratna* says:

> Those who wish to become the Sugata's [Buddha's] Disciples,
> Or Pratyekabuddhas, or likewise Kings of the Dharma –
> Without recourse to this Patience they cannot reach their respective goals.
> They move across, but their eyes are not on the other shore.[5]
>
> (Conze 1973b: 13)

The *Aṣṭa* explains that 'No one can attain any of the fruits of the holy life, or keep it ... unless he patiently accepts the elusiveness of the dharma' (Conze 1973b: 98). And again, 'Whether one wants to train on the level of Disciple, or Pratyekabuddha, or Bodhisattva, – one should listen to this perfection of wisdom, ... and in this very perfection of wisdom should one be trained and exert oneself' (Conze 1973b: 84). What the *Aṣṭa* is saying here is that there is no Arhatship or Pratyekabuddhahood without perfect wisdom, an understanding of emptiness, for it is necessary to understand the way things really are in order to cut attachment and attain *any* degree of sainthood. Attachment to *dharmas* is attachment none the less.[6] Thus the goal of the Hearers is Arhatship, but this goal cannot be attained without understanding the absence of Self in *dharmas* – in other words those who follow any Abhidharma teaching of the inherent existence of *dharmas* cannot attain even their (from a Mahāyāna point of view) limited goal. What characterizes the Mahāyāna is not the teaching of absence of Self in *dharmas* but, according to the great Tibetan scholar Tsong kha pa (1357–1419), the extensive deeds and compassion of the Bodhisattva who is treading the path to perfect Buddhahood for the benefit of all.

So the terminology of the *Perfection of Wisdom* is that of the Abhidharma, but the critique is of the claim to have found some things which really, ultimately exist, i.e. *dharmas*. These early *Prajñāpāramitā* texts constantly ask what *dharma* is referred to by the term *x*; the reply is that no such *dharma* can be found, in reality there is no such thing:

> No wisdom can we get hold of, no highest perfection,
> No Bodhisattva, no thought of enlightenment either.
> When told of this, if not bewildered and in no way anxious,
> A Bodhisattva courses in the Well-Gone's [Sugata's] wisdom.
>
> (Conze 1973b: 9)

The Bodhisattva should not be bewildered. The *Aṣṭa* says:

> And yet, O Lord, if, when this is pointed out, a Bodhisattva's heart does not become cowed, nor stolid, does not despair nor despond, if he does not turn away or become dejected, does not tremble, is not frightened or terrified, it is just this Bodhisattva, this great being who should be instructed in perfect wisdom.
>
> (Conze 1973b: 84)

It is difficult for us to appreciate just how extraordinary these teachings are as religious teachings, and how disturbing they must have seemed to anyone who took them seriously at the time they were first promulgated. For anyone who has tried to practise these teachings in meditation and life the requirement of completely letting go, 'existential relaxation', cutting even subtle attachment, is an extremely difficult one to fulfil, requiring immense training and application, and potentially, if taken seriously, very frightening. This, the *Ratna* tells us, is true renunciation:

> In form, in feeling, will, perception and awareness
> Nowhere in them they find a place to rest on.
> Without a home they wander, dharmas never hold them,
> Nor do they grasp at them – the Jina's Bodhi
> [Buddha's enlightenment] they are bound to gain.
>
> (Conze 1973b: 9–10; cf. 13)

The language would not have been lost on contemporary readers (or reciters). The image of wandering without a home was a potent one.

Other *sūtras* make the point more strongly, but the *Ratna* gains through its pointed yet poetic subtlety. True renunciation is the abandonment of all grasping attachment, and clearly this is a mental state which may or may not be mirrored in the social institution of monasticism.

A final note. The *Perfection of Wisdom* texts repeatedly assert that the Bodhisattva does not engage in discursive thought. This may suggest a problem in relating the absence of discursive thought to *prajñā* as the result of analysis. It seems to me that the *Prajñāpāramitā sūtras*, in speaking from the point of view of the Buddha's non-dual, non-conceptual awareness, give little attention to how the Bodhisattva is to raise his or her perception to that level. Wisdom, I have argued, involves initially *extending* the analysis, to realize as fully as possible, in the first instance intellectually, the truth of emptiness. To conclude that wisdom for the *Perfection of Wisdom* is the result of simply cutting discursive thought, making the mind a blank perhaps, would, I think, be a historical and religious error, perhaps the error referred to in Buddhist hermeneutics as 'confusing the result with the cause'.[7] Otherwise, as Tsong kha pa points out, spiritual, salvific value would follow from fainting or deep, dreamless sleep.

THE BODHISATTVA

According to Haribhadra (late eighth century), those following the Hearer and Pratyekabuddha paths may also be called 'Bodhisattvas' in that they are aiming for an enlightenment (*bodhi*). Thus when specifically Mahāyāna Bodhisattvas are meant, those aiming for full Buddhahood for the benefit of all, the word '*mahāsattva*', meaning Great Being, is added. However, it is quite normal in Buddhist literature to use the word 'Bodhisattva' in a Mahāyāna sense to equal '*bodhisattva-mahāsattva*', i.e. that being who has taken the vow to be reborn, no matter how many times this may be necessary, in order to attain the highest possible goal, that of Complete and Perfect Buddhahood for the benefit of all sentient beings. It is in this sense too that I shall use 'Bodhisattva'.

The concern of the Bodhisattva is with liberation, full Buddhahood, not for himself alone (or herself, of course – this follows throughout), but for all sentient beings. The *Prajñāpāramitā sūtras* contrast this with the narrow scope of the non-Mahāyāna traditions, where their spiritual goal is in the last analysis purely a personal affair:

They make up their minds that 'one single self we shall tame, ... one

> single self we shall lead to final Nirvana.' A Bodhisattva should certainly not in such a way train himself. On the contrary, he should train himself thus: 'My own self I will place in Suchness [the true way of things], and, so that all the world might be helped, I will place all beings into Suchness, and I will lead to Nirvana the whole immeasurable world of beings.'
>
> (*Aṣṭa*, Conze 1973b: 163)

Again, from the *Pañcaviṃśati*:

> What do you think, Sariputra, does it occur to any of the Disciples and Pratyekabuddhas to think that 'after we have known full enlightenment, we should lead all beings to Nirvana ...?'
> Sariputra: No indeed, Lord.
> The Lord: One should therefore know that the wisdom of the Disciples and Pratyekabuddhas bears no comparison to the wisdom of the Bodhisattva.
>
> (Trans. in Conze 1968: 33)

The Bodhisattva generates infinite compassion, and all his acts are directed towards helping others:

> Great compassion ... takes hold of him. He surveys countless beings with his heavenly eye, and what he sees fills him with great agitation. ... And he attends to them with the thought that: 'I shall become a saviour to all those beings, I shall release them from all their sufferings!' But he does not make either this, or anything else, into a sign to which he becomes partial. This also is the great light of a Bodhisattva's wisdom, which allows him to know full enlightenment.
>
> (*Aṣṭa*, Conze 1973b: 238–9)

This last point is crucial. The Bodhisattva's deeds and attitude are all sealed with the perfection of *prajñā* – the Bodhisattva does not, in carrying out his infinite great and compassionate deeds, consider that there is any ultimately, inherently existing being who is helped. This is final, true, and total selflessness. In a famous passage the *Diamond Sūtra* says:

> As many beings as there are in the universe of beings ... all these I must lead to Nirvana. ... And yet, although innumerable beings have thus been led to Nirvana, no being at all has been led to

> Nirvana. ... If in a Bodhisattva the notion of a 'being' should take place, he could not be called a 'Bodhi-being'.
>
> (Trans. in Conze 1958: 25)

The *Perfection of Wisdom* also speaks of the Bodhisattva's cultivation of spiritual and other practices in order to develop various psychic and mundane abilities which he can then use in various ways to help sentient beings both materially and spiritually. Through psychic ability the advanced Bodhisattva is said even to be able to manifest Buddhas as psychic creations for the benefit of beings, so that in this and other ways the clear distinction between a Buddha and an advanced Bodhisattva begins to break down. Moreover, being selfless he turns over all his stock of merit, the result of his many virtuous deeds, for the benefit of others. He develops 'skill-in-means' (or 'skilful means' – *upāya*), the ability to adapt himself and his teachings to the level of his hearers, without attachment to any particular doctrine or formula as being necessarily applicable in all cases. The Bodhisattvas may, in their compassion, visit the hells in order to help hell-beings, and as the Mahāyāna developed so the notion of skill-in-means became a strategy whereby Buddhism could open itself out to new and originally non-Buddhist ideas. The *Kāraṇḍavyūha Sūtra*, for example, has Avalokiteśvara, a Bodhisattva so advanced that he has taken on divine attributes (an example of Conze's 'celestial Bodhisattvas'), apparently sanctioning Hindu doctrines such as Śaivism for those to whom such doctrines would be helpful.

The compassion and wisdom of the Bodhisattvas in the Mahāyāna scriptures are both descriptive and exhortatory. There are wonderful beings who have great abilities and perfect compassion. They have progressed well along the path to Supreme Buddhahood and are able and willing to help sentient beings in whatever ways may be of greatest benefit. On the other hand the follower of the Mahāyāna is exhorted to take the Bodhisattva vow himself, to take these teachings and the stories of Bodhisattvas as models. We know that historically the combination of descriptive and prescriptive planes sometimes gave rise to tension. The perfection of giving was often illustrated with popular but gory tales of the Bodhisattva giving his limbs or body, for example, or burning himself out of devotion and selflessness. Chinese pilgrims to India in classical times describe curious cases of what amounts to religious suicide. I-tsing, in the seventh century, observed that 'The Mahāsattva offered his own eyes and body, but a bhikṣu need not do so'! (Joshi 1967: 110)

The activities and aspiration of the Bodhisattva are well illustrated in the *Aṣṭasāhasrikā* by the story of Sadāprarudita ('Ever Weeping'), who willingly offers his own flesh in order to obtain money to give to the Bodhisattva Dharmodgata, who will teach him the *Prajñāpāramitā* (in spite of the cost of books, nowadays the teachings are somewhat cheaper, and for that reason perhaps less valued!). The flesh is offered to a Brahmin who wishes to carry out a particularly perverse sacrifice but, as in all good heroic tales, the Brahmin turns out to be a god testing the novice Bodhisattva's resolve, and he is restored to wholeness. The story forms an important source for our appreciation of the cult of the book, the *Prajñāpāramitā* text, and the Bodhisattva Dharmodgata is the perfect Dharma preacher, so important to the early Mahāyāna. He is Sadāprarudita's Good Friend, the person who is needed, according to a voice from the sky, in order to acquire and master the *Perfection of Wisdom*. The story is allegorical and visionary – indeed Stephan Beyer has pointed out the frequency of such visionary tales in the early Mahāyāna. Beyer speaks of the visionary origins of the Mahāyāna in general, and the *Prajñāpāramitā* in particular:

> The metaphysics of the Prajñāpāramitā is in fact the metaphysics of the vision and the dream: a universe of glittering and quicksilver change is precisely one that can only be described as empty. The vision and the dream become the tools to dismantle the hard categories we impose upon reality, to reveal the eternal flowing possibility in which the Bodhisattva lives.
>
> (Beyer 1977: 340)

It is frequently said in textbooks that the compassion of the Bodhisattva is so great that he postpones *nirvāṇa*, or turns back from *nirvāṇa*, in order to place all other sentient beings in *nirvāṇa* first. It seems to me, however, that caution and further research is required here. Such a teaching appears *prima facie* to be incoherent, and contains a claim that somehow a Buddha must be deficient in compassion when compared with a Bodhisattva. If all other beings must be placed in *nirvāṇa* before a particular Bodhisattva attains *nirvāṇa* himself there could obviously be only one Bodhisattva. Alternatively, we have the absurd spectacle of a series of Bodhisattvas each trying to hurry the others into *nirvāṇa* in order to preserve his or her vow! Moreover if sentient beings are infinite, a widely held view in the Mahāyāna, then the Bodhisattva is setting himself an impossible task, and no Bodhisattva could ever attain Buddhahood. I asked the late Kensur Pema Gyaltsen, head abbot of Drepung Monastery and one of the most learned Tibetan scholars, about this while he was on a visit to Britain. I explained that it was widely asserted in books available in the West that the Bodhisattva does not become enlightened until he has helped all other sentient beings to enlightenment. The eminent Lama seemed to find this most amusing since, as he put it, all those who had become Bodhisattvas would not become enlightened, while those who had not become Bodhisattvas would! He stated quite categorically that the final view is that this is not how Bodhisattvas behave. In Tibetan practice the merit from virtuous deeds is always directed towards obtaining full Buddhahood in order to be able to help beings most effectively. There is never any mention of postponing or turning back from Buddhahood. Otherwise any Bodhisattva who did become a Buddha would be presumably either deficient in compassion or have broken his vow.

In fact it should be clear that to speak of *nirvāṇa* in a Mahāyāna context is naïve. There are a number of different types of *nirvāṇa* – the *nirvāṇa* of the Arhat, of the Pratyekabuddha, the supreme and compassionte 'non-abiding' *nirvāṇa* of the Buddha, for example, not to mention the separate issue of whether a Buddha ever finally 'goes beyond' beings and enters some kind of final *nirvāṇa*. Generally, the Mahāyāna Bodhisattva does not postpone or turn back from *nirvāṇa*. Rather he or she rejects the *nirvāṇas* of the Arhat and Pratyekabuddhas, at least as final goals, and aims for the full *nirvāṇa* of the Buddha.

It is the textual situation which requires further research. There certainly are texts which speak of the Bodhisattva postponing or turning back from some enlightenment, although they are rare. The notion may have developed mainly in Sino-Japanese Buddhism. According to Kensur Pema Gyaltsen, if a text states this, it is not to be taken literally, it does not embody the final truth. It may be that it embodies a form of exhortatory writing – the Bodhisattva adopts a position of complete renunciation. In renouncing even Buddhahood the Bodhisattva precisely attains Buddhahood. Nancy Lethcoe (1977) claims to detect a difference between the *Aṣṭa* and the *Pañcaviṃśati sūtras* on this issue. The *Aṣṭa* clearly teaches that the Bodhisattva first attains Buddhahood, and only then can he fully help others. The *Pañcaviṃśati*, on the other hand, teaches that some Bodhisattvas will postpone their enlightenment until all beings have become enlightened (ibid., 264). She gives three references to the *Pañcaviṃśati* (60–73, 81, 170), but although in the first two sections there are many references to types of Bodhisattvas, some of whom it is stated *will* attain full enlightenment and help others, I fail to find any obvious reference to compassionate Bodhisattvas postponing

Buddhahood. *Pañcavimśati* 170, however, is different. In Conze's translation (used by Lethcoe) it reads (1979: 124): 'Through this skill in means will I, for the sake of all beings, experience that pain of the hells ... until these beings have won Nirvana. ... Afterwards I will, for the sake of my own self, know full enlightenment. ...' Clearly, the key word here is 'afterwards'. The Sanskrit and Tibetan, however, do not necessarily carry the temporal sense of the English 'afterwards'. They can mean 'thereupon', 'because of that', or 'thereby', all of which convey a very different meaning. I do not want to emphasize the linguistic point, however. My purpose is simply to suggest sensitivity to the initial incoherence and textual uncertainty concerning the Bodhisattva's claimed postponement of *nirvāṇa*, an assertion which appears to have become part of the lore of textbooks on Buddhism. In fact (*pace* Lethcoe), the *Pañcavimśati* also says that the Bodhisattva vows that 'after we have known full enlightenment we should lead all beings to Nirvana' (quoted above, p. 50). One should note, however, that the *Pañcavimśati*'s 'irreversible' Bodhisattvas seem to be able to do all the things a Buddha can. It is possible that at these rarefied levels, in the eyes of non-systematic piety, advanced Bodhisattvas and Buddhas have simply been conflated.

CHAPTER THREE

Madhyamaka

NĀGĀRJUNA AND ARYADEVA

Candrakīrti, at the beginning of his chapter on wisdom in the *Madhyamakāvatāra Bhāṣya*, observes that it is indeed difficult to understand the intention of the sacred scriptures. We are fortunate, Candrakīrti tells us, that there is a person predicted by the Buddha who can be taken as an authority for the exact meaning of the *sūtras*:

> How the Bodhisattva who courses in the perfection of wisdom sees the true nature of *dharmas* has been clearly taught by the Noble Nāgārjuna, who understood exactly the scriptures, in his Madhyamaka treatise, employing reasoning and scriptural testimony. This true nature of *dharmas* is characterized by their absence of inherent existence.
>
> (Cone edition, f. 242a)

The 'Noble' (*ārya*) Nāgārjuna, and his principal disciple Āryadeva, are credited with founding the Madhyamaka ('Middling') as a school, an attempt systematically to set forth, demonstrate, and defend an understanding of the way things really are. The name of Nāgārjuna is the first great name in Buddhist thought since the Buddha, and for that reason (among others) he is sometimes referred to as the 'second Buddha'. Unfortunately we know even less about the life of Nāgārjuna than we do about the Buddha himself. He has been the focus of many legends, however, and these have compensatory value for the scholar in the light they throw on concepts of sainthood and the activities of the spiritual hero. According to Tibetan sources Nāgārjuna was placed in the monastic order as a child in order to escape an astrological prediction of an early death. His subsequent mastery of doctrine, medicine, and alchemy was such that he was invited by the *nāgas*, under-water serpents, to visit their kingdom. While there he discovered the *Prajñāpāramitā sūtras*, which had been lost to the world of men since their exposition by the Buddha. He returned to the world with the *sūtras*, and through his magical ability was able to live for many centuries. Nāgārjuna also became the friend and advisor of a great king, and used his magic in order to keep the king in full vigour and youthfulness. Alas, even with magic and compassion it is impossible to please all of the people all of the time! The crown prince, impatient to succeed to the throne, appealed to Nāgārjuna to commit charitable suicide. He wanted the Master to demonstrate perfect generosity by donating his head. The only weapon which could be used to behead Nāgārjuna was a blade of sacred grass, a result of the time when Nāgārjuna accidentally killed some insects while gathering grass for his meditation cushion. It is said that when the time is ripe Nāgārjuna's head and body will rejoin and again work for the benefit of sentient beings – a rather nice millennarian touch! After death Nāgārjuna was reborn in Sukhāvatī, the Pure Land of Amitābha Buddha.

I leave the reader to meditate on the significance of such a story. Modern scholars favour the theory that there were at least two Nāgārjunas, distinguishing between the philosopher Nāgārjuna, who was probably from the southern or Andhra region, and lived perhaps in the second century CE, and a later Nāgārjuna who was a Tantric alchemist and yogin. In addition, it is possible that works have been attributed by the Buddhist tradition to Nāgārjuna simply because of his doctrinal importance, so that the name 'Nāgārjuna' now refers to a composite being of myth rather than a historical figure. There are thus serious historical and methodological problems in trying to suggest what in fact the 'teachings of Nāgārjuna' were.

Our interest at this point is with the second-century philosopher Nāgārjuna and not the later Tāntrika. Tibetan scholars divide Nāgārjuna's non-Tantric works into three classes, and it is reasonable to start by taking these treatises as works of our second-century Mahāyāna philosopher:

(i) The analytic corpus.

(a) *Madhyamakakārikā* – Nāgārjuna's principal philosophical work.

(b) *Yuktiṣaṣṭikā* – 'Sixty Verses on Reasoning [*yukti*]'.
(c) *Śūnyatāsaptati* – 'Seventy Verses on Emptiness'.
(d) *Vigrahavyāvartanī* – a reply to objections against his work.
(e) *Vaidalyaprakaraṇa* – an attack on the categories of the Hindu epistemologists (Nyāya).
(f) *Vyavahārasiddhi* – a proof of the conventional realm. This work is lost save for a few verses, and some Tibetans substituted the *Ratnāvalī*.

(ii) The collection of hymns. A number of hymns have been attributed to Nāgārjuna, one group of four being termed the *Catuḥstava*, although there is some dispute as to which four should be included.

(iii) The collection of shorter treatises and epistles. This includes two works attributed to Nāgārjuna which he apparently wrote as letters to his friend the king, the *Suhṛllekha* and the *Ratnāvalī* (if it is not included in the analytic corpus above).

A number of other treatises are attributed to Nāgārjuna by the Chinese and Tibetan traditions, some of which may be authentic, although I have mentioned already my doubt as regards the traditional Chinese attribution of the enormous *Ta-chih-tu lun* (*Mahāprajñāpāramitā Śāstra*) to the Master.

As with Nāgārjuna, it is possible to distinguish between a Tantric and a 'philosophical' Aryadeva. Traditionally it has sometimes been held that Nāgārjuna directed his attack at the Abhidharma scholars, while Aryadeva extended the critique to the non-Buddhist philosophical schools. His output was considerably smaller than that attributed to Nāgārjuna, and the most important work of the non-Tantric Aryadeva was a treatise called the *400 verses* (*Catuḥśatakakārikā*).

THE DEVELOPMENT OF THE MADHYAMAKA TRADITION IN INDIA

Tibetan writers, surveying the history of Indian Madhyamaka, have divided Madhyamaka teachers into a number of schools and subschools. There was little systematic attempt at such division in India itself and none, as far as we know, in China. Nevertheless, the Tibetan distinction between Svātantrika and Prāsaṅgika Madhyamaka, and the subsequent division of the former into Sautrāntika-Svātantrika Madhyamaka and Yogācāra-Svātantrika Madhyamaka became standard in Tibet and has been adopted by modern writers on the Madhyamaka.

It appears that the earliest of the 'sectarian' Mādhyamikas ('Madhyamika' – those who follow or pertain to the Madhyama, the Middle) was Buddhapālita (*c.* 470–540), who is sometimes said to have founded the Prāsaṅgika tradition. He apparently wrote just one work, a commentary on Nāgārjuna's *Madhyamakakārikā*, which survives (as do so many Madhyamaka texts) in Tibetan translation. It takes two to make a quarrel, however, and since in this work he shows no awareness of the criticisms of his arch-rival Bhāvaviveka (*c.* 500–70), who is said to have founded the Svātantrika tradition, it is only in retrospect that Buddhapālita can be called a Prāsaṅgika. In fact it was Candrakīrti (*c.* 600–50), who subjected Bhāvaviveka to trenchant criticism in defence of Buddhapālita, who must be deemed the actual founder of Prāsaṅgika Madhyamaka as a self-aware tradition standing in conscious opposition to the Svātantrikas. Most of Bhāvaviveka's works survive only in Tibetan and Chinese translation. They include his commentary to the *Madhyamakakārikā*, known as the *Prajñāpradīpa*, as well as what was probably the first 'encyclopedia of Indian philosophy', the *Madhyamakahṛdaya*, together with an autocommentary called the *Tarkajvālā* – the *Blaze of Reasoning*.

The great Prāsaṅgika is Candrakīrti, whose *Prasannapadā* commentary to the *Madhyamakakārikā* is the only commentary on Nāgārjuna's principal philosophical work surviving in Sanskrit. Candrakīrti's *Madhyamakāvatāra*, together with its *Bhāṣya*, an autocommentary, remain in Tibetan and integrate Madhyamaka philosophy into the Mahāyāna spiritual path. The *Madhyamakāvatāra* and its commentary are the official 'schoolbooks' for the study of Madhyamaka in Tibetan monastic universities to the present day, and they thus occupy the same role in the Madhyamaka curriculum as does the *Abhisamayālaṃkāra* in the study of the perfection of wisdom.

Among Prāsaṅgikas one should also mention Śāntideva (*c.* 695–743), whose *Bodhicaryāvatāra* is, like the *Madhyamakāvatāra*, a statement of the Bodhisattva's path to Buddhahood, but distinguished by a poetic sensitivity and fervour which makes it one of the gems of Buddhist and world spiritual literature.

It is often said that the issue which split the Madhyamaka into Svātantrika and Prāsaṅgika branches was one of methodology, and this certainly does explain the origins of their names although, as so often in the study of Mahāyāna thought, relatively little work has been done on these schools and conclusions are still very provisional.[1] Bhāvaviveka objected to the use by Buddhapālita of *prasaṅga* arguments – that is, arguments which try to convince the opponent of the error of his ways by simply pointing out that the opponent's position entails undesired consequences for the opponent himself. According to Bhāvaviveka this simply will not do. It is necessary also to employ an independent (*svatantra*) inference put into the proper logical structure or syllogistic form recognized by other schools of Indian philosophy, particularly the Buddhist logicians, headed by the brilliant Diṅnaga (fifth–sixth centuries). This dispute may look fairly minor, but perhaps it bulked large in an environment of scholastic precision. It does have its soteriological dimension, however. According to Tsong kha pa, that most acute and sophisticated of Madhyamaka commentators, the difference between the two schools here is not simply one of method, but rather of the most effective way of bringing the opponent to an inferential understanding of emptiness which is, as we have seen, one type of wisdom (*prajñā*). For Candrakīrti, however, rushing to the defence of Buddhapālita, Bhāvaviveka was simply addicted to logic! Note also that for Tsong kha pa, while there is a distinction between Svātantrika and Prāsaṅgika on this issue of method it is not, in spite of their names, their characteristic distinction. The distinctive difference between the two subschools of Madhyamaka lies in the acceptance by the Svātantrika of inherent existence conventionally, although all Mādhyamikas deny its ultimate existence. For the Prāsaṅgika, following Candrakīrti, this is a contradiction in terms and inherent existence is simply a fiction on any level.[2]

The Tibetan tradition terms Bhāvaviveka's school 'Sautrāntika-Svātantrika Madhyamaka' in order to distinguish it from the subsequent development of Yogācāra-Svātantrika Madhyamaka under Śāntarakṣita and his pupil Kamalaśīla (eighth century). The basic text for the Yogācāra-Svātantrika tradition is Śāntarakṣita's *Madhyamakālamkāra*, with an autocommentary and subcommentary by Kamalaśīla. Śāntarakṣita was influenced by the development of Buddhist 'idealism', the Yogācāra or Cittamātra tradition, which he uses as a stage on the path to establish the Madhyamaka position. The principal Cittamātra element in Śāntarakṣita's thought appears to lie in a view that, although ultimately all entities lack inherent existence, conventional objects are not external to the perceiving mind. Bhāvaviveka accepted that conventional objects are genuinely external to consciousness, as aggregates of atoms, and so he is termed a 'Sautrāntika-Svātantrika Madhyamaka' because his position in this respect is like that of the non-Mahāyāna Sautrāntika tradition. Kamalaśīla also wrote a number of independent works, particularly the

Madhyamakāloka, and three *Bhāvanākramas* showing the stages of Madhyamaka practice. Both Śāntarakṣita and Kamalaśīla were important early missionaries to Tibet, and according to the traditional stories Kamalaśīla appears to have been murdered there by anti-Buddhist rivals. Among later Yogācāra-Svātantrikas should also be mentioned Haribhadra (late eighth century), whose *Abhisamayālaṃkārālokā* is the principal Indian commentary to the *Abhisamayālaṃkāra*.

EMPTINESS AND INHERENT EXISTENCE – THE INCOMPATIBLE RIVALS

The concept of self-existence or essence (*svabhāva*) was a development of Abhidharma scholars, where it seems to indicate the defining characteristic of a *dharma*. It is that which makes a *dharma* what it is, as resistance or hardness is the unique and defining characteristic of an earth *dharma*, for example. In the Abhidharma only *dharma*s, ultimate existents, have essences. Conventional existents – tables, chairs, and persons – do not. This is because they are simply mental constructs out of *dharma*s – they therefore lack their own specific and unique existence.

Since the *Perfection of Wisdom sūtras* taught that all entities, including *dharmas*, are only conceptual existents or constructs, it follows that for the *Perfection of Wisdom* there can be no essences at all. The concept of the essence (*svabhāva*), however, seems to undergo a subtle shift in meaning in the Madhyamaka. It comes to signify generally 'inherent existence' in the sense of independent real existence. For *x* to have inherent existence is for *x* to exist in its own right. In a famous discussion in Chapter 15 of his *Madhyamakakārikā*, Nāgārjuna tells us:

> The origination of inherent existence from causes and conditions is illogical, since inherent existence originated from causes and conditions would thereby become contingent.
> How could there be contingent inherent existence, for inherent existence is not contingent, nor is it dependent on another being.
> (Nāgārjuna 1977: vv. 1–2)

Tibetan writers of the tradition founded by Tsong kha pa (the dGe lugs school, pronounced 'Geluk', the 'Way of Virtue') give a series of equivalents for the expression 'inherent existence' as it is used by the Prāsaṅgika Madhyamaka, among which is 'Self', 'truly existing', 'truly established', 'ultimately existing', and 'existing from its own side' – that is, existing completely independently from the mind which apprehends the entity concerned (Hopkins 1983: 36).

When the Madhyamaka speaks of all *dharmas* as empty (*śūnya*) it means specifically that all *dharmas* (and therefore all things) are empty of inherent existence. They have no essence. They are only relative. It is inherent existence which is opposed by the Madhyamaka, not tables and chairs as such, but tables and chairs conceived as inherently existing and therefore, in the Buddhist context, as permanent and fully satisfying. Later writers make a distinction between innate and acquired conceptions of inherent existence. Someone may follow the Abhidharma or some other metaphysical tradition and acquire through learning an 'artificial' conception of the inherent, real, fundamental existence of something or another – atoms, *dharmas*, or the Self, for example. These conceptions can be refuted fairly easily by pointing out that *dharmas*, atoms, or the Self cannot have *inherent* existence since they are causally dependent, they are part of a causal and conceptual flow. 'It is dependent origination [*pratītyasamutpāda*] that we call emptiness [*śūnyatā*]', Nāgārjuna says (*Madhyamakakārikā* (*MK*) 24:18). We might gloss this by saying that it is because entities originate in dependence on causes and conditions that they lack inherent existence, they are empty. In Tibet it is sometimes said that the particular meaning of the important Buddhist term 'dependent origination' (*pratītyasamutpāda*) for the Prāsaṅgika Madhyamaka is origination in dependence upon the designating mind; that is, when we say that all entities without exception are empty of inherent existence because they are dependently originated, one meaning of this particularly stressed by the Prāsaṅgika is that all entities are simply mental constructs – the letter A, for example, which we consider to exist as part of the real 'furniture' of the world, is simply imputed by the mind when */* – \ are brought together in a particular way (this happy example comes from Hopkins 1984: 17). *All* entities without exception do not exist from their own side but are imputed by the mind in this way (including the mind and emptiness themselves).

It is more difficult, however, to refute the innate conception of inherent existence. The claim here is that unless we are in some sense enlightened beings we all, whatever we may think or say, perceive things as having inherent existence. That is, we perceive and behave as though things were existent in their own right, therefore causally independent, and thus permanent. We thereby grasp after them with implicit expectation of permanent satisfaction. This is a version, of course, of the old and basic Buddhist claim that we suffer because we do not perceive things the way they really are; the root cause of the human predicament is a very deep form of ignorance. The refutation of the innate conception of inherent existence requires a correspondingly deep and sustained familiarity with meditation on emptiness.

Inherent existence is the equivalent for the Prāsaṅgika of really, ultimately existing, in the sense of existing from its own side, independent of the imputing, conceptualizing activity of the mind. In reading the Madhyamaka arguments against other schools, on causation, for example, it is crucial to bear in mind that what is being attacked is causation between inherently existent objects. To see entities as empty is to see them as mental constructs, not existing from their own side and therefore ***in that respect*** like illusions and hallucinatory objects. Nāgārjuna says, concerning the casual flow within which *dharmas*, with their *svabhāvas*, are said to occur according to the Abhidharma scholars:

> Whatever comes about conditioned by something else is quiescent from the point of view of inherent existence. Therefore both the process of origination and the act of production itself are quiescent. Like an illusion, a dream, or a castle in the air are production, duration and cessation declared to be.
>
> (*MK* 7:16/34, cf. also *Śūnyatāsaptati* vv. 64–73, trans. in Lindtner 1982: 63–9)

Emptiness itself is in a sense an abstraction. It is the absence of inherent existence and is seen through *prajñā*, analytic understanding in its various forms. Emptiness is not a vague absence, still less an Absolute Reality. It is the absence of inherent existence itself related to the object which is being critically examined in order to find out if it has inherent existence. Emptiness is the ultimate truth (*paramārthasatya*) in this tradition in the sense that it is what is ultimately true about the object being analysed, whatever that object may be. It is not a *thing*, certainly not an inherently existing thing, in its own right. Emptiness, Nāgārjuna asserts, was taught by the Buddhas as an antidote to all *dṛṣṭi*s, a word which must indicate here a viewpoint or dogma holding to the real existence of something as having inherent existence. Those who take emptiness as a *dṛṣṭi* are declared to be extremely difficult to help (*MK* 13:8). Mi bskyod rdo rje (pronounced: Mi kyer dor jay), the Tibetan hierarch of the Karma bKa' brgyud (pronounced: Ka gyer) school (the Eighth Karma pa, 1507–54), refers to two false interpretations of emptiness: one takes emptiness as equalling nihilism: nothing exists at all on any level; the other that emptiness is some sort of really existing, Ultimate Reality or Essence –

perhaps like the Brahman of Hinduism or the Godhead of other religions. Emptiness is thus not for the Madhyamaka the Ultimate Truth in the sense that it is an ultimately existing or inherently existing entity. If the object of analysis were to be emptiness itself then emptiness would also be found to lack inherent existence – just as the object is empty of inherent existence because dependently originated, so too must be its emptiness. Thus we come to emptiness of emptiness (*śūnyatāśūnyatā*; see Hopkins 1983: 433). This is a potentially infinite series, depending on what it is that the opponent is grasping at, for the function of understanding emptiness is simply to cut grasping.

A BRIEF NOTE ON MADHYAMAKA METHOD

Madhyamaka texts critically analyse the claims made by other traditions that something inherently exists. They themselves do not put forward the inherent existence of anything. The broad approach, therefore (at least in Prāsaṅgika Madhyamaka), is to take the claim made by an opponent that something really exists and show to the opponent, through reasoning using principles acceptable to the opponent, that such cannot be the case. Candrakīrti deals with this at length in his *Prasannapadā* commentary to *Madhyamakakārikā* 1:

> There is the setting-forward and proving of his own thesis only insofar as there is the drawing-out of the conclusion of the opponent's thesis. ... This is the best possible refutation, in that the opponent is incapable of establishing his thesis.
>
> (Vaidya 1960: 6, on *MK* 1:1)

This is the essence of the *prasaṅga* method. The Mādhyamika sets out to refute through reasoning his opponent, who advocates inherent existence and is thus bound through egoistic grasping. 'I do not myself have any thesis,' Nāgārjuna says, 'I negate nothing' (*Vigrahavyāvartanī* (*Vig*). vv. 29/63). Nāgārjuna's claim to have no thesis was extensively debated in Tibet even a millennium or more later.[3] There were those who interpreted Nāgārjuna's denial of a thesis as equivalent to an assertion that the Mādhyamika has no position at all and makes no assertions in any sense. He simply refutes. Others, most notably Tsong kha pa and his tradition, maintained that Nāgārjuna's denial of a thesis is only a denial of an inherently existing thesis. For Tsong kha pa, Nāgārjuna clearly has a position, and obviously makes assertions. Any alternative involves paradoxes. In context, Nāgārjuna's text criticizes an opponent who argues that Nāgārjuna must accept the real existence of something, to wit, his own words and arguments – otherwise he could not refute anything. His reply is that his own arguments quite obviously also lack inherent existence, but this does not mean that they lack refutative force. It is like when one illusory or dream entity puts an end to another illusory, dream entity (*Vig.* v. 23). From which it seems to follow that when Nāgārjuna says he does not negate he means that he does not negate as an act involving inherent existence. It is rather like activities between illusory entities. There is a non-inherently existing negation, and therefore a non-inherently existing thesis too.

It is a presupposition of the Madhyamaka analyses that if something did have inherent existence that thing would be resistant to analysis, or, as the Tibetans put it, the more it is searched for the clearer it would become. This is an Abhidharma principle for tracing an ultimate existent. In fact, when searched for, objects get lost. Madhyamaka critiques often start by delimiting the direction of the search. Thus, for example, if *x* has inherent existence it would be found as either identical with its parts, taken separately or as a collection, or as an inherently existing entity apart from them. To use Hopkins's example, the letter A, if it inherently exists, is identical either with any one of *1* – \, or with their shapeless collection, or with a separate entity from them. Clearly it is not found in any of these ways, so it does not inherently exist, that is, it does not exist from its own side, independently of the conceptualizing activity of the mind. According to Tsong kha pa's interpretation of Prāsaṅgika, it *does* exist as a conceptually created entity and it is perfectly correct for the Mādhyamika to make this assertion of existence. Tsong kha pa's rivals, on the other hand, tended to see the function of Madhyamaka as purely therapeutic, the cutting of all attachment through refutation alone. The need to assert or show that anything exists at all in any way was attacked as a move away from Nāgārjuna's purely critical approach and a step towards constructing a philosophical system. This was not what the Madhyamaka was about.

Finally, when the Mādhyamika criticizes a thesis of the opponent he is not to be taken as trying to establish as really existing a thesis which is the negation of that of the opponent. The Mādhyamika simply refutes the thesis that something is the case, and might then also continue to refute the thesis that it is not the case (for some poor deluded person may also become attached to this). As Candrakīrti puts it, it should not be inferred from the fact that an advocate of the absence of inherent existence draws unwelcome conclusions for the one who is attached to inherent existence that the first holds the contradictory position. The Mādhyamika has simply refuted; he is not committed to anything – words are not like policemen with big sticks!

THREE MADHYAMAKA CRITIQUES

Let us look now at some examples of Madhyamaka criticism. These examples are simplified accounts, intended as samplers, indicating Madhyamaka style rather than full and comprehensive expressions of the particular critiques.

On causation

The world of the Abhidharma, as interpreted by Madhyamaka, is one of a series of really existing *dharmas*, most of which are caused by preceding *dharmas* and in their turn can cause those which succeed. Nāgārjuna begins his *Madhyamakakārikā* with a critique of causation. The first verse provides a structure termed by later Mādhyamikas the 'Diamond Slivers' – the argument cuts like a diamond: 'Nowhere are there any entities which have originated from themselves, from another, from both, or from no cause at all.' The most succinct explanation of the argument is supplied by Buddhapālita. It is a classic series of *prasaṅgas*; indeed it was in commenting on this verse that Bhāvaviveka elaborated his attack on Buddhapālita's use of the *prasaṅga* and so inaugurated the Svātantrika/Prāsaṅgika debate:

> 'From themselves' means from their essential nature, and entities do not arise from their own essential natures because: (i) such an origination would be quite pointless, and (ii) it would lead to an infinite regress. If entities already essentially (inherently) exist there is no need to produce them, and if an already essentially existing entity is produced then it is not possible that it should ever be the case that it is not being produced. Thus origination does not occur from the entities themselves.
>
> (Trans. by Williams: see Nāgārjuna 1977)

This last point requires a little explanation. In Buddhist thought generally something is a cause because it produces its effect – if the cause is present then it does indeed bring about its result. If x causes itself then, having caused itself, *x* would be present again. Since *x* is the cause as well as the effect so, being present again, it produces the effect – itself – again. And so on, *ad infinitum*. Buddhapālita continues: 'Nor could it occur from another entity, because it would follow quite logically that everything could arise from everything else.' Entities are not produced by inherently existent, independently real, others. If *x* produced *y*, and they are *inherently* distinct entities, then we have no actual explanation of causation, since *x* is equally inherently distinct from *z*. If we call *y* the effect of *x*, equally *z* would be the effect of *x*, since in both cases the putative cause and effect are inherently quite distinct.

> Neither could there be origination from both self and other, since this argument would be prone to the faults of both positions. Nor from no cause at all, for then everything would be being produced continually and everywhere, and also it would become quite pointless to commence anything.
>
> (Trans. by Williams: see Nāgārjuna 1977)

Real production from no cause at all has two faults. First, since entities come into existence with no cause so the world would become random – things would arise anywhere and everywhere. Second, since there would be no cause for the production of *y* there would be no point in commencing something calculated to bring about *y*.

From all this we can conclude that when cause and effect are searched for they are not found. That is, there cannot exist a cause–effect relationship between inherently existing entities. Causation does not resist analysis; there can be no metaphysical theory of how causation really works. This is not to deny, however, the everyday, unanalysed world where, as we have seen, change, flux, dependent origination precisely entail that all things are empty of inherent existence.

On the Self

Nāgārjuna treats the subject of the Self in Chapter 18 of the *Madhyamakakārikā*. A more extensive analysis, an elaboration of Nāgārjuna's first verse, is given by Candrakīrti in his *Madhyamakāvatāra* 6:150 ff., and it is Candrakīrti's discussion which forms the *locus classicus* for the extensive Tibetan discussions of the subject. In Tibetan Buddhism analysis of the Self forms the first and crucial part of integrating the emptiness teaching into meditation practice. The following account is a simplified explanation based on Tibetan discussions. Nāgārjuna says:

> If the Self were the same as the psycho-physical constituents then it would be subject to birth and destruction. If it were other than the psycho-physical constituents then it would be devoid of the characteristics of these constituents.
>
> (*MK* 18:1)

The Self must be either the same or different from the mind–body collection. But mind and body are constantly changing. If the Self were the body then it would be unconscious. If the mind, then which of the constantly changing mental states is it? The present state has instantly ceased, and thus, if the Self were the present state it would have already perished. If it were the present state at whatever time one says the word 'I' then there must be a whole series of Selves, and already the notion of one enduring Self has collapsed. If the Self were the whole series of mental states from birth to death then the Self would cease to be unitary and become a collection, most of which has either perished or not yet come into existence. It could not then be an inherently existent Self. Likewise all the same problems would occur if the Self is the body plus the mind. Suppose, therefore, that the Self is posited as a really existing entity apart from the psycho-physical constituents. Then not only could such a Self never be apprehended, so that one would have no reason to think that it exists, but crucially there is no sense in which it would fit the description of what we believe to be our *Selves*. It would not be the 'I' which enjoys itself or feels depressed. It would seem to be a complete blank, and as such unnecessary and useless. Any Self which cannot be traced as either the same as, or different from, the changing mental and bodily states cannot exist.

As with causation, the Madhyamaka is not saying that we do not exist, or that we should not use the word 'I'. Rather, we do not exist in the way we think we do, as inherently existent, independent monads. The correct way of understanding our existence is as conceptually created entities superimposed upon our changing mental and bodily states.[4]

On nirvāṇa

In the *Aṣṭasāhasrikā Perfection of Wisdom, nirvāṇa* is delcared to be 'like an illusion, like a dream'. It is in the Madhyamaka that we find arguments to demonstrate such dramatic assertions.

Nirvāṇa, for Nāgārjuna, is 'the calming of all representations, the calming of all verbal differentiations, peace' (*MK* 25:24). It is said to be like the true nature of things (*dharmatā*, i.e. emptiness), not produced and not destroyed – that is, things are always like this; it is the cessation of the realm of verbal utterance and the (dualistic) mind (*MK* 18:7). It is the result of seeing things the way they really are, a seeing which occurs through going beyond the conceptualizing activity of our everyday minds and language, which conditions us to think in terms of inherent existence. 'The characteristic of reality [*tattva*]', Nāgārjuna says, 'is to be not dependent on another, calm, not differentiated by verbal differentiations, beyond discursive thought, without diversity' (*MK* 18:9). The expression 'not dependent on another' is glossed by commentators as meaning known by oneself, directly, not through the indirect medium of another person. This reality is interpreted by Prāsaṅgika teachers as equalling emptiness, i.e. the real way of things, but not an Ultimate, inherently existing Reality.

It is only fair to indicate at this point, however, that there have been both ancient and modern interpreters of Nāgārjuna's thought who have seen him as indicating here as elsewhere a true, positive Ultimate Reality. I shall return to this issue when I discuss the Buddha-essence (Chapter 5). There certainly are texts attributed to Nāgārjuna which do without a doubt give such a 'positive' interpretation of the Madhyamaka reality. Most important here is one of the hymns, the *Dharmadhātustava*. It is to this work, rather than to the strictly philosophical or logical texts, that Tibetan writers who wish to give a 'positive' interpretation of Nāgārjuna's thought refer. I suspect very strongly that the *Dharmadhātustava* is not by the philosopher Nāgārjuna, and it does not seem to cohere with the *Madhyamakakārikā*. It is not possible at our present state of knowledge to show this conclusively, however. Nevertheless, so long as we restrict ourselves to Nāgārjuna's works on philosophy and follow the *Aṣṭasāhasrikā* it seems to me that a positive interpretation of Nāgārjuna's views on the way things really are is rather unlikely.

Since for Nāgārjuna *nirvāṇa* is the result of calming the categorizing, conceptualizing mind, so any tendency to conceptualize *nirvāṇa* is refuted. *Nirvāṇa*, he says, is neither an existent nor a nonexistent, neither both together nor neither alternative. It could not be an existent, since all existents are part of the realm of causal conditioning (*MK* 25:5–6). It would then be subject to decay and perishing (literally: birth and death: *MK* 25:4). It could not be a nonexistent, however, since if there are really no existents so there can be no nonexistents. Nonexistence occurs when something goes out of existence, and also the very notion of nonexistence depends upon the notion of existence. Nonexistents are anyway not independent entities (*MK* 25:7–8). If there is really, from an ultimate point of view, nothing (that is, nothing has inherent existence), then *nirvāṇa* could not come about either. Moreover *nirvāṇa* could not be both an existent and a nonexistent, since these are contradictory (*MK* 25:14). And *nirvāṇa* as a really existing thing which is neither existent nor nonexistent is simply incomprehensible (*MK* 25:16). In fact, Nāgārjuna says:

> There is nothing whatsoever differentiating *saṃsāra* (the round of rebirth) from *nirvāṇa*. There is nothing whatsoever differentiating *nirvāṇa* from *saṃsāra*.
> The limit of *nirvāṇa* is the limit of *saṃsāra*. Between the two there is not the slightest bit of difference.
>
> (*MK* 25:19–20)

According to Tsong kha pa in his commentary to the *Madhyamakakārikā* (f.263b) this is not to be taken as the expression of some mystical identity. Rather, *nirvāṇa* and *saṃsāra* are identical in the sense that they have in all respects the same nature – absence of inherent existence. We should not think that this world is empty but *nirvāṇa* is some really existing alternative realm or world. *Nirvāṇa* is attainable here and now through the correct understanding of the here and now.

THE TWO TRUTHS

In Chapter 24 of the *Madhyamakakārikā* an opponent accuses Nāgārjuna of having destroyed the Buddhist religion with his teaching of emptiness. Nāgārjuna's reply is that:

> The doctrine of the Buddhas is taught with reference to two truths – conventional truth [*lokasaṃvṛtisatya*] and ultimate truth [*paramārthasatya*].
> Those who do not understand the difference between these two truths do not understand the profound essence [*tattva*] of the doctrine of the Buddha.
> Without dependence on everyday practice [*vyavahāra*] the ultimate is not taught. Without resorting to the ultimate, *nirvāṇa* is not attained. If emptiness is coherent then all is coherent. If emptiness is not coherent then likewise all is not coherent.
>
> (*MK* 24:8–10/14)

Nāgārjuna seems to be making two points here. First, his opponent fails to understand an old Buddhist distinction between the two truths (perhaps 'levels of reality' would be better). Thus he takes what is ultimately the case, i.e. things are not found, as being the way the everyday world is. This is patently absurd and would indeed destroy the Buddhist religion. As Candrakīrti points out, 'everyday practice does not exist from the point of view of ultimate truth'. In fact it is crucial for the Madhyamaka to accept the everyday conventional world, as it forms the basis for religious practice and without it enlightenment cannot be attained. Nevertheless, the everyday conventional world must be accepted not as an ultimate world but precisely as what it really is – the everyday conventional world. That is, it must be seen correctly as lacking inherent existence. The other point Nāgārjuna is making is that when the everyday conventional world is thus seen correctly it is apparent that emptiness (the ultimate truth) and the world are not opposed to each other but rather mutually imply each other. While emptiness in itself, directly cognized in a non-dual meditative absorption, is beyond language, as Candrakīrti says, 'not conditioned by others, quiescent, accessible to saints only by direct intuition, beyond all verbal differentiations', still, it is nothing more than the absence of inherent existence. As one of the most important of the transmitters of Buddhism to Tibet, Atiśa (982–1054), a Prāsaṅgika, puts it in his *Satyadvayāvatāra*: 'If one examines with reasoning the conventional as it appears, nothing is found. That nonfindingness is the ultimate. It is the primeval way of things' (*dharmatā*; 21, Lindtner's edn: Atiśa 1981: 192). The problem for Nāgārjuna's opponent lies in his interpretation of 'emptiness' as equalling 'nonexistence'. As Candrakīrti points out, emptiness is taught in order to calm all verbal differentiations, the net of concepts, and therefore it cannot equal another concept, that of nonexistence. Nonexistence is dependent upon existence, and is refuted by the Madhyamaka as much as the latter. In fact: 'The meaning of the expression "dependent origination" is the same as "emptiness", and not "non-existence". Falsely thinking that "emptiness" and "non-existence" are synonyms you criticize us' (Candrakīrti (1960) on *MK* 24:7). Since emptiness and dependent origination mutually imply each other it is *because* things are empty of inherent existence that change occurs. It is the opponent, with his doctrine of inherent existence, who has destroyed Buddhism, since clearly with inherent existence there can be no change and no enlightenment. And Nāgārjuna makes a gentle joke: 'You, levelling at us your own faults, are like a person mounted on a horse who has forgotten the horse' (*MK* 24:15)!

The most important Prāsaṅgika source for the doctrine of two truths is Candrakīrti's *Madhyamakāvatāra* 6:23 ff., together with its commentaries. All entities, Candrakīrti says, have two natures, because there is correct perception and delusory perception. The object of correct perception is reality (*tattva*). That of delusory perception is said to be conventional truth (v.23). Both Candrakīrti and Tsong kha pa are quick to point out that this 'reality' seen by correct perception is not something existing in its own right, with inherent existence, of course. Delusory perception is also of two sorts: that which occurs when the sense organs are working effectively, and that based on defective sense organs (v.24). Perception of the latter type is said by the world, the man in the street, to be delusóry in comparison with perception of the former type, which is accepted by the world. However, even the objects of correct worldly perception are only accepted as true, really true, by the world, and not by enlightened beings (the *āryas*; on *MK* 6:25). Moreover, the imaginary objects of those who philosophize incorrectly, such as the Self, are incorrect even from the point of view of worldly truth.

Let me clarify here what Candrakīrti and other Prāsaṅgikas, like Atiśa and Tsong kha pa, who follow him, are saying. If one searches through reasoning for what is really the case one finds that nothing resists analysis, and thus nothing is really the case. This is the ultimate truth. This perception of reality, the real situation, has as its object emptiness, absence of inherent existence, that is, absence of ultimate existence. Emptiness is not itself an ultimate existent, however. Some of the objects which are empty are maintained in the unenlightened world, on its own bases, as true, since unenlightened beings, through primeval ignorance, perceive things as having inherent existence. Others are held to be false by the world. Those beings who have reached a fair degree of enlightenment, however, do not see conventional entities as really true. They are 'merely conventional' (*saṃvṛtimātra*). This is the proper understanding of the conventional. Atiśa says: 'A *dharma* which has the ability to bring about its goal (i.e. has efficiency), which arises and ceases and satisfies so long as it is not critically examined – this is maintained to be the correct conventional' (v.3). Conventional and ultimate are not two distinct realities, two realms opposed to each other. It should be clear that the ultimate, emptiness, is what is ultimately the case concerning the object under investigation. It is what makes the object a conventional entity and not an ultimate one, as we think it is. Emptiness makes the conventional conventional. Conventional and ultimate are thus not separate. Nevertheless, they are also not the same. A chair and its emptiness of inherent existence are not literally the same thing. Nor is it a question of two different ways of seeing the same thing, as is sometimes stated in modern books on Madhyamaka. The fact that something lacks inherent existence is not just a way of looking at that thing. It is also something which happens to be true of it as well!

MEDITATION AND EMPTINESS – AN IMPRESSIONISTIC OUTLINE

The principal systematic Indian sources for the integration of emptiness teachings into Madhyamaka meditation practice are the three *Bhāvanākramas* of Kamalaśīla, which may indeed have been written originally for a Tibetan audience. In Tibet numerous such works were produced. The dGe lugs contributions have been studied in particular by Jeffrey Hopkins (1974; 1983: esp. 43–123; 1984: 134–44), and I shall follow Hopkins's account.

There is sometimes a tendency in the West to think of meditation and analysis as in some sense opposed. This is a tendency which should be firmly resisted when studying the Madhyamaka. Analysis, investigation of the way things really are, is an activity forming the principal ingredient of insight meditation (*vipaśyanā*), which leads to the different degrees of *prajñā*. The context of the earlier stages of meditation on emptiness may be either formal debate with an opponent or silent, private meditation, having calmed the mind and body. The content in either case will be systematic analysis – 'If an inherently existing entity arises then it can only come from itself, other, both or neither. If from itself, then…'. Meditation on emptiness proceeds through a number of stages. Initially the meditator gains a clear idea of what is, and what is not, being refuted. The object of refutation is inherent existence. The meditator (presupposing, from now on, that he or she is engaged in solitary meditation) clarifies what inherent existence is, and how it differs from mere existence. He may review the faults in attempting to refute existence *as such*, the conventional realm as well, particularly if his problem is to over-negate. He subsequently checks that the reasons given for absence of inherent existence do indeed entail such an absence. For example, in meditating on the emptiness of inherent existence of the Self, he considers that the Self lacks inherent existence because of being neither the same as nor different from the psycho-physical constituents. In order for the meditation to have any power, however, he must first be convinced that if the Self had inherent existence then it would be either the same as or different from the psycho-physical constituents. The meditator then surveys the arguments very carefully and systematically. And he concludes that therefore the subject of analysis lacks inherent existence. With experience the meditator is able to place his mind on this absence alone, the vacuity which is a specific vacuity of absent inherent existence in the object being analysed. His mind in this state has no actual conception of subject and object, although subject and object do still appear. He is said to have attained a conceptual realization of emptiness – conceptual because it is through the medium of an image, it is still not a direct cognition of emptiness. Through repeated familiarization with such meditation the conviction that entities are empty of inherent existence becomes more and more firm and penetrates his awareness. It forms the necessary background to all his religious activity.

The next stage of meditation on emptiness is to attain perfect meditative absorption. Practices for generating stabilization, or calm abiding (*śamatha*), are found throughout the religious world. The meditator gains an ability to place his mind without effort and without wavering on the meditation object. Since meditation on emptiness requires analysis, and analysis is not conducive initially to a one-pointed mind, specific meditation on emptiness is normally postponed at this stage until an ability to generate calm abiding has been acquired. It can take some time. With the calm, still, powerful mind thus developed, our meditator now returns to emptiness, alternating calming meditation with analytic meditation. Eventually a deep state of absorption, one-pointedness (but not yet pure calm abiding), is attained through analytic meditation itself. When analytic meditation actually generates calm abiding one is said to have attained insight (*vipaśyanā*). If this insight is generated with emptiness as the object, one enters what is called the 'Path of Preparation' (*prayogamārga*), which is one of the five successive paths of Buddhist practice (see Chapter 9). Subsequently, in stages, one removes the conceptual elements of this insight into emptiness. When a direct, non-conceptual insight is attained in meditative absorption then one is said to enter the 'Path of Insight' (*darśanamārga*). This is a direct, non-dual cognition of the ultimate. If it is combined with the altruistic concern of the Bodhisattva then our meditator attains the first of the ten Bodhisattva stages (*bhūmi*). All artificial conceptions of inherent existence are completely eradicated. When he arises from his meditation he still sees inherent existence, but he knows that this is not how things are, and he is like a magician viewing his own creations. There is still a very long way to go, however, for he has now so to refine his perception that he eradicates completely even the innate moral and cognitive taints (including the innate conception of inherent existence). He must attain omniscience, Buddhahood, such that no longer even sees inherent existence but sees emptiness in the very same perceptual act as he sees objects.

A FINAL NOTE – MADHYAMAKA IN CHINA AND EAST ASIA

In East Asia the Madhyamaka was generally known as the 'Three Treatise School', after the three Indic texts which served as the root texts for this tradition in Sino-Japanese Buddhism. These treatises were translated into Chinese by the great translator Kumārajīva (344–413), who may be said to have established the Madhyamaka tradition in China, although the principal orientation of the tradition was known for some time prior to Kumārajīva to the early translations of the *Prajñāpāramitā sūtras*. There was nevertheless a strong tendency in these early translations prior to Kumārajīva to the early translations of the *Prajñāpāramitā sūtras*. There environment. The early translator Chih-chien (third century), for example, chose to translate '*śūnya*', '*śūnyatā*', and '*tathatā*' (suchness/thusness; the ultimate way of things) by '*pen-wu*' – original nonexistence – a term used by the Taoist commentator Wang-pi (226–49) to equal the primeval non-being from which things evolve, thus conveying to the Chinese mind at this time a sense of emptiness as the cosmological origin of manifold forms.[5]

The Three Treatises are all, unfortunately, of obscure origin. The *Chung lun* (*Madhyamaka Śāstra*) consists of Nāgārjuna's *Madhyamakakārikā* embedded in a commentary said to be by an Indic teacher whose name in Chinese is given as Ch'ing-mu. It is not possible to be certain of his Indian name or who this teacher was. The *Shih-erh-men lun* (*Dvadaśamukha Śāstra?*) appears in the main to be a collection of verses drawn from Nāgārjuna with a commentary attributed by some to Nāgārjuna and by others to the elusive Ch'ing-mu. The *Pai-lun* (*Śata Śāstra*) is a work by Aryadeva, with a commentary by another obscure figure, Vasu. The verses may bear some relationship to the second part of Aryadeva's *Catuḥśataka*. Sometimes the *Ta-chih-tu lun* (*Mahāprajñāpāramitā Śāstra*) is added to the Three Treatises, producing a Four Treatise School. This text is attributed to Nāgārjuna, in the form in which it now stands incorrectly, and it was also translated (or compiled) by Kumārajīva. Although some works by Bhāvaviveka were translated into Chinese, and commentaries or partial commentaries on the *Madhyamakakārikā* by the Yogācāra (Cittamātra) masters Asaṅga and Sthiramati, neither Buddhapālita's commentary nor the works of Candrakīrti were translated into Chinese – not to mention the later Yogācāra-Svātantrika works. This means that the Chinese Three Treatise School, and therefore the school in Japan and Korea, developed quite independently of the major scholastic disputes and developments in Indian Madhyamaka.

The most important Mādhyamika among Kumārajīva's Chinese disciples was Seng-chao (384–414), but the greatest of the San lun (Three Treatise) masters in China was Chi-tsang (549–623). Chi-tsang's Madhyamaka teachings seem to be rather different from those of his chronological successor Candrakīrti. One of Chi-tsang's pupils, a Korean named Ekwan (a number of important early 'Chinese' Mādhyamikas were in fact Korean) first introduced the Madhyamaka into Japan in 625, but although it contributed to the ideas of other schools it never really flourished as an independent school. In China, too, the Three Treatise School seems to have entered a decline after Chi-tsang, and although it contributed a certain amount to Ch'an (Zen), for example, it eventually perished as a separate school in the ninth century. Three Treatise teachings, on the other hand, have continued to be studied to the present day in East Asian Buddhism.

Two teachings in particular characterize Chi-tsang's interpretation of Madhyamaka. First, there is his principle that 'the refutation of wrong views *is* the illumination of right views'. That is, the Mādhyamika holds no views at all, he simply refutes false views, and the refutation of false views is not in order to establish another view but rather to let go of all attachment to any view and thence to all words and conceptuality. Emptiness is not itself a true doctrine or view, but is a therapeutic device, as Nāgārjuna says, the antidote to all views (*dṛṣṭi*). The Ch'ing-mu commentary likens emptiness to a medicine – if the medicine increases the illness then one is incurable.[6]

Second, there is Chi-tsang's doctrine of the two levels of truth. For Chi-tsang the two levels of truth are not, as they are for Candrakīrti, two natures possessed by all things. Rather, they are levels of teaching which are, as such, not fixed but provisional, taking the student through a step-by-step dialectical ascent to a state of non-conceptuality. This ascent is composed of three phases. At the first level people have conceptions of existence, and these are opposed with emptiness (= nonexistence here?).

At this level existence is conventional truth, emptiness ultimate truth. It is now important to negate emptiness as well, in order that the mind does not become fixed, attached to emptiness and thereby duality. At the second level, therefore, existence and emptiness are conventional truth, non-duality is the ultimate truth. By 'non-duality' here, Chi-tsang explains, neither existence nor emptiness is meant. Third, both duality and non-duality are conventional truth, while neither-duality-nor-non-duality is the ultimate truth (*Erh-ti-chang*, trans. in Chan 1963: 360). This is the denial of all views, all extremes, and with the denial of all views and concepts the mind is able to shine forth in a non-conceptual state of *prajñā*.

In formulating his theory of the two levels of truth Chi-tsang was undoubtedly influenced by the *Vimalakīrtinirdeśa Sūtra*, an important *sūtra* in Chinese Buddhism. In this *sūtra* a similar but extended series of teachings is given in order to explain the meaning of non-duality. Eventually Mañjuśrī, the Bodhisattva particularly associated with wisdom, explains that true non-duality is to say nothing. Vimalakīrti accordingly, when asked for his explanation of non-duality, remains in silence. On the ultimate level there is nothing to speak about. In spite of this, Chi-tsang's teachings are, I suspect, in part due to certain Chinese Taoist concerns, although (*pace* Candrakīrti) they nevertheless do have a basis in Indian Madhyamaka. Fung Yu-lan points out that Chi-tsang's state where all concepts cease is exactly paralleled in the work of the Taoist Chuang-tzu. Wing-tsit Chan comments that Chi-tsang's dialectic is strikingly similar to approaches found in Chuang-tzu.[7] An emphasis on an original, non-conceptual, spontaneous purity beyond all words (which mislead in a very radical way) has always been central to the concerns of Philosophic or Contemplative Taoism.

CHAPTER FOUR

Cittamātra (Mind Only)

BACKGROUND

Nāgārjuna probably lived during the second century CE, and he is associated with a king of the Sātavāhana dynasty, a dynasty which held sway for some time over large areas of Central India, the Deccan. As we have seen, North India during the last century or so BCE and the first three centuries CE was subject to foreign invasions and fragmentation. Impermanence (lack of inherent existence) was present in the very fabric of the socio-political environment! With the rise of the Gupta empire in the fourth century, however, all changed. For two centuries the Gupta empire dominated India, and this domination marks the high point of classical Indian civilization. India's greatest poet and dramatist, Kālidāsa, probably lived at the court of Candra Gupta II (*c.* 376–415). It is from this time also that Chinese pilgrims, in search of *sūtras* to take home to China and translate, started to visit India and, with fine historical sense, they have left us accounts of their travels and observations. The greatest of these pilgrims were Fa-hsien and Hsüan-tsang (the model for Tripiṭaka in the famous *Monkey* stories). Hsüan-tsang visited India not during the Gupta period, however, but during the reign of Harṣa (seventh century), one of the major post-Gupta kings of North India, and it is possible to detect already, in comparison with the Gupta visit of Fa-hsien, a certain decline in social and political stability. Hsüan-tsang has left a detailed description of the enormous Buddhist monastic university of

Nālandā, in present-day Bihar. Such universities were similar to the universities of medieval Europe, and provide the model for Tibetan monastic universities up to the present day, although most in Tibet itself have been destroyed in recent years by the Chinese. They taught not only Buddhism but Hindu thought and other disciplines such as medicine. Universities like Nālandā and Vikramaśīla also trained missionaries in the skills needed in order to transmit Buddhism to Central Asia, China, and Tibet (Buddhism reached Korea and Vietnam via China, and Japan from China and Korea). More ominously for the history of Indian Buddhism, it is from the Gupta period that we can see the flowering of Hinduism in its classical Purāṇic form, the form in which it is now familiar. It is admittedly difficult to show in detail the mutual influences of Hinduism and Buddhism at this time, although the influence of Buddhist thought on Gauḍapāda (seventh century), the founder of Advaita Vedānta, is quite clear. It seems likely that the influence of classical Hinduism on Buddhism was more in the direction of practices – the forms of Mahāyāna devotionalism, for example – than on philosophical thought.

With the coming of the Guptas we find, therefore, socio-economic stability, prosperity, Buddhism a major academic (and land-holding) institution, a dynamic resurgent Hinduism in its classical form, and an environment of intellectual brilliance and sophistication. Asaṅga and Vasubandhu, said to be the founders (together with a very obscure Maitreya) of the Cittamātra tradition, appear most likely to have lived during the early part of this Gupta period.

It would be wrong to suppose that the first stage of Mahāyāna was characterized by the production of new scriptures, and that this stage was followed by their systematic exposition through philosophic schools. The production of Mahāyāna *sūtras* seems to have continued throughout most, if not all, of the history of Mahāyāna in India – not to mention the 'spurious' *sūtras* of Central Asia and China. Although they are characteristic of the earliest phase of Indian Mahāyāna, *Perfection of Wisdom sūtras*, for example, continued to be produced for many centuries alongside scriptures representing a conceptually later phase of Mahāyāna. One should be cautious also about assuming that within any one phase of Mahāyāna the earliest *sūtras* predate systematic treatises (*śāstras*). The earliest *sūtra* clearly of the Cittamātra tradition, the *Saṃdhinirmocana Sūtra*, seems to postdate at least in part the earliest systematic treatise, the encyclopedic *Yogācārabhūmi*.

The *Saṃdhinirmocana Sūtra* is a fairly short and systematic scripture, although it still grew over a period of time. New teachings characteristic of the Cittamātra tradition are found mainly in Chapters 5–7. As a *sūtra* the *Saṃdhinirmocana Sūtra* is quite aware that it represents a new tendency in Buddhism. It speaks of 'three turnings of the Wheel of Dharma'. This phrasing follows an old and recognized Buddhist precedent. The Buddha's very first *sūtra* was called the *Dharmacakrapravartana Sūtra* – the Turning of the Wheel of Dharma. In the *Aṣṭasāhasrikā* the gods rejoice at the teaching of the Buddha, proclaiming: 'We now, indeed, see the second turning of the wheel of dharma taking place' (trans. in Conze 1973b: 150). Of course, the *sūtra* adds that in reality no turning actually occurs! The *Saṃdhinirmocana* shows an awareness of the thread of Buddhist intellectual history, a need to explain the 'turnings of the Wheel' and to resolve these into a final, definitive explanation. The *sūtra* explains that formerly the Buddha taught in Varanasi (Benares) the non-Mahāyāna Hearer teachings of the Four Noble Truths and so forth. This was a wonderful teaching, but it was not the final teaching; it required interpreting and had to be understood correctly. It subsequently became a basis for disagreement. The Buddha also taught that all *dharmas* lack inherent existence. This was the second turning of the Wheel of Dharma, also marvellous, but it too required interpreting and subsequently became a basis for disagreement. The final teaching, however, the teaching of the *Saṃdhinirmocana Sūtra* itself, is completely explicit, absolutely marvellous, cannot be surpassed, it is not a basis for disagreement, there is no higher teaching, its meaning is to be taken literally (see Lamotte 1935: 7: 30).

The distinction between texts which have to be interpreted and those which can be taken literally (*neyārtha/nītārtha*) forms the basis of Buddhist hermeneutics and was an ancient one, found in all Buddhist schools. Tsong kha pa devoted a whole treatise to explaining how this distinction is made in the different Mahāyāna traditions (trans. in Thurman 1984). According to Tsong kha pa for the Madhyamaka, following a *sūtra* called the *Akṣayamatinirdeśa*, texts to be taken literally or of definitive meaning are those which teach emptiness. By way of contrast, the *Saṃdhinirmocana Sūtra* states that the *Perfection of Wisdom* and Madhyamaka teachings of emptiness were only a skilful means employed by the Buddha, they were not his final teaching. According to this scripture some of those who heard the Buddha's teaching of emptiness understood that it was not to be taken completely literally but had to be interpreted. They meditated and realized accordingly. Others were honest and good folk who did not understand but recognized the profundity of the emptiness scriptures and had faith in them. Since they did not understand the *sūtras* they could not meditate, of course. Yet others were wicked, and took the teaching of universal emptiness literally. They over-negated, destroying the Dharma. Some took this as the Buddha's true teaching, others, from the same basis, concluded that the emptiness teachings, the *Prajñāpāramitā*, could not be the word of the Buddha (7: 18–23). These have fallen into an abyss of wrong views. For the *Saṃdhinirmocana Sūtra*, therefore, the Buddha did not intend complete emptiness, and there has been an over-negation. Something, as we shall see, really exists!

THE CITTAMĀTRA TRADITION – SCHOLARS AND TEXTS

All Tibetans know the story of Asaṅga (310–90?). The saint strove for many years to have a vision of the celestial Bodhisattva Maitreya, at that time residing in the Tuṣita heaven awaiting his time to return to earth as the next Buddha. Despairing of the results of his meditation Asaṅga gave up, but when, full of compassion, he stooped to help a suffering dog by the roadside that dog became Maitreya himself. Maitreya is always there, but he is only seen through the eyes of compassionate holiness. Maitreya took Asaṅga to Tuṣita and there taught him five new texts:

(i) *Abhisamayālaṃkāra* – the treatise on *Perfection of Wisdom* practice mentioned in Chapter 2.
(ii) *Madhyāntavibhāga* – 'The Discrimination of Middle from Extremes'.
(iii) *Dharmadharmatāvibhāga* – 'The Discrimination of *dharmas* and their True Nature'.
(iv) *Mahāyānasūtrālaṃkāra* – 'The Ornament of the Mahāyāna Sūtras'.
(v) Finally, the *Ratnagotravibhāga*, often known as the *Uttaratantra*, a treatise on the *tathāgatagarbha* or Buddha–essence doctrines which will be examined in the next chapter.

It seems to me unlikely that the *Abhisamayālaṃkāra* and the *Ratnagotravibhāga* stem from the same hand as the other three texts, but it is quite possible that these other three do have a single author. Modern scholars, doubting the divine, have disagreed over whether this charming story indicates that Asaṅga himself really composed these texts, or whether they can be traced to a genuine human author called Maitreya, perhaps Asaṅga's teacher, sometimes referred to as Maitreyanātha to distinguish him from any 'mythological' figure. Erich Frauwallner has argued that had Asaṅga considered himself inspired in a vision by the Bodhisattva Maitreya he would have written not philosophical treatises (*śāstras*) but rather *sūtras*. Since these three texts are, according to Frauwallner, unitary philosophical works, and differ somewhat from works known to be by Asaṅga, so this indicates an authorship by Maitreyanātha rather than by the Bodhisattva Maitreya (Frauwallner 1956: 297). I leave the matter open!

Among works attributed to Asaṅga himself ar ethe *Abhidharmasamuccaya*, a text which constructs a Mahāyāna Cittamātra Abhidharma and indicates that the Mahāyāna was by no means completely opposed to the Abhidharma, the *Mahāyānasaṃgraha*, an important general treatise on Cittamātra-Yogācāra doctrine, and the *Yogācārabhūmi* – the Stages of Yogācāra. The *Yogācārabhūmi*, however, is attributed by the Chinese tradition to Maitreya, and is almost certainly the work of a school, a compilation over some time, lacking a number of characteristic Cittamātra doctrines and rather earlier than Asaṅga.

Vasubandhu is said to have been Asaṅga's brother, the author of the *Abhidharmakośa* and its commentary (*Bhāṣya*), the principal source in Tibet (and extant in Sanskrit) for the study of the non-Mahāyāna Sarvāstivāda-Vaibhāṣika Abhidharma. Asaṅga is held to have subsequently converted his brother to Mahāyāna.[1] Two important Cittamātra works attributed to Vasubandhu are the *Viṃśatikā* (*20 Verses*) and the *Triṃśikā* (*30 Verses*). Among the other works said to be by Vasubandhu the brother of Asaṅga are commentaries on the *Madhyāntavibhāga* and *Dharmadharmatāvibhāga*, and a series of verses known as the *Trisvabhāvanirdeśa*, the Teaching on the Three Aspects. A commentary to the *Mahāyānasūtrālaṃkāra* may be by Asaṅga or by Vasubandhu.

Two other important Indian writers on Cittamātra should also be mentioned – Sthiramati and Dharmapāla. Both these masters appear to have lived during the sixth century, and were roughly contemporaneous with the Svātantrika-Mādhyamika Bhāvaviveka, with whom they engaged in written debate. Sthiramati and Dharmapāla represent different subschools of Cittamātra. Sthiramati's tradition was associated with the university of Valabhī, founded in the sixth century by Sthiramati's teacher Guṇamati, who had left Nālandā. Dharmapāla, who died at the early age of 32, represented the Nālandā tradition, although it is unclear how far he also innovated. Hsüan-tsang studied Cittamātra at Nālandā and upon his return to China established the Fa-hsiang school purporting to follow the interpretation of Dharmapāla. The basic text of this school in China was the *Ch'eng-wei-shih lun* (*Vijñaptimātratāsiddhi*), a translation of Vasubandhu's *Triṃśikā* together with a commentary composed of ten Indian commentaries, with precedence given to that by Dharmapāla. Among the most important Cittamātra works of Sthiramati were his commentaries on the *Triṃśikā* and the *Madhyāntavibhāga*, both of which survive in Sanskrit. The *Ch'eng-wei-shih lun* itself is our main source for Dharmapāla's views, although some other works do survive in Chinese translation.

THE THREE ASPECTS (*TRISVABHĀVA*)

The expression *Cittamātra*, together with *Vijñaptimātra* and sometimes *Vijñānavāda* which are also used for this school, all refer to its principal classical doctrine, which is that of Mind (*citta/vijñāna*) Only (*mātra*). Another name, possibly older, is *Yogācāra*, which seems to refer to monks dedicated particularly to the practice of yoga, here meaning meditation. It is possible that some of the key doctrines of Cittamātra, classical Yogācāra, were the product initially of reflection on meditative experience. This can be seen already at a very early, pre-Cittamātra stage in the *Pratyutpanna Sūtra*. In Chapter 3 of that *sūtra* questions are asked about the status of Buddhas seen and teachings received in meditation. How is it possible? The answer is that 'Whatever belongs to this triple world ... is nothing but thought [*cittamātra*]. Why is that? Namely, however I discriminate things ... so they appear' (trans. in Harrison 1979: 37). The Buddha is produced by mind, or thought, as is my own body – although true to the Madhyamaka orientation of this *sūtra* the mind is also stated to be lacking in inherent existence. When we turn to the earliest specifically Cittamātra scripture, the *Saṃdhinirmocana Sūtra*, we again find that the doctrine that all is only mind is introduced in the context of a discussion of meditation. The Buddha is asked whether the images perceived in meditation are different or not different from the mind? The answer is that they are not different. The image is said to be only perception (*vijñaptimātra*; for this expression see Hall 1986). Nevertheless, people consider that there are also material objects in the world, really existing outside the mind. Are these not different from the mind? The Buddha replies that they are indeed not different – but deluded, unenlightened people do not understand the teaching of 'only perception' (8: 7–8). As

Lambert Schmithausen has stressed, the 'formulation of universal idealism' in Cittamātra arose out of a generalization of reflections on meditative practice, and not originally from purely theoretical or doctrinal, philosophical, concerns (Schmithausen 1973a: 176). Moreover, the fact that all is experienced in meditation to be only mind enables the yogin to engage in the world and manipulate it in what appears to be a wholly miraculous way.[2]

Cittamātra is a complex and sophisticated tradition, much less studied in the West than Madhyamaka. It certainly should not be presupposed that all or even most of the Cittamātra masters and texts teach exactly the same doctrine. Nevertheless, they do have some teachings in common, and central to Cittamātra thought is that of the Three Aspects.[3] The teaching of the Three Aspects is for the *Saṃdhinirmocana Sūtra* the final correct doctrine, requiring no interpretation or adaptation, the antidote to the nihilistic interpretation of emptiness.

All things which can be known can be subsumed under these Three Aspects. The first Aspect is called the constructed or conceptualized aspect (*parikalpitasvabhāva*). The *Saṃdhinirmocana Sūtra* connects it with the falsifying activity of language. It is the realm of words which attribute inherent existence to things (6: 4). More informatively, the *Mahāyānasaṃgraha* and its commentaries explain that the conceptualized or constructed aspect is appearance as an object when really there are only perceptions (*vijñaptimātra*). By 'object' here is meant both poles of an experience, both experiencer and that which is experienced, referred to in Cittamātra terminology as 'grasper' and 'grasped' (*grāhaka/grāhya*; *Mahāyānasaṃgraha* 2: 3). The conceptualized aspect is the world as it is experienced by everyday unenlightened folk, the world of really existing subjects confronting really existing and separate objects. It is how things appear to us, the realm of subject–object duality. These things do not actually exist at all (*Triṃśikā* v.20), things are not really like that.

The second Aspect, the dependent aspect (*paratantrasvabhāva*), is, according to the *Saṃdhinirmocana Sūtra*, the dependent origination of *dharmas*, that is, the causal flow (6: 5). According to the *Trisvabhāvanirdeśa* it is that *which* appears, in opposition to the *way* in which it appears, which is the first Aspect, the conceptualized aspect (v.2). In other words, it is the substratum for the erroneous partition into inherently existing subjects and objects which marks the conceptualized aspect.

In order to understand what is being said here, one should try and imagine all things, objects of experience and oneself, the one who is experiencing, as just a flow of perceptions. We do not know that there is something 'out there'. We have only experiences of colours, shapes, tactile data, and so on. We also do not know that we ourselves are anything other than a further series of experiences. Taken together, there is only an ever-changing flow of perceptions – *vijñaptimātra*. Due to our beginningless ignorance we construct these perceptions into enduring subjects and objects confronting each other. This is irrational, things are not really like that, and it leads to suffering and frustration. The constructed objects are the conceptualized aspect. The flow of perceptions which forms the basis for our mistaken constructions is the dependent aspect.

In itself the dependent aspect is, of course, beyond language, since language is the realm of the conceptualized aspect – language necessarily falsifies, constructs inherently existing entities. Indicating its nature, we might say that the dependent aspect is the flow of experience which is erroneously partitioned. The *Mahāyānasaṃgraha* describes it as the support for the manifestation of non-existent and fictive things (2: 2). Note, however, that for the Cittamātra falsification (*pace* the Madhyamaka) requires a really existing substratum. This point is strongly made in the very earliest phase of Yogācāra thought, in the *Yogācārabhūmi*. One has to avoid both under- and over-negation. Under-negation is to take for inherently existing realities entities which are merely the creation of language, in other words, the conceptualized aspect. Over-negation is to deny the substratum which really, ultimately (*paramārtha*) exists, albeit inexpressibly, and to say that nothing exists at all. Both these faults are ruinous to religious practice. There must be a real substratum, for without a real substratum erroneous construction, the conceptualized aspect, could never take place.[4] Moreover, if the dependent aspect as substratum did not exist, then likewise liberation, seeing things the way they really are, could also not occur. There would be simply universal nonexistence (*Mahāyānasaṃgraha* 2: 25).

The final Aspect is called the perfected aspect (*pariniṣpannasvabhāva*). According to the *Saṃdhinirmocana Sūtra* it is the 'Suchness' or 'Thusness' (*tathatā*), the true nature of things, which is discovered in meditation (6: 6). It is said to be the complete absence, in the dependent aspect, of objects – that is, the objects of the conceptualized aspect (*Mahāyānasaṃgraha* 2: 4). This is not as difficult as it sounds. What it amounts to is that through meditation we come to know that our flow of perceptions, of experiences, really lacks the fixed enduring subjects and objects which we have constructed out of it. There is only the flow of experiences. The perfected aspect is, therefore, the fact of non-duality, there is neither subject nor object but only a single flow. It is also emptiness, explained for this tradition as meaning that one thing is empty of another. That is, the flow of perceptions – the dependent aspect – is empty of enduring entities – the conceptualized aspect. What remains, the substratum which is empty of those enduring entities, the flow of perceptions themselves, nevertheless does exist (Willis 1979: 163; Thurman 1984: 214). One of the commentaries to the *Mahāyānasaṃgraha* explains all the Three Aspects with reference to the example of water seen in a mirage. The water as perception rather than real water is the dependent aspect. The water considered by a person hallucinating to be real water is the conceptualized aspect, while the complete absence of real water in the water as image is the perfected aspect (on 2: 4).

Were there to be no dependent aspect there could likewise be no liberation, for without a flow of perceptions there would be nothing at all! According to the *Mahāyānasaṃgraha*, no dependent aspect, no perfected aspect (2: 25). Elsewhere it is explained that the dependent aspect is conceptualized aspect in one part, and perfected aspect in another. The first part is *saṃsāra*, the second *nirvāṇa* (2: 28). That is, the dependent aspect, the flow of perceptions, experiences, as substratum for erroneous construction, the conceptualized aspect, is the substratum for *saṃsāra*; as substratum for realizing the true nature of things it is the substratum for *nirvāṇa*. In everyday life we deluded people do as a matter of fact hypostatize our experiences, which in reality are all there is, and construct them into enduring objects and enduring selves. This is *saṃsara*, the round of rebirth, frustration, and suffering. It is based on a fundamentally wrong understanding of what is really there. Through realizing this in meditation, coming to understand that objects and the Self are just a flow of experiences with no enduring elements set in opposition to each other (no duality), we attain enlightenment. This very same flow of experiences can be a basis for suffering in the unenlightened man, but also a basis for liberation in the saint. It becomes possible, therefore, to talk of two types of dependent aspect. The tainted dependent aspect is those phenomena, those perceptions, which are then projected, as it were, into 'really existing' subjects and objects. Pure dependent aspect is the post-meditational experience of the saint who has seen in his meditation the way things really are. It is a flow of purified perceptions, perceptions without the ignorance of construction into enduring entities.[5]

MIND

According to the eighteenth-century Tibetan lama dKon mchog 'jigs med dbang po (pronounced: Kern chok jik may wong bo) a Cittamātrin, one who follows the Cittamātra tradition, is a Buddhist who asserts that entities as dependent, that is, the flow of perceptions, really exist but that external objects do not (trans. in Sopa and Hopkins 1976:107). Another Tibetan, Mi pham (1846–1914), states quite categorically that for the Cittamātra the non-dual mind, mind or consciousness devoid of subject and object, really, absolutely exists (Guenther 1972:113). Maitreya(nātha) begins his *Madhyāntavibhāga* with a clear assertion of existence which serves to differentiate the Cittamātra from the Madhyamaka: 'The imagination of the nonexistent (*abhūtaparikalpa*) exists. In it duality does not exist. Emptiness, however, exists in it' (cf. trans. by Friedmann in Sthiramati 1937: 10). This school, therefore, holds that something exists. Sthiramati adds in his subcommentary that the imagination of the nonexistent exists 'from the point of view of inherent existence'. Sthiramati goes on to explain that nevertheless it is not true that there is here a contradiction with the *Perfection of Wisdom sūtras* which maintain that all is empty, since the imagination of the nonexistent is free from duality: 'Emptiness here means being free from subject and object, and that is the imagination of the nonexistent. Emptiness is not nonexistence.' Thus we have a reinterpretation of the notion of emptiness, which has ceased to mean 'absence of inherent existence', since the imagination of the nonexistent, whatever it is, is empty but nevertheless has inherent existence. The fundamental opposition between emptiness and inherent existence in the Madhyamaka no longer applies. Our new opposition is emptiness versus subject–object dichotomy. The imagination of the nonexistent, Sthiramati says, 'has real [*dravyasat*] existence. Its phenomena, sense data etc., do not exist apart from it. They are unreal as independent entities . . .' (trans. by Friedmann, in Sthiramati 1937:11).

What precisely is this imagination of the nonexistent? It is already clear from the way the term has been used that it must correspond in some way to mind or consciousness, that is, the flow of perceptions and experiences, but consciousness understood apart from its normal dualistic connotations. Sthiramati states: 'It is the bare reality, free from the differentiation into subject and object. Because sense-data etc. are not perceived outside the consciousness, the consciousness arises in the appearance of sense data etc, as in a dream (Sthiramati 1937:11; cf.

Griffiths 1986: 87). The fundamental point here is that the imagination of the nonexistent is the same as the non-dual flow of perceptions which manifests itself (erroneously) as exterior and interior objects. Maitreyanātha explains the particular characteristic of this imagination of the nonexistent as consciousness: 'Consciousness arises in the appearance of things, sentient beings, substance and ideas; its external object does not exist...' (v.3; Sthiramati 1937: 14). The declaration in the *Madhyāntavibhāga* that the imagination of the nonexistent exists should be taken therefore along with Sthiramati's assertion in his commentary to the *Triṃśikā* that the *Triṃśikā* was composed in order to counter two extremes – the one that objects inherently exist in the way that consciousness does, and the other that consciousness does not inherently exist at all (cf. Thurman 1984: 228). This inherently existing non-dual consciousness is also stated to be the same as the dependent aspect (*Madhyāntavibhāga* 1:6; *Mahāyānasūtrālaṃkāra* 11:40). When, however, the dependent aspect is referred to as the imagination of the nonexistent it appears to be the tainted dependent aspect which is being considered, the dependent aspect which is the substratum for *saṃsāra*, which has as a matter of fact been constructed into subject and object.

It is the doctrine of consciousness or mind as the basis for so-called 'external' objects which gave the Cittamātra tradition its name. Apparently external objects are constituted by consciousness and do not exist apart from it. Vasubandhu begins his *Viṃśatikā*: 'All this is only perception [*vijñaptimātra*], since consciousness manifests itself in the form of nonexistent objects.' There is only a flow of perceptions. This flow, however, really exists, and it is mental by nature, for in terms of the Buddhist division of things it has to be either mental or physical. The flow of experiences could scarcely be a physical or material flow. There may be a danger in calling this 'idealism', for it is rather unlike forms of idealism familiar from Western philosophy. Nevertheless, if 'idealism' means that subjects and objects are no more than a flow of experiences, perceptions, they are of the same nature (*ekadravya*), and these experiences, as experiences, are mental, then this could be called a form of 'dynamic idealism' (cf. Griffiths 1986: 82–3).[6]

Certain objections were recognized by the Cittamātra as capable of being levelled at their doctrine of consciousness. Vasubandhu, in his *Viṃśatikā*, undertook to prove the invalidity of a number of these:

(i) Spatio-temporal determination would be impossible – experiences of object *x* are not occurrent everywhere and at every time so there must be some external basis for our experiences.

(ii) Many people experience *x* and not just one person, as in the case of an hallucination.

(iii) Hallucinations can be determined because they do not have pragmatic results. It does not follow that entities which we generally accept as real can be placed in the same class.

In reply Vasubandhu argues that these are no objections, they fail to show that perception-only as a teaching is unreasonable. Spatio-temporal determination can be explained on the analogy of dream experience, where a complete and unreal world is created with objects felt to have spatio-temporal localization in spite of the fact that they do not exist apart from the mind which is cognizing them. Furthermore the second objection can be met by recourse to the wider Buddhist religious framework. The hells and their tortures which are taught by Buddhist traditions as the result of wicked deeds, to be endured for a very long time until purified, are experienced as the collective produce of the previous intentions (*karma*) of those hell inmates. The torturers and guardians of hell obviously cannot really exist, or they would have been reborn in hell themselves and would experience the suffering associated with it. If this were the case then how could they gleefully inflict sufferings upon their fellow inmates? Thus they must be illusory, and yet they are experienced by a number of people. Finally, as in a dream objects have pragmatic purpose within that dream, and likewise in hell, so in everyday life. Furthermore, as physical activity can be directed towards unreal objects in a dream due, it is said, to nervous irritation on the part of the dreamer, so too in everyday life.

In addition to showing that the perception-only doctrine has not been refuted, Vasubandhu also attempted positively to establish the doctrine by showing that there can be no other theory adequate to explain how it is we experience objects. The 'external' object cannot be a unitary whole, since it is never experienced apart from its parts. Neither can it be made up out of parts, since these can be reduced further to their parts, and eventually to atoms. Atoms, however, are described as imperceptible, and thus gross objects as aggregates of atoms also could not be perceived. Moreover, atoms cannot exist. If atoms are defined as the smallest pieces of reality then they cannot combine with other atoms in part (through partial contact), for then it would follow that atoms have parts and are thus in theory capable of further division. If they combined with other atoms totally then no matter how many atoms combined they would still occupy only the space of one atom and would thus still be imperceptible. So there can exist neither atoms nor their combination. And if the object existed as an independent reality apart from its parts one would be able to perceive the object all in one go. Thus the only way to explain perception of objects is on the analogy of a dream.

This is a typical example of Indian philosophical style. I make no comment on its coherence. Such reasoning is, of course, also part of that reasoning which makes up insight (*vipaśyanā*) meditation in the Cittamātra tradition. The next stage in this meditation, having negated external objects with the teaching of only mind, is said to be to negate mind itself and dwell in non-duality. The *Madhyāntavibhāga* states that 'because of the nonexistence of its object, consciousness [*vijñāna*] also does not exist' (1: 3). From the Abhidharma scholars it had been taken that it is of the nature of consciousness to be conscious of something. If I know, then I know something; if I see, I see something, and so on. Knowing or seeing without anything known or seen is simply not knowing or seeing at all. Thus if there is no object for consciousness so there cannot be the corresponding consciousness.[7] Recently certain scholars have argued from such assertions that mind in the Cittamātra tradition therefore has no greater reality than any other entity.[8] I remain unconvinced, however. It is clear in these cases that the negation of mind (*citta/vijñāna*) is not a negation of the really existing non-dual stream of perceptions which are by their very nature mental, but only of the mind as subject, that is, the perceptions which have been constructed into the subject, the perceiver, the mind as Self. Sthiramati comments:

> Because it discerns, it is *vijñāna*, consciousness; since it has no real object it neither can have the nature of a knower, a perceiver. Therefore, because the external object does not really exist, the consciousness does not exist in reality as a perceiver. But it is not the case that it does not exist as the reflection of things, sentient beings, ego-substances and ideas. For if the consciousness should not exist in that capacity, we should have to admit the absurdity of absolute nonexistence.
>
> (Sthiramati 1937: 22–3; Friedmann's translation slightly modified)

What Sthiramati is saying here is that the flow of perceptions must exist, otherwise there would be nothing. Thus mind in that sense, as the non-dual flow of perceptions, is not being denied.

The *Mahāyānasūtrālaṃkāra* states that in negating mind in this context of meditation the wise man depends on non-duality and 'dwells in the *dharma*-realm, the *dharma*-expanse' (*dharmadhātu*; 6: 8). One of the commentaries to this verse in the *Mahāyānasaṃgraha* makes it clear that the non-duality of the *dharma*-realm is the same as the non-duality of subject and object (the conceptualized aspect). It does not therefore negate the dependent aspect, the flow of perceptions and experiences. The commentary adds that 'the *dharma*-realm thus seen is not false, it is the true *dharma*-realm' (trans. in Lamotte 1938: 178). The commentary to the *Mahāyānasūtrālaṃkāra* itself (13: 16–19) speaks of the *dharma*-realm as an intrinsically pure consciousness, the Suchness or Thusness which is consciousness (*cittatathatā*). The point is explained quite clearly in the *Mahāyānasaṃgraha*. The dependent aspect, as we have seen, has two dimensions – the substratum for *saṃsāra*, the conceptualized aspect, and the substratum for *nirvāṇa*, the perfected aspect. In its first dimension it is tainted (= the imagination of the nonexistent). In its second dimension it is pure. And, says the *Mahāyānasaṃgraha*, when one has burnt perception (*vijñapti*) with the fire of non-conceptual awareness (*nirvikalpajñāna*) the perfected aspect which is true appears, and the aspect which is imagination of the nonexistent does not appear (3: 29). In other words there remains a really existing, pure, non-conceptual, non-dual flow of awareness.[9]

SUBSTRATUM CONSCIOUSNESS, CONSCIOUSNESS, AND IMMACULATE CONSCIOUSNESS

All the phenomenal world depends in some sense on consciousness. However, the Cittamātra tradition was not content to leave the matter at this point. Rather, it distinguished eight types of consciousness: the five sense consciousnesses plus the mind (*manovijñāna*) – a sense which on the one hand apprehends psychic events, and on the other synthesizes experiences supplied by the other five senses – the 'tainted mind' (*kliṣṭamanas*), and the substratum consciousness (*ālayavijñāna*; literally 'storehouse consciousness', rendered into Tibetan as the 'consciousness which is the substratum of all'). The tainted mind takes the substratum consciousness as its object and mistakenly considers the substratum consciousness to be a true Self. These eight forms are the working out of the discrimination into subject and object. The substratum consciousness can be explained as this working out seen from the subjective perspective, the cause responsible for the whole cosmic manifestation. It is likened by Vasubandhu to a great torrent of water or river (*Triṃśikā* v.5; cf.

Saṃdhinirmocana 5: 5), which is changing every moment but which nevertheless preserves a certain identity. According to Sthiramati it is actually the same substance as the imagination of the nonexistent (on *Madhyāntavibhāga* 1: 3; cf. *Mahāyānasaṃgraha* 1: 61). Elsewhere, as we might expect, it is also identified with the dependent aspect (see Kiyota 1962: 21; but cf. Griffiths 1986: 95). This substratum consciousness can be seen under a number of facets, but its chief function is to serve as a repository for the 'seeds' (*bīja*) which explain phenomenal existence in general and personal experiences which result from previous deeds in particular. The substratum consciousness is an ever-changing stream which underlies saṃsāric existence. It is said to be 'perfumed' by phenomenal acts, and the seeds which are the result of this perfuming reach fruition at certain times to manifest as good, bad, or indifferent phenomena. The substratum consciousness, seen as a defiled form of consciousness (or perhaps subconsciousness), is personal in a sense, individual, continually changing and yet serving to give a degree of personal identity and to explain why it is that certain karmic results pertain to this particular individual. The seeds are momentary, but they give rise to a perfumed series which eventually culminates in the result, including here, from seeds of a particular type, the whole 'inter-subjective' phenomenal world (cf. Griffiths 1986: 91 ff.). This inter-subjective world is the product of seeds which are common to all substratum consciousnesses, the results of common previous experiences stretching back through beginningless time. There was, however, some dispute over whether all seeds were the results of perfuming, or whether there were some seeds which were latent from all eternity in the substratum. According to Dharmapāla, followed by Hsüan-tsang in *Ch'eng-wei-shihlun*, there were seeds of both type in the substratum consciousness, so that not all seeds were the results of *karma* (Hsüan-tsang 1973: 117–21). One interesting result of all this, to be noted in passing, is that the Cittamātra tradition maintained that certain people possess only seeds for Arhatship or Pratyekabuddhahood, and not for full Buddhahood, so that some sentient beings would never become full Buddhas. More radically, there are some beings who lack good seeds altogether, so that by the very nature of things those beings can never become enlightened. This is perhaps as close as Buddhism came to a theory of eternal damnation – although there are, of course, notable differences (ibid, 123–5).

Although it performs some of the functions of a Self, the Cittamātra tradition denied vehemently that with the substratum consciousness it had smuggled in a Self by the back door. In the *Saṃdhinirmocana Sūtra* the Buddha forcefully states that he had not taught the substratum consciousness to the immature since they would only conceive it to be a Self (5: 7). It is indeed the substratum consciousness which for this tradition is the conventional self, the referent of the word 'I', and is misapprehended by the tainted mind and taken as a real substantial Self, a permanent and stable 'I' or 'Me'. This is incorrect, however. The substratum consciousness is an ever-changing stream, no doubt an attempt to explain the evolution of the world from consciousness, and certain problems of personal identity, but in no way something to be grasped or attached to as a Self. According to Asaṅga and Vasubandhu it 'ceases' at enlightenment.[10] Since the substratum consciousness appears to be identical in substance with the imagination of the nonexistent, that is, the tainted dependent aspect, its cessation in the Mahāyāna context does not necessarily entail a complete cessation of consciousness or experience. Indeed, Asaṅga speaks in the *Mahāyānasaṃgraha* of the cessation of the personal, individual, constructions of consciousness, but not of the common, inter-subjective world, which becomes the object of a purified vision for the enlightened yogin (1: 60). Otherwise, of course, an enlightened Buddha would be incapable of helping anyone. What happens at the point when the substratum consciousness 'ceases' was, however, the subject of an intense debate, particularly in China.

According to the Indian missionary Paramārtha (499–569), who founded in China the She-lun school of Cittamātra, when the substratum consciousness ceases there remains, shining in its own purity, a ninth consciousness, the 'immaculate consciousness' (*amalavijñāna*). This consciousness is the permanent, ultimate, true reality. According to the later Fa-hsiang school of Cittamātra, founded by Hsüan-tsang following Dharmapāla, however, the cessation of the substratum consciousness is only a cessation of the substratum consciousness inasmuch as it is tainted. The pure consciousness which remains is the same substance as the substratum consciousness, under a different name.[11] This dispute seems, as such, to have been little known in India, although the seventh-century Korean commentator Wŏnch'ŭk (Yuan-ts'ö) in his commentary on the *Saṃdhinirmocana Sūtra* identified Paramārtha with the tradition of Sthiramati, and portrayed the dispute as one of those arising from the split between the school of Valabhī and that of Nālandā (Demiéville 1973: 43–4). Since the substratum consciousness, as the imagination of the nonexistent, equals in substance the tainted dependent aspect, it follows that the purified consciousness is a purified version of what was, when tainted, the substratum consciousness. This appears to correspond with Hsüan-tsang's tradition – we can either speak of this purified consciousness as the purified substratum consciousness or, keeping 'substratum consciousness' for tainted consciousness, refer to it as an 'immaculate consciousness' (*amalavijñāna*). In substance, however, they are the same thing. Nevertheless, in Paramārtha's tradition there seems to have been a strong desire to make the immaculate consciousness an ultimate reality in the fullest possible sense, and therefore literally itself the perfected aspect in opposition to the conceptualized and dependent aspects.[12] From this perspective the immaculate consciousness must be quite different in substance from the substratum consciousness. It is known that Paramārtha (unlike, as far as we can tell, Sthiramati) was associated with the doctrine of the *tathāgatagarbha*, the Buddha-essence, which will be the subject of the next chapter, and it is quite possible that this doctrine may have provided a basis for his teaching of the absolute and immutable immaculate consciousness.

YET MORE DISPUTES WITHIN THE CITTAMĀTRA TRADITION

It appears from the *Ch'eng-wei-shih lun* that Dharmapāla's tradition took very seriously the *Triṃśikā* teaching of transformation (*pariṇāma*) of consciousness. Indeed within this tradition consciousness as the flow of perceptions appears to have been thought of as a kind of substance or almost a subtle matter which can be divided into parts. Consciousness, it is said, genuinely transforms itself into two parts (*bhāga*). The first part is the subjective awareness, called the 'seeing part' (*darśanabhāga*). The other part is that which is apprehended (*nimittabhāga*). These correspond to subject and object. The consciousness itself, which undergoes this transformation, is called the 'reflexive' or 'self-aware' part (*svasaṃvittibhāga*), or sometimes the 'essential part' (*svabhāvikabhāga*). This third part is what consciousness is in itself – all consciousness for the Cittamātra tradition is self-aware, it knows itself, knows that it knows, at the same time as, in everyday life, it knows objects. According to Dharmapāla's tradition there is also a fourth part, which knows this self-aware part, although he seems to have avoided an infinite regress by stopping at this point (Hsüan-tsang 1973: 137–45). Since these are genuine transformations of consciousness the mistake lies not in the notion of subject and object as such, but rather in considering them to be inherently separate entities when really they are the same substance, consciousness. Duality is false, not the world seen through non-dual perception. Thus the conceptualized aspect is the conception of duality. The actual subjects and objects themselves, seen as non-dual images of consciousness, are true and make up the dependent aspect.

For Sthiramati, however, from the final point of view none of this has taken place. There is no real transformation of consciousness, it is all the result of mistaken apprehension. In reality, meaning from the point of view of an enlightened being, there is only the non-dual flow of pure consciousness. There is no actual partition of consciousness into different parts – this is only our way of speaking from an unenlightened perspective. There are, therefore, no subjects and objects. The very notion of subject and object is duality, and thus erroneous perception.[13]

These disputes may also relate to the 'with form/without form' (*sākāra/nirākāra*) debate. This topic was the major subject of contention in late Indian Cittamātra. The problem centred on the issue of whether consciousness took the form (*ākāra*) of the object or not. If it did, then an awareness which perceives that form is not mistaken in at least one major respect. If consciousness does take the form 'blue', say, then an awareness which perceives blue is correct inasmuch as it perceives blue, although it is mistaken, of course, in thinking that blue is an independent external reality.

From the point of view of deluded everyday cognition, consciousness has indeed apparently taken the form of the object, and so there is no dispute. But the problem arises when we consider enlightened cognition, particularly that of the Buddha. A Buddha has no delusion, but constantly enjoys a pure non-conceptual awareness. If the form which consciousness takes as blue is genuinely true, albeit free from duality in terms of substance ('with form' position) then it could be seen even by the Buddha's non-conceptual awareness. If, however, it is false and truly there is only a pure radiant flow of consciousness which is like a mirror free of all images ('without form' position) then the Buddha would not see forms at all.

It seems to me difficult to understand how, granted the 'without form' perspective, an enlightened Buddha can therefore aid sentient beings in their spiritual and mundane welfare, since, continually immersed in non-conceptual awareness, an enlightened Buddha would not even see the common world, let alone beings which inhabit it. The Buddha's omniscience would be aware of no more than its own nature. It is possible that partisans of the 'without form' position answered this problem with reference to the pure spontaneity of the Buddha's activity, not needing actually to apprehend beings in order to help them. One is tempted to suggest that the topic may be a Holy Mystery, but one can be sure that given the complexity of the Cittamātra tradition, and the sophisticated intellectual culture from which it came, there is somewhere in the literature an answer to it!

CHAPTER FIVE

The *tathāgatagarbha* (Buddha-essence/ Buddha-nature)

It would be wrong to think of the Tathāgatagarbha tradition in Buddhism as a school in the way that the Madhyamaka and Yogācāra-Cittamātra traditions are schools. Although the root treatise of the tradition, the *Ratnagotravibhāga*, together with its commentary, the *Vyākhyā*, appear to have been composed in India perhaps as early as the mid-third century CE,[1] if we can judge by quotations in other works the *Ratnagotravibhāga* and its commentary seem to have exerted no obvious or direct influence on the development of Indian Buddhist philosophical thought prior to the eleventh century. In Tibet, where there are said to be only two Mahāyāna philosophical schools, Madhyamaka and Cittamātra, scholars have differed sharply over the allegiance of the *Ratnagotravibhāga*. The very fact of their disagreement suggests that the Tathāgatagarbha tradition cannot be obviously equated with either of the two schools, and in China, where the Tathāgatagarbha teaching was of crucial importance, Fa-tsang in the seventh century saw the Tathāgatagarbha doctrine as a distinct tradition from Cittamātra and Madhyamaka, and spoke of the Tathāgatagarbha *sūtras* as representing a fourth turning of the ever-mobile Dharma Wheel. There may be some doctrinal connection, as yet unclear, between the Tathāgatagarbha tenets and the teaching of Paramārtha's She-lun Cittamātra in China, and also the 'without form' Cittamātra. Nevertheless, a number of important Cittamātra doctrines, such as the Three Aspects and the substratum consciousness, are missing from our earliest Tathāgatagarbha sources. It must be admitted, however, that the history of early Cittamātra is obscure in the extreme and largely unknown. Takasaki has argued that the Tathāgatagarbha tradition started as a distinct Buddhist tradition but was prevented from forming a separate school through subsequent absorption into the Cittamātra, particularly through the identity of the *tathāgatagarbha*, the Buddha-essence or Buddha-nature, with the substratum consciousness. This suggestion is asserted most notably and influentially in the *Laṅkāvatāra Sūtra*.[2] In spite of this, the importance of the Tathāgatagarbha teaching is sufficiently great, and its doctrinal allegiance sufficiently obscure, to warrant here, perhaps, a separate though cautious treatment.

SOME TATHĀGATAGARBHA *SŪTRAS*

Probably the earliest scripture to teach specifically the Tathāgatagarbha doctrine was the appropriately named *Tathāgatagarbha Sūtra*, a relatively short *sūtra* consisting almost entirely of nine examples to illustrate the way the Buddha-nature is contained hidden within sentient beings. According to the Chinese version of the *sūtra* the Buddha observes with his divine eye that

> all the living beings, though they are among the defilements of hatred, anger and ignorance, have the Buddha's wisdom, Buddha's Eye, Buddha's Body sitting firmly in the form of meditation. – Thus, in spite of their being covered with defilements, transmigrating from one path ... to another, they are possessed of the Matrix of the Tathāgata [*tathāgatagarbha*], endowed with virtues, always pure, and hence are not different from me. – Having thus observed, the Buddha preached the doctrine in order to remove the defilements and manifest the Buddha-nature (within the living beings).
>
> (Trans. in Takasaki 1958: 51)[3]

The *sūtra* adds that this is the nature of things, that whether Buddhas occur or do not occur nevertheless beings are always the *tathāgatagarbha* (or, as it is interpreted in one Tibetan version, *have* the *tathāgatagarbha*). The teaching appears to be that sentient beings are in reality already enlightened, but there is admittedly some tension here with other parts of the *sūtra* which speak of beings becoming Buddhas at some point in the future. This tension between innate, inherent enlightenment and becoming enlightened is a tension at the root of the Tathāgatagarbha tradition, different resolutions of which are central to subsequent doctrinal elaboration. The assertion in the *Tathāgatagarbha Sūtra* that all sentient beings have within them a fully enlightened Buddha should be taken along with an earlier assertion in another *sūtra* that all beings have within them the Tathāgata-awareness.[4] Sentient beings have within them something of the Buddha, inherently pure but apparently in an obscured, tainted state. Enlightenment lies in removing the taints in order to allow this inherently pure nature to shine forth. The *tathāgatagarbha*, the Buddha-nature, or, more literally, the Tathāgata-embryo or Tathāgata-womb, is that within each being which enables enlightenment to take place. The claim that all sentient beings have this element is the claim that all sentient beings have it within them to attain full Buddhahood.

The Mahāyāna *Mahāparinirvāṇa Sūtra* (not to be confused with the non-Mahāyāna *sūtra* of the same name, represented in the Pāli tradition by the *Mahāparinibbāna Sutta*) is, in contrast to the *Tathāgatagarbha Sūtra*, a long *sūtra* which exists in a number of versions the textual history of which is extremely complicated. This *sūtra* is particularly noteworthy in our present context for two reasons. First, the latest sections of the *sūtra* translated into Chinese (with rather obscure origins) teach the universality of enlightenment, the presence of the *tathāgatagarbha* and eventual Buddhahood even in the case of really wicked, evil people who apparently have no spiritual basis whatsoever (the *icchāntikas*) and who were given no hope by the Cittamātra tradition. The publication of these sections in China caused something of a stir, particularly in the circle around Tao-sheng (fourth–fifth centuries). Tao-sheng had already taught that all beings will eventually attain Buddhahood, in spite of the fact that the earlier sections of the *Mahāparinirvāṇa Sūtra* said otherwise in the case of the *icchāntikas*, the 'no-hopers'. He was accordingly branded a heretic. When the later sections were translated he was vindicated and much admired for his wisdom and understanding.[5]

The second reason why the *Mahāparinirvāṇa Sūtra* is important for our purposes is that it boldly asserts that the *tathāgatagarbha*, the Buddha-nature, is nothing other than the Self (*ātman*). This is in direct contrast with other *sūtras* such as the *Laṅkāvatāra Sūtra* which are very careful to avoid the use of terms like 'Self' in connection with the *tathāgatagarbha*. According to the *Mahāparinirvāṇa Sūtra*: '"Self" is the meaning of "*tathāgatagarbha*". The Buddha-element certainly exists in all sentient beings. Moreover it is obscured by various defilements and is therefore not able to be seen by sentient beings in the way in which it exists.'[6] Of course, this Self is not a Self in the worldly sense taught by non-Buddhist thinkers, or maintained to exist by the much-maligned 'man in the street'. The Buddha taught the non-Self doctrine in order to overcome the egoistic Self which is the basis for attachment and grasping (see the translation in Ruegg 1973: 81–2). Elsewhere in the large and heterogeneous *Mahāparinirvāṇa Sūtra* the Buddha seems rather to portray his teaching of the *tathāgatagarbha* as a Self as a strategy to convert non-Buddhists. It is said that some non-Buddhist ascetics see the Buddha and would follow him were he not a nihilist who taught no-Self. The Buddha knows their thoughts: 'I do not say that all sentient beings lack a Self. I always say that sentient beings have the Buddha-nature *(svabhāva)*. Is not that very Buddha-nature a Self? So I do not teach a nihilistic doctrine.'[7] The Buddha adds that it is because all sentient beings do not see the Buddha-nature that he teaches impermanence, no-Self, unhappiness, and impurity. It is this that is thought to be a nihilistic doctrine. He has taught Self where there is really no-Self, and no-Self where there is really Self. This is not false but skilful means. Here the Buddha-nature is really no-Self, but it is said to be a Self in a manner of speaking. Elsewhere the *sūtra* speaks of three misunderstandings: (i) where there is no Self to conceive of a Self; (ii) where there is Self to conceive of no Self; and (iii) to meditate on no Self, maintaining that according to worldly beings there is a Self but in the teaching of the Buddha there is no such Self, and what is more there does not exist even the name of the *tathāgatagarbha* (f.147a). The Buddha teaches no-Self in certain contexts, but also a Self (True Self) in others. What exactly that Self is in the *Mahāparinirvāṇa Sūtra*, however, is not determined beyond its being the possibility within each sentient being to become a Buddha (cf. Liu 1982: esp. 82 ff.).

One thing anyway is clear. The *Mahāparinirvāṇa Sūtra* teaches a really existing, permanent element (Tibetan: *yang dag khams*) in sentient beings. It is this element which enables sentient beings to become Buddhas. It is beyond egoistic self-grasping – indeed the very opposite of self-grasping – but it otherwise fulfils several of the requirements of a Self in the Indian tradition. Whether this is called the Real, True, Transcendental Self or not is as such immaterial, but what is historically interesting is that this *sūtra* in particular (although joined by some other Tathāgatagarbha *sūtras*) is prepared to use the word 'Self' (*ātman*) for this element. However one looks at it the *Mahāparinirvāṇa Sūtra* is quite self-consciously modifying or criticizing the no-Self traditions of Buddhism. Early Buddhism had spoken of the four cardinal errors of seeing permanence where there is impermanence, happiness where there is only suffering. Self where there is no Self, and purity where there is impurity. This *sūtra* is quite categoric in asserting that the error here lies in looking in the wrong direction – in other words that there is an equal error in seeing impermanence where there is permanence, suffering where there is happiness, no-Self where there is Self, and impurity where there is purity, in failing to see the positive element in Buddhahood which contrasts with the negative realm of unenlightenment.

These Tathāgatagarbha *sūtras* are associated with the Gupta period, the high period of vigorous classical Hindu culture. There is some evidence in the *Mahāparinirvāṇa Sūtra* itself of yet another crisis in the wake of the Hindu renaissance (Nakamura 1980: 213–14). It is tempting to speak of Hindu influence on Buddhism at this point, but simply to talk of influences is almost always too easy. One tradition will only ever influence another if the tradition which is influenced is capable of making sense of the influences in terms of its own tradition. The influenced tradition is already halfway there, there is never a complete change of direction. There was already within Buddhism a long tradition of positive language about *nirvāṇa* and the Buddha, relating this to an experiential core found within in meditation. Having said that, of course the *Mahāparinirvāṇa Sūtra* itself admits Hindu influence in a sense when it refers to the Buddha using the term 'Self' in order to win over non-Buddhist ascetics. Nevertheless, it would be wrong to think in particular of the transcendental Self-Brahman of Advaita Vedānta as necessarily influencing Buddhism at this point. It is by no means clear that the Self which is really no-Self of the *Mahāparinirvaṇa Sūtra* is at all comparable to the Advaita Brahman, and anyway these Tathāgatagarbha *sūtras* are earlier than Gauḍapāda (seventh century), the founder of the Hindu Advaita school, who appears to have been considerably influenced himself by Buddhism – possibly the very form of Buddhism which was evolved in the Tathāgatagarbha texts.

Perhaps the most important Tathāgatagarbha *sūtra*, at least in terms of citations in later Indian sources, is the *Śrīmālādevīsiṃhanāda Sūtra*. It has been suggested that this *sūtra* was originally a Mahāsaṃghika scripture composed in the Deccan/South India (Andhra) during the third century CE.[8] The point remains controversial, however. The text as it stands draws a sharp contrast between the non-Mahāyāna saints on the one hand and fully enlightened Buddha on the other. The Arhats and Pratyekabuddhas have not finished with *karma*, they will be reborn, they are far from the '*nirvāṇa*-realm' (Buddhahood; pp. 80 ff.). The *tathāgatagarbha* is the domain of the Buddha alone, it is not realized by the non-Mahāyāna saints and is not within the realm of logic and reasoning (p. 96). For the *Śrīmālā Sūtra*, 'whoever does not doubt that the Tathāgatagarbha is wrapped-up in all the defilement-store, also does not doubt that the Dharmakāya of the Tathāgata is liberated from all the defilement store' (p. 96). The *dharmakāya* is the 'Dharma-body' of the Buddha, it is what the Buddha is in himself, what he really is, or in other words, it is generally the final, true, ultimate, reality or state of things.[9] The *dharmakāya* is:

> beginningless, uncreate, unborn, undying, free from death; permanent, steadfast, calm, eternal; intrinsically pure, free from all the defilement-store; and accompanied by Buddha natures more numerous than the sands of the Ganges, which are nondiscrete, knowing as liberated, and inconceivable. This Dharmakāya of the Tathāgata when not free from the store of defilement is referred to as the Tathāgatagarbha. (p. 98)

In this *sūtra*, therefore, '*tathāgatagarbha*' is the name given to the *dharmakāya*, which is in reality permanent, when it is, as it were, obscured by defilements in the unenlightened person. Moreover this *dharmakāya*, far from being a characterless Absolute, is possessed of innumerable good qualities. In a crucial passage the *Śrīmālā Sūtra* explains that the *tathāgatagarbha* is empty, void, but not empty in the Madhyamaka sense of lacking inherent existence. Rather,

> the Tathāgatagarbha is void of all the defilement-stores, which are discrete and knowing as not liberated [or 'apart from knowledge which does not lead to liberation'; Chang 1983: 378] ... the Tathāgatagarbha is not void of the Buddha *dharmas* which are nondiscrete, inconceivable, more numerous than the sands of the Ganges, and knowing as liberated. (p. 99)

'Empty' or 'void' here means, as in the Cittamātra tradition, that a substratum lacks something. The substratum here is referred to as '*tathāgatagarbha*' or '*dharmakāya*' depending on whether we are speaking of unenlightened beings with obscurations or enlightened beings. The *tathāgatagarbha* is said to be a substratum which is permanent, steadfast, and eternal (pp. 104–5). It is also the basis for *saṃsāra*, the round of rebirth. Using language rather like that of certain Hindu traditions (the *Bhagavadgītā*, for example), it is implied that from a conventional everyday point of view we can speak of the *tathāgatagarbha* as undergoing rebirth, although actually neither is it born nor does it die (pp. 104–5). Moreover: 'if there were no Tathāgatagarbha, there would be neither aversion towards suffering nor longing, eagerness, and aspiration towards Nirvāṇa' (p. 105). The *tathāgatagarbha* is the basis of aspiration towards *nirvāṇa* because it is the *tathāgatagarbha* which experiences suffering. There can be no experience and retention (no learning from experience) in the case of an impermanent flow of everyday consciousness (pp. 105–6). Something permanent is needed, it is implied, to unify experience and thereby draw spiritually significant lessons. This is, however, no Self. There is no Self within the realm of impure *saṃsāra*, and the *tathāgatagarbha* is the very basis of *saṃsāra*:

> the Tathāgatagarbha is neither self nor sentient being, nor soul, nor personality. The Tathāgatagarbha is not the domain of beings who fall into the belief in a real personality, who adhere to wayward views, whose thoughts are distracted by voidness.... (p. 106)

The *dharmakāya*, however,

> has the perfection of permanence [or 'transcendent permanence' etc.], the perfection of pleasure, the perfection of self, the perfection of purity. Whatever sentient beings see the Dharmakāya of the Tathāgata that way, see correctly. (p. 102)

Since the *tathāgatagarbha* is only the name given to the same 'thing' which in enlightenment is the *dharmakāya*, and the *dharmakāya* has the perfection of Self, so the *tathāgatagarbha* is not Self only inasmuch as it is saṃsāric, egoistic. From an enlightened perspective the same 'thing' can be spoken of as a True or Transcendent Self. And finally, the *Śrīmālā Sūtra* makes it clear that this substratum, the appearance of which as defiled entails *saṃsāra*, the realization of the inherent purity of which is *nirvāṇa*, is in reality intrinsically pure, radiant consciousness (pp. 106–7). This consciousness is intrinsically pure, never defiled, and yet its apparent defilement is the cause of bondage. This is a mystery understandable only to the Buddhas and advanced Bodhisattvas, and approachable only through faith:

> It is difficult to understand the meaning of the intrinsically pure consciousness in a condition of defilement. ... the consciousness intrinsically pure is difficult to understand; and the defilement of that consciousness is difficult to understand. (pp. 106–7)

Such may also serve as an encouragement to faltering students!

THE *TATHĀGATAGARBHA* IN THE *RATNAGOTRAVIBHĀGA*

The *Ratnagotravibhāga* (otherwise known as the *Uttaratantra*) is said in Tibet to be a treatise of Maitreya – Bodhisattva or human author as the case may be. The commentary is attributed to Asaṅga. Maitreya was regarded, in Central Asia and probably India from about the eighth century, as the author. In China, however, where the *Ratnagotravibhāga* and its commentary were translated in 511 CE, from the time of Fa-tsang (seventh century) onwards they were both regarded as the work of a certain Sāramati. This Sāramati appears to be unknown in the Indo-Tibetan tradition. In point of fact the *Ratnagotravibhāga* may well be a heterogeneous text (Ruegg 1969: 11), and the issue of authorship as such is probably insoluble at the present time. It would be wrong to assume automatically, however, that the *Ratnagotravibhāga* stems from the same origins or circle as the Cittamātra texts attributed to Maitreya and Asaṅga.

One of the features of Tibetan Buddhism in contrast with that of East Asia is the strong tendency to approach the *sūtras* indirectly through the medium of exegetical treatises if at all. The *Ratnagotravibhāga* has played a relatively small role in East Asian Buddhism, where the primacy has always been given to *sūtra* study. In addition, the *Ratnagotravibhāga* seems to have been overshadowed and eventually eclipsed by the *Ta-ch'eng ch'i-hsin lun* ('Awakening of Faith in the Mahāyāna'), a treatise attributed to Aśvaghoṣa (first or second century CE) which was more congenial perhaps to Chinese taste and was almost certainly composed in China itself. In Tibet, on the other hand, all discussion of the *tathāgatagarbha* starts from the interpretation of the *Ratnagotravibhāga* and its *Vyākhyā*. The commentary, however, is itself largely composed of *sūtra* excerpts together with their systematic clarificatory exposition. As such the teaching of the *Ratnagotravibhāga* is really an exposition of the teaching found already most notably in the *Śrīmālā Sūtra*.

The *Ratnagotravibhāga* (which will be taken to include the commentary) speaks of two types of Suchness (or Thusness – *tathatā* – another word for the ultimate way of things) – tainted and untainted or immaculate Suchness. The tainted Suchness, in other words the true nature obscured, is the *tathāgatagarbha*. The immaculate Suchness is the *dharmakāya*.[10] According to Takasaki the relation of the *tathāgatagarbha* to the Absolute (by which he means here the *dharmakāya*) is that of cause to result (p. 24). Since, however, these are both Suchness there is no real difference of base or substratum, which is the same throughout. The *tathāgatagarbha* and the *dharmakāya* are in reality, as we have seen, the same thing – the same substratum or substance. In itself Suchness is said to be 'unchangeable by nature, sublime and perfectly pure' (p. 287). The commentary explains that what we are referring to here is consciousness, radiant by nature, pure and non-dual. That the tainted Suchness (= *tathāgatagarbha*) can at the same time be pure and yet defiled; that even defiled beings have within them the qualities of a Buddha; that the untainted Suchness can be not defiled and yet purified; and that the Buddha's activities are everywhere perfectly spontaneous and non-conceptual, and are yet perfectly apt – all these four points are said to be inconceivable, a Holy Mystery (pp. 188 ff.):

> The Highest Truth of the Buddhas
> Can be understood only by faith,
> Indeed, the eyeless one cannot see
> The blazing disc of the sun.
>
> (p. 296; cf. pp. 380 ff.)

Since all sentient beings have within them the *tathāgatagarbha* as tainted consciousness, and since that consciousness when pure is the *dharmkāya*; since also this consciousness has never really been tainted (its inherent nature is pure), and untainted consciousness, the *dharmakāya*, is non-dual, makes no distinctions, so it is possible to speak of the Buddha's *dharmakāya*, his Dharma-body, or pure radiant consciousness, as all-pervading (pp. 189 ff., 233–4). Likewise the *dharmakāya* pervading all as the Tathāgata's pure awareness (*jñāna*) is in reality unchanging. It only appears from the position of primeval ignorance, delusion, to be tainted (pp. 234 ff.). Nevertheless, from the position of ignorance the *Ratnagotravibhāga* speaks of the Buddha-essence as tainted in the case of ordinary beings, partly tainted and partly purified in the case of Bodhisattvas, and perfectly pure in the case of Buddhas (pp. 230 ff.). All these impurities are merely adventitious, they are not essential, they are not part of the pure consciousness itself. The Buddha qualities, on the other hand, are essential to it, so that when the mind is cleaned, polished, as it were, the Buddha qualities (the ten powers of perfect knowledge etc., see pp. 338 ff.) will naturally shine forth. Thus:

> Here there is nothing to be removed
> And absolutely nothing to be added;
> The Truth should be perceived as it is,
> And he who sees the Truth becomes liberated.

> The Essence (of the Buddha) is (by nature) devoid [empty]
> Of the accidental (pollutions) which differ from it;
> But it is by no means devoid of the highest properties
> Which are, essentially, indivisible from it.
>
> (pp. 300–1)

In reality there is no defiling element to be removed, no purifying element to be added, since the Buddha qualities are an intrinsic part of the *dharmakāya* itself, and the *dharmakāya* is inherent in sentient beings as the *tathāgatagarbha*. The real meaning of emptiness, the commentary says, is that one thing lacks another. What remains, as with the Cittamātra, is really there. In this sense the Buddha-essence is indeed empty – it is empty of adventitious defilements which simply do not exist at all from the point of view of its own innate purity.[11]

Finally, let us note one point where the *Ratnagotravibhāga* appears, perhaps, to modify or strive to ameliorate the teaching of the Tathāgatagarbha *sūtras*. Our text is concerned to explain the *sūtra* references to the *tathāgatagarbha/dharmkāya* as the perfection of Self. According to the Sanskrit version of the text, 'Self' here is interpreted to be another name for 'no-Self', as is sometimes found in works (such as the *Perfection of Wisdom sūtras*) which use superficially paradoxical expressions such as 'standing by way of no standing'. The Chinese version, however, could well be older and appears to be rather different. The Buddha is said to have a True Self (*shih-wo*) which is beyond being and non-being.[12] It is possible that later versions of the *Ratnagotravibhāga* text attempted to neutralize here (or perhaps 'clarify' would be a better word) the apparently radical assertion of Self found in the Tathāgatagarbha *sūtra* tradition.

TIBET – THE *GZHAN STONG* AND *RANG STONG* DISPUTE

In portraying the *tathāgatagarbha* theory found in the *sūtras* and *Ratnagotravibhāga* I have assumed that these texts mean what they say. In terms of the categories of Buddhist hermeneutics I have spoken as though the Tathāgatagarbha *sūtras* were to be taken literally or as definitive works, and their meaning is quite explicit. The *tathāgatagarbha* teaching, however, appears to be rather different from that of Prāsaṅgika Madhyamaka, and were I a Tibetan scholar who took the Prāsaṅgika Madhyamaka emptiness doctrine as the highest teaching of the Buddha I would have to interpret the *tathāgatagarbha* teaching in order to dissolve any apparent disagreement. In Tibet we find a major doctrinal rift between those teachers and traditions which took the *tathāgatagarbha* doctrines literally, and saw them as representing the final, highest, doctrinal teachings of the Buddha, and those teachers and schools which insisted that these are not as they stand literal teachings but were taught by the Buddha with a specific purpose in order to help particular people.

Pre-eminent among those traditions for whom the *tathāgatagarbha* teachings were to be interpreted was (and is) the dGe lugs pa school, sometimes known in China and the West as the Yellow Hats, founded by Tsong kha pa in the late fourteenth century. This is, incidentally, the tradition to which His Holiness the Dalai Lama belongs. According to Tsong kha pa (following the *Laṅkāvatāra Sūtra* and Candrakīrti) the difference between the *tathāgatagarbha* doctrine and the Self or soul teachings of non-Buddhists lies in the Buddha's intention in giving the *tathāgatagarbha* teaching. If this doctrine were taken literally it would indeed be no different from the non-Buddhist Self theory. The Buddha, however, taught the *tathāgatagarbha* teaching for a purpose, he did not intend it to be taken as it stands as a literally true doctrine. Rather, through his compassion, he intended it as a means to introduce non-Buddhists to Buddhism. Moreover, when the Buddha spoke of the *tathāgatagarbha* what he was really referring to, the real truth behind his teaching, was none other than emptiness, *śūnyatā* (see translation by Thurman 1984: 347–50). After all, the *tathāgatagarbha* is said to be that within sentient beings which enables them to attain Buddhahood. This is emptiness, absence of inherent existence, which enables sentient beings to change into Buddhas. Understood correctly, in this way, there is *then* no problem in taking the Tathāgatagarbha texts as texts teaching the final truth.

The *tathāgatagarbha* is not just any emptiness, however. Rather it is specifically emptiness of inherent existence when applied to a sentient being's mind, his mental continuum. That is, emptiness here is the emptiness of inherent existence of the mind, which entails that it is a changing mind, a mental flow (remember that to be empty and to be caused are the same, so that if the mind changes then it must be empty of inherent existence). Thus when we say that all sentient beings have within them the Buddha-essence or Buddha-nature we mean that all sentient beings have minds which can change and become Buddha's minds. Since in Tibetan Buddhism the flow of mind is generally said to be eternal, with no beginning or end, so we can say that the mind, and therefore its emptiness, are eternal (see Hopkins 1983: 382). It is moreover this emptiness which is referred to when we speak of the mind's 'intrinsic purity'. When the mind is defiled in the unenlightened state this emptiness is called the *tathāgatagarbha*. When the mind has become pure through following the path and attaining Buddhahood so emptiness is then referred to in the dGe lugs tradition as the Buddha's Essence Body (*svabhāvikakāya*). The Buddha's pure mind in that state is his Gnosis or Wisdom Body (*jñānakāya*), while the two taken together, the Buddha's mind as a flow empty of inherent existence, is what this tradition calls the *dharmakāya*.[13] Two important points follow from this dGe lugs account, which is clearly an attempt to render consistent the teachings of Prāsaṅgika Madhyamaka and those of the Tathāgatagarbha tradition. First, it is quite wrong to take literally the assertions made in some Tathāgatagarbha texts that all sentient beings are already enlightened. If that were true then there would be no need to practise the Buddhist religion. This also means that the *tathāgatagarbha* itself is strictly the fundamental cause of Buddhahood, and is in no way identical with the result, *dharmakāya* or Essence Body as the case may be, except in the sense that both defiled mind and Buddha's mind are empty of inherent existence. This also makes the second crucial point. The system of thought represented by the dGe lugs tradition is known in Tibet as *rang stong* (pronounced: rang tong) – literally 'self-empty' – which is to say that even the *dharmakāya*, and, of course, emptiness itself, are all empty of inherent existence. They are not 'truly established', there is no Absolute in the sense of an ultimate really existing entity (mKhas grub rje 1968: 53). We have already seen that there is no such thing in Prāsaṅgika Madhyamaka thought.

The rival view in Tibet is known as *gzhan stong* (pronounced: zhen tong) – other-empty – and it has been particularly, although by no means exclusively, associated with the Jo nang pa school.[14] In the Jo nang tradition the *tathāgatagarbha* teachings appear to be taken quite literally. There is an ultimate reality, an Absolute, something which really inherently exists. It is eternal, unchanging, an element which exists in all sentient beings and is the same, absolutely the same, in obscuration and enlightenment. All beings have within them the pure radiant non-dual consciousness (or awareness/wisdom/gnosis – *jñāna*) of a fully enlightened Buddha. This consciousness is obscured by adventitious defilements which do not really exist. In the obscured state this non-dual consciousness is spoken of as the *tathāgatagarbha*; in enlightenment it is the *dharmakāya* or Essence Body; but in reality these are exactly the same thing, so that even unenlightened beings have within them the non-dual consciousness of a Buddha, complete with the many remarkable qualities of a Buddha's consciousness. This tradition is known as *gzhan stong*, other-empty, because, following the *Śrīmālā Sūtra*, it teaches that this Ultimate is empty of adventitious defilements which are intrinsically other than it, but is not empty of its own inherent existence and is also not empty of the Buddha qualities which are part of its own very nature.

The Jo nang pas referred to the *gzhan stong* doctrines as the Great Madhyamaka,[15] maintaining that these were not only the teachings of Maitreya and Asaṅga but also the final teachings of Nāgārjuna and Aryadeva. It is generally granted that Nāgārjuna's works of philosophical reasoning such as the *Madhyamakakārikā* seem not to teach an inherently existing Ultimate (i.e. they are *rang stong*), but the Jo nang pas and others insisted that Nāgārjuna's explicit final teaching of an inherently existing Ultimate can be found in certain of his hymns, particularly the *Dharmadhātustava*. The self-empty teachings are said by the Jo nang pas to be correct as far as reasoning goes, as a lower teaching, clearing away erroneous views, but one has eventually to go beyond mere reasoning. When one goes beyond reasoning one realizes something new, a real, inherently existing Absolute beyond all conceptualization but accessible in spiritual intuition and otherwise available, as the Tathāgatagarbha texts stress, only to faith.

The differences between self-empty and other-empty teachings are deeply entrenched and were vigorously debated. From the self-empty point of view the other-empty approach, and the Jo nang pa school in particular, has all but ceased to be Buddhist since it takes literally a teaching which if taken literally is tantamount to the Self doctrine of non-Buddhists. Western scholars too have sometimes given the impression that the Jo nang school and its other-empty doctrine were a strange non-Buddhist aberration. This is, I think, misleading and rests on an essentialistic notion of what Buddhism 'really is'. There may conceivably have been Hindu influences on the development of the other-empty doctrine, as indeed on the original Tathāgatagarbha teachings. Nevertheless, the Jo nang tradition appears to have done nothing more than taken literally certain doctrines which were almost certainly taken literally by some people in India and, as we shall see, were and are very widespread in East Asian Buddhism. Moreover within Tibet itself the other-empty doctrines have been widely accepted among non-dGe lugs scholars, and many contemporary teachers of the rNying ma (pronounced: Nying ma) and bKa' brgyud schools in particular openly accept some form of other-empty teaching as the highest Buddhist doctrinal assertion. This has been very much the case since the growth of a tradition in early nineteenth-century non-dGe lugs Tibetan thought, still very influential, known as the Ris med (pronounced: Ri may) or Non-partiality movement. This movement sought to diminish existing sectarian disputes and harmonize differences, often through emphasizing the Absolute Reality of *gzhan stong* as that which goes beyond reasoning and dispute, thus stressing the purely functional therapeutic role of Prāsaṅgika Madhyamaka reasoning and the superiority (of course) of the *Ratnagotravibhāga* as the text which reveals and invites faith in an all-pervading Buddha-nature.

THE *TA-CH'ENG CH'I-HSIN LUN* AND THE *TATHĀGATAGARBHA* IN EAST ASIA

It is striking and indeed remarkable that so many of the principal 'Indian' sources for a study of East Asian Buddha-essence theory were almost certainly of Central Asian or Chinese composition. In particular the two most important exegetical treatises, the *Ta-ch'eng ch'i-hsin lun*, attributed to Aśvaghoṣa, and the *Fo-hsing lun*, attributed to Vasubandhu, were almost undoubtedly composed in China, although not necessarily by Chinese. The *Fo-hsing lun* (sometimes given the Sanskrit title of *Buddhagotra Śāstra*) was probably composed by its purported translator, Paramārtha.[16] The *Ta-ch'eng ch'i-hsin lun* (given the Sanskrit title *Mahāyānaśraddhotpāda Śāstra*) is usually referred to in English as the *Awakening of Faith in the Mahāyāna*. According to Walter Liebenthal the *śāstra* was 'composed probably soon after 534 A.D. by a Confucian scholar who posed as a monk (?), and had assumed the clerical name Tao-ch'ung' (Liebenthal 1961: 42; cf. Liebenthal 1959). Liebenthal's conclusions are controversial, however, but either way there can now be little doubt that the *Awakening of Faith* was originally composed in the Chinese language.

The *Awakening of Faith* sees the Buddha-essence doctrine as a cosmological theory, an explanation of the true nature of the cosmos, and this feature characterizes Chinese discussions of the *tathāgatagarbha*. Generally in Indo-Tibetan Buddhism it was the soteriological dimension of the Buddha-essence theory which was stressed – the Buddha-essence is that within sentient beings which enables sentient beings to become enlightened. For the *Awakening of Faith*, however: 'The principle is "the

Mind of the sentient being." This Mind includes in itself all states of being of the phenomenal and the transcendental world.'[17] According to the commentator Fa-tsang (643–712), this One Mind is the *tathāgatagarbha* (p. 32). The *Awakening of Faith* itself takes the *tathāgatagarbha* as the substratum of *saṃsāra* and *nirvāṇa* (pp. 77–8). This Mind has two aspects – the Mind as Suchness or Thusness, that is, the Absolute Reality itself, and the Mind as phenomena. Between them these two aspects embrace all there is (p. 31). Fa-tsang again comments that Absolute and phenomena are not differentiated in essence, they include each other, for the One Mind is the essence of both (p. 32). The essential nature of the Mind is unborn, imperishable, beyond language. Differentiation (i.e. phenomena) arises through illusion, fundamental ignorance of one's true nature (pp. 32–3; cf. p. 48). The Absolute Reality is empty:

> because from the beginning it has never been related to any defiled states of existence, it is free from all marks of individual distinction of things, and it has nothing to do with thoughts conceived by a deluded mind. (p. 34)

Nevertheless, to avoid misunderstandings: 'the true Mind is eternal, permanent, immutable, pure, and self-sufficient; therefore it is called "nonempty"' (p. 35; cf. p. 76).

This is clearly a cosmological version (a Chinese version?) of similar comments made in the *Śrīmālā Sūtra* and repeated in the *Ratnagotravibhāga*. Relating the preceding to the individual and liberation (the soteriological dimension) the *Awakening of Faith* asserts: 'Consciousness has two aspects which embrace all states of existence and create all states of existence. They are: (1) the aspect of enlightenment, and (2) the aspect of nonenlightenment' (pp. 36–7). The aspect of enlightenment itself can also be divided into original enlightenment and the actualization of enlightenment. The first of these, original enlightenment, refers to the fact that Mind in itself, truly, is free from thoughts and all pervading, analogous to empty space (p. 37). It is also like a mirror which in itself is empty of images. The world appears in it as reflections, but it is actually undefiled and pure. It 'universally illumines the mind of man and induces him to cultivate his capacity for goodness' (pp. 42–3; cf. p. 48). This primevally enlightened One Mind is referred to as the *dharmakāya* (p. 37). From the phenomenal point of view the fundamental delusion or ignorance is the result of (or identified with) mental agitation, like waves on a previously calm ocean (pp. 44–5):

> The Mind, though pure in its self nature from the beginning, is accompanied by ignorance. Being defiled by ignorance, a defiled (state of) Mind comes into being. But, though defiled, the Mind itself is eternal and immutable. Only the Enlightened Ones are able to understand what this means. (p. 50)

Ignorance, and therefore bondage, lies in mental activity. This is in radical contrast with, say, Tsong kha pa's approach to Buddhism, but it corresponds with what we have seen of Chinese Madhyamaka and its Taoist precedents:

> All thoughts, as soon as they are conjured up, are to be discarded, and even the thought of discarding them is to be put away . . . (thus one is to conform to the essential nature of Reality [*dharmatā*] through this practice of cessation). (p. 96; material in parenthesis taken from Fa-tsang)

Through cutting discursive activity the mind is 'returned' to the state it was always really in, that of pure, mirror-like, radiant stillness. Since this is its own natural state it is thereby quite possible for enlightenment to occur not as the direct result of a long period of moral and spiritual cultivation but rather at any time, suddenly or apparently spontaneously (cf. Gregory 1983b: esp. 36 ff.).

It is interesting to compare the preceding with the Taoist *Huai-nan-tzu*, which dates from perhaps the second century BCE. In Richard Wilhelm's paraphrase:

> the essence of man is calm and pure in its original state, and only becomes cloudy and restless through contact with the objects that cause desires and emotions. . . . This original pure essence dwells in man. It will be temporarily covered, just as the clouds cover the stars . . . it is easy to foster this essence; since it is originally good and spoiled only by reacting to external influences, it is enough to remove the external causes and man will right himself all of his own accord.
>
> (Wilhelm 1985; 108–9)

The notion that the inherent nature of man is, as it were, something divine also harmonized splendidly with the Confucian emphasis on the innate goodness of man, while the teaching that *this* world is in reality the Absolute suited the this-worldly orientation of Chinese culture, with its suspicion of monasticism. Chinese civilization was thus predisposed to the acceptance of a teaching wherein the sage discovers within himself a Self which is also the real essence of the natural world, through learning to calm the mind, cut discursiveness, allowing it to rest in its own purity and goodness. There are precedents for all of this in Indian Buddhism, and in Tibet there are some parallels, but it is only in East Asian Buddhism that these tendencies become the mainstream Buddhist tradition. There are no precedents, however, as far as I know, in Indo-Tibetan Buddhism for one of the conclusions drawn from combining the cosmological doctrine of the all-pervading Buddha-essence with an aversity to all forms of dualistic discrimination. In several Sino-Japanese traditions not only sentient beings but also the vegetable and mineral kingdoms are said to possess the *tathāgatagarbha*. Since possession of the *tathāgatagarbha* is what enables a being to attain enlightenment so the conclusion was drawn that even stones and blades of grass are to be saved, led to enlightenment (perhaps theologians might say 'redeemed') by the compassionate Bodhisattvas and Buddhas (see Ruegg 1969: 152–3, n.1; Shaw 1985: 111 ff.).

It is impossible to underestimate, in my opinion, the importance of the Buddha-essence theory in general, and the *Awakening of Faith* in particular, for East Asian Buddhism. Among the earliest commentaries to the *Awakening of Faith* are treatises not only by Chinese but also Korean scholars (Wǒnhyo (617–86), for example; see Lai 1985: 75ff.), while in Japan Prince Shōtoku Taishi (574–622), sometimes referred to as the 'father of Japanese Buddhism', is said to have written a commentary on the *Śrīmālā Sūtra*. This should be contrasted with the almost complete absence of Indian commentaries on Tathāgatagarbha texts. The many references to Mind, One Mind, and True Self in East Asian Buddhism can to a substantial degree be traced directly or indirectly to this tradition, and the fact that a commentary on the *Awakening of Faith* in Chinese is spuriously attributed to Nāgārjuna has also meant that, rather as in the Tibetan *gzhan stong* traditions, Buddha-essence theory has sometimes been used in East Asia to interpret non-Tathāgatagarbha traditions, in this case Madhyamaka. At the same time the importance of the *Awakening of Faith*, a Chinese creation, in East Asian Buddhism means that one must be careful not to use uncritically models of interpretation derived from Sino-Japanese Buddhism in understanding doctrines of Indian Buddhism (and, to a lesser extent, vice versa). The real point is that yet again one must be sensitive to the immense diversity within Mahāyāna Buddhism.

DŌGEN ON THE BUDDHA-NATURE

Dōgen (1200–53) is generally considered to have been the greatest Japanese philosophical thinker as well as an important religious reformer. The early death of his parents when Dōgen was quite young gave him a vivid and intense awareness of impermanence which he found deeply troubling. As a young monk, dissatisfied with extant traditions of Japanese Buddhism, Dōgen travelled to China seeking the true understanding of Buddhism which, he felt, had been transmitted directly from Śākyamuni Buddha and handed down in an unbroken succession from teacher to pupil. On his return to Japan in 1227 Dōgen introduced the tradition of Ts'ao-tung Ch'an, known in Japan as Sōtō Zen.

The words *ch'an* and *zen* derive from the Sanskrit *dhyāna*, meaning 'meditation'. According to tradition Zen first arose when Śākyamuni Buddha held up a flower and winked. Only Mahākāśyapa understood, and smiled. He thus became the first Patriarch of the Zen tradition. What Mahākāśyapa understood I, alas, do not know! The story, however, indicates the direct, wordless nature of much of Zen teaching, cutting through the trappings of discursive thought. It is said that Zen (Ch'an) was transmitted from India to China by the twenty-eighth Patriarch, Bodhidharma, in the late fifth century CE, although the historicity of Bodhidharma has been doubted. Attributed to Bodhidharma is a saying which characterizes the approach of Zen and also indicates a certain influence of Buddha-essence thought: 'Outside the Scriptures a special tradition; not depending on books and letters; pointing directly to the Mind of man; having seen the Essence one becomes a Buddha.'[18] There has been a strong aversion in some Zen traditions to the forms of traditional religion and the discursive fabrications of philosophical thought, combined with an apparently eccentric behaviour both in order to awaken others to their own True Nature and also as a reflection of the spontaneous unrestricted activity of the perfectly empty and clear Mind. An aversion to ritual and words, the eccentric Sage, an Outsider – these are common between Ch'an and Taoism, although they can be seen also in the sometimes iconoclastic activities of the wandering yogins or *siddhas* in later Indian Buddhism.

The well-known use of insoluble problems in Zen ('What is the sound of one hand clapping?') to break discursive thought, together with stories of sudden enlightenment occurring in strange contexts (as when the Master shut a pupil's leg in the gate) are largely characteristic not of Dōgen's Sōtō Zen but of the rival Rinzai (Chinese: Lin chi) Zen tradition.

It was Rinzai Zen that was associated with the samurai and therefore the martial arts, and it is Rinzai Zen which is well known in the West through the works of D. T. Suzuki. In contrast Dōgen established an austere form of Zen, his monasteries deep in the mountains, and refused any compromise with secular authority. Sōtō Zen has remained close to the soil and the people, so much so that there is a Japanese saying, 'Rinzai for the shōgun; Sōtō for the peasants'. The practice of Dōgen's Zen is sustained *zazen* – sitting meditation.

Dōgen devoted an important section of his major work, the *Shōbōgenzō*, to the Buddha-nature, and his treatment of the topic was significant to his vision of the world and Zen practice within it. He starts from a section of the *Mahāparinirvāṇa Sūtra*, which Dōgen reads as: 'All is sentient being, all beings are (all being is) the Buddha nature; Tathāgata is permanent, non-being, being and change' (trans. in Masao 1971: 30–1). For Dōgen, therefore, it is not that all sentient beings *have* the Buddha-nature. Rather, the expression 'sentient being' refers to everything, and everything *is* the Buddha-nature. It is dualistic to think of beings having the Buddha-nature. All beings, sentient and insentient, are the Buddha-nature. Dōgen says: 'Grass, trees, and lands are mind; thus they are sentient beings. Because they are sentient beings they are Buddha-nature. Sun, moon, and stars are mind; thus they are sentient beings; thus they are Buddha-nature' (*Shōbōgenzō*, trans. by Nishiyama in Dōgen Zenji 1983: IV, 134). One has to be careful to understand Dōgen correctly here, however. He is not saying, as appears to be the case in the *Awakening of Faith*, that from the point of view of the ultimate truth all is Mind and the world of phenomena does not exist, as reflections do not exist for the mirror itself. The Buddha-nature is not an essence 'hidden' in things, behind them, as it were: 'flowers opening, leaves falling in themselves are substance of suchness. Nevertheless fools think that there can be no flower opening, no leaf falling in the realm of True Essence' (Masao 1971: 55). For Dōgen the world of phenomena really and quite literally is the Buddha-nature:

> The real aspect is all things. All things are this aspect, this character, this body, this mind, this world, this wind and this rain, this sequence of daily going, living, sitting, and lying down, this series of melancholy, joy, action, and inaction, this stick and wand, this Buddha's smile, this transmission and reception of the doctrine, this study and practice, this evergreen pine and ever unbreakable bamboo.
>
> (Trans. in Nakamura 1964: 352)

Beings are already Buddhas; as Francis Cook has put it, 'the total being just as it is is Buddha'. Dōgen accordingly rejects any notion that the Buddha-nature is a seed (Cook 1983: 19–20). It is already the flower. This very world of impermanence is the Buddha-nature, 'Buddhism has never spoken of nirvana apart from birth-and-death' (Masao 1971: 63):

> Impermanence is the Buddhahood... The impermanence of grass, trees, and forests is verily the Buddhahood. The impermanence of the person's body and mind is verily the Buddahood. The impermanence of the (land) country and scenery is verily the Buddhahood.
>
> (Nakamura 1964: 352)

The 'divinity', as it were, of trees and mountains harmonized particularly well with Japanese Shintō belief that the natural world is full of spirits, while Dōgen's awareness of impermanence in nature also reflects the Japanese love of nature and sensitivity to its changing moods (the cherry blossom; see Nakamura 1964: 359).

Since we are already and quite literally enlightened so Dōgen seems to be open to Tsong kha pa's criticism of *gzhan stong* – that with such a teaching there can be no basis for Buddhist practice. For Dōgen this appears to be true, if practice is seen as an activity motivated by a desire for a particular result to which it is directed. In reality there is nothing to be attained, and practice and enlightenment are the same thing:

> To think that practice and enlightenment are not identical is a non-Buddhist view.... Therefore, even though you are instructed to practice, do not think that there is any attainment outside of practice itself, because practice must be considered to point directly to intrinsic realization.
>
> (Trans. in Cook 1983: 17)

Practice is itself the manifestation of an intrinsic realization – this is the correct way to interpret Dōgen's comment that 'Although this Dharma (the Buddhist truth) is amply present in every person, unless one practices, it is not manifested; unless there is realization, it is not attained' (Masao 1971: 60). The attainment is a no-attainment, it is not the result of aiming at anything. Enlightenment for Dōgen is (as for all Buddhists) seeing things the way they really are. Since all things and all times are the Buddha-nature, Dōgen's enlightenment is seeing perfectly as it is the present moment 'a profound at-one-ness with the event at hand, in total openness to its wonder and perfection as manifesting absolute reality' (Cook 1983: 24–5). It is as simple as that!

CHAPTER SIX

Hua-yen – the Flower Garland tradition

BUDDHISM IN CHINA

In the last chapter I mentioned the commentator to the *Awakening of Faith*, Fa-tsang. Fa-tsang was, according to traditional reckoning, the third patriarch of the school known in China as Hua-yen, and in Japan as Kegon. The expression 'Hua-yen' means 'Flower Garland', and is the Chinese name of a Mahāyāna *sūtra*, the vast *Avataṃsaka Sūtra*. One feature of East Asian in contrast to Indo-Tibetan Buddhism, was the development of schools based on the study of particular *sūtras*. Each such school saw its scripture as the culmination of the Buddha's teaching, his highest utterance or final word, the *sūtras* of the other schools ranked in a step-like progression to this highest expression of the Buddha's doctrine. It was in these schools, such as Hua-yen and T'ien-t'ai, that a truly Chinese version of Buddhist philosophy was created. This Chinese emphasis on the *sūtra* contrasts with the Tibetan attitude, for example, where it was (and is) felt that *sūtras* are too difficult to understand – poetic, vague, unsystematic, or superficially contradictory, perhaps – without approaching them through a thorough grounding in Madhyamaka and Cittamātra philosophy. In the great Chinese schools philosophy arises out of reading the *sūtras*; in Tibet Indian schools of philosophy, thoroughly mastered, are used as hermeneutic tools in order to understand the *sūtras* themselves. One reason for this Chinese emphasis on *sūtras* and their exegesis, one suspects, is that study of the

Original Master's utterances and commentary on their meaning was very much part of traditional Confucian learning.

There is a tendency sometimes to compartmentalize Indian and Chinese civilizations, to see the great geographical barriers of the Himalayas and Burmese jungles as for ever separating the two cultures, rendering contact and cultural diffusion a spasmodic and fragmentary enterprise. Historically this picture is quite false. Indian and Chinese civilizations met in Central Asia, and Buddhism spread to China through the passes of Kashmir and Afghanistan along well-trod trade routes. To the north-west from the Ganges plain the route runs to Shrinagar, thence to Leh in Ladakh, and over the Karakorams to Yarkand, on the edge of the treacherous Takla Makan desert. Trade routes run south and north of the Takla Makan, joining at Kashgar in the west and Tun-huang in the east. Yarkand is on the southern route, as also is Khotan. On the northern route is Kucha and Turfan. All of these were major centres of trade and cultural diffusion on the Silk Route, running from the Chinese capital of Ch'ang-an (Sian) westwards eventually to reach the Mediterranean coastal ports of Antioch and Tyre. In the wake of Alexander the Great's incursions into North-West India (fourth century BCE) Greek kingdoms were established in Bactria, north of modern Afghanistan, and Greek kings periodically invaded the Ganges valley. At least one Indo-Greek monarch, Milinda (Menandros), is reputed to have become a Buddhist monk and died an Arhat. The earliest portrayal of the Buddha figure in Indian art was arguably in the Gandhāra region (modern Afghanistan/Pakistan/Kashmir) under a strong Hellenistic influence.

By the end of the first century BCE the Greeks had been ousted from Bactria and North-West India by various Iranian tribes. From the beginning of the first century CE the Kuṣāṇa empire, centred in Bactria, took in the whole of North India as well as large areas of western Central Asia. The Kuṣāṇas were enthusiastic Buddhists. There still remain a number of bone relics enclosed within beautiful Kuṣāṇa reliquaries excavated from Kuṣāṇa *stūpas*. The presence of one empire from the Ganges valley to the Silk Route undoubtedly contributed immensely to the dissemination of Buddhism, spread by travelling laymen, particularly merchants, and peripatetic monks. The spread of Buddhism had a civilizing, as well as perhaps a pacifying, effect. It no doubt received active support and patronage from the Kuṣāṇa aristocracy and royal house. At the same time in China the Later Han Dynasty (25–220 CE) held sway over most of China and the eastern end of the Silk Route. Thus Indian and Chinese cultures were in direct contact, and it was through the rich

Sino-Indian mercantile communities of Central Asia that Buddhism spread to China. With the collapse of the Kuṣāṇas and Later Han, oasis centres such as Khotan and Kashgar became independent states where for hundreds of years Buddhism ideologically unified Iranian, Indian, and Chinese civilizations.

Of course, many things reached China via the Silk Route (barbarian invaders and disease among them) without thereby becoming Chinese. The Chinese were intensely xenophobic, and a foreign religion, and barbarians in strange garb, could at the most be curious. In addition, the Confucian Chinese found certain aspects of Buddhism morally and socially repellent. Monks who renounced the world might fail to pay proper respect to their ancestors. The very notion of rebirth appeared to put ancestor worship into question. What was seen as the world-negating dimension of Buddhism contrasted noticeably with a Chinese emphasis on the world of the senses and political-cum-social relationships. Why should loyal Heaven-fearing Chinese follow strange Indian customs? After all, there was no mention of the Buddha in the Confucian classics nor even in Taoist sources. There were periodic persecutions of Buddhism throughout the first thousand years of Chinese Buddhist history. As late as the T'ang dynasty, probably the high point of Chinese Buddhism, a century or so after Fa-tsang, Han-yü (768–824), disgusted that the Emperor Hsien-tsung, Son of Heaven, should pay respect to a relic of the Buddha, like a good Confucian even at the risk of his own life petitioned the throne in his famous *Memorial on the Bone of the Buddha*. Buddhism, he argued, has no magic power – it does not confer longevity, a principal concern of the this-worldly Chinese. What is the point of weird religious rites if they do not confer longevity? The sages of old, prior to the arrival of Buddhism, lived for ages. When Buddhism arrived during the Later Han dynasty the lives of the emperors and their dynasties grew shorter. This much was true. Buddhism remained a foreign religion in China until the collapse of the Later Han dynasty. It was in the spiritual vacuum created by the Period of Disunity (221–589), short lives and short reigns, that Buddhism really began to influence the cultured elite who alone, through their internalization of the foreign religion, could render it truly Chinese. In times of disunity and political fragmentation the Chinese turned to individualism and retreat, characteristically Taoist virtues, and attempted to live alone in harmony with the Source of Things. It was under the wing of Taoism that Buddhism began to gain a foothold in intellectual circles. The cultured elite at this time were interested in Buddhist meditation. Buddhist ideas were explained using Taoist terminology, and it was suggested that the Taoist Lao-tzu might have travelled to India, either becoming or teaching the Buddha. The first phase of Chinese intellectual absorption of Buddhism was one of Buddho-Taoist synthesis.

'"I stand in awe of supernatural beings," said Confucius, "but keep them at a distance."' For Han-yü the spectacle of an emperor worshipping a bone was an 'absurd pantomime':

> The Buddha was born a barbarian; he was unacquainted with the language of the Middle Kingdom, and his dress was of a different cut. His tongue did not speak nor was his body clothed in the manner prescribed by kings of old; he knew nothing of the duty of minister to prince or the relationship of son to father.... There is... all the less reason now that he has been dead so long for allowing this decayed and rotten bone, this filthy and disgusting relic to enter the Forbidden Palace.... I beg that this bone be handed over to the authorities to throw into water or fire, that Buddhism be destroyed root and branch for ever....
>
> (Trans. by J. K. Rideout in Birch 1967: 269–70)

Han-yü's influential friends deflected the fury of the Son of Heaven, and his punishment was commuted to banishment, or, if you prefer, he became a governor far away in the south, an area infested with crocodiles!

Buddhism in China was spread during its first thousand years through the influence of translator-missionaries from India and Sino-Indian Central Asia such as Lokakṣema (147–86), the great Kumārajīva (344–413), and Paramārtha (499–569), as well as by Chinese such as Fa-hsien (?340–?420), Hsüan-tsang (596–664), and I-tsing (635–713) who undertook the hazardous journey to India by land or sea in order to obtain scriptures for China. Sometimes these journeys were taken with imperial patronage, and further land grants and patronage of temple building meant that as time passed so Chinese Buddhist monasteries tended to gain in power and temporal prestige. In spite of this (or partly, perhaps, because of it) the monasteries and monks were closely supervised by the government, always suspicious of foreign customs which remained for ever strange. Chinese monks for their part, after initial protest, undertook such un-Indian practices as prostrating to the emperor. Always in the background was the rivalry and opposition of Confucians and the growing Taoist church. Major persecutions occurred in 446, 574, and, in particular, 842–5. During this last persecution 260,500 fully ordained monks and nuns were forcibly returned to lay life.

The Period of Disunity ended with the triumph of the Sui (581–618) and then the T'ang dynasties. Once more Chinese imperial control spread into Central Asia, where it eventually met the forces of militant Islam. At the Battle of the Talas River (751), in what is now Russian Turkestan, the T'ang forces were decisively defeated by the Arabs. The days of Buddhism in western Central Asia were numbered. Within China under the T'ang we see extensive state patronage, large monasteries, and a vast Buddhist literature of translated and indigenous works. The tenets of Buddhism had been more or less disentangled from Taoism. T'ang Buddhist doctrine shows a move from introduction to absorption and creative internalization. Among the predominantly practice-oriented Buddhist traditions which become progressively more important as time passes, particularly after the 842–5 persecution, we find Ch'an (Zen) on the one hand, with its stress on meditation verging sometimes on an antinomian anti-intellectualism, and deep devotion to a Buddha, particularly Amitābha, on the other. In the great T'ang philosophical synthesis of Hua-yen we find, in the words of Wing-tsit Chan, 'the highest development of Chinese Buddhist thought ... (which) with the philosophy of T'ien-t'ai, forms the metaphysical basis of Chinese Buddhism in the last millennium' (Chan 1963: 406).

THE *AVATAṂSAKA SŪTRA*

The *Avataṃsaka Sūtra* is longer than the Bible, and a single title is apt to give a misleading impression of unity. In fact the *sūtra* as it stands is a heterogeneous work, a collection of texts some of which certainly circulated separately. Other parts were probably composed at the time of compilation in order to fill obvious gaps in the composite text. Only two sections survive in their entirety in Sanskrit, both of which were without doubt originally separate texts – the *Daśabhūmika Sūtra* on the ten stages of the Bodhisattva's path to enlightenment, and what is now the climax of the *Avataṃsaka*, the *Gaṇḍavyūha Sūtra*. The *Daśabhūmika Sūtra* itself was first translated into Chinese during the third century CE. A comprehensive translation of the *Avataṃsaka* into Chinese was made by Bodhibhadra in 418–20, and a further translation was made by Śikṣānanda during the closing years of the seventh century. The Śikṣānanda translation is some 10 per cent longer than that by Bodhibhadra – which serves to remind us that the Mahāyāna *sūtras* in classical times were not fixed but underwent revision, expansion, and sometimes contraction.

Consequently we should be wary of referring to a *sūtra* recension as *the sūtra*.

The original texts translated as the *Avataṃsaka Sūtra* were brought to China from Khotan, in Central Asia. The texts refer to China and Kashgar, so it is likely that compilation and even authorship of at least some portions of the comprehensive work took place within the Indic cultural sphere of Central Asia. The *Avataṃsaka Sūtra* sets out to portray the cosmos as it is seen by a Buddha or very advanced Bodhisattvas. As such it is not a philosophical *sūtra*, although there are sections which are philosophically stimulating. Luis Gomez has referred to the teaching of its climax, the *Gaṇḍavyūha Sūtra*, as one of 'speculative mysticism' (Gomez 1967: lxxviii). Whereas the Buddhist philosophical schools portray a certain rivalry between Madhyamaka and Cittamātra the *Gaṇḍavyūha* speaks both of all things lacking inherent existence and a pure untainted awareness or consciousness (*amalacitta*) as the ground of all phenomena:

> Endless action arises from the mind; from action (arises) the multifarious world. Having understood that the world's true nature is mind, you display bodies of your own in harmony with the world. Having realized that this world is like a dream, and that all Buddhas are like mere reflections, that all principles [*dharma*] are like an echo, you move unimpeded in the world.
>
> (Trans. in Gomez 1967: lxxxi)

Because all things lack inherent existence so the Bodhisattva's mind can, through meditation, 'pervade' or 'enter into' all things and he or she can move 'unimpededly'. The *Gaṇḍavyūha* views the world not from the point of view of ontology but from inside the Buddha's – or an advanced Bodhisattva's – experience. As such, the world of the *Gaṇḍavyūha* is one of magic and the visionary (cf. Beyer 1977). It is a world where things happen at a distance through working on one's own mind simply because things lack inherent existence and therefore lack concrete difference. Or, put another way (a way which may be philosophically different, but is not different for the *sūtra*), things happen at a distance according to the Bodhisattva's will, or he can pass through walls, because there is no distance, no mural hardness, since all is a continuum of consciousness. This is experienced through meditation. The world of the *Avataṃsaka Sūtra*, the world of the Buddha, is a world of vision, of magic, of miracle. As a result of meditative absorption the Buddhas and Bodhisattvas have the power, a magical power, to create. The motive for their acts of creation is great compassion. Through visualization the mind creates an image. If all is lacking in inherent existence, all is dream-like or illusory. Moreover if (as Buddhists have always believed) all follows the mind – as the mind is so is the world – it follows that the images created in meditation by the Buddhas will have as much reality as anything else (Gomez 1967: lxxix; cf. lxxxv). If all lacks inherent existence, or all is Mind, then not only are these images, these magical interventions, as real as anything else, but also, as mind, or lacking in inherent existence, they reveal the true nature of things as much as anything else. Since the Buddha uses his magical interventions, his transformations, solely for the benefit of sentient beings, their use will reveal the true nature of things *more* openly, more revealingly, than other things. In the world as seen by the Buddhas 'fictions' become 'reality' and 'reality' becomes 'fiction'.

What is the world of the Buddha? Who, for that matter, is the Buddha? The Buddha of the *Avataṃsaka Sūtra* is not Śākyamuni, the so-called historical Buddha who lived and died in India. That Buddha was indeed nothing more than a transformation, a magical intervention. The *Avataṃsaka Sūtra*'s Buddha, *the* Buddha, is Vairocana, or Mahāvairocana, the Great Illumination Buddha. He does not teach in the *sūtra*, but approves of teachings given by his vast retinue of advanced Bodhisattvas. Vairocana is just unutterably amazing:

> The realm of the Buddhas is inconceivable;
> No sentient being can fathom it....
> The Buddha constantly emits great beams of light;
> In each light beam are innumerable Buddhas....
> The Buddha-body is pure and always tranquil;
> The radiance of its light extends throughout the world;...
> The Buddha's freedom cannot be measured –
> It fills the cosmos and all space....
> The Buddha body responds to all – none do not see it.
> With various techniques it teaches the living,
> Sound like thunder, showering the rain of truth....
> All virtuous activities in the world
> Come from the Buddha's light....
>
> (Trans. in Cleary 1984/6: I, Bk 1)

His deeds, his magical interventions, are equally vast and astonishing:

> In all atoms of all lands
> Buddha enters, each and every one,

Producing miracle displays for sentient beings:
Such is the way of Vairocana. . . .
The techniques of the Buddhas are inconceivable,
All appearing in accord with beings' minds. . . .
In each atom the Buddhas of all times
Appear, according to inclinations;
While their essential nature neither comes nor goes,
By their vow power they pervade the worlds.

(ibid., I, Bk 4)

We have here, I think, a two-fold approach to the Buddha. There is the Buddha as he is in himself, and also his transformations – the Buddha for himself and for others. The Buddha for himself is said or implied at various places in this vast and heterogeneous *sūtra* to be the universe itself, to be the same as 'absence of inherent existence' or emptiness, and to be the Buddha's all-pervading omniscient consciousness. From the visionary, experiential perspective of the *sūtra* these are not necessarily contradictory. The universe of the *Avataṃsaka Sūtra* is called the *dharmadhātu* – the Dharma-realm. This is not the universe as seen by us, however. Rather, the *dharmadhātu* is the universe seen correctly, the quick-silver universe of the visionary perspective wherein all is empty and therefore is seen as a flow lacking hard edges. This is described by the *sūtra* as a universe of radiance, luminosity with no shadows. Such is experienced by the meditator. His mind expands, 'the solid outlines of individuality melt away and the feeling of finiteness no more oppresses (him)' (Suzuki 1968: 149–50). In the *Gaṇḍavyūha* Sudhana the Pilgrim, our hero, 'felt as if both his body and mind completely melted away; he saw that all thoughts departed away from his consciousness; in his mind there were no impediments, and all intoxications vanished' (trans. in Suzuki 1968: 199n). This universe *is* the Buddha. At the same time what makes it this universe, what gives it the flow, is emptiness. It is a Universe of Truth, this is the way things really are. Thus:

Clearly to know that all *dharmas*
Are without any self-essence at all;
To understand the nature of *dharmas* in this way
Is to see Vairocana.[1]

Moreover in this state where all is perceived correctly all is seen as a mental creation. One's mind can therefore penetrate all things, and the Buddha is this all-penetrating, all-transforming awareness.[2] This penetrating awareness has many powers to help others and is, as all-penetrating, present in all beings.[3]

There is one particular feature of the world as seen by a Buddha which is repeatedly stressed and for which the *Avataṃsaka Sutra* is justly famous. This is interpenetration. In a world with no hard edges, the world of luminous flow without shadows, all things infinitely interpenetrate:

> They ... perceive that the fields full of assemblies, the beings and aeons which are as many as all the dust particles, are all present in every particle of dust. They perceive that the many fields and assemblies and the beings and the aeons are all reflected in each particle of dust.
>
> (Trans. in Gomez 1967: lxxxviii)

The world as seen by the Buddhas, the *dharmadhātu*, the way things really are, is one of infinite interpenetration. Inside everything is everything else. And yet all things are not confused. As a description of the way things are in our unenlightened world this seems incredible. But the *dharmadhātu* is the world as seen by the Buddha wherein there is no question of *the* world (an objectively real world) as distinct from meditative vision. Thus the *sūtra* is less concerned with describing the world this way as with recounting the Bodhisattva's attainments by which he can see the world in such a light, and the Bodhisattva's miraculous powers by which, through his magical interventions in this world with no fixed hard boundaries, he can cause things to interpenetrate. The Buddha:

> has the miraculous power of manifesting all the images of the Dharmadhātu within one single particle of dust ... of revealing all the Buddhas of the past with their successive doings within a single pore of his skin ... of evolving clouds of transformation from a single pore of his skin and making them fill all the Buddha lands ... of revealing in a single pore of his skin the whole history of all the worlds in the ten quarters from their first appearance until their final destruction.
>
> (Trans. in Suzuki 1968: 157)

The *Gaṇḍavyūha Sūtra* is the climax of this extraordinary story. It is a Pilgrim's Progress in which our hero, Sudhana, on the Bodhisattva Mañjuśrī's advice, travels throughout India from one teacher to another, gradually advancing in spiritual growth.[4] Since the *Avataṃsaka Sūtra* is a *sūtra* of spiritual experience, so the *Gaṇḍavyūha* is accordingly less narrative than an unfolding panorama of Sudhana's experiences. Among his spiritual friends, his teachers (fifty-three in all), many are lay people, from all social groups. Of particular interest is Vasumitrā, the prostitute. She is none the less an advanced Bodhisattva. The doctrine of Skilful Means knows no bounds. For some suffering sentient beings the best way to receive the teaching of the Buddha is through Vasumitrā's technique of embraces and kisses: 'Some, with only an embrace, obtain renunciation of passion and attain the Bodhisattva meditation.... Some, with only a kiss...' (trans. by Wilson, in Paul 1979: 161). Religion, it seems, can be fun! Eventually Sudhana meets the Bodhisattva Maitreya. Maitreya shows him a great tower, the Tower of Vairocana, which represents the dharmadhātu, the Universe itself as seen in the Buddha's vision. Sudhana enters the tower. The experience is overwhelming:

> To Sudhana's wondering gaze, the interior of the Tower reveals itself as being as wide as the sky.... Moreover within the tower there are hundreds of thousands of towers, each one as exquisitely adorned... and each one, while preserving its individual existence, at the same time offering no obstruction to all the rest.... He sees Maitreya and other Bodhisattvas entering into *samādhi* [meditative absorption] and emitting from the pores of their skin multitudes of transformation bodies of various kinds. He also hears all the teachings of the Buddha melodiously issuing from every single pore of the skin of all the Bodhisattvas. He beholds all the Buddhas, together with their respective assemblies, and is the spectator of their different activities. In one particularly high, spacious, and exquisitely decorated tower, of incomparable beauty, he sees at one glance the entire trichiliocosm... and in each one of these worlds he see Maitreya's descent to earth, his nativity, and all the subsequent events of his final existence.... He sees, moreover, pillars emitting multicoloured radiance....
>
> (From the summary by Sangharakshita 1985: 229–31)

Sudhana sees himself and his career in each of the towers. From the egoistic perspective it is admittedly difficult even to imagine what such an experience could possibly feel like.

Lastly, onto this stage which is already the *dharmadhātu* we must introduce the person who, for the *Avataṃsaka Sūtra*, is the greatest Bodhisattva of them all. This is Samantabhadra. In a sense, Samantabhadra's life, experiences, and being are the underlying theme of the whole vast *sūtra*. Samantabhadra is a Bodhisattva, or Buddha (at such rarefied levels distinctions tend to get blurred), who is used by the *sūtra* as the model, the path, and the goal. The *Gaṇḍavyūha*'s Prayer of Samantabhadra forms an oft-repeated set of Bodhisattva vows, a devotional hymn beginning with what is called the 'Seven-limbed Service':

(i) Prostration:

> I reverently prostrate myself before all the Victorious Ones (Buddhas), multiplying my obeisances as if with bodies as numerous as the dust particles in the earth. . . .
> I rejoice in the belief that the entire Universe is filled with the Victorious Ones; even on the tip of a grain of sand, Buddhas as numerous as particles of dust exist, each of them sitting in the center surrounded by bodhisattvas.
>
> (Trans. in Bary *et al.* 1972: 173)

(ii) Making grand mental and real offerings.
(iii) Confession.
(iv) Rejoicing in the merit of oneself and others.
(v) Requesting the Enlightened Beings to turn the Wheel of the Doctrine.
(vi) Requesting them also not to enter into the selfish type of *nirvāṇa* which would abandon sentient beings.
(vii) Finally, dedication of the merit gained through performing this Seven-limbed Service towards the development of one's spiritual path to enlightenment for the benefit of all sentient beings.

Samantabhadra, and the practitioner, then make a number of great Bodhisattva vows. For example:

> May all beings in the ten quarters always be happy and healthy; may they be endowed with the benefits of piety, may they be successful and their wishes be fulfilled. . . .
> Allow me to work for the welfare of creatures, as long as the lands and roads exist in the ten quarters, relieving anxieties, extinguishing pain. . . .
> Allow me to work till the end of time, adjusting myself to the lives of beings, fulfilling the life of Enlightenment. . . .
> May I see the Buddhas while practicing the course to Enlightenment; on the tip of a particle of dust there are fields as

> numerous as particles of dust, and in each of these fields there are innumerable Buddhas. . . .
>
> (ibid., 174 ff.)

Our pilgrim, Sudhana wishes to see Samantabhadra. To do so he has to develop 'a great mind vast as space, an unhindered mind relinquishing all worlds and free from attachments, an unobstructed mind . . . an unimpeded mind'. And:

> He perceives ten auspicious signs and ten kinds of light and then Samantabhadra sitting in the Buddha's assembly. Observing Samantabhadra, he sees in every pore every feature of the mundane and spiritual worlds, and finally he sees himself in Samantabhadra's being, traversing infinite realms, coursing in a sphere of endless, inexhaustible knowledge, ultimately becoming equal to Samantabhadra and the Buddha, filling the cosmos.
>
> (Cleary 1983: 9)

And Thomas Cleary finishes, 'This concludes what many have considered the most grandiose, the most comprehensive, and the most beautifully arrayed of the Buddhist scriptures.'

THE HUA-YEN TRADITION IN CHINA

The phenomenon of patriarchs is a particular feature of East Asian Buddhism, in cultures dominated by the Confucian reverence for ancestors. Within the Hua-yen tradition in China there are said to have been five patriarchs: Tu-shun (557–640), Chih-yen (?600–68), Fa-tsangh Cheng-kuan (?738–?839), and Tsung-mi (780–841). This patriarchal scheme, however, is apt to be confusing for the modern scholar of Hua-yen. The earliest use of the expression 'Hua-yen school' (*tsung*) appears to have been with Cheng-kuan. Fa-tsang was the systematizer of the tradition and is therefore often spoken of as the actual creator of Hua-yen as a school. Nevertheless, creative Hua-yen elements were present before Tu-shun and after Tsung-mi, and we should not assume that even the patriarchs of Hua-yen all held exactly the same view (see Gimello 1983: 321).

Hua-yen thought is, perhaps, less philosophy than the systematic explanation of the *dharmadhātu*, the world of visionary experience and magic. It is sometimes said to be the philosophical or doctrinal articulation of Ch'an (Zen) meditation. Argument frequently gives way to assertion. Tu-shun, the first patriarch, was known in his day not as a philosophical thinker but rather as a wonder-worker, particularly renowned for his healing abilities. It is said that when he led the monks to meditate on Li Mountain all the many insects of the locality left at Tu-shun's request, so that the monks could plant vegetables for food without infringing the precept against killing. Another time a terrible dragon left at Tu-shun's arrival in the tormented neighbourhood. According to a widely held view Tu-shun was in fact Mañjuśrī himself. He was one of a number of great Chinese Buddhist teachers who lived close to the people and whose magical functions were important both for the spread of Buddhism and for the physical welfare of the masses. One story records how he, like Jesus, miraculously made a relatively small amount of food suffice for a much larger number than expected at the meal. Tu-shun's own religious practices may well have centred on reciting the *Avataṃsaka Sūtra*. Miracles brought about by reciting the Mahāyāna *sūtras*, miracles promised by the *sūtras* themselves, are frequent features of East Asian Buddhism, and a number of stories of miraculous interventions through reciting the *Avataṃsaka Sūtra* survive. The hermit monk P'u-an (530–609), for example, through the power of the *sūtra* successfully moved a large boulder which might otherwise have fallen on his flimsy hermitage, froze to the ground a group of archers who, incited by a jealous rival, wished to murder him, and even raised a dead follower to life. All this, P'u-an insisted, was not due to his own merits but to the power of the *Avataṃsaka Sūtra*.

Tu-shun and P'u-an were miracle-working contemplatives who lived in the country close to the peasantry.[5] Fa-tsang too, according to tradition, as a youth lived the ascetic life, sustained by weeds, on T'ai-pei Mountain. He remained a layman until, at the age of 28, and a disciple of the second Hua-yen patriarch Chih-yen, he was appointed abbot of a new monastery by the T'ang empress Wu Tse-t'ien. Fa-tsang then became ordained. It is said that wonders took place at Fa-tsang's sermons – lights emanated from his mouth and the earth shook (Chang 1971: 237–8). While Tu-shun was a friend of the masses, however, Fa-tsang and the systematic Hua-yen synthesis he created were closely associated with the political and spiritual aspirations of the notorious Empress Wu and her court.

Empress Wu (625–705) was the only woman in Chinese history to become emperor in her own right. As such she has been mercilessly vilified and condemned by Confucian historians ever since. At odds with Confucian orthodoxy, and the daughter of a pious Buddhist mother, Empress Wu made Buddhism the *de facto* state religion of China. She sought to find in Buddhism an ideology which could rival that of Confucius and provide a basis for female rulership. She utilized the Mahāyāna doctrine that a Bodhisattva can appear in female form for the benefit of sentient beings, and she also portrayed herself as a *cakravartin*, the Wheel-turning Emperor who, in Buddhist legend, establishes social harmony and ensures Utopia. Empress Wu was naturally attracted by the *tathāgatagarbha* doctrines which depict the core of each sentient being, male or female, that which really matters, as the same – particularly since the *tathāgatagarbha* teaching is prominently set forth in the *Śrīmālā Sūtra*, in which the principal figure is a Buddhist queen. Fa-tsang himself was strongly influenced by the *Awakening of Faith*'s Buddha-essence doctrine, which he used as a basis upon which to construct his Hua-yen philosophy of mutual identity and mutual interpenetration. Empress Wu was also attracted by the *Avataṃsaka Sūtra* in her attempt to create a state ideology of Buddhism. The *Gaṇḍavyūha Sūtra* gave an important role as Bodhisattva teachers to women – even those lay women whose morality was, to uninitiated eyes, open to question. Moreover, the *Avataṃsaka Sūtra*, with its doctrine of a central Buddha surrounded by infinite Bodhisattvas, pervading with his mind all of reality, present in all things, all ranked in harmonious interdependence, provided the empress with an interesting model for a political theory which related empress to court and thence to people and satellite states.[6] In Japan too the Emperor Shōmu (724–48) set out to rule on the basis of Hua-yen, and to that end he sponsored the building of Tōdaiji, the monastery which is still the seat of Kegon (Hua-yen) teaching in Japan, with its enormous bronze statue of Mahāvairocana, the emperor writ large.

The political significance of Hua-yen may well have suggested itself to Empress Wu in the course of Fa-tsang's famous demonstration of interpenetration. Fa-tsang appears to have been a good teacher, a master of visual aids with a very Chinese way of bringing Indian abstraction down to earth. On a number of occasions Empress Wu, not surprisingly, seems to have had some difficulty in grasping the intricacies of Hua-yen thought. On one occasion when she had experienced problems with the doctrine of interpenetration Fa-tsang called for a candle and placed it surrounded by mirrors on every side. When lit, the candle was reflected in each mirror, and each of the reflections in every other mirror so that in any one mirror were the images of all the others. One demonstration is worth a thousand words, they say! Unfortunately the close association of Empress Wu with the Hua-yen cannot have helped the popularity of Hua-yen among Confucian literati after her death. Hua-yen as a separate school did not survive the ninth-century persecution, but its thought became the central teaching of that fund of doctrinal material appropriated by the primarily practice-oriented schools of Ch'an and the Pure Land tradition which survived the persecution and prospered.

HUA-YEN THOUGHT – FA-TSANG'S *TREATISE ON THE GOLDEN LION (CHIN-SHIH-TZU CHANG)*

Among the many works of Fa-tsang his *Treatise on the Golden Lion* is particularly noteworthy as a short summary of Hua-yen thought composed with the intention of making it accessible to a lay audience. For our purposes it has the added attraction of being easily available in English translation.[7]

> The *Golden Lion* arose out of poor Empress Wu's puzzlement:
> Fa Tsang pointed to the golden lion guarding the palace hall and used it as a metaphor to illustrate the teachings. The doctrines were thereby made extremely clear and easy to understand, and the Empress quickly came to a full comprehension of the essence of the teaching.[8]

Hua-yen thought is complex and often obscure. It is very easy to mistake what are in reality, perhaps, instructions for meditation or descriptions of mystic vision for philosophical statements depicting the true way of things. If Empress Wu experienced difficulties she could speak personally with Fa-tsang. For us the problems are so much greater, and the *Golden Lion*, perhaps because of its brevity, nevertheless remains, it seems to me, an obscure document.

Fa-tsang begins with Hua-yen ontology. Gold is lacking its own inherent existence and it is for this reason that a craftsman can fashion an object of it – say, Empress Wu's lion. The lion comes into existence in dependence upon cause and conditions, but gold is always in some form or another. The gold of the golden lion stands for *li*, usually translated as 'principle' or 'noumenon', while the lion (shape) is *shih*, phenomenon. The dyad *li*/*shih* were standard terms of indigenous Chinese philosophy, and the term *li* had already been appropriated by Chinese Buddhist thinkers prior to Fa-tsang to equal the Buddha-nature: 'Like the Tao, *li* is the absolute principle behind, in, or above phenomenal changes. The Buddha-nature defined in terms of *li* is, therefore, *an essential, transcendent entity* ... a priori, perfect and complete' (Lai 1977: 75–

italics in original). The Hua-yen noumenon, Fa-tsang's gold, however, is not something above and behind phenomena. Phenomena are not emanations from the absolute noumenon. Rather, phenomena *are* noumenon – the lion is gold, there is no gold behind the lion, the lion is not an emanation of gold. Gold only exists as having some form or another, in this case that of a lion. There is no gold without form which then takes on, as it were, some form or another. The phenomenal is the noumenal in phenomenal form. This approach harmonized well with the traditional Chinese this-worldly outlook. The Ultimate is not elsewhere but here and now, in even the smallest, meanest thing. In particular it was easy to blend the Hua-yen emphasis on phenomena as being noumenon with the Taoist appreciation of Nature and a vision of enlightenment as living in harmony with Nature or the natural flow of things.[9] Like Nature, or the Tao, the Hua-yen noumenon is, in a sense, not an aloof, unchanging Absolute but, precisely because it lacks its own inherent existence in the Madhyamaka sense, it is dynamic. Gold, through a skilled craftsman, can take on a wide range of different forms.

Nevertheless, Fa-tsang continues, the lion shape is only a shape. In itself the lion is unreal – there is only gold. The lion seems to exist, but the gold *qua* gold is in another sense unchanging. We might say that from the point of view of gold, the gold has remained constant. From the point of view of gold there has been no change – it is not the concern of gold if someone has fashioned it into a lion, that is, they have imposed a lion-image onto it. But equally, since gold always has *a* shape, the gold *qua* gold does not impede, or stand in the way of, its shape or form. It is only through form that gold *is*, even though from the point of view of gold itself there is no lion form.

Since there is only gold, Fa-tsang argues, then when the lion-shape comes into existence it is in fact the gold that comes into existence. This is, on the surface, paradoxical in the extreme. It helps to remember that gold always has a shape, although the shape is nothing in addition to the gold itself. Thus if gold takes on a lion-shape it ceases to be gold in, say, bar-shape, and becomes gold in lion-shape. Since 'gold' is short for 'gold in *x*-shape', when the golden lion comes into existence, that is, gold in lion-shape, we can say that gold comes into existence. Nevertheless, whether the lion-shape occurs or ceases the gold *qua* gold neither increases nor decreases. Thus, from an ultimate point of view phenomena are, in Buddhist parlance, unborn.

It is all very well to talk of gold and lions, but these stand for *li* and *shih*, noumenon and phenomenon. What, according to Fa-tsang, are *li* and *shih*? There is little problem concerning phenomena. These are the ordinary phenomena of the universe. Fa-tsang's interpretation of noumenon, however, is a subject of dispute among scholars. Fa-tsang certainly refers to noumenon as emptiness, and he demonstrates some understanding of the Madhyamaka doctrine that emptiness is the same as absence of inherent existence. For this reason a number of modern scholars, particularly Francis Cook, have argued that Fa-tsang's noumenon is in reality nothing other than emptiness, understood in its strictly Madhyamaka sense as absence of inherent existence. For Cook there is no Hua-yen philosophy as such – Hua-yen is simply Madhyamaka with the Indian negativism replaced by a Chinese emphasis on the natural world and the way things actually do exist.[10]

There is a tendency among modern scholars to reduce all of Mahāyāna philosophy to a series of footnotes to Nāgārjuna. This tendency should, I think, be firmly resisted. Mahāyāna thought is not so monolithic. It is agreed on all counts that Fa-tsang was strongly influenced by the *Awakening of Faith*, and his noumenon is said to to be identical with the *tathāgatagarbha*.[11] In China Nāgārjuna himself was thought to be a commentator to the *Awakening of Faith*, and therefore to hold a *tathāgatagarbha* doctrine. Thus Nāgārjuna's sense of 'emptiness' was often taken to imply more than just 'absence of inherent existence'. It seems that the different senses of 'emptiness' found in Indian Buddhist thought were not always clearly distinguished in China. Moreover Francis Cook's theory tends to ignore Hua-yen sources which speak of the Universe as in reality the One Mind, and at the moment I still favour the older view that Fa-tsang's noumenon is in fact this One Mind. The imagery used – gold/lion; water/wave – suggests that the noumenon is more than just absence of inherent existence. The Chinese word *li* also carries with it a more positive connotation. One text, attributed to Tu-shun but now thought to be by Fa-tsang, refers to the noumenon as 'the true thusness of mind' and phenomena as 'birth-and-death of mind'.[12] In his *Return to the Source* Fa-tsang speaks of the 'one essence', the undefiled essence, the *tathāgatagarbha* 'that is inherently pure, complete and luminous', and quotes the *Awakening of Faith* on this essence as having 'the meaning of mind inherently pure'.[13] Elsewhere Fa-tsang explains that according to the *Awakening of Faith*, the ontology of which he places above that of Madhyamaka, 'all things are nothing but Absolute Mind' (Gregory 1983b: 36–7). Indeed in China and Japan the *Awakening of Faith* was often thought to be a Hua-yen text. Tsung-mi, the fifth Hua-yen patriarch, himself criticizes the Madhyamaka doctrine of emptiness interpreted as the final teaching, and speaks of the ultimate truth as 'a single, true, spiritual Nature, uncreated and imperishable'. This is the *tathāgatagarbha* and the 'True Mind' (in Bary *et al.* 1972: 179 ff.). It seems that inasmuch as Hua-yen scholars did distinguish the Madhyamaka emptiness as absence of inherent existence alone, to that extent they saw the Hua-yen noumenon as beyond the Ultimate Truth of Madhyamaka.

Thus far Fa-tsang's ontology. He uses this ontology in order to clarify and explain the characteristic Hua-yen doctrines of mutual identity and mutual interpenetration. This explanation is called the 'Ten Mysterious Gates', of which the first is the most important and, in Hua-yen fashion, is said to contain the others. This first gate is termed 'simultaneous complete correspondence'. Both gold and lion exist simultaneously; both, Fa-tsang says, are perfect and complete. There are two ways of interpreting this obscure point.[14] First, noumenon and phenomena mutually penetrate and are identical – there is no opposition between the two, the one does not cancel out the other. Second, Fa-tsang explains elsewhere that since all things arise interdependently (following Madhyamaka), and since the links of interdependence expand throughout the entire universe and at all time (past, present, and future depend upon each other, which is to say the total *dharmadhātu* arises simultaneously), so in the totality of interdependence, the *dharmadhātu*, all phenomena are mutually penetrating and identical. This is how I understand what Fa-tsang is trying to say here. First, since all phenomena are nothing more than noumenon in a particular form, and the form does not in itself exist, so all phenomena are identical. Moreover, noumenon cannot in itself be divided. One piece of gold and another piece of gold, as gold, are not different. The difference lies in spatial separation, and that is something to do with shape or form, not the gold *qua* gold. Since a phenomenon is only noumenon, and since between any two 'instantiations' of noumenon there is, as noumenon, no difference, so each phenomenon is in fact the same as any other phenomenon. Furthermore, since each instantiation of noumenon is noumenon itself (noumenon cannot be divided), so each phenomenon is also all phenomena. Mutual identity and interpenetration. Second, since the *dharmadhātu* is a totality of interdependent elements, and according to Madhyamaka teaching each entity lacks inherent existence and only *is* in terms of an infinite network of causal interrelationships so, if any entity were taken away, the entire Universe would collapse ('No man is an island . . .'). This means that each entity is a cause for the totality. Moreover the totality is, of course, a cause for each entity. Since each entity is a cause, *the* cause, for the totality – that without which the totality could not occur – *and nothing more* (for Madhyamaka 'to be' is only explicable in terms of causal relationships), so each entity is the same as any other entity. Again, if any one entity were removed, that totality would not occur. Thus each entity exerts total causal power. But if each entity in the Universe exerts total causal power each entity must contain each other entity. Once more, mutual identity and interpenetration. And yet, of course, none of this prevents each entity from occupying its own place in the totality – each entity remains discrete and entities do not obstruct each other.

Lastly, lest all this talk of gold and lions has confused, Fa-tsang reminds us that this is not a novel physics or a lesson for craftsmen. Both gold and lion in reality adopt various forms in accordance with the mind, a transformation of Mind Only. And here, perhaps, we should leave Fa-tsang and his *Treatise on the Golden Lion*. He has much more to say in even that short text, but we have met the main points and gained some idea, a sampler, of the nature, complex and obscure, of Hua-yen thought. It is an attempt to express in rational terms a spiritual vision. Some (among whom I am not necessarily one) would consider that attempt doomed to failure!

A NOTE ON SOME ASPECTS OF HUA-YEN PRACTICE

Hua-yen, in common with much of East Asian Buddhism, particularly Ch'an, for which it provides a philosophical foundation, favours the teaching of sudden enlightenment. This is not only because the Buddha-nature, the One Mind, is already present, pure and radiant, untainted in all sentient beings, but also because the Hua-yen doctrines of identity and interpenetration entail that Buddhahood is already present at the first stage of the Bodhisattva's path to enlightenment. 'On each stage', Fa-tsang says, 'one is thus both a Bodhisattva and a Buddha.' This takes place from the very beginning. According to Fa-tsang if the Bodhisattva has begun, has perfected his or her faith, he or she is already a Buddha, with all that this means in terms of the *Avataṃsaka Sūtra*. The Bodhisattva must see himself or herself as a Buddha, and behave accordingly. For Li T'ung-hsüan (635–730), who contributed a great deal towards developing a practical spirituality on the basis of the *Avataṃsaka Sūtra* and Hua-yen thought, followed by the great Korean monk Chinul (twelfth century):

> the first access of faith in the mind of the practitioner is in itself the culmination of the entire path, the very realization of final

> Buddhahood. ... 'Faith' or confidence in the possibility of enlightenment is nothing but enlightenment itself, *in an anticipatory and causative modality*.[15]

To Fa-tsang the Sudden Teaching was necessary because the noumenon, Suchness or Thusness, is beyond language and therefore beyond stages of practice, which have at the best a provisional validity. Practice cannot create a state of enlightenment which is not there already, and thus there can be no causal relationship between practice and enlightenment. In spite of this, there is no implication that in East Asian Buddhism those who hold the teaching of Sudden Enlightenment sit and wait for enlightenment to happen. Rather, moral and meditative practice bring out what one already is.

The *Avataṃsaka Sūtra* and its recitation formed the central concern of a number of Chinese lay Buddhist societies. It seems that these societies were a major feature of Chinese Buddhist practice. Originally they were founded in order to sponsor vegetarian feasts which were held on holy days, as thanksgivings, and so on. The result of taking part in this sponsorship would be merit, a principal concern of laity throughout the Buddhist world. Subsequently the societies convened in order to generate merit through chanting a favourite *sūtra*. This merit could be used for a number of purposes – bringing prosperity or children, helping one's ancestors, or it could be dedicated towards a favourable future rebirth or even the highest Mahāyāna purpose, the welfare of all sentient beings. The *Avataṃsaka Sūtra* was a particularly favoured *sūtra* for such societies, probably due to the miraculous powers associated with this work, itself the result, perhaps, of the *sūtra*'s staggering visionary and miraculous content. It seems likely that *Avataṃsaka* societies developed around miracle-working monks such as P'u-an or Tu-shun, for whom chanting the *Avataṃsaka Sūtra* formed their principal daily practice. These monks organized the lay fraternity, and developed a cult centred on the *sūtra* itself, rather than on themselves as miracle workers. Such popular cults and feasts, it has been argued, fitted naturally into Chinese society, taking the place of communal feasts founded on sacrifices to local deities. As time passed so lay recitation of the *sūtra* became more important than the feasts themselves. Some of these *Avataṃsaka* societies were very large indeed, and highly organized. Over the centuries such societies contributed to the growth of secret societies which were to trouble central government in later Chinese history. With the collapse of state and state patronage in late T'ang times the lay *Avataṃsaka* societies also became more important as patrons of the Buddhist order and Buddhist works. This growing importance of local patronage is reflected in the growing practical and popular concern of Hua-yen in the late T'ang as it ceased to be an independent school and subsequently gradually fused with traditions like Ch'an which were practical, down to earth, and enjoyed widespread popular support (see Gregory 1983a: 278 ff.).

THE *AVATAṂSAKA SŪTRA* AND VAIROCANA IN BUDDHIST ART

Set in the jungles of Java, the *stūpa* complex of Borobudur is one of the enduring monuments of Mahāyāna Buddhist civilization. The whole forms a *maṇḍala*, a cosmogram in the shape of a terraced hill. The hill is composed of, in ascending order, five rectangular and four circular levels. The circular levels contain three circles of small *stūpas*, culminating in a great central *stūpa*. Sculptures and friezes in the galleries and niches of the rectangular levels indicate that as the worshipper ascends the monument he or she passes from the lower levels of the cosmos to the Buddhas above, and eventually to the central Buddha. These sculptures and friezes instruct the practitioner in *karma* and rebirth, tell the life story of Śākyamuni Buddha, and illustrate popular Jātaka tales, stories of the Buddha's previous lives as a Bodhisattva. They also illustrate the entire text of the *Gaṇḍavyūha Sūtra*. Thus we have a panel in which Sudhana, full of joy, is depicted jumping up three steps in one leap. The Bodhisattva vows to be a refuge for all beings, and is depicted accompanied by beings from the hells and other realms of rebirth. In one panel Samantabhadra, portrayed with an insignia of a lotus with one stalk and three buds, stretches out his hand to stroke Sudhana on the head. Offerings of music to the Buddha are illustrated by a lively scene of a central Buddha in tranquil meditation surrounded by vigorous drummers, figures blowing trumpets, and other instrumentalists. In one of the Samantabhadra vows it is said that his aspiration will end only 'when space comes to an end'. This is cleverly depicted by the Bodhisattva flying through the air, presumably trying to find the end of space.[16]

It is in Central Asia, not surprisingly, perhaps, that we find the earliest artistic creations clearly depicting features associated with the *Avataṃsaka Sūtra*. These are representations of the Buddha Vairocana as a cosmic Buddha, a Buddha containing within himself all the other Buddhas and all features of the universe. From the sixth-century Khotan region there remains a painted panel of a standing Buddha surrounded by a nimbus, bearing other Buddhas on his chest. Again, on the northern Central Asian trade route, from Kyzyl, near Kucha, there survives a sixth-or seventh-century cave painting of a standing Buddha. This Buddha has right hand raised, five Buddhas across his chest, and further figures down his legs. Figures also radiate out into his nimbus. In a further almost contemporary wall painting from Karashahr, the nimbus is composed of ocean scenes (the cosmic ocean?) with lotuses, underwater serpents (*nāgas*), and ducks. Once more there are Buddhas and other figures across the chest, arms, and legs, while two figures on the knees have been identified as the sun and moon. Finally, a particularly famous seventh-century wall painting from Balawaste, on the southern route, depicts Vairocana in meditation, his torso and arms covered in cosmic symbols with sun and moon on his shoulders and the cosmic mountain Meru on his chest. There also survives a contemporaneous bronze-gilt statue of Vairocana, traced to Central Asia, again a standing figure, bearing Mount Meru, sun and moon on his front, and the paths of rebirth on his back.[17]

These figures from Central Asia depict in a very vivid way the cosmic nature of Vairocana. Another way of depicting this was through sheer size. Such technique was used effectively in China and Japan where, as we have seen, there was a political tendency to identify Vairocana with the emperor. From about the fifth century in China, following without doubt Indian and Central Asian models, huge cave temples were constructed, adorned with statues and paintings many of which have survived the ravages of time and barbarians. Cave temples had obvious advantages. They were durable and easy to keep in good repair (no leaking roofs), and they could be kept warm in winter and cool in summer. One also suspects that they provided a psychological image of emanation from one mass and return to unity. Among the most important of the cave temple complexes is that of Lung-men, near Lo-yang in Northern China. The construction of temples and images at Lung-men was given enthusiastic support by Empress Wu. The shrines were hollowed out of the sandstone cliffs of a river gorge, and the central carved figure is an enormous Vairocana Buddha, some 15 metres from the base of the pedestal to the tip of his halo. This figure took three years to carve, from 672 to 675. It was carved, therefore, during the reign of Empress Wu and the lifetime of Fa-tsang himself. The figure is solid, aloof, and majestic, wearing a monastic robe of simple folds. Small, very small, Buddha figures are depicted in the halo, radiating from the central cosmic Buddha.[18]

Hua-yen Buddhism came to Japan in the eighth century. It was brought from China by a number of Chinese missionaries, and also by an Indian, Bodhisena. The Emperor Shōmu, Bodhisena, together with Gyōgi, surnamed 'the Bodhisattva' – a priest who spread Buddhism, engaged in public works, and advised the emperor – and also Rōben, the abbot, jointly founded the monastery of Tōdaiji. This monastery is to the present day the centre of Kegon (Hua-yen) Buddhism in Japan, with 70,486 adherents in 1970.[19] From the beginning Japanese Buddhism was closely tied to the welfare of the state, and this was never more so than during the Nara period (710–94). When, in 735–7, a smallpox epidemic ravaged Japan the emperor ordained that every province should have a 5 metre high image of the Buddha and a copy of the *Perfection of Wisdom*. Subsequent edicts founded monasteries and *stūpas*. All monasteries were to be supervised by Tōdaiji. But the principal anti-smallpox precaution, indeed the dominant concern of the age, was the construction at Tōdaiji of an enormous bronze image of Vairocana, over 16 metres high. It is said that the Shintō Sun Goddess gave her permission for the enterprise. Vairocana, she said, is the Sun – a useful basis for Buddhist–Shintō syncretism and further Buddhist missionary activity. The figure was probably based on the great Chinese images, but the Tōdaiji Buddha was cast, in sections, out of metal. The first discovery of gold in Japan soon after the completion of the statue was held to be a miraculous blessing and enabled the whole image to be gilded. The wooden building which housed the Tōdaiji Vairocana remains the largest wooden structure ever built. Unfortunately, however, it was burnt down in the twelfth century, and also its replacement in the sixteenth century (one advantage of caves). The present building is only two-thirds of the original size, but is still the largest wooden building in the world under a single roof. The Vairocana figure itself is unimpressive apart from its size, since over the years it has been badly damaged, particularly due to fire, and badly restored.

The Bodhisattva Samantabhadra (Japanese: Fugen) is often portrayed in Japanese art, usually associated with his 'vehicle', a white elephant. The portrayal of Samantabhadra is more due to his connection with the favourite Japanese *sūtra*, however, the *Lotus Sūtra*, than with the Kegon tradition. It is to this *sūtra*, therefore, that we now turn.

PART II

Compassion

CHAPTER SEVEN

The *Saddharmapuṇḍarīka* (*Lotus*) *Sūtra* and its influences

There were once two Japanese priests, Hōgon and Renzō. Hōgon practised reciting the *Avataṃsaka Sūtra*, while Renzō, was a devotee of the *Saddharmapuṇḍarīka* (*Lotus*) *Sūtra*. As a result of the power of the *Avataṃska Sūtra*, and Hōgon's virtue, a deity regularly supplied Hōgon with food. Out of his charity, and perhaps also a little spiritual pride, Hōgon requested one day that the deity provide enough food for two, and invited Renzō to dine. Alas, in spite of the deity's agreement, on the appointed day no food appeared. Evening came, and Renzō, realizing perhaps that he had something better to do, returned home. As soon as he left the hermitage the deity appeared, laden with food. At first sight one might suppose that Renzō was lacking in virtue – but nothing could be further from the truth. Renzō, through the power of the *Lotus Sūtra*, came accompanied by so many invisible protector deities that the poor deity of the *Avataṃsaka Sūtra* could not get through the door! Hōgon, duly impressed, abandoned reciting the *Avataṃsaka Sūtra* and became a fervent supporter of the *Lotus Sūtra*. As so often, religious practice is a matter of power, and the greater magical power lay with the *Lotus Sūtra*.

This story, and many like it, comes from the *Hokkegenki*, an eleventh-century collection of miraculous tales attesting to the efficacy of faith in, reciting, copying, and generally promulgating the *Lotus Sūtra* (trans. in Dykstra 1983: 59–60). For many East Asian Buddhists since early times the *Lotus Sūtra* is the nearest Buddhist equivalent to a bible – one revealed work containing the final truth, itself sufficient for salvation. For many contemporary Japanese Buddhists who follow the lead of Nichiren (1222–82), the *Lotus Sūtra* is not only sufficient for salvation but is the only *sūtra* adequate to the task during the present epoch of spiritual decline (Japanese: *mappō*). From China we are told of a court official who recited the whole *sūtra* once every day for 30 years, and 3 times a day after the age of 80. A certain Chinese abbot recited the *Lotus* 37,000 times in 30 years. If we can believe the *Hokkegenki*, there were Japanese who recited the complete *sūtra* more than 30 times a day and 1,000 times a month![1]

Any text which inspires such fervent enthusiasm (and not a little of East Asian art and literature) deserves closer examination. The Sanskrit text of the *Lotus Sūtra* survives in a number of different versions, mainly fragmentary, the textual history of which is complex. The earliest extant Chinese translation was made by Dharmarakṣa in 286 CE (revised 290 CE). The version which conquered East Asia, however, and therefore by far the most significant version given the *sūtra*'s importance in East Asian Buddhism, was the *Lotus* translated by Kumārajīva and his team of translators in 406.[2] One should never assume, incidentally, that because we are dealing with a *sūtra* originally composed in India an extant Sanskrit text must, where they differ, represent an earlier or more authentic version of the text than any Chinese translation. The codification of the Canon, the printing and preservation of texts in China, has meant that Chinese translations will often be much earlier than any Sanskrit manuscript. To think of an extant Sanskrit text as *the*, or even *an*, original is fraught with textual and historical problems.

Kumārajīva's *Lotus Sūtra* consists of twenty-eight chapters. It is not a homogeneous work. Japanese scholars, who have carried out extensive study of the *Lotus Sūtra*, are inclined to see the oldest parts of the text as having been composed between the first century BCE and the first century CE (Chapters 1–9, plus Chapter 17). Most of the text had appeared by the end of the second century.[3]

The *Lotus* is a dramatic *sūtra*. There are frequent changes of scene and, apart from its message, the success of the *sūtra* has been due perhaps in no small part to its use of several striking parables. The antiquity of the *sūtra* is vividly attested by its need to establish its authority against those who would ridicule both the *sūtra* and its preachers. According to Sino-Japanese tradition the *Lotus Sūtra* was the final teaching of the Buddha, preached immediately before he manifested his *parinirvāṇa*, his death – or, in the light of the teaching of the *Lotus Sūtra* itself, his disappearance from human view.

In the *sūtra* the Buddha, Śākyamuni Buddha, is at pains to make it quite clear to his audience that he, as a Buddha, is infinitely superior both cognitively and spiritually to those who have attained other religious goals, Buddhist and non-Buddhist:

> The Hero of the World is incalculable.
> Among gods, worldlings,
> And all varieties of living beings,
> None can know the Buddha.
> As to the Buddha's strengths, ... his sorts of fearlessness, ...
> His deliverances, ... and his samādhis,
> As well as the other dharmas of a Buddha,
> None can fathom them. (p. 23)

Nevertheless he, the Buddha, has employed his skill-in-means and devices (*upāya/upāyakauśalya*) in order to adapt his teaching to the level of his hearers. This teaching of skill-in-means, or skilful means, is a key doctrine of the Mahāyāna, and one of the key teachings of the *Lotus Sūtra*. It was undoubtedly one of the factors responsible for the success of the *Lotus Sūtra* in East Asia. Among the principal problems which faced Buddhist missionaries during the early transmission of Buddhism to China, and thence, of course, to other countries in East Asia, was on the one hand the quantity of apparently contradictory teachings attributed to the Buddha, and on the other a pressing need to adapt the Buddhist message to suit cultures very different from those in India. Broadly speaking, the doctrine of skilful means maintains that the Buddha himself adapted his teaching to the level of his hearers. Thus most, if not all, of the Buddha's teachings have a relative value and only a relative truth. They are to be used like ladders, or, to use an age-old Buddhist image, like a raft employed to cross a river. There is no point in carrying the raft once the journey has been completed and its function fulfilled. When used, such a teaching transcends itself. Thus although the corpus of teachings attributed to the Buddha, if taken as a whole, embodies many contradictions, these contradictions are only apparent. Teachings are appropriate to the context in which they are given. Their truth is relative and so the contradiction evaporates.[4]

The doctrine of skilful means prompted the Chinese Buddhist philosophical schools to produce schema known as *p'an chiao*. Each school ranks the Buddha's teaching in progression leading up to the highest teaching, the 'most true' teaching, embodied in the principal *sūtra* of that school. Thus each school explains the purpose for teaching each doctrine, and the reason why only its own *sūtra* embodies the final teaching – inasmuch as the final teaching can be captured in words. Moreover the doctrine of skill-in-means, operating within a philosophical framework where all phenomena have but relative existence, entails almost infinite flexibility in adapting the teaching of the Buddha to suit changing circumstances. The Buddha teaches out of his infinite compassion for sentient beings. All teachings are exactly appropriate to the level of those for whom they were intended. Any adaptation whatsoever, provided it is animated by the Bodhisattva's compassion and wisdom, and is suitable for the recipient, is a part of Buddhism. The Buddha, or a Bodhisattva, is quite capable of teaching even non-Buddhist teachings if that is for the benefit of beings. In point of fact, the teaching of skilful means in Mahāyāna Buddhism comes to extend beyond simply adapting the doctrine to the level of the hearers to refer to any behaviour by the Buddha or Bodhisattvas which is perhaps not what one might expect, but which is done through the motivation of compassion, animated by wisdom, for the benefit of others. This is well illustrated by another *sūtra* entirely devoted to skilful means, with the shortened title of *Upāyakauśalya Sūtra*. This *sūtra* contains a series of questions and answers concerning legendary events in the life of Siddhārtha, explaining that they were not what they appeared to be, but served the higher purpose of the Buddha's teaching. For example, why did the Buddha, free of karmic hindrances and omniscient, once return empty-handed from his begging round? This was, it seems, out of his compassion for monks in the future who similarly will return occasionally empty-handed (Chang 1983: 459). Sometimes the person who composed the *sūtra* seems to have been at a loss, or had to use some ingenuity, to explain a feature of the Buddha's conduct. Why did the Buddha, when still a Bodhisattva just after his birth, walk seven steps?

> If it has been more beneficial to sentient beings to walk six steps than to walk seven steps, the Bodhisattva would have walked six steps. If it had been more beneficial to sentient beings to walk eight steps than to walk seven steps, the Bodhisattva would have walked eight steps. Since it was most beneficial to sentient beings to walk seven steps, he walked seven steps, not six or eight, with no one supporting him.
>
> (Chang 1983: 445)

The teaching of skilful means is of some importance when considering Mahāyāna ethics, since all is subordinated to the overriding concern of a truly compassionate motivation accompanied by wisdom. All is relative.

Thus it can be skill-in-means for a Bodhisattva to act in a way contrary to the 'narrower' moral or monastic code of others. The *Upāyakauśalya Sūtra* recounts how the Buddha in a previous life as a celibate religious student had sexual intercourse in order to save a poor girl who threatened to die for love of him (p. 433)! A story well-known in Mahāyāna circles tells similarly how in a previous life the Buddha killed a man. This was the only way to prevent that man from killing 500 others and consequently falling to the lowest hell for a very long time. The Bodhisattva's act was motivated by pure compassion; he realized he was acting against the moral code but he was realistically prepared to suffer in hell himself out of his love for others. As a result, the *sūtra* assures us, not only did the Bodhisattva progress spiritually and avoid hell, but the potential murderer was also reborn in a heavenly realm (pp. 456–7). Stories like this have provided the basis for Mahāyāna Buddhist participation in violence – e.g. violence by Tibetan monks in defence of the Dharma against the Chinese Communist invasion. Paradoxically, justification in Mahayana *sūtras* for killing by a Bodhisattva has also been used by the Chinese Communists to persuade Chinese Buddhists to take part in the class war and to support the People's Liberation Army.[5] In the *Hokkegenki* we are told of the skilful means of a Japanese devotee of the *Lotus Sūtra* who insisted on repeatedly stealing so that he could carry out missionary work, spreading the *Lotus Sūtra* in prison. The chief of police was told in a dream that 'In order to save criminals in prison, the holy man Shunchō stayed there seven times. This was nothing but the expedience of various Buddhas who concealed their glory from sentient beings in order to make contact with them' (Dykstra 1983: 51).

The teaching of skill-in-means is a crucial ancillary of one of the other principal doctrines of the *Lotus Sūtra*, that of the One Vehicle (*ekayāna*). The *sūtra* explains that when the Buddha mentioned the topic of skill-in-means a number of Arhats and other followers began to feel uneasy:

> Now, why has the World-Honored One made this speech earnestly praising expedient devices [skilful means]? The Dharma which the Buddha has gained is very hard to understand. He has something to say, whose meaning is hard to know, and which no voice-hearer or pratyekabuddha can attain. The Buddha has preached the doctrine of unique deliverance, which means that we, too, gaining this Dharma, shall reach nirvāṇa. Yet now we do not know where this doctrine tends. (pp. 25–6)

That is, although it is agreed that the Buddha is in certain respects superior to Arhats and Pratyekabuddhas, as regards their having attained liberation, the goal, freedom from rebirth, Arhats, Pratyekabuddhas, and Buddhas are all on the same level. They are all enlightened. Now the Buddha is portrayed arguing that he taught many provisional ways and goals: his doctrine was taught out of skill adapted to the level of his hearers, with the implied possibility that the goals of Arhatship and Pratyekabuddhahood are no real goals at all, they are merely provisional devices, and there is a great gulf separating Arhatship and Pratyekabuddahood from the true goal of full and complete Buddhahood.

At first, we are told, the Buddha refused to elaborate on the position newly stated, even when beseeched by Śāriputra:

> Cease, cease! No need to speak.
> My dharma is subtle and hard to imagine.
> Those of overwheening pride,
> If they hear it, shall surely neither revere it nor believe in it. (p. 28)

There is a tradition, however, that the Buddha will not refuse a request three times. Upon being begged three times by Sāriputra to elaborate, the Buddha does decide to preach. At this we told that 5,000 of the gathering got up and left the assembly:

> For what reason? This group had deep and grave roots of sin and overwheening pride, imagining themselves to have attained and to have borne witness to what in fact they had not. Having such faults as these, therefore they did not stay. The World-Honored One, silent, did not restrain them. At that time the Buddha declared to Śāriputra: 'My assembly has no more branches and leaves, it has only firm fruit. Śāriputra, it is just as well that such arrogant ones as these have withdrawn'. (p. 29)

We can see in this episode, perhaps, a reflection of what really happened in the monastic assembly when a follower of the Mahāyāna rose to preach the new doctrine. Those who dissented withdrew in silence, privately reserving their scorn. The Mahāyānists, on the other hand, placed in the mouth of the Buddha a scathing criticism of the arrogance, the lack of openness and flexibility, on the part of those who believed themselves to have attained, or to be well on the path to, the highest spiritual goal, and were not open to the new perspective.

What is this new perspective? It is the perspective of the One Vehicle. At the time the *Lotus Sūtra* was compiled it was accepted on all counts that there were Arhats, Pratyekabuddhas, and Buddhas. Most were following the path to Arhatship. Somewhere, sometimes, perhaps, there were Pratyekabuddhas, while certain rare beings such as Siddhārtha Gautama became Buddhas. It was agreed that the attributes of these were different, the Buddha was in certain respects superior, but all were truly enlightened – after death none would be reborn. We have seen in the *Lotus Sūtra*, however, and indeed in texts belonging to certain non-Mahā yāna traditions, a gradual devaluation of Arhats and Pratyekabuddhas, and an elevation of the Buddha and his attainments. The *Lotus Sūtra* marks the culmination of this process. There is in reality only One Vehicle (*yāna*), not three. This One Vehicle is the Supreme Buddha Vehicle. Just as the Buddha is infinitely superior to the Arhat and the Pratyekabuddha, so the only final vehicle is the One Vehicle to Perfect Buddhahood. *All* will eventually become Buddhas – the doctrine of the three vehicles was in reality nothing more than the Buddha's skilful means:

> Knowing that the beings have various desires and objects to which their thoughts are profoundly attached, following their basic nature, by resort to the expedient power of various means, parables, and phrases, I preach the Dharma to them. Śāriputra, I do this only in order that they may gain the One Buddha Vehicle and knowledge of all modes. Sāriputra, in the world of the ten directions there are not even two vehicles. How much the less can there be three! (p. 31)

It is only because Buddhas who appear at the decay of a cosmic epoch find that beings are so full of demerit and evil that they would not understand such doctrines that they teach the other vehicles. This is their skill-in-means, their use of expedients. The ways of the Arhat and the Pratyekabuddha are simply skilful devices to save those who would not believe if they were told about the only true goal, the full and complete *nirvāṇa* of a Buddha (p. 31). There is really no such thing as Arhatship and Pratyekabuddhahood as Buddhist goals. These were taught simply to encourage people. All will eventually take the path of the Bodhisattva and progress to Perfect Buddhahood – including those who consider themselves to have attained already the goals of Arhatship and Pratyekabuddhahood. Much space in the *Lotus Sūtra* is taken up with the Buddha predicting how the great Arhats in his entourage, people like Śāriputra, the hero of the Abhidharmikas, will eventually become Full Buddhas. Śāriputra had embarked on the Bodhisattva path aeons ago – he had just forgotten it, that is all!

There is some evidence from the *Lotus Sūtra* itself that there may have been persecution of those who insisted, perhaps with evangelical zeal, on shouting the new teachings at people who would rather not hear them.[6] In one of the later sections of the *sūtra* we are told of the insistent Bodhisattva Sadāparibhūta, who would pounce on his fellow Buddhists with the words, 'I profoundly revere you all! I dare not hold you in contempt. What is the reason? You are all treading the bodhisattva path, and shall succeed in becoming Buddhas!' The result was that some

> reviled him with a foul mouth, saying, 'This know-nothing bhikṣu! Whence does he come? He himself says, "I do not hold you in contempt," yet he presumes to prophesy to us that we will succeed in becoming Buddhas! We have no need of such idle prophecies!' In this way, throughout the passage of many years, he was constantly subjected to abuse; yet he did not give way to anger, but constantly said, 'You shall become Buddhas!' When he spoke these words, some in the multitude would beat him with sticks and staves, with tiles and stones. He would run away and abide at a distance, yet he would still proclaim in a loud voice, 'I dare not hold you all in contempt. You shall all become Buddhas!' (pp. 280–1)

Skilful means and the doctrine of the One Vehicle form the subjects of the main parables for which the *Lotus Sūtra* is justly renowned. The first parable is that of the burning house. Summarized, it tells how three sons of a wealthy man are trapped inside a burning house while playing. So absorbed are they in their games that they are unaware of the fire. The father, well-trained in those skilful devices needed by all parents, resolves to persuade the children to come out by offering them various new playthings. They like playing in carriages drawn by animals. He offers them goat carriages, deer carriages, and ox carriages. The children cannot wait, and they rush into their father's arms. What does he now do? He gives them each a wonderful carriage, the very best, drawn by a white ox (Chapter 13). The parable requires little interpretation. The father is the Buddha. The burning house is the house of *saṃsāra*, within which sentient beings, absorbed in their playthings, are trapped. The Buddha offers various vehicles (*yānas*) as bribes, according to the tastes of sentient beings, but when they have taken up the practices and are saved from *saṃsāra* he gives them all the very best, the only, solitary One Vehicle of Buddhahood. The question is asked whether the father, or the Buddha, lied to his children? He did not. In a world of relativity (and the *Lotus Sūtra* appears to accept the Madhayamaka doctrine of emptiness), and a world where spiritual progress is paramount, truth very often depends upon context. The Buddha describes himself as the Father of Beings (p. 61). Whatever he says is true and not false. He simply uses skilful means out of compassion in order to save his children.

Elsewhere in the *Lotus Sūtra* we find a parable of the Prodigal Son, this time spoken not by the Buddha himself but by several of his overjoyed followers. A man's son has left home, wandered away, and fallen into dire poverty. Meanwhile his father's business by contrast has prospered in another city, and his father has become a very rich man. The son arrives one day at his father's house. While the son no longer recognizes his father or his new mansion, the father instantly recognises his son and sends a servant to fetch him. The son, alas, is terrified. The father accordingly realizes that he must introduce him in gradual stages to the truth that he is the son of the father and heir to all this wealth. The father offers his son very menial and dirty work (attaining of Arhatship!). He does the job well, and the father gradually promotes him. Eventually the father starts to treat him like a son. At long last the father, about to die, announces to all that this man really is his son and natural heir. The son is, of course, overjoyed. The parable is obvious – as all good parables should be (Chapter 4). The Buddha's teaching, again, is likened to the rain which pours down equally on all plants. This rain is nevertheless absorbed and used by each plant according to its nature (Chapter 5). This parable, well-known in East Asia, inspired a lovely Japanese poem by Shunzei (1114–1204):

> Spring's fine rain
> both in the distance and right here
> both on grasses and trees
> is evenly dyeing everything
> everywhere in its new green.
>
> (Trans. in LaFleur 1983: 94)

The impact of the Buddha's teaching of universal Buddhahood is illustrated by the case of a poor man who fell asleep while drinking with a wealthy friend. The friend, having to leave, sewed a jewel into his poor friend's garment. The poor man eventually wanders off, to resume his life of poverty. When the two meet again the rich man is astonished. Why is his friend so poor when he has this jewel on his person? He is really wealthy. He can have all that he ever hoped for. Like this is the joy of discovering that one is really destined for Buddhahood (Chapter 8). The nature of Arhatship and Pratyekabuddhahood as goals is illustrated by the parable of the Place of Jewels (Chapter 7). The Buddha is like a guide leading men to the Place of Jewels, a fabulous Utopia, perhaps. The followers become tired and want to give up. The guide, however, is the best sort of guide – he is also a magician. He creates a magical city in which they can rest before going on to their true destination. Likewise the Buddha creates the magical city of Arhatship and Pratyekabuddhahood.[7]

This, therefore, is the principal message of the first half of the *Lotus Sūtra* – the Buddha's skilful means, the doctrine of the One Vehicle, and the complete joy of the Buddha's disciples in finding that they will, indeed they must, attain Perfect Buddhahood. There are in reality no such goals as Arhatship and Pratyekabuddhahood. While we are still in the first part of the *Lotus Sūtra* extraordinary events start to take place, events which foreshadow the equally shattering message of the second part of the *sūtra*. To the astonishment of the assembly the *Lotus* depicts the appearance of another Buddha, one from the past, previously unknown, called Prabhūtaratna (Chapter 11). This Buddha appears in the sky inside a floating *stūpa*. He had so admired the *Lotus Sūtra* that he vowed to be present whenever it is preached. We can see reflected here a number of assertions. First, the *Lotus Sūtra* is not new, but its preaching is part of the ministry of every Buddha. Second, there can be more than one Buddha existing at the same time and in the same region. Third, and this was the most radical implication of all, there is here a denial of a cardinal teaching found among non-Mahāyāna schools, the teaching that the Buddha after his *parinirvāṇa*, or apparent *parinirvāṇa* (death), has gone completely beyond any further recall or reference, has to all intents and purposes ceased as far as those who are left are concerned. For Prabhūtaratna is supposed to be dead, and yet here he is radiantly vigorous.

It is this teaching, the doctrine that the Buddha remains, has not abandoned his children but is still here helping in many infinite compassionate ways, which forms the centrepiece of the *Lotus Sūtra*'s second half. The Buddha has not really died. He is like a great doctor whose sons have been poisoned. He quickly mixes the antidote, but the minds of some of the sons are so deranged that they ignore the medicine. The father fakes his own death and retires elsewhere. Brought to their senses by shock the sons take the antidote. The father then reappears. His death was a skilful device (Chapter 16). The Buddha is still with us. Furthermore, the Buddha's life can be projected far into the past. In the *sūtra* the Buddha explains that he has converted countless individuals, many myriads of *koṭis* (i.e. a large number – the *sūtras* relish the breathless multiplication of immense figures). At this, Maitreya, the coming Buddha, asks in astonishment how it can be that the Buddha teaches so many beings in the span of a mere forty years since his enlightenment?

> In this way, since my attainment of Buddhahood it has been a very great interval of time. My life-span is incalculable asaṃkhyeyakalpas [rather a lot of aeons], ever enduring, never perishing. O good men! The life-span I achieved in my former treading of the bodhisattva path even now is not exhausted, for it is twice the above number. Yet even now, though in reality I am not to pass into extinction [enter *parinirvāṇa*], yet I proclaim that I am about to accept extinction. By resort to these expedient devices the Thus Come One teaches and converts the beings. (p. 239)

It is often said that in the *Lotus Sūtra* the Buddha is deified. In Japanese Buddhism it is certainly taught that the Buddha of the *Lotus Sūtra* is eternal. However, there is a problem with the notion of an eternal Buddha. If the Buddha is eternal then no one who is not already a Buddha could attain Buddhahood. If the *Lotus Sūtra* taught an eternal Buddha it would accordingly destroy the notion that all will eventually attain Buddhahood – unless, that is, the *Lotus Sūtra* also held to a doctrine of the *tathāgatagarbha*. In China, particularly in the T'ien-t'ai tradition, the *Lotus Sūtra* was linked with the *Mahāparinirvāṇa Sūtra*, which, as we have seen, advocates the *tathāgatagarbha*, and also with the *Awakening of Faith*. However, there is little or no evidence from the *Lotus Sūtra* itself that it accepts the *tathāgatagarbha* teaching. Thus I suspect that the East Asian doctrine of an eternal Buddha in the *Lotus Sūtra* results from the systematization of the teachings of the *Sūtra* within the context of T'ien-t'ai (Japanese: Tendai) thought, which draws on other Mahāyāna material to teach a cosmic Buddha rather like the Mahāvairocana of Hua-yen Buddhism. The quotation above is apparently contradictory. It speaks of the Buddha attaining enlightenment in time, and seems to give a finite figure to the length of his subsequent life. Nevertheless, it also speaks of the Buddha's life as 'ever enduring, never perishing'. In Buddhist theory the length of a life is contingent upon merit. This is why the Buddha in the *Lotus Sūtra* speaks of the life-span he has achieved through his many good deeds on the Bodhisattva path. Thus I suggest that the quotation above is to be taken as indicating an enormously long but still finite length to the Buddha's life. His life as a Buddha both begins and ends in time, and references to its eternity are typical examples of *sūtra* hyperbole. Nevertheless, whether the Buddha is literally eternal or not, the Buddha of the *Lotus Sūtra* is religiously eternal – for the devotee he is, as it were, always there.[8]

The feature of laudatory self-reference, a feature of the early Mahāyāna *sūtras*, is very much to the fore in the *Lotus Sūtra*. If a person hears just one verse of the *sūtra* and rejoices in it for even a moment the Buddha predicts that person to Full Buddhahood. The *sūtra* should not only be recited and promulgated but worshipped as if it were the Buddha himself with 'sundry offerings of flower perfume, necklaces, powdered incense, perfumed paste, burnt incense, silk canopies and banners, garments or music' (p. 174; cf. Chapters 20–3). Moreover the sin of maligning this *sūtra* and its preachers is much worse than constantly maligning the Buddha (p. 175). Those who preach the *sūtra* will themselves see the Buddha (pp. 180–2) – the *Lotus Sūtra* enjoins active missionary work in promulgating the *sūtra* and its teachings (Chapter 22). If a person promulgates the *sūtra* even a little bit he or she will receive a favourable rebirth and be strikingly handsome – 'His teeth shall not be wide-spaced, yellow or black. His lips shall not be thick, pursed or thin. In short, he shall have no disagreeable features' (p. 262)! The preacher too is to be revered as a Buddha. If a person is ill and hears this *sūtra* he shall recover and neither grow old nor die (p. 301). Many other miracles will accompany the *sūtra*'s devotees. Their senses will all become perfect – indeed superhuman (Chapter 19). Divine young boys will come and minister to the devotees. When the preacher preaches, if there are no human beings to hear supernatural beings will arrive instead. Of course, the modern reader is apt to take such assertions symbolically or as exaggerations for effect. Perhaps this has always been the case, but in Ancient Japan there were nevertheless many stories of miraculous happenings accompanying the *Lotus Sūtra's* devotees.[9]

The magical power of the *Lotus Sūtra* has no doubt been one reason for its popularity. Another reason is the way in which the *sūtra* praises even a little act of faith and devotion as having apparently quite disproportionate results. If a person makes offerings to the Buddha's relic *stūpas*, if a child builds *stūpas* in play out of mud, if someone makes statues and worships them, or sponsors such activities, prostrates himself or herself, or even raises just one hand, if a person recites 'Adoration to the Buddha' just once, even with a distracted mind, that person is on the path to Buddhahood.[10]

The importance of Pure Land Buddhism in Japan, centred on rebirth in Sukhāvatī, the Pure Land of Amitābha or Amitāyus Buddha in the West, has meant that the few references to this land and Amitābha/Amitāyus in the *Lotus Sūtra* have tended to associate this *sūtra* in the Japanese mind with rebirth in the Pure Land.[11] It is noticeable that faith in the *sūtra* and its practices almost invariably entails a rebirth in the Pure Land according to the stories in the *Hokkegenki* (e.g. Dykstra 1983: 79). Moreover, the *sūtra* is said to be so powerful that it can even save the most incorrigible sinners. Chapter 12 of the *Lotus Sūtra*, probably the last major section to be interpolated into the text, tells how in a previous life the Buddha offered himself as a lifelong servant to someone who could preach to him the Mahāyāna. Eventually a hermit offered to preach the *Lotus Sūtra*. That hermit is in the present life none other than the Buddha's erring cousin, Devadatta. The evil Devadatta is in reality the Buddha's best friend. Thanks to Devadatta the Buddha has been able to practice throughout his lifetimes the various virtues, especially, perhaps, the virtue of patience! Devadatta too is predicted to future Buddhahood. In Japan the stated ability of the *sūtra* to save the wicked gave it a great advantage over many other *sūtras*. An evil priest engaged in many non-Buddhist acts, such as hunting, fishing, and eating meat. Nevertheless he regularly recited the *Lotus Sūtra* at night with great faith. He was accordingly reborn in the Pure Land.[12] A layman who regularly took part in hunting and all the other sins of an active courtly life placed his entire hope in a passage of the Devadatta chapter which declared that he who has faith in the *sūtra* will avoid an unfortunate rebirth. During his final illness he repeatedly recited just this chapter. He too was reborn in the Pure Land (Dykstra 1983: 122–3). Even a robber, because of his devotion to the saving virtues of the 'celestial' Bodhisattva Avalokiteśvara (*Lotus*: Chapter 25) was protected from injury by Avalokiteśvara when attacked by forces of the law (ibid., 132–3). The *sūtra* states that:

> . . . one might encounter royally ordained woes,
> Facing execution and the imminent end of one's life.
> By virtue of one's constant mindfulness of Sound-Observer
> [Avalokiteśvara]
> The knives would thereupon break in pieces,
> Or, one might be confined in a pillory,
> One's hands and one's feet in stocks.
> By virtue of mindfulness of Sound-Observer
> One would freely gain release. (p. 317)

Avalokiteśvara, a Bodhisattva so advanced that he has taken on 'celestial' qualities, grants children to the barren and saves from all kinds of woes. A purely spiritual compassion is a compassion of very limited use and benefit. Why should the compassion of a great Bodhisattva be limited only to the spiritual?[13]

Not only are the wicked greatly encouraged by the *Lotus Sūtra*, but also that other group so often discriminated against in early Buddhist writings – women. In the same chapter of the *sūtra* in which Devadatta is predicted to Perfect Buddhahood, a Nāga princess appears, barely 8 years old. She has become an advanced Bodhisattva in a moment due to the preaching of Mañjuśrī, another celestial Bodhisattva. The monkish Śāriputra, in spite of the other miracles he has seen, is now really taken aback. How can such spiritual progress happen to a female? With her supernatural power the Nāga princess before his very eyes is instantly transformed into a male and attains Buddhahood. True, in the *Lotus Sūtra* it does appear to be necessary that the girl becomes a male. Nevertheless in other Mahāyāna *sūtras* the situation is perhaps more liberal. In a famous section of the *Vimalakīrtinirdeśa Sūtra* a goddess, in order to demonstrate one more to Śāriputra that sex differences are all part of the realm of phenomenal illusion, transforms herself into a male and Śāriputra, to his panic, into a female. The poor monk was no doubt concerned about all the Vinaya rules he was unavoidably infringing![14] Out of her compassion the goddess then returns them both to their conventional forms. We have seen already that the principal figure in the *Śrīmālā Sūtra* is a queen. Many Tibetans (and Western Buddhists, for that matter) are deeply devoted to the lovely Tārā, who declared that she would always act in female form for the benefit of sentient beings (see Chapter 10 below).

The final feature of the *Lotus Sūtra* we must note, a feature which has been of some influence in East Asian Buddhist practice, is that of body burning. Chapter 23 of the *Lotus Sūtra* recounts how the Bodhisattva Bhaiṣajyarājā in a previous life wished to make the most perfect offering to the Buddha. He accordingly offered his body by setting fire to it. The body burned for a very long time, and he was eventually reborn in a Pure Land. 'Good man this is called the prime gift' (p. 295). Supposing someone wishes to become enlightened:

> if he can burn a finger or even a toe as an offering to a Buddha-stūpa, he shall exceed one who uses realm or walled city, wife or children, or even all the lands, mountains, forests, rivers, ponds, and sundry precious objects in the whole thousand-millionfold world as offerings. (p. 298)

I confess it is difficult to know how to take these assertions. Certainly

Indian *sūtras* delight in hyperbole, and one is tempted to take these stories and recommendations as poetic exhortations to renunication rather than literal invitations to cremation. However, there can be no doubt that Chinese pilgrims to India describe cases where Buddhists engaged in mortifying the flesh and religious suicide (Joshi 1967: 108–11). In East Asian Buddhism, burning joints or the whole body as an act of devotion was taken very seriously indeed. Fa-tsang himself is said to have burnt a finger off out of religious enthusiasm. Burning fingers was a not-uncommon practice in Chinese Buddhist monasteries up to very recent times. Holmes Welch tells of an informant who burnt one finger each year for four years in succession. Hsü-yün, a renowned and respected abbot, burnt a finger off in 1897 out of filial piety, in order to help, through transferring the merit thus obtained, his mother who had died while bearing him (Welch 1967: 324–5). The burning was apparently a spiritual experience; healing was very rapid. In Japan, Joshō burned off a finger as a penance for accidentally touching a woman (Dykstra 1983: 66).

There are recorded cases of complete self-immolation in the nineteenth century, while the *Hokkegenki* records stories of similar events in Japan. The reader is reminded, perhaps, of the self-immolation by Vietnamese monks in the 1960s. The cases here are, however, rather different. The Vietnamese immolations were by way of political protest rather than a direct attempt to offer devotion to the Buddhas.[15] Nevertheless, the form of suicide, burning, was undoubtedly indicated by the age-old precedent of the *Lotus Sūtra*. If one is going to make a political protest through suicide one might as well do it in a blaze of publicity! I should add that my own knowledge of Tibetan monks suggests that in general they strongly disapprove (exceptional Bodhisattva acts apart) of harming the body or destroying it out of religious enthusiasm. They will all say that the body is the vehicle of enlightenment. It exists in order to be able to help others. A human rebirth is a very rare opportunity for spiritual growth. It is not to be thrown away unless its loss will be of enormous benefit to sentient beings.

A NOTE ON T'IEN-T'AI (TENDAI)

The T'ien-t'ai sect is usually classed with Hua-yen as representing characteristically Chinese responses to Buddhism, its creative internationalization. Although there are, of course, detailed differences between the two schools, both are broadly similar in approach and tenet. Both are strongly syncretistic, both created *p'an-chiao* systems for ranking *sūtras*, culminating in the *Lotus Sūtra* for T'ien-t'ai and the *Avataṃsaka Sūtra* for Hua-yen. Both schools stressed the doctrine of the One Mind, the universal Buddha-nature, and the one primeval Buddha who is equal to the universe. Both schools emphasized doctrines of interpenetration, Sudden Enlightenment, and the presence of Truth in even the slightest things of everyday life. Tien-t'ai was, however, the earlier of the two schools. Its great systematizer was Chih-i (538–97), a contemporary of the Chinese Mādhyamika Chi-tsang, and a century earlier than Fa-tsang. Chih-i chose to make his home on Mt T'ien-t'ai, hence the name of the school.

For Chih-i the final purpose of the Buddha coming into the world was to preach the *Lotus Sūtra*. This *sūtra* is both the highest and chronologically the final teaching of the Buddha. One problem for those East Asian Buddhists who would treat the *Lotus Sūtra* as the final teaching of the Buddha, however, was the enormous popularity of the *Mahāparinirvāṇa Sūtra*, by definition the *sūtra* of the Buddha's last days. The T'ien-t'ai tradition, therefore, classed the two *sūtras* together in its *p'an-chiao* schema of ranking. The final teaching is that of the *Lotus Sūtra*, but the Buddha preached the *Mahāparinirvāṇa* in order to stress his permanence for those who were too slow to grasp sufficiently the teaching of the *Lotus Sūtra* (Hurvitz 1963: 237 ff.). One result of this was to assimilate the *Lotus Sūtra*'s teaching of the Buddha and the ultimate universality of Buddhahood with the *Mahāparinirvāṇa* doctrine of the Buddha-nature. For Chih-i the enormous figures for the Buddha's life-span in the *Lotus* serve to indicate that the True Buddha is eternal, beyond time and space altogether.[16] T'ien-t'ai accordingly makes a notional distinction between the Eternal Buddha (origin) and his manifestations for the benefit of beings (traces). The former is sometimes referred to, with the Hua-yen, as Vairocana, while the latter is pre-eminently Śākyamuni. These are only notional distinctions, however. Actually Śākyamuni is none other than the Original Primeval Buddha (as are we all). All things interpenetrate.

There is available an interesting seventeenth-century Japanese colour woodblock print which indicates the essence of Tendai teachings in one pictorial representation. Imagine, if you will, a large circle divided into ten sections. Each of the six lower sections illustrate a realm of rebirth – gods, humans, anti-gods (*asuras*), animals, hungry ghosts, and hells – while the four higher sections depict the Arhats, Pratyekabuddhas, Bodhisattvas, and finally, at the very peak of existence, the Buddha realm. In the centre is the Chinese character *hsin*, Mind, the still centre of the wheel, the source of bondage and liberation. An accompanying text explains that each world contains all others, one instant of thought contains 3,000 worlds (a popular T'ien-t'ai slogan). The outline of the circle, and the lines separating the realms, are not unbroken lines but are made up of many small circles. Each time the *Lotus Sūtra* is recited 10,000 times, or (even better) 100,000 times, one small circle is linked in. When all are completed the devotee will reach the Buddha's Pure Land – a vivid way of representing some sort of spiritual progress![17]

As a result of the association of T'ien-t'ai with the Sui dynasty in China (581–618) the sect suffered a decline under the T'ang corresponding to the increasing fortunes of Hua-yen. T'ien-t'ai all but ceased and most of its texts were lose due to the ninth-century persecution of Buddhism, and the tradition and its texts had to be reintroduced from Japan and Korea. The tradition had been introduced as a sect into Japan by Saichō (767–822), who travelled to China and studied at Mt T'ien-t'ai. This introduction was in the face of considerable opposition from the older schools of Nara Buddhism, such as Kegon. We have seen that Buddhism in Japan was from the beginning associated with the state and political/social activity. The monasteries were expected to devote considerable time to rituals for the protection of the state and for various this-worldly benefits. The magical power of ritual and text was thus important. In exchange the state extended its toleration of the foreign religion and sometimes its considerable patronage. The close connection of Buddhist monasteries with politics caused frequent problems throughout Japanese history, however, and there is some reason to believe that the move of the capital from Nara eventually to Heiankyō (Kyōto, hence the 'Heian Era') in 794 was in order to escape the influence of the overmighty prelates of aristocratic Nara Buddhism.[18] Saichō established the Tendai teachings at his small new temple on Mt Hiei. This mountain was very close to the new capital, and it was felt by the Nara sects that Saichō had perhaps influenced Emperor Kammu in his decision on a site for the capital. Although Saichō had fled from what he saw as the corruption of Nara Buddhism, such was the connection between Japanese Buddhism and politics that his Tendai sect, perhaps as a counterbalance to Nara, received extensive patronage from the court. Saichō, an austere and righteous monk, declared his monastery to be a Centre for the Protection of the Nation. His monks spent an intense period of twelve years studying on Mt Hiei, where moral perfection was seen as a vital part of the Buddhist path. On graduation, Saichō declared:

> Those who are capable in both action and speech shall remain permanently on the mountain as leaders of the order: these are the treasure of the nation. Those who are capable in speech but not in action shall be teachers of the nation, and those capable in action but not in speech shall be the functionaries of the nation.
>
> (Trans. in Bary *et al.* 1972: 286)

Among the functionaries, some would engage in agriculture and engineering works for the benefit of the populace. Like political involvement, the willingness of religious practitioners to engage in such activities stands in stark contrast with traditional Indian attitudes and is another important feature of Japanese Buddhism.

By the time Oda Nobunaga burnt the monastery of Enryakuji on Mt Hiei in 1571 for siding with his enemies, it consisted of some 3,000 buildings and the monastery was extremely wealthy. Its history had also been extremely wild. During the second half of the tenth century a dispute within the Tendai tradition broke into armed hostility. Ryōgen the abbot, favoured by the court, is said to have organized a band of mercenaries in order to suppress his rivals. Soon monastic armies were being used against the government, and by the eleventh century it was not uncommon to send armed bands into the streets of Kyōto in order to enforce sectarian interests. These bands might take with them sacred objects, thus turning opposition into sacrilege. Emperor Shirakawa (1073–86) once commented that three things were beyond his control: the river's floods, the fortunes of gambling, and the monks of Mt Hiei.[19] During the thirteenth century the armed bands of Enryakuji apparently attacked the capital more than twenty times.

What are we to make of such events? Many Japanese saw them as a true sign that they were living in the final days of the Dharma, the era of total spiritual decline (Japanese: *mappō*). There is a temptation to see such depressing activities as purely secular matters of economics and power politics, and therefore not the concern of Buddhism as such. This would be a mistake, however. The separation of religion from secular or material life is familiar in the modern world (an indication of religious decline?) but is not a feature of the traditional Mahāyāna Buddhist world-view, particularly in Japan. As we shall see when we examine the teaching of Nichiren, there is well-known and influential Mahāyāna *sūtra* material permitting killing if it promotes the interest of the Dharma – including killing those who slander the true Doctrine, and therefore, by a reasonable inference, one's own sect. According to the *Mahāparinirvāṇa Sūtra* lay followers should take up arms to defend the monastic community.[20] Thus although among the motivations for violence there may have been political and economic factors we cannot conclude that the violence by its very nature had nothing to do with religious concerns and was contrary to the teaching and spirit of Buddhism. The prosperity of one's own sect was seen as very definitely a religious matter. We may not like the fact that Mahāyāna Buddhism permits killing, but the texts are there and are as much part of Buddhism as a historical phenomenon as are the acts themselves.

NICHIREN AND NICHIRENISM

In Anglo-Saxon England it was widely felt that the year 1000 CE would usher in the end of the world and the Second Coming of Christ. In Japan at about the same time numerous disasters and moral decline indicated that the era of *mappō* had begun, the era of the Last Days, the final days of the Dharma. This era is characterized in the scriptures as an age when the true spirit of the Dharma has become extinct. The late Heian period saw military monks, moral bankruptcy, imperial weakness, revolts, and vicious feudal warfare. Most Japanese identify the beginning of *mappō* with the burning of the temple of Chōkokuji in 1052. Nichiren, however, seems to have thought of it as beginning in 1034. Either way, Japanese religiosity after this time can only be understood in the context of one overriding problem – how can one be a Buddhist, how is the Buddhist religion to survive, during the Last Days – the era of cosmic and religious disaster when apparently none of the normal sources for religious inspiration can be relied upon?[21]

The period which followed that of the Heian is known as the Kamakura (1185–1333), once more named after a town, this time some 300 miles east of Kyōto and its negative enfeebling influences. Kamakura was chosen as its base by the Minamotos, short-lived victors in the warfare which characterized the fall of Heian. Contrary to what one might expect, perhaps, the theory of *mappō* was a creative influence on the Buddhism of the Kamakura period, as it sought to find a basis for personal and societal religious harmony and solace. On the one hand, we find the simple faith of devotion to the Buddha Amitābha and his all-embracing, all-helping compassion developed by Hōnen (1133–1212) and his disciple Shinran (1173–1262). On the other, Dōgen returned from

China with his austere Sōtō Zen, stressing personal inner cultivation stripped of necessary reliance on outer elements.

Nichiren's solution to the problems of the age was, however, rather different. Nichiren was a prophet. Basing himself on the *Lotus Sūtra* he fiercely and fearlessly denounced the errors of his day, including those of all other sects, and called on the government to implement the Truth, suppressing deviant doctrine and establishing Japan as the Land of Truth, the *Lotus Sūtra* under the emperor in Kyōto. This Truth would subsequently spread from Japan to embrace the whole world, reversing spiritual decline and ushering in the Pure Land of Śākyamuni Buddha on this very earth.

Nichiren was born in 1222. He came from a poor background, and became a novice monk at the age of 11. He studied Tendai on Mt Hiei, and then all the other Buddhist sects in Japan at that time. He was extremely well read in the scriptures. Even those scholars who disagreed with him – and he was very unpopular – admitted Nichiren's learning. Nichiren was not a ranter but a skilled 'theologian' who could support his views with reasoned argument and, most importantly, scriptural testimony.

The initial results of Nichiren's study are contained in his famous *Risshō Ankoku Ron*, the *Essay on the Establishment of Righteousness and the Security of the Country*. This treatise was presented by Nichiren in 1260 to the Hōjōs, who had taken over from the Minamotos as the dominant power in the land, and contains many of the elements of Nichiren's style and teaching. It is in the form of a dialogue between a Visitor and Nichiren himself, the Master. Why is the world in such a terrible state, the Visitor asks?

> We have seen many signs in heaven and earth: a famine, a plague; the whole country is filled with misery. Horses and cows are dying on the roadsides, and so are men, and there is no one to bury them. One half of the population is stricken, and there is no house that has escaped scot-free.... look around at the misery of the age, at the decay of Buddhism. What can be, think you, the cause of all this?
>
> (Trans. in Lloyd 1911: 307, 309)

The answer, according to Nichiren, is that men are so evil that all the protector deities have left the country and been replaced by demons. Japan is literally a country possessed. This is indeed what the scriptures say. Nichiren can refer to a chapter of the *Suvarṇabhāsottama Sūtra* for example, a particularly popular *sūtra* in Japan partly because of its political comments on the role of kingship. In this *sūtra* the Four Great Divine Kings describe how they will forsake a country where the *sūtra* is not upheld and evil is done. Terrible disasters will follow as a result.[22] In this and other *sūtras* the causes of these disasters are delineated. People are following false gods. In China too, Nichiren observes, invasions and other disasters occurred when the emperor attacked Buddhism. In particular, Hōnen's sect centred on devotion to Amitābha is singled out for merciless criticism. Subsequently Nichiren referred to the Amitābha practice as 'Hell without interval', the Zen tradition as the 'Heavenly Demon', the Shingon (Tantric) sect as a force which 'ruins the country', and the Ritsu sect, a sect concerned with the study and correct observance of the Vinaya, as 'the traitor to the country' (see Petzold 1977: 94 ff). Nichiren drew an exact parallel between the situation within Buddhism and that in Japan itself. Just as in Japan there were many trying to govern, while true rulership lay in the emperor, in Buddhism there were many rival Buddhas and *sūtras*, each championed by a different sect, while the true Buddha is the eternal Śākyamuni Buddha of the *Lotus Sūtra*. Deviation from this truth had in both cases led to disaster. There should be one emperor and one Buddha. As Nichiren puts it elsewhere:

> Although every individual tries to get ahead of all others, yet the Sovereign must be one; if two Kings co-exist in one country there cannot be peace; if there are two masters in one home, then family dissensions will break out. It is not otherwise in Buddhism. Apart from what it is, one Scripture must be the great King of all Buddhist Scriptures.
>
> (Trans. in Petzold 1977: 49–50)

Since the country's disasters came from upholding false teachings, it is the duty of the government to suppress false doctrines. Nichiren recognizes that some Buddhists may find this conclusion unpalatable, but it is clearly stated in the *sūtras*. In the *Mahāparinirvāṇa Sūtra* the Buddha describes how in a previous life he killed several Brahmins to prevent them from slandering Buddhism, and to save them from the punishment they might otherwise have incurred through continuing their slander. In the same *sūtra* it is said that the followers of the Mahāyāna ought to keep weapons and ignore the moral code if such is necessary in order to protect the Dharma. In the *Gaṇḍavyūha Sūtra* one of Sudhana's 'Good Friends', King Anala, is 'said to have made killing into a divine service' in order to reform people through punishment.[23] True, according to Asaṅga, followed by Fa-tsang, only a very great Bodhisattva can so discard the normal moral code. Nichiren, however, considered himself to be a great Bodhisattva, and suppression of errors was necessary in the age of *mappō* in order to protect the people from disaster. There is some dispute as to whether Nichiren thought it was necessary at that time actually to kill 'heretics'. He seems rather to imply that the government should institute withdrawal of lay support, thus starving the miscreants in order to bring them to the Truth (Petzold 1977: 77). However, Nichiren undoubtedly sanctioned fighting by his followers in a just cause: 'In this life you are participating in the life of the "furious spirits", and yet you will surely be born in Buddha's land after death' (ibid., 83). Scriptural support for killing was used not only in Japan. Every enthusiast for the martial arts has heard of the Chinese Buddhist warrior monks of Shao-lin. The Chinese Communists were able through such justification to collect money from Chinese Buddhists for a fighter aircraft named *Chinese Buddhist*, used against the American 'demons' in Korea (Welch 1972: 278)! As Demiéville points out, it is indeed a paradox that Mahāyāna Buddhism, in making the moral code flexible in the interests of compassion, ends up justifying killing to an extent far greater than non-Mahāyāna Buddhism.

Disasters, Nichiren said, will continue until Truth is followed and propagated. Indeed there are further disasters still to come, particularly foreign invasion. The subsequent attempted invasion of Japan by the Mongols under Kublai Khan may have suggested to some that Nichiren be taken a little more seriously. Prior to that, however, he had been injured in a mob attack, very nearly executed (saved, it is said, by divine intervention), and exiled. He died, still taken seriously by very few, in 1282.

For Nichiren, in the era of *mappō* one can be saved only through faith in the *Lotus Sūtra*. According to Nichiren's teaching the *Lotus Sūtra* is perfect, the final truth; in the age of *mappō* the people require a simple teaching; the age of *mappō* is indeed the time to proclaim this teaching of the *Lotus*; Japan is the country where it should be proclaimed and from which it will spread over all the world; and all other systems already established in Japan have done their allotted task in preparing the way for this final teaching, and must now give way to it. The content of Nichiren's *Lotus Sūtra* teaching is contained in his Three Great Secret Laws. These are, in Japanese, *honzon* (or *gohonzon*), *daimoku*, and *kaidan*.

The term *honzon* refers to the focus or chief object of reverence in Nichiren's system. For Nichiren *the* Buddha is Śākyamuni, the eternal Buddha of the *Lotus Sūtra*, and for this reason the actual final teaching is contained not in the *Lotus Sūtra* in its entirety but rather in those sections of the second part of the *sūtra* which deal with the cosmic Buddha Śākyamuni. This Buddha is therefore the primary object of reverence. However, the actual physical *honzon* (at least for the subsect known as Nichiren Shōshū) is a *mandara* (Sanskrit: *maṇḍala*), a representation of the cosmos centred on Sākyamuni, designed by Nichiren and based on the *Lotus Sūtra*. In the centre is the formula *Nam Myō hō renge kyō* – Adoration (or Reverence) to the *Lotus Sūtra*. Around it are written the names of the cardinal directions, Śākyamuni, Prabhūtaratna, and other beings who appear in the *Lotus Sūtra*, each in his appropriate position. In Nichiren Shōshū the name of Nichiren is also given a prominent place. The *honzon* is thus an abstract representation of the totality since, with Tendai, Śākyamuni as the eternal Buddha is also the cosmic Buddha.

Daimoku refers to the formula *Nam* (or with some Nichiren traditions *Namu*) *Myō hō renge kyō*, or its actual chanting, often accompanied by a rhythmic beat on a drum. The title of the *Lotus Sūtra*, followed Chih-i's commentary, is considered to contain all that follows in seed. According to Nichiren, to utter this title with faith is enough to save one from hell and will itself lead to perfection:

> To utter the sacred Title with the conviction that the three are one – the three being the Buddha Śākyamuni who from eternity has realized Buddhahood; the Lotus of Truth which leads all beings without exception to Buddhahood; and we beings in all realms of existence – to utter the sacred title is the Heritage of the Sole Great Thing concerning Life and Death.... This is the essence of what is promulgated by Nichiren. If it should be fulfilled, the great vow of propagating the Truth over all the world would be fulfilled.
>
> (Trans. by Sansom in Eliot 1935: 428)

For Nichiren this phrase is more profitable than the entire text of the *Sūtra*. Chanting this title is the practice for the period of *mappō*, and is the highest practice of Buddhism. To quote from a Nichiren scholar, Gyōkei Umada:

> When a man gazes at the Maṇḍala and recites the Sacred Title, heart and soul, subjectivity and objectivity become fused into one whole, and the worshipper realizes in himself the excellent qualities of the Supreme Being, and thereby his short life is made eternal and his limited virtue infinite.... herein lies the consummation of the creed of the Nichiren Sect: the peace of mind of all believers and religious

life. The result of all this is the realization of the Buddha Land in the present state of existence.

(Quoted in Petzold 1977: 36–7)

Finally, the *kaidan* is the place for receiving the moral precepts, or the place of ordination. The interpretation of this varies from subsect to subsect. The *kaidan* can be the place in a believer's home where the *honzon* is set up and regularly worshipped. It could also be a central place of initiation into the sect. But Nichiren also speaks of the *kaidan* as if it were a secret spot within one's own heart, as well as the place where in the future, with the establishment of Truth the world over, an enormous initiation hall for all people will be erected, apparently in Japan:

> Then the golden age . . . will be realized in these days of degeneration and corruption. . . . Then the establishment of the Holy See will be completed, by imperial grant and the edict of the Dictator, at a spot comparable in its excellence with the Paradise of the Vulture Peak [where Śākyamuni preached the Mahāyāna *sūtras*]. We have only to wait for the coming of the time.
>
> (Anesaki, in Petzold 1977: 64–5)

Like all good prophets, Nichiren was persecuted, and made a virtue of suffering. A number of his followers over the years have been martyred for their unyielding opposition to Falsehood. Nichiren was fond of identifying himself with the persistently persecuted Bodhisattva Sadā paribhūta of the *Lotus Sūtra.* In his later years his attention was particularly drawn to Chapter 15 of the *sūtra*, where the Buddha according to Nichiren entrusted the *Lotus Sūtra* (or its title) to a certain old man named Viśiṣṭacāritra, who would be chief of the Bodhisattvas who would propagate the *Lotus Sūtra* during the era of *mappō*. The general view is that Nichiren saw the references to Viśiṣṭacāritra as a prophecy concerning himself, and identified himself with the reincarnation of Viśiṣṭacāritra. Certainly, Nichiren did see himself as something rather special by virtue of his propagation of the *Lotus*, the highest teaching, at that time:

> those who propagate the Lotus of Truth are indeed the parents of all men living in Japan. . . . I, Nichiren, am the master and lord of the sovereign, as well as of all the Buddhists of other schools. Notwithstanding this, the rulers and the people treat us thus maliciously.
>
> (Anesaki in Petzold 1977: 58: see 43–4)

The prophet Nichiren goes on to warn them that the Mongols are coming to chastise the people for their infidelity. The truth of his prophecy will prove the authenticity of his teaching and mission.

After Nichiren's death a number of subsects arose. In the Nichiren Shōshū (to which the lay movement Soka Gakkai is affiliated) Nichiren is now himself seen as the Buddha of the *mappō* era. This has led inevitably to a supramundane Nichiren who turns out to be identical with the eternal cosmic Buddha of the *Lotus Sūtra*. Śākyamuni begins once more to loose significance. The Soka Gakkai is a powerful lay Buddhist organization well known in the West through the works of its president, Daisaku Ikeda. Soka Gakkai is closely involved in politics, and was at one time directly connected with Kōmeitō, the Clean Government Party. Kōmeitō has had considerable electoral success (it describes itself as a 'middle of the road' party), although direct connection with Soka Gakkai was severed in 1970 following a minor scandal. Soka Gakkai is a prosperous organization with a large following in Japan, although it has been criticized sometimes in particular for its practice of *shakubuku*, a rather fierce form of gaining converts through what has often appeared to be a form of emotional and verbal bludgeoning.

Of some interest also is the Nihonzan Myōhonji. This sect was founded early in the twentieth century, and was originally, like so many Nichiren sects, strongly nationalistic (Japan as a basis for world conversion). The founder, Nichidatsu Fuji, however, became a radical pacifist as a result of the devastation wrought by the Second World War. Nihonzan Myōhonji has spread throughout the Orient, and has temples in India. As part of its campaign for world peace it has financed the construction of *stūpas*, 'peace pagodas', across the world, including two in England, one at the New Town of Milton Keynes in Buckinghamshire, and one in London. Followers of Nihonzan Myōhonji are active at peace demonstrations, beating drums and chanting adoration to the name of the *Lotus Sūtra*.

Another modern Japanese lay movement which originates from Nichiren's teachings is the Risshō Kosei Kai. Works in English by the president, Nikkyō Niwano, particularly commentaries on the *Lotus Sūtra*, are well known. In 1965 President Niwano visited Pope Paul VI and attended the opening of the Fourth Session of the Second Vatican Council. Risshō Kosei Kai, Nichiren Shōshū, and Soka Gakkai, in common with a number of other modern Japanese Buddhist movements, stress the lay element in Mahāyāna Buddhism, group therapy, and the way in which the practice of Buddhism can improve one's material and spiritual welfare in this life. They see Buddhist practice as involving active missionary propagation, and definite social benefits. According to Nikkyō Niwano, to bring a person into the (Buddhist) Way is to raise up humanity, and is perhaps the only way to create a 'truly ideal society' (Niwano 1981: 42). Since mind and matter are connected, so changing the mind through Buddhism inevitably affects the material surroundings and thence prosperity:

> there is nothing odd about a person who has through faith undergone a change of heart, a change in his or her way of thinking, having the blessings of money or other material things come his or her way. ... improvement and change for the better are natural consequences.
>
> (ibid., 125–6)

Eventually all will arrive at the one teaching, and all will live according to the doctrine of the Buddha. This will be, in a sense, the Pure Land (ibid., 135–6). Or, as it is put in the Soka Gakkai:

> To become Buddha means to live everywhere a joyous pleasant life, from the moment you get up in the morning to the time you go to sleep in the evening. To call a life happy and pleasant, when it is without clothing or money, with sickness in the home and debt collectors at the door – that is of no use.
>
> (Quoted by Dumoulin 1976: 263)

Such a teaching obviously harmonizes with the pressing needs of Japan's postwar reconstruction and economic growth. How easily it harmonizes with Buddhism as it has existed in history, and particularly as it existed in India, is, however, a moot point!

CHAPTER EIGHT

On the bodies of the Buddha

PROLEGOMENON TO THE MAHĀYĀNA

There is a Zen saying that if one meets the Buddha on the road one should kill him. It is tempting to see this as another Japanese exhortation to holy violence, but the lesson is inspired, perhaps, by yet another *sūtra*, contained in the *Ratnakūṭa* collection. In this *sūtra* a group of virtuous Bodhisattvas are depressed at the thought that no matter how moral they are in this life their spiritual progress will be hindered by the immoral deeds they did during their infinite past lives, 'killing their fathers, mothers or Arhats; destroying Buddhist temples or stūpas; or disrupting the Saṃgha'. As a skilful means in order to help these Bodhisattvas let go of the conception of Self which is at the root of their spiritual anguish, Mañjuśrī, the Bodhisattva particularly associated with wisdom, took up a sharp sword and lunged towards the Buddha with the intention of killing him. The sword is Mañjuśrī's sword of wisdom, his principal iconographic feature in Buddhist art. The Buddha deflected this apparently murderous intent. The point of the lesson was, it seems, two-fold. First, the Buddha who appears before the assembly is empty of inherent existence, and he is thus 'killed' when he is seen this way. Second, since all things lack inherent existence if the Bodhisattvas can gain an insight into emptiness, their past wicked deeds can be understood as ultimately illusory and no real barrier to spiritual progress. Recognizing the moral dangers of this teaching, the *sūtra* adds that those in the assembly whose spiritual progress was mediocre, through the Buddha's power, failed to see Mañjuśrī with his sword and hear the Buddha's teaching on the subject.[1]

Supposing one meets the Buddha on the road (and restrains one's homicidal tendencies), who or what exactly would one meet? Certainly the Buddha would appear as a physical human being clad in a monk's robe. And yet he would not be simply another monk. He would have a special impact by virtue of what he had attained, by virtue of his not being just another human being but rather a Buddha:

> His peaceful countenance was neither happy nor sad. He seemed to be smiling gently inwardly. With a secret smile, not unlike that of a healthy child, he walked along, peacefully, quietly. He wore his gown and walked along exactly like the other monks, but his face and his step, his peaceful downward glance, his peaceful downward-hanging hand, and every finger of his hand spoke of peace, spoke of completeness, sought nothing, imitated nothing, reflected a continuous quiet, an unfading light, an invulnerable peace.
>
> (Hesse 1951: 22)

In two ways, it seems to me, the Buddha as a *Buddha* extends beyond the physical human being. On the one hand he is not an isolated individual in history (now long dead) but rather exemplifies in his own person the Truth which he has discovered. There is a saying often repeated in Buddhist texts that whether a Buddha appears or does not appear, the true nature of things remains for ever. There is a sense in which the Buddha as a physical human being exemplifies this true nature of things – not in the sense that he created it, or it only exists in him, but rather in the sense that it exists *as realized* in him, and therefore is transmitted as realization through him to others. Second, in the Indian context, or in the context of meditative attainment and therefore magical intervention, the physical Buddha met on the road through his attainments can render all about him, and himself, other than they appear to be. He is a being of power, a master of magical transformations. Thus the Buddha we meet has three dimensions – his physical presence as a saffron-robed monk, his exemplification of the true nature of things which entails that he is truly free, an enlightened being, and his compassionate ability and desire to engage in magical interventions for the benefit of others, his occupation of the fluid quick-silver world of magic which we saw when examining the *Avataṃsaka Sūtra*. These three dimensions indicate the incarnation of perfect wisdom (knowing the true nature of things) and compassion (magical intervention), the two definitive constituents of Buddhahood, in a physical body of the monk whom we have been fortunate enough to meet. However, we become enlightened not through our encounter as such but through following his teachings until we embody them in our own physical presence. The Buddha's body (and his magical interventions) are tools subservient to the cognition by others of the Truth. Thus with our sharp sword of wisdom we 'kill' the physical Buddha, we go beyond the physical to the true nature which he incarnates and exemplifies. Viewed in this perspective, of course, the actual physical death of the Buddha, the Enlightened One, was no insurmountable tragedy.

There seems no reason to doubt that Śākyamuni Buddha, Siddhārtha Gautama, was a being who lived and died in India at a particular time in history. His influence on his followers was presumably deep and life transforming, although his wider influence during his lifetime on the areas of North India where he lived and preached was perhaps slight. It is tempting to think that over a period of centuries, following the death of the Master, Śākyamuni's grieving followers, losing sight of the historical individual, gradually deified the Buddha until he took his place alongside the teeming myriads of India's other gods and goddesses. This process by which a historical individual is deified is one of exaggeration and exaggerated reverence. It is essentially a process of falsification, the creation of a massive delusion.

Such a model is, I think, misleading. The Buddha was never simply a human being, and is not seen this way by any Buddhist tradition. He always embodies our three dimensions – physical, 'spiritual' (for want of a better word; exemplifying the true nature of things), and magical. If after the Buddha's death interest shifts from the physical to the spiritual and magical (eventually embracing also the Buddha seen in meditative absorption) this is only natural and embodies a change of emphasis rather than growing falsification. Moreover, the image of deification is apt to convey for Western readers a radical de-(or super-) humanization which is misleading in the Indian context. Divinization, investing a being with divine attributes, was common in Ancient India, and by no means carried with it the dramatic implications which we assume in a monotheistic culture – that the being divinized enters a radically different order from common humanity. As A. L. Basham has put it, 'Divinity was cheap in ancient India' (Basham 1967: 88). The king, Brahmins, holy ascetics, and cows were referred to as gods (or goddesses). According to certain of the law books, gold and clarified butter were also gods. Trees could be gods, and a god dwelt in the hearth of every home as Agni, the Fire. It was natural to refer to the Buddha in terms also used of gods. Such indicated little more than an attitude of deep respect and humility on the part of his followers. In a world which lacks the rigid dichotomy of sacred from profane, God from Creation, where the borders between divine and human are fluid, so there was never any question of anyone referring to Siddhārtha Gautama, once he had become the Buddha, the Enlightened One, as merely another human being. Nevertheless, the Buddha has discovered truths unknown to the Brahmin priests and their gods. In a Buddhist cosmos where human beings through virtuous deeds can become gods, and gods through the exhaustion of their merit fall to the deepest hells, the Buddha had gone beyond the cycle of transmigration, beyond gods and humans. No matter whether he is referred to out of respect as having certain divine attributes, as a Buddha, an enlightened being, he is set over and against both gods and men. Even in the Theravāda tradition, where the human aspects of the Buddha are most prominent, the Lord denies that he is a man or a god. Rather, he is a Buddha, as were all the Buddhas before him, and those who will come after.

The word *kāya*, usually translated as 'body', is a systematically ambiguous word in Pāli and Sanskrit. This ambiguity is an important part of its range of uses in the Buddhist treatment of the Buddha himself. In the fifth century CE the Theravāda commentator Buddhaghosa explained that the word could be used to refer in particular to a body, or to any group.[2] Thus the word *kāya* when used of the Buddha can refer to his actual body, primarily the physical body, and also to any group or collection of elements which make up or in some sense pertain to the Buddha.

Throughout the Buddhist world the minimum for becoming a Buddhist is to 'take refuge' from the depth of one's heart in the Buddha, his Doctrine, and the Community. But what exactly is one taking refuge in when one takes refuge in the Buddha? This question was posed in particular by one of the non-Mahāyāna traditions of Buddhism, the Vaibhāṣika (Sarvāstivāda). A person should not take refuge in the physical body of the Buddha, it was argued, since the physical body is impure (oozing and smelly, a common Indian observation with extensive cultural implications). Moreover, the physical body of the Buddha, although endowed with the eighty minor marks, such as copper-coloured, glossy and prominent nails, and the thirty-two major marks, e.g. soft skin, wheel marks on the soles of the feet, white hair between the eyebrows, is still not the characterizing feature of a Buddha.[3] The Vaibhāṣika tradition holds that the Buddha through his magic power, his magical transformations, can manifest created or fictitious bodies as and where he pleases, but one could scarcely see these as the object of the Buddha Refuge. Rather, when we take refuge in the Buddha so we take refuge in his Dharma-body, his *dharmakāya*. The word '*dharma*' in *dharmakāya* refers here to *dharmas*, the ultimates which form the subject matter of the Abhidharma. The *dharmakāya* is that which characterizes the Buddha as Buddha, that is, the collection (*kāya*) of pure elements (*dharmas*) possessed in the fullest degree by the Buddha - various kinds of knowledges and understandings, together with the Buddha's five pure psycho-physical constituents: pure physical matter, sensations, conceptions, further mental contents such as volitions and so on, and consciousness. They are said to be be pure because they are without any admixture of moral and cognitive taints. One takes refuge in the Buddha's *dharmakāya* in the same way that one might respect a monk, not because he is a physical being as such but because he possesses the qualities of a monk.[4] The Buddha's Dharma-body is thus the flow of Buddha-qualities, and in taking refuge in the Buddha one takes refuge in just this *dharmakāya*, those qualities which the Buddha's doctrine sets forth and teaches. The *dharmakāya* is here set over and against the mere physical body of the Buddha. It is that which the Buddha is setting forth for his followers. The Mahāyāna stress on the *dharmakāya* is in its origins not a radical metaphysical departure, or a deification, but a continuation of this trend. The Mahāyāna treatment of the Buddha's physical body, on the other hand, in terms of our tripartite schema stresses more and more the magical dimension of the Buddha's being, a response to the apparent physical death of Siddhārtha Gautama on the one hand, and an encounter with the Buddhas of spiritual experience on the other. Physical becomes magical transformation - an unsurprising development given the philosophy of both Madhyamaka and Cittamātra. The impetus for this treatment of the Buddha lay no doubt with the supramundane teachings of the Mahāsaṃghikas, which we examined in the first chapter.

THE BODIES OF THE BUDDHA AND THE PHILOSOPHY OF EMPTINESS

The extant Sanskrit text of the *Aṣṭasāhasrikā (8,000 verse) Perfection of Wisdom* makes a clear distinction between the physical body of the

Buddha (*rūpakāya*) and his *dharmakāya*. Those who represent the Buddha through his physical attributes are described as foolish, 'For a Tathagata cannot be seen from his form-body [physical body]. The Dharma-bodies are the Tathagatas . . .' (Trans. in Conze 1973b: 291). The contrast of the Buddha's physical form with his *dharmakāya*, to the disparagement of the former, was a practical, we might say institutional, as well as a doctrinal move. Those who would oppose the 'innovations' of the Mahāyāna, the introduction of teachings not taught by the 'historical' Buddha, were thereby accused of adhering with unjustifiable rigidity to the physical Buddha rather than to the *dharmakāya* which all agreed the Buddha himself said would lead the Community after his death. Moreover, it is argued in a recent article by Yuichi Kajiyama that a particular concern of the *Aṣṭasāhasrikā* was the criticism of *stūpa* worship. Reverence of the physical body of the Buddha in the centuries after the death of the Lord was equivalent to worshipping the *stūpas* containing the Buddha's relics. Disparagement and devaluation of the Buddha's physical body was criticism of *stūpa* worship; praising the Buddha's Dharma-body was replacing *stūpa* worship with a new cult based on the worship of the *Perfection of Wisdom* itself (Kajiyama 1985 12 ff.). We know, of course, that many early Mahāyāna *sūtras* such as the *Aṣṭasāhasrikā* and the *Lotus Sūtra* did indeed advocate the importance of elevating the *sūtra* and its worship. What Kajiyama highlights is the practical basis of the *sūtra*'s praise of the *dharmakāya* and the *Perfection of Wisdom*, and its disparagement of the physical body enshrined in a *stūpa*. It also follows that the first dimension of the meaning of *dharmakāya* in the *Aṣṭasāhasrikā* is *Perfection of Wisdom*, precisely the *sūtra* itself, the *dharmakāya* as Dharma, as the Doctrine.[5] This harmonizes with Lewis Lancaster's study of the oldest versions of the *Aṣṭasāhasrikā* preserved in very early Chinese translations (Lancaster 1975). Lancaster has found that most of the references to the *dharmakāya* in the Sanskrit text are later interpolations (including the quotation above). That is, the *sūtra* grew over a number of centuries, and one direction of growth was in elaborating its treatment of the *dharmakāya*. In the earliest version of the text the Buddha's actual body is an excellent but conditioned physical body, while the expression *dharmakāya* refers simply to the collection of the Buddha's *sūtras*. If we follow Kajiyama then the specific reference is to the *Prajñāpāramitā sūtras* themselves.

As Kajiyama points out, however, the term *prajñāpāramitā* in the *Aṣṭasāhasrikā* has a range of meanings, including the true nature of things (*dharmatā*=*śūnyatā*) and its cognition. Thus while the expression *dharmakāya* in the oldest *Perfection of Wisdom* literature was used to equal the Buddha's teaching, inasmuch as the Buddha's spiritual body, his teaching, is his body because, like him, it exemplifies the true nature of things, that true nature of things itself is that which is to be realized. Just as in the Vaibhāṣika tradition *dharma* in *dharmakāya* was taken to equal the essential ultimates (*dharmas*) which, possessed to a full degree, make up the Buddha's realization, in the *Perfection of Wisdom* literature the *dharmakāya* comes to refer not only to the Doctrine which sets forth the true nature of things, but also to the realization and the true nature of things itself. The *dharmakāya* is the body, or collection, of ultimate truths (*śūnyatā*: emptinesses); or, it is the mental *dharmas* cognizing the ultimate truth (= *prajñā*). The Buddha has died, but there remains the truth which he indicated, and its realization is still possible. Those whose concern is with historical issues of authenticity, or relics, when the important thing is realization, are indeed foolish.

There are thus at least three interconnected dimensions to the *dharmakāya* in *Prajñāpāramitā* texts. First, the *dharmakāya* is the collection of teachings, particularly the *Prajñāpāramitā* itself. Second, it is the collection of pure *dharmas* possessed by the Buddha, specifically pure mental *dharmas* cognizing emptiness. And third, it is emptiness itself, the true nature of things. The *dharmakāya* in all these senses is contrasted with the Buddha's physical body, that which lived and died and is preserved in *stūpas*. The appeal to the spiritual body (*dharmakāya*) rather than the form-body (*rūpakāya*) was an appeal to the spirit rather than to the form!

The familiar, later, three body schema is not found in the early *Perfection of Widsom* texts. Nor is it found in the writings of Nāgārjuna. In conformity with the *Aṣṭasāhasrikā*, Nāgārjuna speaks of a physical body and a *dharmakāya*. The Buddha's physical body is the result of his collection of merit, his compassionate deeds performed throughout infinite past lives. It is the incarnation of his compassion – a physical body of a Buddha exists for others. The Buddha's *dharmakāya*, on the other hand, arises from his collection of wisdom, from the Buddha's insight into emptiness. These two collections, Nāgārjuna explains, are the causes of Buddhahood (*Ratnāvalī* 3:10–13). Accumulating merit and wisdom is the essence of the Mahāyāna path, the path to full Buddhahood. Nāgārjuna's attitude to the Buddha is further illustrated by the *Catuḥstava*, a collection of four hymns attributed with reasonable reliability to the Master. In the *Niraupamyastava* – the *Hymn to the Incomparable One* – Nāgārjuna describes in poetic, almost devotional, terms the wonders of the Buddha and his understanding of emptiness. And then Nāgārjuna raises his praises to a new and higher level: 'Even if you are not seen in a physical sense, it is said that you are seen. For by seeing the Dharma you are indeed well seen. (And yet) there is no seeing the true nature of things (*dharmatā*).'[6] The true nature of things cannot be seen with the physical eyes, as was the physical body of the Buddha. Yet the Buddha manifests in accordance with the needs of others, teaching, for example, three vehicles although in reality there is only one (vv. 18–21). And: 'Your body is permanent, stable, primevally tranquil. It is of the nature of the Dharma ...'[7] Nevertheless the Buddha demonstrates an apparent death (*parinirvāṇa*), although those who have faith in the Buddha can indeed see him in the innumerable realms of the cosmos (vv. 22–3). There is no clear distinction in Nāgārjuna's hymn between the Buddha as an actual being who is in some sense transcendent (*lokottara*) but who manifests wordly activity out of skilful means, remaining after his apparent death in order to inspire his followers (cf. *Lotus Sūtra*), and the true body of the Buddha, which is his Dharma, or that which is indicated by his teachings, the true nature of things (*dharmatā*), emptiness. Rather, Nāgārjuna plays with both of these notions, contrasting them with the Buddha's physical appearance. A clear distinction between these two eventually gives rise to the three-body schema. Nāgārjuna's failure to make the distinction is doctrinally confusing, perhaps, but poetically rather pleasing.

In another of Nāgārjuna's hymns, the *Paramārthastava – Hymn to the Ultimate* – Nāgārjuna speaks of the Buddha in his ultimate aspect, to all intents and purposes the ultimate, true way of things itself. Almost the entire hymn is composed of negatives – the Buddha is neither non-being nor being, neither annihilation nor permanence, not non-eternal, not eternal. He falls into no category of duality (Tucci 1932: 322, v.4). He has no colour, no size, no spatial location and so on (vv. 5–7). He cannot therefore be praised (vv. 9–10). And Nāgārjuna ends with another of his gentle jokes: 'I have praised the Well-gone [Sugata – an epithet of the Buddha] who is neither gone nor come, and who is devoid of any going' (v.11, Tucci's trans.).

The *Ta-chih-tu lun* (*Mahāprajñāpāramitā Śāstra*), attributed to Nāgārjuna by Chinese tradition, on the other hand, while making a marked distinction between the Buddha's physical body and his *dharmakāya*, appears to mean by the *dharmakāya* not emptiness but rather the supramundane qualities of the Buddha.[8] This is not really surprising, since there is evidence that the enormous *Ta-chih-tu lun* originated among

Vaibhāṣikas, probably from Kashmir, who had adopted the Mahāyāna. This interpretation of the *dharmakāya* is fundamentally that of the Vaibāṣika but it suggests that such an interpretation of the Buddha's highest body was possibly current among certain Mādhyamikas at the time of the translator Kumārajīva in the late fourth and early fifth centuries. By way of contrast, however, the Svātantrika Mādhyamika Bhāvaviveka (*c.* 500–70) speaks of the *dharmakāya* as beyond language and conception, neither existent nor nonexistent and so on. It is tranquil, the calming of all verbal differentiations.[9] We know from elsewhere in the same text that this is an exact characterization of the true state of things (reality: *tattva*), that is to say, emptiness.[10] For the Prāsaṅgika Mādhyamikas also, Prajñākaramati (tenth century) writes of the *dharmakāya* as having the nature of the ultimate reality.[11] Clearly, therefore, from the contrast of physical body and *dharmakāya* in the *Aṣṭasāhasrikā* and Nāgārjuna we find a fairly consistent pattern among later Mādhyamika theorists in using the term *dharmakāya* as an equivalent for emptiness, the ultimate truth. Nevertheless, inasmuch as the *dharmakāya* is referred to within the context of Buddhology, so the *dharmakāya* is, I think, not so much a personification of emptiness as that which is set forth or exemplified in the Buddha's very being. It is his true nature, the lesson of which he embodies. Since the *dharmakāya* is the true being of others as well (all are empty of inherent existence) so all, through having the *dharmakāya* within, as it were, can embody the *dharmakāya* – that is, all can become fully enlightened Buddhas.

CITTAMĀTRA – THE SYSTEM DEVELOPS

Cittamātra texts frequently refer to the bodies of the Buddha. Particularly important as sources for their schema, however, are the *Mahāyānasūtrālaṃkāra* (*M.sūtr.āl.*) and its commentary, and Asaṅga's *Mahāyānasaṃgraha* (*M. Saṃg.*).

The Cittamātra tradition generally speaks of the Buddha possessing three bodies. The first is referred to as either the *dharmakāya* or the *svābhāvikakāya* – the Essence or Essential Body. These are two ways of referring to the same thing, although from different angles. The same body is said to be the *dharmakāya*, because it is the support of *dharmas*, and the Essence Body because it is self-contained and does not contain anything contingent or adventitious.[12] This *svābhāvikakāya* is the essence of the Buddhas, the ultimate, the purified Thusness or Suchness

(*M.sūtr.al.* comm. on 21:60–1). Or, as a commentary to the *Mahāyānasaṃgraha* puts it, the Essence Body is the true nature of things taken as a body (on 10: 1). Recalling our discussion in Chapter 4, it is clear that the Cittamātra Essence Body, the Buddha's highest 'body', is in fact his non-dual purified flow of consciousness, the essence of being a Buddha.[13] Put into the complex technical terminology of the Cittamātra tradition, the Essence Body, the *Mahāyānasaṃgraha* informs us, is the dependent aspect as pure, immaculate, and it is characterized by a 'revolution of the basis' inasmuch as the dependent aspect as tainted has been destroyed and the dependent aspect as pure revealed.[14] This *dharmakāya* is permanent (non-dual consciousness is in reality always the case), and it is the support for other *dharmas* inasmuch as consciousness forms the basis for phenomenal illusion. More significantly, in the context of Buddhology, the *dharmakāya* is the basis for the other two bodies of the Buddha inasmuch as these further bodies represent the Buddha's compassion. They are not ultimately true, but just as the phenomenal illusion of the unenlightened is constructed on the basis of consciousness, so the further bodies of the Buddha are constructed out of compassion on the basis of non-dual pure consciousness (*M.sūtr.āl.* 9: 60).

To the extent to which the *svābhāvikakāya/dharmakāya* is the Buddha's consciousness, it is possible to say from the conventional, phenomenal point of view that the *dharmakāya* is the collection of good mental qualities which characterize being a Buddha. Cittamātra texts are thus able to harmonize their teaching with those works which speak, as we have seen, of the Buddha's *dharmakāya* as his collection of pure elements.[15] The *dharmakāya* is also said to be the same as the Dharma-realm, the *dharmadhātu* (see above, Chapter 6, p. 123; *M.Saṃg.* comm. on 10:31). The *dharmadhātu* is really the cosmos, the totality, seen in the light of its essential or fundamental aspect, what it really is. To speak of the *dharmadhātu* and the *dharmakāya* as one is to say that what the Buddha exemplifies, the essence of the Buddha, his true nature, is no different from the essence or true nature of all things – all things thus in a sense exemplify the Buddha. Put another way, the essential body of the Buddha is the essential or fundamental dimension of the cosmos – a point of religious and spiritual significance particularly developed, as we have seen, in East Asian Buddhism.

Our texts pose the serious question as to whether there can be only one Buddha, or whether there are many.[16] The answer is neither – or both! If we refer simply to the level of the true nature of things then there is no way of distinguishing one Buddha from another. On this level they have no real physical bodies to differentiate them. Moreover, since their true nature is the same, each Buddha as basis (= *dharmakāya* as the basis for other bodies) is the same. Furthermore, their intentions to act for the benefit of others are the same, and their activities – manifesting enlightenment out of compassion for others, and so on – are the same. On the other hand one cannot say that all Buddhas are literally and in all respects the same, or there would be only one Buddha. If that were true then when one being became a fully enlightened Buddha so all beings would become enlightened. Alternatively, if there were only one Buddha then it would be pointless for other unenlightened beings to strive to become enlightened. A further interesting point made in this context by the *Mahāyānasūtrālaṃkāra* commentary is that there could not be just one primeval Buddha (a view suggested in some other Buddhist traditions), an *ādibuddha*, always enlightened, since there can be no Buddha without the twin accumulations of merit and wisdom, and there can be no such accumulations without a previous Buddha. It is absurd to have a Buddha without any beginning (on 9:77). If there is just one primeval Buddha, say Śākyamuni understood in his transcendend aspect, then no other being could become enlightened. If, on the other hand, unenlightened beings can become enlightened after all by accumulating merit and wisdom, they require a previous Buddha in order to indicate the way. Thus there would not be one primeval Buddha.

The second body of the Buddha is known as the *Sāṃbhogikakāya* – the Body of Complete Enjoyment. It is a physical body (*rūpakāya*), although not perhaps a body of gross material form. It manifests in different ways and at different places according to the needs of sentient beings (*M.Saṃg.* 10:35). No matter how excellent, the Enjoyment Body is an impermanent body.[17] It is in fact the glorified body of the Buddha, adorned with the thirty-two and the eighty marks, which appears seated on a lotus throne in a Pure Land preaching the Mahāyāna to the assembly. The traditional view in Mahāyāna countries is that the Enjoyment Body preaches only to those Bodhisattvas advanced enough to attain a Pure Land, and the Mahāyāna *sūtras* are actually the result of the Enjoyment Body's preaching rather than that of the so-called historical Buddha Siddhārtha Gautama, who appeared not in a Pure Land but in Ancient India. Historically, however, there are problems with this traditional account. The early Mahāyāna *sūtras* frequently speak as though they are being taught in India, and enumerate Hearers and Arhats as well as Bodhisattvas among their listeners. Of course, it is possible to explain this – the Hearers and Arhats were really Bodhisattvas, like

Śāriputra in the *Lotus Sūtra*, who had forgotten their mission. Nevertheless one suspects that in reality the view that all the Mahāyāna *sūtras* were the preaching of the Enjoyment Body in a Pure Land took some centuries to develop, and may indeed represent the final response of the Mahāyāna to the question of textual authenticity.

The Enjoyment Body is in many respects the most important body of the Buddha (Nagao 1973: esp. 35 ff). It is the actual Buddha in his supramundane form, normally said to be the Buddha of Buddhist devotion, a transcendent being animated through pure compassion. It is as an Enjoyment Body that a being actually attains Buddhahood – as we shall see, the third body of the Buddha, his Transformation Body, the corporeal 'human' Buddha Siddhārtha Gautama, was a mere image manifesting becoming enlightened for the benefit of beings. Certain texts, most notably the Cittamātra tradition represented by Hsüan-tsang's *Ch'eng-wei-shih lun*, speak of two aspects to the Enjoyment Body – the Enjoyment Body in its private sense, as experienced and enjoyed by the Buddhas themselves, and the Enjoyment Body for others, which is the Buddha appearing with his various marks for the benefit and enjoyment of the Bodhisattvas.[18] This would appear to be a later development possibly connected with the wish to find a place for the old *dharmakāya*, the Buddha's pure attributes, various knowledges, and so on, which would not taint the purity of the Cittamātra *svābhāvikakāya/dharmakāya* as non-dual consciousness, unqualified and beyond all language.

Little needs to be said of the Buddha's Transformation Bodies (*nairmāṇikakāya*). The Buddha whom the non-Mahāyāna tradition lauds as *the* Buddha, the constant reference point for all doctrine and attempts at innovation, turns out to be simply a manifestation out of compassion, an 'eject', a conjuring trick, as it were, from the Enjoyment Body for the benefit of those whose attainments are so weak that they are unable to reach a Pure Land, or who are not yet capable of appreciating the Mahāyāna. The Transformation Body Buddhas manifest in whatever way is necessary for others.[19] Such manifestations may teach any teaching, Buddhist or non-Buddhist, out of compassionate skilful means. Often Transformation Bodies show the birth, renunciation, enlightenment, and death associated with the life of Siddhārtha Gautama, but not necessarily. A Transformation Body can manifest in any suitable way, even as an animal (see the Jātaka tales), in order to teach a particular point. Buddhists have no objection to seeing the historical Jesus Christ as a Transformation Body Buddha – a manifestation from an Enjoyment Body out of compassion in a form suitable to his particular time and place.

Moreover a Buddha can, of course, manifest infinite Transformation Bodies of different types at any one time. Thus through the two physical bodies of the Buddha the Cittamātra schema encompasses the Mahāyāna doctrine of the immense status and acts of the Buddha, Mahāyāna devotion to the all-compassionate Lord, and also such aspects of religious doctrine and practice as the correct way to relate to other religions and to adapt doctrinally and institutionally to changing circumstances.

A NOTE ON THE dGE LUGS SCHEMA OF THE BUDDHA'S BODIES

Before leaving the topic of the bodies of the Buddha it seems worthwhile to look briefly at the schema (non-Tantric; the dGe lugs Tantric schema is slightly different) found in the dGe lugs tradition of Tibetan Buddhism. This is for a number of reasons. First, in philosophy the dGe lugs tries to follow very closely its understanding of Candrakīrti's Prāsaṅgika Madhyamaka, and yet in its treatment of the Buddha bodies the dGe lugs provides a schema which synthesizes in certain respects both Madhyamaka and Cittamātra treatments. The origins of the dGe lugs schema are as yet obscure, but it almost certainly originates from the Yogācāra-Svātantrika Madhyamaka tradition of Haribhadra's commentaries on the *Abhisamayālaṃkāra*. In the Yogācāra-Svātantrika Madhyamaka we find precisely an attempt to bring together Madhyamaka and Cittamātra.

Second, in looking at the dGe lugs treatment we can see the complex way in which later Buddhist scholasticism elaborated and developed its inheritance in terms of further distinctions and subdivisions. Moreover, the dGe lugs view is still very much alive among Tibetans today, and as Tibetan Buddhism becomes popular in the West many people have become interested in the dGe lugs teachings. These are generally the teachings of His Holiness the Dalai Lama, for example, himself a dGe lugs hierarch.

In the dGe lugs the *dharmakāya* has two aspects, known as the Essence Body (*svābhāvikakāya*) and the Wisdom Body, or Body of Gnosis (*jñānakāya*). The Essence Body also has two aspects. First, it is the absence of inherent existence (emptiness – *śūnyatā*) as it pertains to the Buddha's omniscient and non-dual stream of consciousness. This aspect of the Essence Body has always been the case. Even before the Buddha became enlightened his mind stream lacked inherent existence, and it was this lack which enabled it to change into an enlightened mind stream. One can therefore say that in a sense the Essence Body of the Buddha is always there, even in unenlightened beings. It is that seed of the Buddha within each one which enables him or her to become fully enlightened. It is this, therefore, which is referred to by the dGe lugs tradition as the *tathāgatagarbha*. The other aspect of the Essence Body is also an absence, this time the absence of all cognitive and moral obscurations in the Buddha's mind. This absence has not always been present, of course, but happened automatically or spontaneously when a being became a Buddha. In both respects the Essence Body for the dGe lugs is an emptiness (empty of inherent existence or empty of cognitive and moral obscurations), and since the dGe lugs is rigorously Prāsaṅgika Madhyamaka so the Essence Body alone is an ultimate truth. The other bodies, no matter how exalted, are conventional truths.

The Wisdom Body or Body of Gnosis is the Buddha's omniscient non-dual consciousness itself. This is the Cittamātra *svābhāvikakāya* or *dharmakāya*. The *dharmakāya* for the dGe lugs, therefore, is in substance the non-dual mind stream of the Buddha, understood as empty of inherent existence and all obscurations, and therefore perfect and capable of infinite flexibility in order to help sentient beings. The Buddha's omnisicent consciousness constantly perceives emptiness in all things, and the things themselves, in the very same mental act. Each of the Buddha's senses is omniscient, each sense can therefore do the work of each other sense. His consciousness, his Wisdom Body, is omnipresent inasmuch as the Buddha is non-dualistically aware of all things.[20]

All Bodhisattvas become fully enlightened not on this earth but in one of the highest realms.[21] A Buddha then immediately manifests his Enjoyment Body, ornamented with the various marks, surrounded by a Pure Land and a retinue of advanced Bodhisattvas, teaching the Mahāyāna. The Enjoyment Body and Pure Land are made of his own omniscient wisdom consciousness, and not gross matter. Moreover all that the Enjoyment Body sees are seen as not being separate phenomena from his own mind. He occupies, therefore, the strange magical world of the *dharmadhātu* familiar from the *Avataṃsaka Sūtra*. At the same time the Buddha spontaneously manifests myriads of Transformation Bodies according to the needs of sentient beings. There is no need for a Buddha to ponder which is the best way to help sentient beings.[22] The Enjoyment Body Buddha remains until there are no suffering sentient beings left unenlightened. The *dharmakāya*, the Buddha's omniscient mind stream and its attendant emptinesses, remains for ever – there can be no end to a continuum of consciousness, for what could cause it to cease?

The dGe lugs distinguishes various types of Transformation Bodies. There are those which manifest like Siddhārtha Gautama, and perform the different deeds (twelve in the standard list) of a human Buddha. Others can be artisans or craftsmen. There is a story in which a proud god-musician was humbled by the Buddha appearing as a better musician. Each played on fewer and fewer strings. The god played excellently on only one string, but the Buddha continued playing sweetly with no strings at all (Dhargyey 1976: 208)! Sometimes the Buddha can appear as an animal, or even an apparently inanimate object such as a tree, or a bridge to save those caught on the wrong side of a ravine. The Buddha can also appear in a heavenly realm, as in the case of Maitreya, who all Buddhist traditions hold will be the next Buddha on this earth. He is at present residing in the Tuṣita heaven awaiting the opportune time for his descent to earth. Of course, no one is actually enlightened on our polluted plant! From this perspective Maitreya is already really a Buddha, or is an emanation, a Transformation Body, of one who has long been a Buddha.[23]

The whole dGe lugs schema can best be summed up in a diagram as in Figure 1.

A FINAL NOTE: THE 'NON-ABIDING *NIRVĀṆA*' AND THE LIFESPAN OF THE BUDDHA

In the second chapter, while discussing the meanings of *nirvāna* in the Mahāyāna, I mentioned the supreme and compassionate 'non-abiding' (*apratiṣṭhita*) *nirvāṇa* of the Buddha and contrasted it with the *nirvāṇas* attained by the Arhats and Pratyekabuddhas. I also mentioned a further point concerning whether the Buddha in the Mahāyāna ever eventually, at some point in the unimaginable future, will attain *parinirvāṇa* and go completely beyond recall or reference by suffering sentient beings. The expression 'non-abiding *nirvāṇa*' was probably introduced as a term, although not necessarily as a concept, by the Cittamātra tradition. It is best understood initially from the side not of a Buddha but of a Bodhisattva, an aspirant on the path to Buddhahood. It is crucial in his or her practice that the Bodhisattva renounces *saṃsāra*, the round of misapprehension and false behaviour, and also any conception of *nirvāṇa* as not just the negation of greed, hatred and delusion but also a transcendence of the institutions and persons of *saṃsāra*. That is, the Bodhisattva in going beyond duality, abandons greed, hatred, and delusion

Dharmakāya	Ultimate Truth	– Essence Body	(i) Absence of inherent existence in the Buddha's mind stream. (ii) Absence of cognitive and moral obscurations in the Buddha's mind stream.
	Conventional Truth	– Wisdom Body	Buddha's omniscient mind stream.
Rūpakaya (form-body)		– Enjoyment Body	Arises in heavenly realm. Occupies a Pure Land. Teaches Mahāyāna to advanced Bodhisattvas. Emanates myriads of:
		– Transformation Body	Artisans, animals or objects, certain beings in heavens, Buddhas on earth, manifesting twelve deeds, such as birth, enlightenment, and death. Teaches in whatever way is necessary to help beings.

FIGURE 1 *The dGe lugs schema of the Buddha's bodies*

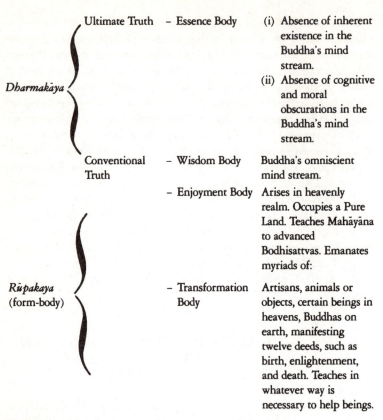

but does not abandon sentient beings; he or she attains wisdom but preserves compassion. If *nirvāṇa* is understood as not just abandoning greed, hatred, and delusion but also abandoning in this life the institutions and persons of 'the world', and after death returning no more to help those institutions and persons (i.e. Arhatship), then the Bodhisattva renounces also *nirvāṇa*. Thus the *nirvāṇa* that is attained by the Bodhisattva when he or she attains Buddhahood is not that type of *nirvāṇa*. Rather, it is a non-abiding *nirvāṇa*, which is to say that it is a *nirvāṇa* which embodies two dimensions – the upward movement away from *saṃsāra*, away from greed, hatred, and delusion, and a downward movement returning to the maelstrom of *saṃsāric* institutions and persons out of compassion (see Nagao 1981: 61 ff.). The Buddha abides neither in *saṃsāra*, for he is a Buddha, nor in *nirvāṇa* in the sense that he has abandoned suffering sentient beings. In a sense he has a foot (or a lotus) in both camps, while in another sense he is in neither. He has gone beyond all duality and all clinging – he clings neither to the world nor to transcendence.

Will the fully enlightened Buddha ever attain to *parinirvāṇa*? Clearly, this problem concerns pre-eminently the Enjoyment Body. There is no question of the *dharmakāya* attaining *parinirvāṇa*, for the *dharmakāya* does not attain anything at all. It is permanent, remaining for ever in its own nature. Things are always empty of inherent existence; the continuum of pure radiant consciousness never ceases. The Buddha's Transformation Bodies, on the other hand, in one sense can be said to attain *parinirvāṇa*, but in another sense do not. The Transformation Body is a manifestation for the benefit of beings, and among the deeds of Transformation Bodies is the manifestation of *parinirvāṇa*. Thus the Transformation Body can attain *parinirvāṇa*. Nevertheless, since the manifestation is unreal, just a show, the *parinirvāṇa* is also unreal, just a show.

If we look at the Enjoyment Body, the transcendent glorified Buddha, then we can detect two theories on the eternality of the Buddha (Poussin 1928/48: 3, 803 ff). According to such texts as the *Ta-chih-tu lun*, the *Lotus Sūtra* (text, rather than its East Asian interpretation) and the *Suvarṇabhāsottama Sūtra*, after an enormously long period of time the Buddha will eventually enter *parinirvāṇa*, although according to the first of these the Buddha's Transformation Bodies will continue in order to help sentient beings.[24] These texts clearly operate with the (older?) notion that the length of a Buddha's life, as with all beings, is the result of his merit gained in the past. Since the Buddha's merit, while immense, cannot be literally infinite (as it is the result of finite acts), the Buddha's lifespan must in reality be finite (cf. *Suvarṇabhāsottama Sūtra* 1970: 5–8). In other texts, however, apparently later in date, such as the *Buddhabhūmi Śāstra*, the Buddhas never enter *parinirvāṇa*. Part of the problem is that some texts view beings as infinite, and other (Cittamātra) texts maintain that there are some beings who as a matter of fact will never attain enlightenment. The Buddhas remain, therefore, either to continue to save infinite sentient beings, or to try and provide more pleasant rebirths for those who will never put an end to the round of *saṃsāra* (Poussin 1928/48: 3, 806–9). Here we find the extreme point of the Mahāyāna emphasis on compassion: the love of the Buddhas is so great that they are resolved never to enter the final *nirvāṇa* of complete quiescence and peace, but rather to remain and help other beings. Of course, inasmuch as the Buddhas see things correctly, so, as the *Prajñāpāramitā Sūtras* state, no beings are really saved, and there is no *nirvāṇa* to attain. What more do fully enlightened Buddhas have to gain by entering any further state called *parinirvāṇa?* They act tirelessly for the sake of sentient beings, for in Buddhas there are no negative experiences such as tiredness. And from the side of suffering sentient beings themselves the Enjoyment Body Buddhas remain exerting their infinite compassionate deeds so long as a single being remains unenlightened.

The path of the Bodhisattva

TIBET AND TANTRA

The Buddhism which came to Tibet from the seventh century onwards came from two directions. On the one hand there were Chinese influences, particularly forms associated with Ch'an (Zen). On the other, and growing progressively in importance until all but eclipsing the Chinese influences, there were the developed forms of Buddhism found in India at the time. It is the Tibetan boast that it alone, of all the countries to which Buddhism spread, received and practises the complete range of teachings found in Indian Buddhism. This includes in pride of place the Tantric forms which mark late Buddhism in India. An extensive discussion of Tantra would take us beyond the scope of this book. It is possible to indicate in a few words, however, the nature of Tantric Buddhism, particularly as it is found in the Highest Yoga class (*anuttarayoga*) given principal place in the Tibetan traditions.

The concern of Tantric Buddhism is largely with ritual and meditative practices. In terms of the Mahāyāna dichotomy of wisdom and means, therefore, the Tantras are primarily concerned with means, that is, the means of becoming fully enlightened and the manifold expression of the Buddha's compassionate ability to help others. Since, as we have seen, the realm of compassion/means is for the Mahāyāna a realm of magical intervention and transformation, so Tantric practices, as practices particularly concerned with means, are seen in Tibetan Buddhism as in the broadest sense magical practices for transforming mundane reality into a form most suited to help others. More concretely, in Tantric practice the meditator first invokes and visualizes a particular Buddha. After praising the Buddha as an external being he (or she, Tārā, for example) is absorbed into the practitioner's mind which takes on the divine aspect of great bliss. With this blissful mind the mediator reduces the world of experience to what it really is, empty or mind-dependent. Through working on his or her own mind the practitioner is then able to transform the world. The meditator, through visualization, chanting, and perhaps appropriate gestures, intervenes in 'the' world and transforms himself or herself into the appropriate Buddha, and the world of his or her experience into the divine world, the Pure Land of that Buddha, a world within which magic and miracles occur for the benefit of others.

This is perfectly understandable from what we have seen of earlier Mahāyāna in, say, the *Avataṃsaka* tradition.[1] The world is mind-dependent. For the Buddha it is a world of constant magical transformation. In Tantric practice from the beginning – after necessary initiation, for Tantric Buddhism is strictly esoteric – the practitioner tries to see himself as the appropriate Buddha, and the world as a divine, magical realm. Gradually this becomes more real; gradually the meditator brings into play a subtle physiology, a subtle (astral?) body usually dormant or semi-dormant within the gross material body. This subtle body (owing something, I suspect, to ancient Indian medical theories) really becomes a divine body, it is transmuted into that of a Buddha. Gradually also the hold of the gross world of inherently existing separate objects is loosened, and the meditator develops an ability to transform the world, to perform miracles. Tantric Buddhism, Vajrayāna, is thus not seen, in Tibet at least, as a totally different 'vehicle' of Buddhism but is rather a particular form of Mahāyāna practice. It is usually placed squarely within the Mahāyāna framework of emptiness and compassionate motivation.[2] Tibetans will state, moreover, that it is through Highest Yoga Tantra practice alone that a person can become a fully enlightened Buddha in one lifetime – indeed, it is sometimes said that it is only through having final recourse to the highest Tantric practices that one can become a Buddha at all. Hence the reputation of Tibetan Buddhism for magic and mystery! Hence also the complex iconography (for visualization and transformation) and the elaborate ritual (rendering divine, taking upon oneself divine attributes) of Tibetan Buddhism. Moreover, since these practices require (at least as they are presented in the dGe lugs tradition) prior understanding and training in Mahāyāna thought and behaviour, an awareness of emptiness and the Bodhisattva path in order to understand the rationale for Tantra, for magical transformation, followed by personal initiation and careful guidance, for the practices have their psychological and perhaps also their social risks, we find in late Indian and Tibetan Buddhism the overriding importance of the teacher, a guru or lama. This is so much a feature of Tibetan Buddhism that it is sometimes called 'Lamaism' – a term offensive, however, to Tibetans, who consider, with a large degree of truth that their Buddhism is simply Indian Buddhism of the type that was transmitted to Tibet from the seventh century onwards.[3]

BUDDHISM REACHES THE LAND OF SNOWS

The transmission of Buddhism to Tibet appears to have begun in earnest during the reign of the great emperor Srong btsan sgam po (pronounced: Song tsen gam po), who died *c.* 650 CE. There can be little doubt that Srong btsan sgam po was a remarkable man, who began a period of phenomenal Tibetan expansion which created over the next 200 years a vast empire in Central Asia which repeatedly defeated imperial Chinese armies and at one stage captured the Chinese capital of Ch'ang-an (763) and established a short-lived puppet Chinese emperor. Tibetan imperial expansion led to surplus wealth which could finance the trappings of newly discovered and newly desired civilization. Buddhism was already well established in the areas overrun by Tibetan armies; it was an adaptable, civilizing force with willing missionaries. Among his wives Srong btsan sgam po is said to have married two princesses, one Chinese and one Nepalese, who brought from their homelands Buddhist artefacts and ideas. According to tradition, the king had temples built in Lhasa (then known as Rasa) in order to house the Buddhist statues given by his queens. These are the oldest temples and the earliest statues of Tibetan Buddhism. However, while none of this is very surprising, it scarcely amounts to a wholesale propagation of the Buddhist faith. Later pious Tibetan tradition portrays Srong btsan sgam po (said to be an emanation of Avalokiteśvara) as a Buddhist convert and enthusiastic propagandist for Buddhism, but as far as we can tell the transmission of Buddhism was actually a far slower process. Per Kvaerne has pointed out that contemporary documents make no mention of Buddhism, and King Srong btsan sgam po appears to have died and been buried still adhering to the old pre-Buddhist cult centred on the divinity of the king and involving blood sacrifice.[4] As late as 727 a Chinese traveller to India commented: 'As far as the country of Tibet in the East is concerned, there are no monasteries there, and the teachings of Buddha are unknown' (quoted in Hoffmann 1975: 127).

Buddhism is first mentioned in official documents during the reign of Khri srong lde brtsan (pr.: Tri song day tsen; 740–*c.*798 – Kvaerne, or 755–97 – Hoffmann). This king was an enthusiastic supporter of the new faith, and is seen by Tibetan tradition as the second of the three Dharma kings, an emanation of Mañjuśrī. It is clear from surviving records and later tradition that the introduction of Buddhism into Tibet was closely involved with political struggles and controversy between the king and his powerful nobles. Those members of the aristocracy opposed to the king tended to form a faction allied with the priests of the pre-Buddhist cults. This pre-Buddhist religion is often referred to by modern writers as Bon, and is said to be a form of shamanism. On both counts there are problems here. This religion cannot be identified in any simple manner with the Bon religion as it has continued down to the present day. Bon as we know it emerges into history under Buddhist influence perhaps during the eleventh century. Furthermore, the old pre-Buddhist religion of Tibet (which was not necessarily as indigenous religion itself) was a cult mainly connected with royal funeral ceremonies and was not, as far as we can tell, shamanistic in any way.[5]

It is also often stated that the Buddhism of Tibet is some strange hybrid, the result of Indian Buddhism mixing with this pre-Buddhist religion. Again, there is no clear evidence for this. Certainly, Buddhism in each country to which it has spread has absorbed some of the local cults and culture. It happened in China and Japan as much as Tibet. Tibetan texts themselves speak of local deities tamed by Buddhist saints, usually yogins with a strong involvement in Tantric magic, such as Padmasambhava (eighth century). These local deities pledge to protect Buddhism, they are converted, and their cults become part of local Buddhist practice. This absorption of the local cults indicates a Mahāyāna concern to control local forces in order to protect person, property, and religion. It is not uniquely Tibetan. The local deities rarely if ever have any direct connection with the path to Buddhahood – they are worldly (*laukika*) and not supramundane (*lokottara*). Nevertheless, their conversion is essential to the conversion of a country, and reflects a Mahāyāna involvement with the whole of life as a skilful means to benefit beings, and a Tantric involvement in all experience as part of divine expression, a Buddha's Pure Land. Thus, although Buddhism in Tibet has a local flavour, and reflects the tastes and interests of the Tibetan people, still, this is not unusual in Buddhism and is far from indicating Tibetan Buddhism as a strange hybrid religion. Indeed, many of the features of Tibetan Buddhism which initially strike one as unusual can be traced to forms of Buddhism present in India at the time of transmission to Tibet, particularly the Buddhism of the Pāla dynasties of Bengal/Bihar (eighth to ninth/tenth centuries).

If we follow traditional accounts, King Khri srong lde brtsan invited the great Indian scholar Śāntarakṣita to Tibet. The Indian scholar laid the foundations for the first monastery in Tibet, at bSam yas (pr.: Samyay). Nevertheless, the story runs, Tibetan demons hindered Śāntarakṣita's progress, and he returned to India having advised that the king invite the yogin Padmasambhava to Tibet in order to quell through magic its demons and bind them to the service of the Dharma. This Padmasasmbhava did with spectacular success. Some scholars have seen in the figures of Śāntarakṣita and padmasambhava two contrasting types of Buddhist adept, models of sainthood, prevalent in Indian Buddhism at this time – the scholarly abbot, and the wandering Tantric yogin, a *siddha*, a magician who cannot be placed in any category, and is free from all external constraints. The *siddha's* actions may shock, may be antinomian: he or she is a person of power operating for the benefit of beings from the position of a Buddha, behind and beyond all laws. The relationships between monastic Buddhism and the *siddha*, who may or may not be a monk, have not always been easy. Some Tibetan traditions veer more towards the one as a model or towards the other. But these are only types – Śāntarakṣita practised the Tantras as did the great Tibetan monastic scholars such as Sa skya Paṇḍita (1182–1251) and Tsong kha pa (1357–1419). *Siddhas* such as Padmasambhava and Nāropa (956–1040) did not neglect the study of doctrine as taught in the great monastic universities, and the Tibetan traditions which trace their lineage in particular to these *siddhas*, the rNying ma pa (pr.: Nying ma pa) and bKa' brgyud (pr.: Ka gyer), have also produced great monastic scholars. As the founder of the rNying ma pa tradition, Padmasambhava has been revered from about the fourteenth century onwards as a totally miraculous being, a Second Buddha, eclipsing almost completely Śākyamuni. In the earliest sources, however, there is little evidence for the quite exceptional status of Padmasambhava. Be that as it may, it is said that as a result of Padmasambhava's activities Śāntarakṣita was able to return to Tibet, bSam yas monastery was completed, and the first Tibetan monks were trained. It was also during the reign of King Khri srong lde brtsan that the bSam yas debates occurred. Because of the direct relevance of these debates to the Buddhist path, however, they will be treated in the next section.

It is clear from the records that Khri srong lde brtsan elevated the monkhood to a very high position indeed, beyond that of his ministers and the other nobility. In so doing he contributed substantially to the alienation of his aristocracy. Much of this was in keeping with Indian precedent (and contrasts with China), but it aggravated still further relationships with the non-Buddhist nobility, and also with the peasantry, who were nevertheless required by law to support the monks. The third Dharma king, Ral pa can (pr.: Rel pa chen; d.838 – Kvaerne, or 836 – Shakabpa), an emanation of the Bodhisattva Vajrapāṇi, showed even more enthusiasm for Buddhism. He is said to have tied pieces of string to his long hair, the other ends of which were tied to strips of cloth. These pieces of cloth were spread out on the ground for the monks to sit on. Eventually Ral pa can was murdered by two disaffected ministers, who placed his anti-Buddhist brother, gLang dar ma, on the throne. gLang dar ma instituted a persecution of Buddhism, closing monasteries, confiscating their estates, and forcing monks to marry and become huntsmen or followers of the non-Buddhist cults. At least two monks were executed. gLang dar ma was himself killed by a Buddhist monk and yogin, dPal gyi rdo rje (pr.: Bel gyee dor jay) who, out of skilful means animated by compassion, decided to save the Dharma and also the king by preventing him from carrying out further crimes (842). By the death of gLang dar ma Buddhism had all but perished in Central Tibet. Thus ends the period known as the First Diffusion of the Dharma in Tibet. It also inaugurates the end of Tibetan imperialism. The Tibetan empire eventually fragmented into the clans and countries from which it arose. Buddhism, meanwhile, entered a period of decadence, with lawless '*siddhas*' aparently acting out of megalomanic immorality in the belief that they were already Buddhas and beyond all good and evil.

Slowly, however, the Dharma and monasticism revived. Instrumental in bringing about a Second Diffusion of the Dharma in Tibet was the king of a region in western Tibet, who subsequently became a monk-king, known as Ye shes 'od (pr.: Ye shay er). This king built monasteries and sent youths to India in order to study as monks and train as translators. It is said that Ye shes 'od particularly wanted to invite the great Indian scholar and saint Atiśa to Tibet, and according to a cherished tradition, when the monk-king was captured by a Muslim Turkic tribe and thrown into prison, he insisted that his nephew Byang chub 'od (pr.: Jang chup er) use the ransom raised for his release to invite Atiśa to revive Buddhism in Tibet. Ye shes 'od accordingly died in prison, a martyr to the Dharma, and Atiśa (982–1054) spent many years in Tibet teaching, translating, and establishing a form of Buddhism firmly based on scholarship, morality, and a strict monastic tradition within which Tantric practice nevertheless had a legitimate place. Atiśa (whose principal disciple was a Tibetan layman, 'Brom ston (pr.: Drom tern)) wrote for his pupils in Tibet a short treatise known as the *Bodhipathapradīpa*, the *Lamp on the Path to Enlightenment*, in which he created a system integrating all Buddhist practices as he had received them from his many teachers into a gradual path based on morality and culminating in the development of compassion and wisdom completed through Tantric practice. This treatise, the root text for Atiśa's bKa' gdams pa (pr.: Ka dam pa) school, has been enormously influential in Tibetan religious thought.

During Atiśa's time, Tibetans were also founding schools. The layman-translator Mar pa (1012–96) travelled a number of times to India, and together with his disciple, the famous yogin and poet Mi la ras pa (pr.: Mi la ray pa; 1040–1123), and the latter's disciple sGam po pa (1079–1153), established the bKa' brgyud – a tradition which has subsequently split into several lineages. Among the most famous of these bKa' brgyud lineages is that of the Karma pa (divided itself into the Red Hat Karma pa and the Black Hat Karma pa), which appears to have introduced the idea of succession through reincarnation. It is said that when the second Black Hat Karma pa, head of the Black Hat lineage, died in 1283 a child was recognized as his reincarnation and trained to occupy once more his religious and administrative position. This phenomenon of 'incarnate lamas' was subsequently adopted by other traditions (the Dalai Lama is perhaps the best-known case), and is a feature of the form of Buddhism found in Tibet and Mongolia.

Politically, the period after the collapse of the Tibetan imperial dynasty is marked by the gradual centralization of power in the hands of the one organization which could offer some form of stability in a time of near-anarchy, the monasteries. Even before the arrival of the Mongols Tibet had seen the growth of powerful monastic centres headed by 'prince-abbots' and sometimes allied to local kings. When Tibet hurried to submit to the terrifying Mongol scourge, Prince Godan, who was grandson of Genghis Khan and interested in religion and particularly magic, invited the monk reputed to be the holiest in all Tibet, the head of the Sa skya tradition, Sa skya Paṇḍita Kun dga' rgyal mtshan (pr.: Kern ga gyel tsen; 1182–1251), to visit him in his camp. Impressed, Godan became his patron and handed over the whole of Tibet to the learned abbot. Sa skya Paṇḍita was succeeded by his nephew 'Phags pa (pr.: Pak pa; 1235–80), the teacher of Kublai Khan, the Khan who became Mongol emperor of China. This period saw not only the establishment of Sa skya power over Tibet, but also immense Sa skya influence in Mongolia and China. The Tibetans appeared to have replaced a material empire with one of the spirit! Unfortunately the Tibetan lamas were often accused by the Chinese of arrogance and worldliness. Their connection with the barbarian Mongolian conquerors did little to help their popularity in China, and Sa skya power began to wane with the collapse of the Mongol empire. Over the centuries within Tibet Sa skya gradually lost political control (but not spiritual influence) to other 'princely-monastic' traditions, particularly the bKa' brgyud lineage known as the Phag mo gru pa (pr.: Pak mo dru pa).

The preceding traditions of Tibetan Buddhism are sometimes known, following Chinese custom, as 'Red Hats' (the Black Hat Karma pa notwithstanding). This marks a contrast with the most recent of the Tibetan schools, Tsong kha pa's Yellow Hat dGe lugs pa. Tsong kha pa sought to return to the Indian sources, particularly as they had been systematized in Atiśa's synthesis. He stressed monastic austerity and formidable learning. Tsong kha pa founded the first dGe lugs monastery, dGa' ldan (pr.: Gan den), close to Lhasa, in 1409. The other two great dGe lugs monastic universities, 'Bras spungs (pr.: Dre pung) and Sera, were founded also near to Lhasa in 1416 and 1419 respectively. One of Tsong kha pa's pupils, dGe 'dun grub (pr.: Gen dun drup), founded bKra shis lhun po (pr.: Tra she hlun po) monastery some distance south-west of Lhasa. On the death of dGe 'dun grub his reincarnation was discovered in dGe 'dun rgya mtsho (pr.: . . . gya tso), and on the latter's death in bSod nams rgya mtsho (pr.: Sir nam gya tso; 1543–88). This bSod nams rgya mtsho reintroduced Buddhism to Mongolia, finally converting the Mongols who ever since have been enthusiastic and often very learned supporters of the dGe lugs tradition. The Mongol khan, Altan Khan, was so impressed with the learning and spirituality of bSod nams rgya mtsho that he called him an 'ocean' (Mongolian: *dalai*), and bSod nams rgya mtsho thus became the Third Dalai Lama, for his two previous incarnations were given the title respectively. When bSod nams rgya mtsho's own reincarnation, the Fourth Dalai Lama, was found in a Mongol family as the great-grandson of Altan Khan, Mongol support for the dGe lugs tradition was complete. Politically, on the other hand, the situation had deteriorated. The growing power of the dGe lugs monasteries had led to a religio-political rivalry with other political powers, particularly the Karma pa bKa' brgyud. Geographically this rivalry represented an old rivalry between Central Tibet, dominated by Lhasa and the dGe lugs, and southern Tibet (gTsang) whose king supported the Karma pa and resented Lhasa ambitions and pretensions. The situation became most unpleasant, with armed bands, sometimes monks, allied to each side sacking each other's monasteries, although at times both Dalai Lamas and Karma pa hierarchs intervened to mediate and defuse a potentially dangerous situation. Nevertheless, the story is not very edifying. Suffice to say that this anarchy ended when, during the mid-seventeenth century, the Mongol Gushri Khan defeated and killed the king of gTsang and gave political control of Tibet to the Fifth Dalai Lama, Ngag dbang blo bzang rgya mtsho (pr.: Nga wang lo zang gya tso; 1617–82), a learned and yet politically gifted monk and ruler. From that time on the Dalai Lamas, providing they reach maturity, have been in theory at least the political leaders of the Tibetan people.[6]

THE EIGHTH-CENTURY DEBATES

Let us return now to the time of Khri srong lde brtsan. We have seen that during the first diffusion of Buddhism in Tibet the establishment of Buddhism *vis-à-vis* the non-Buddhist cults was also involved with political rivalry between the king and his powerful nobles. Within Buddhism there were further rivalries, however. King Srong btsan sgam po is said to have had two Buddhist wives, one from Nepal and the other from China. We know that Chinese wives of subsequent kings were associated with Chinese Buddhist missionaries. It seems likely that Indian wives also had their missionaries. This meant that a number of rather different forms of Buddhism were introduced together into Tibet. It seems that partisans of these different traditions were by the time of Khri srong lde brtsan in a state of open antagonism, with advocates of one approach threatening to kill those of another (Houston 1980: 32). In particular, these different approaches polarized into that represented by a Chinese monk (*ho-shang*) named, appropriately enough, Mahāyāna, and the approach of Śāntarakṣita and his disciple Kamalaśīla. The Chinese monk appears to have been a follower of some form of Ch'an, although exactly which form is disputed by scholars. Śāntarakṣita is said to have died some time before the debate (or debates – it is now thought that in reality there may have been a series of controversies lasting, perhaps, for some years). The side of Śāntarakṣita was represented by Kamalaśīla. Late sources lead us to believe that Kamalaśīla's faction was very much in the minority. The debate was of great importance to later Tibetan thought and its view of its antecedents and development. Accounts are contained in a number of later works which seem to agree in essentials, although this may be because they all depend on the same original. There are also Chinese accounts of the debate. We are told that it was held in the presence of the king, and Mahāyāna was the first to speak:

> If you commit virtuous or non-virtuous deeds, because you go to heavens and hells, (you still) are not liberated from *saṃsāra*. The path to Buddhahood is obscured ... Whoever does not think anything; the one who does not ponder will become completely liberated from *saṃsāra* ... he is instantaneously enlightened. He is equal to one who has mastered the tenth *bhūmi*.[7]

In other words, enlightenment not only has nothing to do with morality, but it is positively hindered by good and bad deeds, which lead to heaven and hell and bind one still further in the round of rebirth. Enlightenment lies in cutting all thought, all mental activity, and must necessarily be instantaneous (or 'simultaneous' – there are problems of interpretation and translation here). There can be no stages, necessarily conceptual, to non-conceptual awareness.

If we can follow the Tibetan Bu ston (1290–1364), Kamalaśīla replied to Mahāyāna that if his opponent were right then there could be no wisdom (*prajñā*) gained through conceptual activity. But surely liberating wisdom is precisely the *result* of conceptual activity, of analysing to find out whether an entity has or has not inherent existence. In a state of no thought at all how can there be insight? How can there be renunciation of the wrong view if one has not attained to the right view? Moreover, Kamalaśīla's colleagues pointed out, to attain enlightenment suddenly is to abandon the path of gradual cultivation through the six perfections of giving, morality, and so on. And if one accepts a sudden enlightenment which cannot be cultivated then what is to be done? There can be no religious practice at all! Mahāyāna's approach is one which contradicts the scriptures, destroys morality and compassion, and also destroys any possibility of generating actual insight.[8] The king, we are told, was persuaded by these arguments and judged Kamalaśīla's party the winner. Henceforth, he decreed, everyone should follow the teachings of Nāgārjuna and engage assiduously in the practice of morality and the perfections. Mahāyāna and his followers were expelled from Tibet.

It has been suggested that since Khri srong lde brtsan wished to improve the morality of his semi-barbaric people he was likely from the beginning to accept the testimony of Kamalaśīla and his party (Houston 1980: 9). Certainly, it was not in the interests of the king to advocate a position which denied the value of good deeds and placed the spiritual practitioner outside the nexus of moral (and legal) control. Moreover it was also not in his interests to side too closely with Chinese Buddhism, for Tibet was still at war with China. Throughout subsequent Tibetan thought the view of Ho-shang Mahāyāna has frequently been taken as one of the archetypal 'wrong views', a dangerous misinterpretation. Tsong kha pa will often accuse his opponents of falling unintentionally into this heresy, inasmuch as they tend to deny the role of analysis in generating insight into emptiness. It should be clear that some of the tension between the two approaches can be traced to an opposition between the Madhyamaka view of emptiness as an absence of inherent existence in the object under investigation, and the *tathāgatagarbha* perspective on emptiness, so influential in Chinese Buddhism including Ch'an, which sees emptiness as the radiant pure mind empty of its conceptual accretions. This second approach sees concepts, and mental activity which is necessarily conceptual, as obscurations, clouds covering an innate pure radiance (an image which is repeated by Mahāyāna, according to Bu ston, in describing his position). By way of contrast, our first approach divides conceptual activity into profitable and unprofitable. It thus sees emptiness in *saṃsāra*, rather than in radical contrast to it.

In recent years scholars have gained access to a number of very early fragmentary writings found at the Central Asian oasis site of Tun-huang. This site was under Tibetan imperial control for some time, and the writings, in Tibetan, give perhaps a rather clearer account of what Mahāyāna's views actually were. It is known that as a matter of fact Mahāyāna himself did not ignore morality, but was quite prepared to administer the monastic vows. According to one of these fragments the practitioner should accumulate merit and practise the perfections, although the ultimate is beyond them (Gomez 1983: 118, 127). The picture we get from these fragments is that Mahāyāna saw the root cause of *saṃsāra* as discrimination (*vikalpa*; ibid, 107). Thus enlightenment comes from cutting the discriminating mind. However, this does not seem to refer to a striving to cut all thoughts altogether, for that too would be a clinging:

> When he enters a state of deep contemplation, he looks into his own mind. There being no-mind, he does not engage in thought. If

> thoughts of discrimination arise, he should become aware of them.... Whatever thoughts arise, one does not examine.... He does not examine any dharma whatsoever. If he becomes aware in this way of the arising (of thoughts, he perceives) the absence of self-existence.... After sitting (in this manner) for a long time, the mind will become tame, and one will realize that his awareness is also discriminating mind.... Awareness itself is without name or form ... the awareness and place where it occurs cannot be obtained by any search. There is no way of reflecting on the inconceivable. Not to cling even to this absence of thought is (the immediate access of) the Tathagatas.
>
> (Trans. in Gomez 1983: 108–9)

In this way there can be liberation in each moment of thought:

> But if one were to experience non-examination and does not act according to these concepts, or accept them, or become attached to them, then every instant of mind is liberated at each moment.
>
> (ibid., 125)

These practices have something in common with Zen, and also with the Tibetan rNying ma pa tradition known as *rDzogs chen* (pr.: Dzok chen), the Great Perfection. They are certainly far subtler than the traditional Tibetan accounts of Mahāyāna's views. But what of Mahāyāna's attitudes to morality and the perfections? In fact he shows a tendency to reinterpret the perfections of giving, morality, and so on in a way consonant with his meditative practice. Thus: 'When one enters non-examination, he brings to perfection great morality, because there is no arising of any faults in any of the three doors (of conduct)' (Gomez 1983: 122). One interpretation of this is that morality etc. have their place *after* one has attained to direct insight through cutting all conceptualization. Such an approach also has Zen parallels – a version of it is held by Dōgen, for example.

According to the traditional Tibetan account, Kamalaśīla was subsequently murdered, although it is not clear by whom. Before his sad death, however, he wrote three works, known as the three *Bhāvanākramas*, summarizing the path as he saw and taught it, and also his criticisms of the approach of Ho-shang Mahāyāna. This approach, Kamalaśīla observes, is to reject correct analysis which leads to understanding. With no understanding, moral taints and impurities cannot be overcome. Moreover, to attain enlightenment it is necessary to complete the two collections of merit and wisdom. Merit comes through the means of giving, morality, and so on. These people destroy the Mahāyāna, they over-inflate their own views, are without respect for the wise, and ignore the Buddha's words. Being destroyed themselves, they seek to destroy others. Their words are infected with the poison of contradiction, violate logic and scriptural tradition, and they should be rejected by the wise.[9] Thus Kamalaśīla's view of the quietism and antinomianism sometimes associated with Zen! In the first *Bhāvanākrama* in particular Kamalaśīla systematically explains the stages of the path as he understands and advocates it. This text together with Atiśa's *Bodhipathapradīpa* and the author's own commentary are among the most important Indian sources for the progressive stages on the path to enlightenment in Tibet. The path begins for the Mahāyāna with compassion, for, say Kamalaśīla, 'compassion alone is the root cause of all the qualities of the Buddha'.[10] It is to this path, and compassion in particular, therefore, that we now turn.

COMPASSION AND THE *BODHICITTA*

According to Atiśa in his *Bodhipathapradīpa*, beings can be divided in terms of their scope or aspirations into three types – the lesser, the middling, and the superior. Those of lesser scope take as their goal themselves alone – they are selfish – and act simply for the pleasures of *saṃsāra*, either in this life or in some future rebirth. Other texts will state that as a scope or aspiration this does not deserve the name 'religious' at all. Those in the second category, that of middling aspiration, turn their backs on the pleasures of existence and renounce immoral deeds. They act in order to bring about their own pacification, in other words in order to attain enlightenment as an Arhat. But those of highest, superior scope seek to bring a complete end to all the sufferings of others, since the suffering of others is indeed their own suffering. Atiśa has written the *Bodhipathapradīpa* for this last category, the superior beings who follow the Bodhisattva path of the Mahāyāna.[11]

Thus we have ordinary worldly beings, those who are on the path to the *nirvāṇa* of an Arhat, and finally the Bodhisattva whose aspiration lies in removing the sufferings of all sentient beings. The distinctions between these persons rest on their aspirations. One corollary of this – a corollary Tibetans are quick to point out – is that the distinction between Mahāyāna and non-Mahāyāna is not as such one of schools, traditions,

Vinaya, robes, or philosophy. It is one of motivation, the reason for following the religious path. As such, there could in theory be a Mahāyānist, one with the highest motivation of complete Buddhahood for the sake of all sentient beings, following the Theravāda tradition.[12] This fits with what we know of the historical origins of the Mahāyāna, embedded firmly within the non-Mahāyāna traditions. One can speak of a particular philosophy, say the Sarvāstivāda or Sautrāntika systems, as a non-Mahāyāna philosophy, and the Madhyamaka and Cittamātra as Mahāyāna philosophies, but one cannot say for certain of a particular person whether he or she is a Mahāyānist, or not without knowing whether that person has developed the Mahāyāna motivation. There are said to be many who hold to Mahāyāna philosophies, and also carry out Mahāyāna rituals, who are not genuine followers of the Mahāyāna. Their real aspiration may be their own liberation, or even worldly goals such as fame or money.

Developing the authentic Mahāyāna motivation is called 'generating *bodhicitta*', the Mind of Enlightenment or Awakening Mind. This *bodhicitta* results from deep compassion for the suffering of others. His Holiness the Dalai Lama has said somewhere, speaking from the Madhyamaka perspective, that in Mahāyāna there are no absolutes, but if there were one it would be compassion. Compassion is not an ontological absolute, but it is an ethical absolute for the Mahāyāna. In the first chapter of his *Bodhicaryāvatāra*, one of the great spiritual poems of mankind, Śāntideva (695–743) praises compassion and the *bodhicitta* in the following terms:

> It is like the supreme gold-making elixir,
> For it transforms the unclean body we have taken
> Into the priceless jewel of a Buddha-Form.
> Therefore firmly seize this Awakening Mind.
>
> How can I fathom the depths
> Of the goodness of this jewel of the mind,
> The panacea that relieves the world of pain
> And is the source of all its joy?[13]

This compassion is the basis and motivating force of the Bodhisattva, from it springs the entire edifice of the Mahāyāna. Kamalaśīla states that 'The Buddhas, the Blessed Ones, attained to their omniscience by embracing compassion; and they so rejoice in the welfare of the world that they remain therein, nor do the Blessed Ones abide in nirvana, because of their compassion' (trans. in Beyer 1974: 100). According to the

Dalai Lama,

> We should have this [compassion] from the depths of our heart, as if it were nailed there. Such compassion is not merely concerned with a few sentient beings such as friends and relatives, but extends up to the limits of the cosmos, in all directions and towards all beings throughout space.
>
> (T. Gyatso 1979: 111)

Truly generating this deep compassion and the resultant *bodhicitta* is a completely life-transforming experience; one ceases to be an ordinary being and becomes a 'Son or Daughter of the Buddhas' (*Bodhicaryāvatāra* 1: 9). This is not simply an idle thought: 'Wouldn't it be nice to be a Buddha for the sake of all sentient beings!' Rather it results from a very specific and sustained series of meditations.

First, it is presupposed in the Tibetan traditions of the 'graduated path' that very few practitioners are capable of beginning straight away with the Bodhisattva motivation. We all begin with the first scope, that of self-concern with the pleasures of this and other worlds – whether we realize it or not. Preliminary meditations are used, therefore, in order to raise the aspiration of the practitioner from this 'sensual' scope to one of conern for liberation from *saṃsāra* altogether – in other words, the motivation of the Arhat. More specifically, Tsong kha pa speaks of the 'three principal aspects of the path' – renunciation, compassion, and emptiness. It is necessary to have renunciation before one can truly begin to generate compassion.[14] To this end a series of graded meditations are recommended. One first meditates on the rarity and value of a human rebirth, a birth with time and the ability to understand and practise the Dharma. Next the meditator contemplates impermanence and death, the fact that death comes to everyone and is certain, although the time of death is uncertain. At the time of death only one's spiritual development will be of help. This generates enthusiasm for practising the Dharma straight away, 'as if there were no tomorrow'. One meditates on *karma* and rebirth, which helps to develop the moral basis for spiritual practice. If the meditator practises these meditations systematically then by this stage he or she will have given rise to a spiritual and moral perspective and a genuine concern with virtue which will lead to favourable future rebirths. Next one contemplates the various forms of rebirth and suffering throughout the six realms (gods, titans or anti-gods (*asuras*), humans, hungry ghosts (*pretas*), animals, and hell realms). The practitioner visualizes each of the six destinies and their sufferings, their ultimate unsatisfactoriness. Only after repeatedly meditating like this will a feeling of complete renunciation for all rebirth in *saṃsāra*, and a desire for Arhatship, arise. It is then, and only then, that meditation intended to generate *bodhicitta* has any real meaning.[15]

The Third Dalai Lama, bSod nams rgya mtsho, states that:

> there is a need to look to the goal of complete Buddhahood, which is ultimate fulfillment from both one's own and others' point of view. Moreover, one should not think to gain Buddhahood merely for one's own benefit. One should want it purely in order to be able to more efficiently and deeply benefit sentient beings. Just as you have fallen into the ocean of samsaric misery, so have all others; and they, like you, know only frustration and misery.
>
> (Trans. by Mullin in S. Gyatso 1982: 109–10)

The causes of generating *bodhicitta* in general, and the meditations in particular, differ somewhat in different texts. In later Indian and Tibetan Buddhism, however, there are frequently said to be two meditations which, practised carefully and repeatedly, will lead eventually to the arising of *bodhicitta*.

The first meditation is called the 'six causes and one effect'. As a preliminary the meditator is required to produce a feeling of equanimity or equality, 'an unbiased attitude' towards all sentient beings. He or she visualizes in front an enemy, a friend, and one to whom feelings are neutral. All are really alike. In the endless series of rebirths each has been a friend, an enemy, and neutral many times, each has helped and hindered. None is really, inherently, a friend or enemy. Each, even in this life, can become enemy or friend, or a person to whom one no longer has any feeling. Thus we generate a feeling of equanimity, of equality towards all. Now, briefly, for the six causes and one effect: (i) Since we have all had infinite births in the past, so each sentient being no matter how lowly has been our mother in this or previous births infinite times (and every other relationship, of course). (ii) As our mothers, beings have been immensely kind to us, undergoing great sufferings and trouble for our sake.[16] (iii) At the present time all our 'mother sentient beings' are undergoing great sufferings. What can we do? We have a duty, an obligation, to repay their kindness by helping them all to the uttermost limit of our ability. The Third Dalai Lama states:

> Like members in a drunken procession staggering towards a cliff, they are stumbling over the precipice of evil into the suffering of

cyclic existence and the lower realms. Think, 'If I do not do something for these pathetic, feeble beings, who will? ... Were I to ignore these kind beings and work only for my personal liberation from samsara, what lack of conscience and consideration!'

(S. Gyatso 1982: 116)

(iv) and (v) In the light of this the meditator generates great love, 'May these mother sentient beings have happiness, and may I contribute towards their happiness', and great compassion, 'May they be free of suffering, and may I help them to become free'. (vi) Finally, one decides to take upon oneself the responsibility for helping all sentient beings. However, the next question is whether it is actually possible to do very much to help even a few beings, let alone every single one? Meditating in this way, the practitioner concludes that it is only possible to fulfil one's aspirations and duty to all sentient beings by becoming a fully enlightened Buddha, with all the abilities and powers of a Buddha to help others.

Thus one generates the 'one effect', the *bodhicitta*, the altruistic aspiration to perfect enlightenment for the benefit of all sentient beings.

The second meditation for developing *bodhicitta* is called 'Exchanging self and others'. First, one meditates that all are equal in that all beings, like me, desire happiness and the avoidance of suffering. Śāntideva says:

Hence I should dispel the misery of others
Because it is suffering, just like my own,
And I should benefit others
Because they are sentient beings, just like myself.

When both myself and others
Are similar in that we wish to be happy,
What is so special about me?
Why do I strive for my happiness alone?[17]

Next, one becomes aware that each person individually is as important as I am, and therefore, objectively, since others are greater in number than I am so, as an aggregate, others are always more important than myself. Thus, in helping, it is rational to help others rather than myself. The meditator may at this point repeat the equanimity meditation given above. Then, he or she meditates on the faults and problems involved in cherishing self rather than others. Śāntideva states that

All misery in the world derives from
Desiring happiness for oneself;

> All happiness in the world arises from
> Desiring the happiness of others.
>
> (Trans. in T. Gyatso 1979: 139)

The result is that one is able to 'exchange self with others'. The Dalai Lama strongly asserts that ' "The only purpose of my existence is to be used by others and to serve others". This idea, this attitude, this determination must arise from the depths of one's heart, from the very depths of one's mind' (ibid., 140).

The foregoing is linked with a practice known as 'giving and taking', in which the meditator visualizes in front of him or her beings suffering in various situations or realms, and imagines that he or she is taking on their sufferings with the inhaling breath, and breathing out happiness, which transmutes the negative situation of sentient beings into one of happiness and bliss. Tibetans will often state that when this practice is perfected, a Bodhisattva can genuinely take onto himself or herself the sufferings and illnesses of others.[18]

Thus arises the *bodhicitta*. Atiśa describes a ritual for taking the Bodhisattva vows in front of a suitable master.[19] The original idea appears to have been that one would make a resolution in front of the Buddha himself. According to a later version of the ceremony, three times the aspirant repeats:

> May all the buddhas and bodhisattvas abiding in the ten directions deign to take notice of me! May the master deign to take notice of me! I, named so-and-so, by virtue of wholesome roots developed from giving, from morality and from meditation in this and other rebirths – that I have done, had done, or appreciated the doing of – just as previous tathāgata, arhat, completely fulfilled lord buddhas and bodhisattvas great heroes abiding on a high stage, first generated the thought towards supreme, right and full awakening, so likewise, from this time forth until reaching the site of awakening, in order to ferry over the stranded, to release the bound, to revive the breathless, to bring to nirvana those not yet in nirvana, I generate a thought towards supreme, right and full great awakening.
>
> (Trans. by Tatz in Gyaltsen 1982: 30)

With the completion of this ceremony the aspirant is a Bodhisattva, and is deemed to have undertaken certain commitments, including never abandoning any sentient being, or retreating into the lower aspiration of the Arhat vehicle. The most moving statement of the aspirations and hopes of a Bodhisattva who has generated *bodhicitta* is found, as always, in Śāntideva:

> May I be the doctor and the medicine
> And may I be the nurse
> For all sick beings in the world
> Until everyone is healed.
>
> May a rain of food and drink descend
> To clear away the pain of thirst and hunger
> And during the aeon of famine
> May I myself change into food and drink.
>
> I become an inexhaustible treasure
> For those who are poor and destitute;
> May I turn into all things they could need
> And may these be placed close beside them. (3: 8–10)

According to the texts, it is only said to be *bodhicitta* if the compassion is embedded in an awareness of emptiness. Thus *bodhicitta* is said to have the nature of emptiness and compasson. Ever since at least as early as the *Saṃdhinirmocana Sūtra*, however, it has been asserted that there are two types of *bodhicitta* – the ultimate and the conventional or relative *bodhicittas*. Ultimate *bodhicitta* is, according to the *sūtra*, 'beyond this world, cannot be formulated by concept or speech, is extremely radiant, the image of the Ultimate, immaculate, unshakeable, and very bright like the steady glow of a lamp on a calm night'.[20] Since the *Saṃdhinirmocana Sūtra* is a Cittamātra text, it seems likely that ultimate *bodhicitta* (etymology: enlightenment mind) is the pure radiant mind of an enlightened being, possessed of compassion. For Sthiramati, in common with the *Saṃdhinirmocana Sūtra*, the *bodhicitta* is equal to the *dharmakāya* 'as it manifests itself in the human heart' (Suzuki 1963: 299; cf. the *tathāgatagarbha*). From the point of view of a Prāsaṅgika like Tsong kha pa, too, there is no problem in seeing the ultimate *bodhicitta* as the mind stream of a Bodhisattva or Buddha endowed with compassion and directly cognizing emptiness (cf. Hopkins 1984: 56).

Conventional *bodhicitta*, the moral *bodhicitta*, *bodhicitta* properly speaking, is also of two types – aspiring and engaging *bodhicittas*. Śāntideva says:

> As is understood by the distinction

between aspiring to go and (actually) going,
So the wise understand in turn
The distinction between these two. (1: 16)

Kamalaśīla does not differ substantially from this:

> Now this intention is the initial yearning for Buddhahood: 'Oh, that I might be a Buddha, for the sake of all beings!' And the setting forth [engaging] is the actual making of a vow to become a Buddha, and the actual accumulation of the stocks of merit and knowledge.[21]

Thus the Bodhisattva who truly wishes to help others, or, even better, who spontaneously produces the wish to help sentient beings whenever he or she sees suffering, has generated aspiring *bodhicitta*. Actually engaging in the practices of the Bodhisattva path, the perfections and so forth, with this as a basis, is the engaging *bodhicitta*. It is along this path that we shall now follow.

BODHISATTVA STAGES, PATHS AND PERFECTIONS

With the arising of the *bodhicitta*, according to the *Sūtra on the Ten Stages*, the *Daśabhūmika Sūtra*, the Bodhisattva enters the first of the stages (*bhūmi*) on the path to Buddhahood, a stage known as 'Joyous'. It appears, however, that there must have been circulating at one time a number of schemes on the Bodhisattva's path, for a text such as the *Bodhisattvabhūmi* has quite a different plan. As time passed some attempt was made to bring these different schemes into line, and we find this in the systematic plan given, for example, in Kamalaśīla's *Bhāvanākrama* (and briefly by Atiśa), and followed in Tibet by, say, the dGe lugs tradition.

According to the plan of the *Bhāvanākrama*, the Bodhisattva, once *bodhicitta* has arisen, has not yet attained the first Bodhisattva stage, but must strive in wisdom and means, without neglecting either (as does Ho-shang Mahāyāna). 'Means' here refers to the five perfections of giving, morality, patience, effort, and meditative concentration. 'Wisdom' refers to the perfection of wisdom. Thus it is important for the Bodhisattva to combine the three types of wisdom – from study, deep consideration, and meditation – with skilful means which will prevent any neglect of the welfare of others. In particular, Kamalaśīla advocates that the Bodhisattva now devote time to meditative practice and the development, if it has not been developed before, of perfect calm abiding (*śamatha*). He thus gains the ability to enter the various trances and meditative states familiar from other systems of meditation. With the attainment of calm abiding our Bodhisattva can learn to combine it with analytic insight into emptiness.

Both Kamalaśīla (implicitly) and Atiśa relate this process in the Bodhisattva's development after the arising of *bodhicitta* to a stage known as the Path of Accumulation (*sambhāramārga*). The schema of five 'paths' to enlightenment is known from non-Mahāyāna sources, and seems originally to have marked a different plan of the path from that of the ten stages. In Atiśa's and Kamalaśīla's schemes, and subsequently in Tibet, the two plans of 'paths' and 'stages' are combined in a way which does not always appear very satisfactory.[22]

The Path of Accumulation is entered, according to dGe lugs writers, when there arises a fully developed *bodhicitta*. This path has a number of stages, each of which is indicated by various attainments. For example, during the first stage of the Path of Accumulation one masters the Four Objects of Close Contemplation (*smṛtyupathāna* – trans. from Dhargyey 1976: 188). That is, one understands through close meditative examination the body, feelings, the mind, and all *dharmas*. In the third and final stage the meditator is said to develop through cultivating calm abiding the ability to visit celestial realms in order to make offerings and acquire merit, and also the ability to see teachers, and statues of the Buddha, as actual Buddhas.[23]

As we have seen in Chapter 3 on Madhyamaka above, when analytic meditation on emptiness itself generates calm abiding, then one is said to enter the second of the five paths, the Path of Preparation (*prayogamārga*). Kamalaśīla makes it clear that while a Bodhisattva at this stage is still technically an ordinary person (*pṛthagjana*) and not an Arya, a Noble Being, nevertheless he or she is quite beyond the stage and attainments of the average 'man in the street'. The Path of Preparation has four stages, known as heat, peak, patience, and supreme mundane *dharmas*, which indicate progressively deeper understanding and experience of emptiness, refining away all conceptual awareness and dualistic apprehension. Various attainments accompany his progress. He will never take rebirth again in the lower realms.[24] The Bodhisattva at this stage attains five powers of deep faith, armour-like exertion and perserverance, recollection (of the Four Noble Truths and their ramifications), meditative absorption – the combination of calm abiding and insight – and wisdom, the 'ability to examine the void nature of the Four Noble Truths'.[25]

When our Bodhisattva attains direct, non-conceptual, and non-dual vision of emptiness then he attains the Path of Insight (*darśanamārga*). At this point, according to the systemic account of Kamalaśīla and others, he enters the first Bodhisattva stage (*bhūmi*). At this stage also the Bodhisattva becomes an Arya, a Noble One, and has control over all his future rebirths. He gains many powers and attainments. Indeed, with progressively higher stages the Bodhisattva's attainments are multiplied to multicosmic proportions.[26] For example, it is said of a Bodhisattva at this first stage that he has twelve attainments. After rising from meditation he can, in just one instant:

> 1. see a hundred Buddhas; 2. receive the blessings of a hundred Buddhas; 3. go to a hundred Buddha Lands; 4. illuminate a hundred lands; 5. vibrate a hundred worldly realms; 6. live for a hundred eons; 7. see with true wisdom the past and future for a hundred eons; 8. enter into and rise from a hundred meditative stabilizations; 9. open a hundred different doors of doctrine; 10. ripen a hundred sentient beings; 11. emanate a hundred of his own body; 12. cause each of the hundred bodies to be surrounded by a hundred bodhisattvas.
>
> (Hopkins 1983: 100)

These twelve attainments are multiplied by powers of ten throughout each subsequent stage. Also onto the different stages of the Bodhisattva path are projected the numerical lists of spiritual practices and acquisitions formulated through the centuries of scholastic contemplation of the Buddha's attainments and path (although one should say that unfortunately there is not always consistency in different texts in attributing these to each stage). Thus at the third *bhūmi* the Bodhisattva attains the four meditations (*dhyāna*), the four non-material meditative absorptions, the four *brahmavihāras* of friendliness, compassion, sympathetic joy, and equanimity (surely, in the systematic plan we are looking at, these should have been attained already), and the five supernatural faculties of the divine eye, the divine ear, ability to know the thoughts of others, knowledge of birth and death – the previous births of himself and others – and wonder-working powers such as flying etc. (Dayal 1932: 106 ff.). At the fourth stage the Bodhisattva practises and attains the thirty-seven elements of enlightenment (ibid.: 80 ff.). And so on.

If we return now to our Bodhisattva on the first stage, the 'Joyous' stage, we are told that he (or she) is accordingly filled with joy, and makes ten great vows. Briefly, as enumerated by Dayal these are as follows:

(1) To provide for the worship of all the Buddhas without exception;

> (2) To maintain the religious discipline that has been taught by all the Buddhas and to preserve the teaching of the Buddhas; (3) To see all the incidents in the earthly career of a Buddha; (4) To realise the Thought of Enlightenment [*bodhicitta*], to practise all the duties of a bodhisattva, to acquire all the *pāramitās* [perfections] and purify all the stages of his career; (5) To mature all beings and establish them in the knowledge of the Buddha ... (6) To perceive the whole Universe; (7) To purify and cleanse all the buddha-fields; (8) To enter on the Great Way [Mahāyāna] and to produce a common thought and purpose in all bodhisattvas; (9) To make all actions of the body, speech and mind fruitful and successful; (10) To attain the supreme and perfect Enlightenment and to preach the Doctrine.[27]

The Bodhisattva can see many Buddhas and receive teachings from them. He develops various clairvoyances, can pass through objects and manifest in many forms at a time in order to help others (Dhargyey 1976: 197). In particular, the Bodhisattva at this first *bhūmi* concentrates on cultivating the perfection of giving (*dānapāramitā*) – although it should on no account be thought that the Bodhisattva only gives at this stage. It is rather a question of emphasis; no perfection is neglected at any stage on his path.

It is one of the features of the *Daśabhūmika Sūtra* that it correlates each of the ten stages with a different perfection. The more common scheme of six perfections is perhaps expanded to ten precisely for this purpose. The essence of giving is described as bestowing wealth with an unattached mind. Giving can be classified into three categories: material goods, fearlessness, and the Dharma itself, which is the highest of gifts because it has the highest, most perfect result (sGam po pa 1970: 153 ff.). The gift of fearlessness means to be a refuge to those in fear. According to the *Bodhisattvabhūmi* (a section of the Cittamātra work, the *Yogācārabhūmi*) 'A bodhisattva, when the proper time has come, gives with confidence and respect, with his own hands, and without harming others' (trans. in sGam po pa 1970: 156). However, the perfections become perfections inasmuch as they are embedded in an awareness of emptiness. The Bodhisattva in giving has no awareness of the inherent existence of giver, recipient, and gift. Among the specific objects which it is said a Bodhisattva might give are wealth, material objects such as food or clothing, his life or limbs, wife, children (but not parents), even poison if it is useful and given with compassion.[28] There are many stories, often incorporating folk legends, known throughout the Buddhist world in which Śākyamuni in a previous life as a Bodhisattva gives something terribly valuable freely and without question when asked or invited to do so.[29]

It may be worth mentioning at this point the phenomenon known as 'transference of merit'. An important part of Mahāyāna practice, marked at the end of every ceremony, and indeed every event which might be said to create merit for the participants, is the bestowing of whatever merit may have been attained to the benefit of other sentient beings. This appears to contradict the supposed rigidity of the law of *karma*. It is clear from the preceding that the wish of the Mahāyāna practitioner to give away his merit is part of a general wish to give away anything which may be of benefit, and also a constant reminder of the reason for undertaking the long journey to full enlightenment. That journey is solely for the benefit of others. In terms of the Bodhisattva's *own* motivation and aspirations, the issue of *others'* karmic results is scarcely relevant. The importance is his own intention. Nevertheless, in terms of emptiness and mind-dependence, the magical world of the Mahāyāna, when things are seen to lack inherent existence *karma* does loose its rigidity, and a benevolent intention (backed with insight) can work wonders! Thus the notion of transference of merit fits squarely within the ontology and spirituality of the Mahāyāna. Having said that, however, it should not be thought that the institution of transference of merit is solely or uniquely a Mahāyāna phenomenon. It is found throughout the Buddhist world. Inscriptional evidence in India shows that merit transference was a part of Buddhism from a very early date indeed. Gregory Schopen has clearly indicated that in inscriptions what distinguishes Mahāyāna from non-Mahāyāna transference of merit is that whereas in the latter case the merit is usually transferred to a particular person simply in order that the recipient should have the merit, in Mahāyāna inscriptions merit transference is always for the benefit of all sentient beings, usually in order that they may all attain perfect enlightenment.[30] It is likely that the doctrine of *karma* has rarely in practice been treated in as rigid a manner as some texts would suggest. There are texts which state that *karma* is never lost, no matter what happens, but in the context of Buddhist practice (which is, after all, what Buddhism is all about) it is likely that these texts took on an exhortative character ('Do not do evil deeds and think you can get away with it!'), and were not treated as making rigid doctrinal statements about the nature of things. *Karma* does not entail that a virtuous and generous person cannot give away his or her merit for the benefit of others. Who is to say that this generosity is misplaced in terms of the welfare of the recipient?

The fourth of the five paths is the Path of Cultivation (*bhāvanāmārga*), and all the remaining nine Bodhisattva stages, as well as the other perfections, occur during this path which (short of adopting Tantric practice, which can lead to Buddhahood in one lifetime) is said to take aeons of compassionate activity and striving to follow to its end. At the second *bhūmi*, the Immaculate or Pure, the Bodhisattva is said to be possessed of a perfectly pure morality. He thus practises the second of the perfections, the perfection of morality, and attains to their highest degree the ten good paths of action – three physical: abstention from killing, stealing, and sexual misconduct; four vocal: abstention from lying, slanderous, insulting, and frivolous speech; and three mental: abstention from greedy desire, malice, and false views. In perfecting these one learns to practise their opposites, cherishing and saving life and so on. Correct behaviour becomes natural. The Bodhisattva also commends this morality to others, and becomes their teacher, guide, and protector. Nevertheless, in spite of this morality, as Tsong kha pa points out, following Candrakīrti, 'if they do not abandon the view that phenomena inherently exist, then their ethics will not be pure but will be faulty though apparently proper' (on *Madhyamakāvatāra* 2:3ab, trans. in Hopkins 1980: 195). That is, the morality of one who does not understand emptiness cannot be pure, even if it appears to be so, for it is not the perfection of morality. Of course, the Bodhisattva at this stage also has the many miraculous meditative attainments that we have already seen, and is becoming progressively more wonderfully extraordinary!

According to Tsong kha pa and Candrakīrti, the third *bhūmi*, Luminous, is so called because when it is attained there appears a fire of wisdom which burns all knowables, and a light which extinguishes all elaborations of duality in meditative absorption, while in the Bodhisattva there appears a 'copper-like splendour' (Hopkins 1980: 204). The Bodhisattva thoroughly understands impermanence, and it is at this stage that the virtue of patience becomes perfected. The Bodhisattva is patient and not disturbed, we are told, even when his body is cut 'not just flesh but also bone, not in large sections but bit by bit, not continually but pausing in between, and not finishing in a short time but cutting over a long period' (ibid., 206)! He is perfectly patient and no anger arises. He views those who do the deed with infinite compassion.

According to sGam po pa, patience is of two sorts. First, the Bodhisattva counteracts any wish for hurting, he does not quarrel, does no harm in retaliation, and is not insistent (sGam po pa 1970: 175). Second, patience puts up with misery – that is to say, it means not being 'fatigued by hardships involved in realizing unsurpassable enlightenment and to accept them joyfully' (ibid., 178).[31] Besides perfecting patience at this stage, the Bodhisattva completely destroys desire and hatred, and also reaches various higher meditative absorptions. As a result of this, as we have seen, he attains the five supernatural faculties.

At the fourth stage, called Ignited, or Radiant, the Bodhisattva particularly cultivates the thirty-seven elements of enlightenment. These include the Four Objects of Close Contemplation (*smṛtyupasthāna*) of body, feelings, mind, and all *dharmas*, as well as various 'right exertions' and other miraculous abilities, faculties, powers, and so on (for details see Dayal 1932: 80 ff.). Here, we are told, the Bodhisattva's attachment to any sort of self comes to a complete end.[32] Also at this fourth stage the Bodhisattva acquires the perfection of effort (energy, heroism, or strength: *vīrya*). According to sGam po pa, this is the counteracting of laziness, idleness, faintheartedness, and so on – but, of course, on a heroic scale!

The fifth stage is called Difficult to Conquer, since the Bodhisattva is said to be unable to be conquered by any or all demons, the forces of evil. He practises uniformity and purified intention as regards the doctrines of past, present, and future Buddhas and so on.[33] At this stage our Bodhisattva masters the perfection of meditation. According to sGam po pa, the essence of this perfection lies in the 'tranquillity by which the mind abides within itself by the oneness of the good and wholesome' (sGam po pa 1970: 188). That is, the mind is one-pointed. Indeed, it is precisely at this point that treatises on the ten stages describe the attainment of calm abiding. But this provides obvious problems. We have seen that in the schema which combines the five paths and the ten stages calm abiding was a prerequisite to beginning the ten stages, and it seems out of place to introduce it here.[34] In fact we are dealing with a schema which probably originally progressed through six not ten stages, culminating in one-pointed absorption and wisdom. This schema was expanded to ten, and combined with the miraculous, cosmic scale of the *Daśabhūmika* world. Subsequently, it seems, the schema was grafted onto the five-path model. The result tries to include everything!

Through his meditation at this stage the Bodhisattva comes to know truly and correctly the Four Noble Truths, and also any other sort of truth (such as ultimate and conventional). He is aware, of course, that all *dharmas* lack inherent existence and are akin to illusions, but, according to the *Daśabhūmika Sūtra*, this simply increase his love and compassion all the more (Honda 1968: 176 ff.; Cleary 1986: 49). Since they may be useful, the Bodhisattva at this stage learns various secular arts such as mathematics and medicine, music and history.[35]

The sixth *bhūmi*, Approaching, is the stage at which our aspirant attains the perfection of wisdom. He is said to be concerned with the correct apprehension of dependent origination (*pratītyasamutpāda*). This in itself suggests the antiquity of a schema which culminated in wisdom, for the association of enlightenment with the formulae for dependent origination has been part of Buddhism from early times. Of course, as we have seen, in Madhyamaka dependent origination is associated with the lack of inherent existence. Things are neither born nor do they perish, but they are still involved in the appearance of birth and death. Nevertheless, it is paradoxical to find the Bodhisattva attaining the perfection of wisdom at this point, when direct insight into emptiness, the content of the perfection of wisdom, was a prerequisite to attaining the first *bhūmi*, and all the preceding perfections are only perfections precisely inasmuch as they are underpinned by an awareness of emptiness.

At the sixth *bhūmi* the Bodhisattva, with the mastery of wisdom, could if he so wished abandon the world and enter the peace of (Arhat) *nirvāṇa*. With wisdom he no longer has attachments. Without attachments, craving, the fuel of *saṃsāra* should cease. But the Bodhisattva is a Bodhisattva; he has developed great compassion and the *bodhicitta*. He does not practise for his own benefit but in order to fulfil his obligations to sentient beings. Thus, in a sense, we might say that a sliver of holy attachment (although we call it compassion) remains. There are Mahāyāna texts which make precisely this point.[36] Nevertheless, the compassion of the Bodhisattva is not really attachment as a moral or cognitive fault, for the Bodhisattva knows that there is no inherent existence and therefore he cannot have attachment. It is precisely because there is no inherent existence that the Bodhisattva can act in many miraculous ways for the benefit of others. And with no inherent existence, and no more taints, why should the Bodhisattva abandon the world and seek his own peace? Thus the Bodhisattva aims for the non-abiding *nirvāṇa* which is neither *saṃsāra* nor *nirvāṇa*.

Having refrained from entering a selfish *nirvāṇa* the Bodhisattva spends the remaining stages developing skilful means, entirely devoted to the welfare of others. He is now beyond all Hearers and Pratyekabuddhas, the followers of the non-Mahāyāna traditions.[37] From the eighth stage, the Immovable, the Bodhisattva begins the immense task of eradicating for ever the obscurations to ominiscience. From the seventh onwards he practises a further list of four perfections added to the original group of six: the perfections of skilful means, the vow (supremely highest vow), power, and gnosis or awareness (*jñāna*). At the seventh stage (Gone Afar), also, the Bodhisattva practises fully giving (!), pleasant speech, beneficent conduct, and impartiality. His mind is always absorbed in the Doctrine, even when asleep. He can manifest in whatever form he likes for the benefit of others, including that of an Arhat or, one assumes, a Buddha (cf. Honda 1968: 208; Cleary 1986: 71). Normally by the seventh stage, or the eighth, the progress of the Bodhisattva is said to be irreversible; he is destined for supreme Buddhahood and incapable of reverting to the methods of liberation and aspirations of the Arhats and Pratyekabbudhas. He could at any point attain Arhatship, but he refrains, now irreversibly, from doing so.

In entering the Immovable stage the Bodhisattva is said by the *Daśabhūmika Sūtra* to be like a man who has awakened from a dream, and who has abandoned all false conceptualizations. He begins to see the world in a new way, even when not meditating, a way which will eventually lead to the omniscient awareness of a Buddha (Honda 1968: 219; Cleary 1986: 77). All his activities at and after this stage are spontaneous or automatic, the results of his immense compassion and wisdom. There is no more striving, no more wanting, not even enlightenment. Events take their course naturally for the benefit of beings. All the Buddhas appear before our Bodhisattva and exhort him to attain Buddhahood (Honda 1968: 220; Cleary 1986: 78). He already appears to have many of the powers of a Buddha. He can split his body into infinite (or near infinite) forms, and can now definitely appear in the form of a Buddha if he so wishes for the benefit of others (Honda 1968: 224–5; Cleary 1986: 79–80). He has immense spiritual attainments, 'the details of which would take forever to tell' (Cleary 1986: 88)!

At the ninth stage, that of Good Intelligence, the Bodhisattva is said to acquire the knowledge and duties pertaining to all the vehicles – Arhats, Pratyekabuddhas, Bodhisattvas, and Tathāgatas. He thereby delivers the Buddha's message to all suffering sentient beings. At this stage also, and rather strangely, he finally attains the four analytical knowledge (*pratisaṃvid*) of *dharmas*, meaning, grammar, and exposition. In order words, at this rarefied level, with infinite bodies and incomprehensible miracles, the Bodhisattva masters grammar and becomes a wonderful preacher! Nevertheless, as a preacher the Bodhisattva really is quite special, for he can understand different questions from all the different beings in the entire cosmos in one go, and answer them all, each separately and satisfactorily with just one sound (Honda 1968: 244 ff.; Cleary 1986: 92 ff.)!

Finally the Bodhisattva attains the tenth stage, called the Cloud of Dharma. According to sGam po pa, this stage is so called because a Bodhisattva at this *bhūmi* 'lets the Dharma fall like rain and extinguishes the very subtle glow of conflicting emotions still held by sentient beings. Another reason is that it is covered by meditative absorption and mantras like the sky with clouds' (sGam po pa 1970: 250). The Bodhisattva enters into meditation and appears upon a wonderful jewelled lotus seat known as the Great King of Jewels. Many other Bodhisattvas appear, and light rays permeate all the directions which relieve the misery and sufferings of sentient beings. After further miracles and wonders the Tathāgatas consecrate our Bodhisattva to full Buddhahood (Honda 1968: 259 ff.; Cleary 1986: 101 ff.). He can now put into one atom of dust an entire world region, or put innumerable sentient beings into one pore of his skin, without their suffering injury or indeed noticing. He can manifest all the deeds in the earthly life of a Buddha as many times as he wishes throughout innumerable words (Honda 1968: 270–1; Cleary 1986: 107–8). sGam po pa observes:

> Further, from every pore of his skin he is able to pour out a continual stream of innumerable Buddhas and Bodhisattvas. He can make visible many living beings, gods and men. As Indra, Brahmā, Maheśvara [Hindu gods], a king, a Śrāvaka, a Pratyekabuddha or a Tathāgata he can teach the Dharma as necessary to those who are to be taught.
>
> (sGam po pa 1970: 251)

Such is the tenth stage Bodhisattva. Yet how does this compare with a Buddha? The question is absurd:

> Your question seems to me like that of a man who picks up a few pebbles and says, 'Which is bigger, the endless realms of the earth or these pebbles?' How can you compare the state of enlightening beings [Bodhisattvas] to that of buddhas, the completely enlightened, who have measureless knowledge.
>
> (Trans. in Cleary 1986: 110; cf. Honda 1968: 274)

Beyond the tenth stage is the stage of a Buddha, or the fifth of the five paths, that of No-more Learning (*aśaikṣamārga*). According to Tibetan traditions like the dGe lugs, to attain the final goal of complete Buddhahood requires Tantric practice. But then, according to the *tathāgatagarbha* traditions of Sino-Japanese Buddhism, such as Fa-tsang's Hua-yen, since all things interpenetrate, and the Buddha-nature is always present, one is already a Buddha, and all the stages are contained in the first. As Dōgen puts it, 'only Buddhas become Buddhas' (Cook 1977: 115). All these stages of a gradual path are perhaps confusion! Who is to say who is right?

CHAPTER TEN

Faith and devotion: the cults of Buddhas and Bodhisattvas

ON FAITH

If faith is first contrasted with reason, and seen as not just necessary but also sufficient for salvation, then it is true to say that, with the exception of the Shin traditions in Japan, Buddhism is not a religion where faith plays a central and overriding role. This is not to say, however, that faith is unimportant.

Faith is included, with vigour, mindfulness, concentration, and wisdom, among the five cardinal virtues. In the Abhidharma it is one of the ten virtuous mental states. Defining faith, the *Abhidharmakośa* commentary explains that it is mental clarity (on 2: 25). This definition is not itself very lucid, but it becomes clearer in the light of a discussion contained in a Pāli text, the *Milindapañha*. Faith 'makes serene'. 'When faith arises it arrests the (five) Hindrances, and the heart becomes free from them, clear, serene and undisturbed.' Faith clears the mind of its muddy defilements, as a miraculous gem might clear muddy water for drinking (trans. in Conze 1959: 152).

Thus faith is depicted in terms of its psychological results. It is a mind clear of the five hindrances: sense-desire, ill-will, sloth and torpor, excitedness and worry, and last but by no means least, doubt. These are primarily hindrances to meditative attainment. The *Milinda* also adds, however, that faith 'leaps forward':

> When the Yogin sees that the hearts of others have been set free, he leaps forward, by way of aspiration, to the various Fruits of a holy life, and he makes efforts to attain the yet unattained, to find the yet unfound, to realize the yet unrealized.
>
> (Conze 1959: 153)

In other words, faith provides both the cognitive basis and the volition for spiritual growth. Faith is faith that certain things are the case, and because of this, certain behaviour is appropriate. The result of appropriate behaviour is enlightenment, a transcendence of faith to a knowing of those things which were previously only believed. Again, the *Abhidharmakośa* commentary explains that, according to some, faith (*śraddhā*) is adherence to the doctrine of karmic results (that is, *karma* and rebirth), the Three Jewels, and the Truths, which is to say the Four Noble Truths and their ramifications (on 2: 25). Indian Mahāyāna does not appear to be substantially different. The *Akṣayamati Sūtra* speaks of faith as accepting *karma* and rebirth, the Bodhisattva-ideal, the teachings of emptiness, and the qualities of a Buddha – 'and when in his faith he has left behind all doubts, he brings about in himself those qualities of a Buddha' (trans. in Conze *et al.* 1964: 185). This faith need not be an unreasoned faith. According to an old Buddhist formula, a person first hears the doctrine and then reasons about it. If it makes rational sense then he or she puts it into practice and eventually comes to know directly the truth. The Buddha himself is reported to have said that something should not be held out of respect for him, but only if it makes sense.

Thus far faith, theoretically a reasoned faith, forms the starting point, the basis, for the Buddhist path. Nāgārjuna says that 'Through faith one relies on the practices, Through wisdom one truly knows, Of these two wisdom is the chief, Faith is its prerequisite'.[1] Faith is thereby the first stage of a process the end of which is wisdom. It is the preliminary, an articulation of our inadequacy, eventually transcended by coming to know directly those things which were previously perceived darkly through the cloud of faith. Meditation *particularly* centred on faith was recommended for practitioners of a specific mental type. Those whose minds are dominated by greed are recommended in Theravāda sources, for example, to develop in their practices the faith dimension.[2] But faith here has nothing to do with religious devotion as such. It is merely a practical antidote to a particular moral and spiritual stain. Faith could not begin to have anything to do with reciprocal religious concern (as in the Hindu *bhakti* cults, for example) until it was co-ordinated with a doctrine of

Buddhas and Bodhisattvas who are available and willing to relate to human beings and human concerns. Still, in our discussion of faith we can detect certain elements which may have been conducive to the growth of devotionalism. First, faith embraces faith *in* certain things, one of which is the Buddha himself, and his superior qualities. Second, faith is particularly cultivated by specific mental types. When these two points are combined with the practices and experiences of 'recollection of the Buddha', and with the Mahāyāna idea of enduring Buddhas and powerful compassionate Bodhisattvas, a foundation is constructed for the development of some form of Mahāyāna devotionalism.

BUDDHĀNUSMṚTI – RECOLLECTION OF THE BUDDHA

The *Sutta Nipāta* of the Pāli canon is generally held by scholars to be one of the oldest extant Buddhist texts. At the very end of the *Sutta Nipāta*, in a section also held to be among the oldest strata of that text, is a wonderfully moving and, I think, potentially significant discussion. A Brahmin named Piṅgiya 'the wise' praises the Buddha in heartfelt terms:

> They call him Buddha, Enlightened, Awake, dissolving darkness, with total vision, and knowing the world to its ends. ... This man ... is the man I follow ... This prince, this beam of light, Gotama, was the only one who dissolved the darkness. This man Gotama is a universe of wisdom and a world of understanding.[3]

Why is it, Piṅgiya is asked, that you do not spend all your time with the Buddha, that wonderful teacher? Piṅgiya replies that he himself is old, he cannot follow the Buddha physically, 'my body is decaying'. But:

> there is no moment for me, however small, that is spent away from Gotama, from this universe of wisdom, this world of understanding.... with constant and careful vigilance it is possible for me to see him with my mind as clearly as with my eyes, in night as well as day. And since I spend my nights revering him, there is not, to my mind, a single moment spent away from him.
>
> (vv. 1140, 1142)

In this ancient and extraordinary discussion Piṅgiya indicates that it was possible through his awareness, through his meditation, for him to be constantly in the presence of the Buddha and constantly to revere him.

Towards the end the Buddha himself testifies that Piṅgiya too will go to 'the further shore' of enlightenment.

The interpretation of this discussion is perhaps difficult. One certainly should not assume that we have here a fully-fledged devotionalism. Nevertheless, Piṅgiya's praise of the Buddha and his reference to seeing him with the mind appear to connect with the practice of *buddhānusmṛti*, a practice known from other contexts in the Pāli canon and practised by, as far as we can tell, all schools of Buddhism.

According to the Theravāda commentator Buddhaghosa, a meditator who wishes to practise recollection of the Buddha should go to a favourable spot for retreat:

> and recollect the special qualities of the Enlightened One ... as follows: 'That Blessed One is such since he is accomplished, fully enlightened, endowed with (clear) vision and (virtuous) conduct, sublime, the knower of worlds, the incomparable leader of men to be tamed, the teacher of gods and men, enlightened and blessed'.[4]

The meditator recollects the features of the Buddha systematically and in detail. Among the results of such a meditation are that, in the words of Buddhaghosa, the meditator

> attains the fullness of faith, mindfulness, understanding and merit.... He conquers fear and dread.... He comes to feel as if he were living in the Master's presence. And his body ... becomes as worthy of veneration as a shrine room. His mind tends towards the plane of the Buddhas. (p. 230)

If tempted to wrongdoing, our meditator feels as much shame as if face to face with the Buddha. Even if his spiritual progress stops at this stage, he will progress to a 'happy destiny'. Three points are particularly worth noting here. First, there is the connection of *buddhānusmṛti* with attaining to a higher plane, a happy destiny, or the 'plane of the Buddhas'. Second, through recollection of the Buddha one becomes free from fear. We know from a Sanskrit *sūtra* source that *buddhānusmṛti* was particularly recommended as an antidote to fear (Tsukamoto 1985: 2, 1038–9). And third, through recollecting the Buddha, Buddhaghosa says, the meditator comes to feel as if he were living in the presence of the Buddha himself – so much so, that shame would deter him from evil deeds. How is this possible if the Buddha has died and is beyond recall? Is the result of recollection of the Buddha just a profound hallucination?

Fear, and the desire to see the Buddha, were, I think, important feelings in the centuries, perhaps even the decades, after the death of the Buddha. The *Gaṇḍvyūha Sūtra* speaks for many Buddhists when it states that:

> It is difficult, even in the course of hundreds of kotis of aeons, to hear a Buddha preach;
> How much more to see him, his sight being the supreme remover of all hesitations ...
> Better it is to roast for Kotis of aeons in the three states of woe, terrible though they are,
> Than not to see the Teacher....
> Annulled are all the sufferings when one has seen the Jina, the Lord of the world,
> And it becomes possible to enter on gnosis, the sphere of the supreme Buddhas.
>
> (Trans. in Conze *et al.*, 1964: 188–9)

According to Paul Harrison, although there were a number of recollections common in non-Mahāyāna Buddhism, in Mahāyāna texts only recollections of the Buddha, Doctrine, and Community are important, with recollection of the Buddha by far the most significant. Harrison suggests that while at first the Buddha was someone to be emulated, as time passed and memories faded he became more an object of devotion (Harrison 1978: 37). Rather, I suspect, as time went on so the Buddha became more an object to be reached, an object with whom one might hope to enter into a real relationship as was experienced when he was present on earth. A need for the Buddha to be present, to console, clarify, teach, and perhaps protect, was a significant factor in the development of Buddhism in the centuries after the death of the Master. In particular, I have suggested that the Buddha seen in meditation, and heard to teach ('living in the Master's presence'), was a significant factor in the origins of the Mahāyāna, and Mahāyāna *sūtra* literature. The ancient practice of *buddhānusmṛti* was a practice well adapted to the needs of Śākyamuni's followers in the years after his death.

There is a passage contained in the *Ekottarāgama*, part of the canon which survives in Chinese translation, in which there is given a far more detailed account of recollection of the Buddha than can be found in the Pāli canon. In this *sūtra*, recollection of the Buddha is said to lead to magic powers and even to *nirvāṇa* itself (Harrison 1978: 38). With the Mahāyāna doctrine of infinite Buddhas and Bodhisattvas dwelling in infinite Buddha Lands of the ten directions (a doctrine perhaps itself influenced by the experiences of *buddhānusmṛti*) the practice of recollection of the

Buddha gained still further in importance as a means of contacting those Buddhas and their realms. The *Saptaśatikā Prajñāpāramitā* describes the 'Single Deed Samādhi' by which one can quickly attain supreme enlightenment. The meditators

> should live in seclusion, cast away discursive thoughts, not cling to the appearance of things, concentrate their minds on a Buddha, and recite his name single-mindedly. They should keep their bodies erect and, facing the direction of that Buddha, meditate upon him continuously. If they can maintain mindfulness of the Buddha without interruption from moment to moment, then they will be able to see all the Buddhas of the past, present, and future right in each moment.[5]

What better way to attain enlightenment quickly than to see and receive teachings from not just one but infinite Buddhas? All the more so as social, political, and doctrinal circumstances in India suggested that people were entering the Dark Ages, the Last Days, when enlightenment on this earth (bereft of a Buddha) would be very difficult if not impossible to attain.

There is reason to believe that historically the development and promulgation of *buddhānusmṛti* practices may have something to do with the important meditation schools of Kashmir. We know that Kashmir was renowned throughout Central Asia and China for its teachers of meditation, and texts in which non-Mahāyāna and Mahāyāna elements were mixed, but with a strong emphasis on recollection of the Buddha, composed in Kashmir and translated into Chinese by Kashmiri meditation masters were important in fifth-century Chinese Buddhism.[6] The elaborate and sophisticated Buddhist meditation techniques were among the most important elements that attracted Chinese to the foreign religion. The great missionary Kumārajīva, himself from Central Asia (Kuchā), spent some time in Kashmir and had a close interest in the practice of recollection of the Buddha. *Buddhānusmṛti* was also of deep importance to Hui-yüan (*c.* 334–416), who practised the *pratyutpanna samādhi*, apparently a form of *buddhānusmṛti*, and corresponded on the subject with Kumārajīva. Accordingly, let us look more closely at the *pratyutpanna samādhi*, and Hui-yüan's experience of it.

THE *PRATYUTPANNA SAMĀDHI*, AND HUI-YÜAN

The *Pratyutpanna Sūtra* was first translated into Chinese by Lokakṣema in perhaps 179 CE. This makes it one of the earliest Chinese translations of a Buddhist *sūtra*. It contains the earliest datable literary reference to Amitāyus (= Amitābha) and his Buddha Field, his Pure Land, in the west. Among the many interesting and unusual features of this early *sūtra* is the detail with which it describes and discusses the *pratyutpanna samādhi*, which appears to be the principal message of the *sūtra*.

The basis for practising the *pratyutpanna samādhi* is a strict morality. A practitioner, lay or monastic, male or female, is requested to fulfil completely the moral code before entering into retreat. The meditator then retires to a secluded place and reflects on which direction the Buddha Amitāyus dwells. He or she then concentrates on that Buddha, presumably facing the correct direction. The meditation conforms with what we have seen already of *buddhānusmṛti* practices. The practitioner contemplates the Buddha as being directly in front:

> the bodhisattva should ... fix his mind on those Tathāgatas ... as sitting on the Buddha-throne and teaching the Dharma. He should fix his mind on the Tathāgatas as being endowed with the best of all modes ... fair in appearance, beautiful, pleasing to look upon, and endowed with perfect development of body [etc.].[7]

Elsewhere cognitive as well as bodily excellences of the Buddha are noted and contemplated. Moreover, our meditator is exhorted not to give rise to the notion of 'self' in any way for three months, or sleep, or sit down 'except to perform the bodily functions' for three months (p. 44). Thus he should concentrate on Amitāyus

> for one day and night, for two, three, four, five, six, or seven days and nights. If he concentrates on the Tathāgata Amitāyus with undistracted thought for seven days and nights, then when seven days and nights have elapsed he shall see the Lord, the Tathāgata Amitāyus. If he does not see that Lord by day, then in a dream while sleeping the face of the Lord ... will appear. (p. 43)

And having seen the Buddha, our meditator can worship him, and receive teachings. This seeing of the Buddha is not with the 'divine eye', it is not the result of magic powers. The meditator does not need to develop the various supernatural faculties such as the divine eye which, as we saw in the last chapter, are only developed at the third Bodhisattva stage, and were thought in other texts to be the means by which one can see the Buddhas of the ten directions. The Buddhas seen in the *pratyutpanna samādhi* are said to be apprehended on the analogy of dreams. This is possible because all is empty of inherent existence, and all is likewise Mind Only (pp. 46 ff.).

In September 402, Hui-yüan and 123 others, monastic and lay, took a vow before an image of Amitāyus/Amitābha at Lu Shan, Lu Mountain, the monastic community which Hui-yüan had established and where he lived for many years before his death. The group was a 'mutual support' group, and their vow a covenant to help each other to be reborn in Sukhāvatī the Happy Place, Amitāyus' Pure Land in the west.[8] Hui-yüan's posthumous prestige in Chinese Buddhism was very great indeed, and it is from the time of the Lu Shan vow that subsequent devotees date the arrival of Pure Land Buddhism in China. Hui-yüan's group was, as Zürcher notes, 'a religious conterpart of the cliques of gentry politicians who monopolized the top functions in the bureaucratic hierarchy' (Zürcher 1972: 220). If one practitioner attained Sukhāvatī earlier than the others, he would return or manifest in some form in order to help the others. The method to be used in treading the path to Amitāyus' Pure Land was to be the *pratyutpanna samādhi*.

We know that subsequently, however, Hui-yüan faced some doubts as to how to assess the visions seen as a result of the *pratyutpanna samādhi*. Were they all, in the words of Etienne Lamotte, *de l'autosuggestion pure*? This subject forms one of the topics of Hui-yüan's correspondence with Kumārajīva when the latter was in the Chinese capital of Ch'ang-an (405/6 onwards). The problem reflects perhaps a controversy which was already raging, probably again originating from Kashmir, between the partisans of the divine eye and those of the *pratyutpanna samādhi* as the most effective (and easiest) way of seeing the Buddhas.[9] Kumārajīva advised Hui-yüan that the experiences gained through the *pratyutpanna samādhi* could be very valuable, although his general attitude seems to have been decidedly lukewarm. All the Buddhas are anyway empty of inherent existence, and one should not become attached to these experiences (Tsukamoto 1985: 2, 853–4). It is worth noting that in spite of its importance at this stage in China, the *Pratyutpanna Sūtra* does not appear to have been an important *sūtra* in the doctrinal development of Indian Buddhism.

One feature which led to the growth of Pure Land Buddhism in China, however, was a pessimism and consequential spiritual escapism which accompanied the political traumas of the centuries prior to the T'ang dynasty (prior to 618 CE). This pessimism was very much felt during the lifetime of Hui-yüan, and was renewed during the declining years of the T'ang, especially after the rebellion of An Lu-shan (755–63; see Weinstein 1987: 59 ff.). Moreover, in the centuries during which Buddhism was transmitted to China the doctrine of *karma* had proved particularly compelling and in a way attractive to the Chinese mind, although it also created a nervousness about the future and a further pessimism about the potential of 'fallen man'. Hui-yüan himself was a strict moral disciplinarian. He is said to have died while his fellow monks searched the scriptures in order to find whether it was permissible to give him honey and water to drink. The aged Hui-yüan had refused medicinal alcohol (Zürcher 1972: 253). There is no doubt that the *Pratyutpanna Sūtra*'s emphasis on morality was one of the factors which attracted him to the *sūtra*. The other was that it indicated a way of meeting the Buddha, a sage, in order to have questions answered and doubts cleared. To meet a true sage was very difficult in Hui-yüan's China (Tsukamoto 1985: 2, 845–6). After death Hui-yüan hoped for rebirth in the presence of Amitāyus. The Neo-Taoists too sought a life after death living in harmony with Nature (Liebenthal 1955: 50–1). Ascent of the Holy Man to a heavenly abode was very much part of Chinese culture, and Hui-yüan's reported description of Sukhāvatī in his biography carries with it the authentic flavour of a Taoist paradise – in spite of the fact that Hui-yüan also shows a clear awareness that rebirth in the Buddha's Pure Land is for the purpose of improving facilities for the final attainment of *nirvāṇa* (Zürcher 1972: 245).

There is another aspect of Pure Land teaching which I suspect made it attractive to the Chinese mind. The search for longevity had long been a Chinese concern, particularly among Taoist magicians and alchemists. We know of an important later Pure Land scholar, T'an-luan (476–542), who sought through Taoist techniques to attain long life in order to devote himself further to the study of Buddhism. According to the traditional account, T'an-luan subsequently met an Indian missionary, Bodhiruci. T'an-luan put to him a straightforward question:

> 'Is there any Indian Buddhist scripture which is superior to the Taoist scripture, *Book of Immortals*, in the teaching of prolonging life?' Bodhiruci spat on the ground and shouted in anger. 'How dare you say such a thing. The Taoist book is quite insignificant in comparison with Buddhist *sūtras*. Where in this country can you find the true teaching of attaining eternal life? By practicing Taoism you may prolong your life beyond the fixed limit, but like other people you must meet death sooner or later....'
>
> (Trans. in Matsumoto 1986: 37)

Bodhiruci taught T'an-luan of Amitāyus and his practice (the name means 'Infinite Life'). Through the method of Amitāyus one can attain to immortality (Amitāyus and his Pure Land), and also to ultimate liberation, *nirvāṇa*. In the search for longevity the Buddha's Pure Land was infinitely superior to Taoist magic, and the potions which killed at least one Chinese emperor who sought to prolong his life!

THE NOTION OF A BUDDHA FIELD (*BUDDHAKṢETRA*)

From the perspective of Buddhist cosmology space, like time, is infinite. Infinite space is full of infinite universes, world systems, stretching to the ten directions (the four cardinal points, four intermediate directions, up and down). Within these infinite reaches some universes are known as Buddha Fields or Buddha Lands. Generally, this term denotes an area, a cosmos, where a Buddha exerts his spiritual influence.

The concept of a Buddha Field, while of considerable importance in Mahāyāna thought, is not unique to the Mahāyāna. The *Mahāvastu*, which is a Lokottaravāda text, points out that there are many, many universes or world systems which are devoid of a Buddha, for Buddhas are relatively very rare. Moreover, the *Mahāvastu* notes, there cannot be two Buddhas in the same Buddha Field, for this would imply that one Buddha is not adequate to his task. And even though Buddhas are relatively rare, still, throughout the infinite universes there are innumerable Buddhas, and innumerable tenth-stage Bodhisattvas who are about to become Buddhas. Each leads infinite beings to liberation, and yet there is no chance that eventually all will be liberated and no one will be left. For with infinite sentient beings, even if infinite Buddhas each liberates another infinite beings, still there are infinite suffering sentient beings left (trans. by Jones in *Mahāvastu* 1949–56: I, 96 ff.)!

Human beings live in a world sphere called *Sahā*, in the south, for which the current Buddha is Śākyamuni. The notion of a Buddha Field seems to have arisen from a consideration of Śākyamuni's knowledge on the one hand – the field of his awareness – and his authority and influence on the other – his field of activity (see Rowell, 1935: esp. 379–81; 1937). In addition, one can refer to the actual geographical area where the Buddha was born – although in the case of Śākyamuni it was a grove rather than a field! Naturally the sizes of these three fields are different. The Buddha's knowledge (and from a Mahāyāna perspective, his compassion) is infinite, although his direct spiritual power is exerted over a vast but finite area, his Buddha Field in the primary sense, the area in the centre of which the Buddha arose.

The principal function of a Buddha is to teach sentient beings in his Buddha Field. But the Buddha Field in this primary sense is not simply a place where the Buddha happens to have appeared. Rather, during his career as a Bodhisattva the Buddha-to-be is said to 'purify' his Buddha Field, and the Buddha Field is the result of his great compassion. In other words, the very existence of a Buddha Field depends upon the Buddha's wonderful career as a Bodhisattva. The Buddha's infinite deeds of wisdom and compassion have created his Buddha Field as an area where he can 'ripen' sentient beings. Beings themselves also contribute, for it is a place where they have been reborn through their deeds, as beings potentially able to be ripened. Moreover, a Bodhisattva can himself be reborn in the Buddha Field of a Buddha, in the Buddha's direct presence, or travel there in meditation. The Buddha Field is precisely a place where conditions are obviously advantageous to his spiritual progress. Thus a Buddha Field is both a place where a Bodhisattva can see the Buddha and pursue his or her career, and also the goal of the Bodhisattva's striving, his own Buddha Field purified for sentient beings through his own efforts (Rowell 1935: 385 ff., 406 ff.). And from his place within his realm one text informs us that three times a day, and three times a night, the Buddha surveys his Buddha Field in order to see who can be morally and spiritually helped (Lamotte 1962: 396–7).

So the Bodhisattva purifies his Buddha Field, and the realm within which the Buddha exerts his activity is the result of his purifying deeds as a Bodhisattva. This gives rise to a problem. It is agreed on all counts that the Sahā world of Śākyamuni is not a very pure place.[10] This world is indeed a thoroughly impure Buddha Field. Mahāyāna texts speak of three types of Buddha Field: pure, impure, and mixed. For example, in an impure Buddha Field there are non-Buddhists, suffering beings, differences of lineage etc., immoral beings, lower realms such as hells, inferior conduct and Inferior Vehicles (the non-Mahāyāna traditions), and so on. Bodhisattvas of excellent conduct, and the actual appearance of a Buddha, are rare.[11] This world of Śākyamuni is pretty grim for the pious follower of Mahāyāna! A pure Buddha Field, on the other hand, such as Amitāyus' Sukhāvatī, is something like this:

> well adorned, having no filth or evil, no tiles or pebbles, no thorns or thistles, no excrement or other impurities. Its soil shall be flat and even, having no high or low, no hills or crevices. It shall have vaiḍūrya [lapis lazuli] for earth, and jewelled trees in rows. With cords made of gold shall its highways be bordered. It shall be

> everywhere clean and pure, with jewelled flowers scattered about.
> (From *Lotus Sūtra*, trans. in Hurvitz 1976: 120)

Such a Pure Land has a Buddha who lives for a very long time (perhaps for all eternity), who does not abandon his flock, as Śākyamuni appears to have done after only forty or so years. There are many Bodhisattvas in that realm, and the devil, Māra, and his evil host cannot work their wicked ways. Obviously such a Pure Land is an excellent place for developing the path to enlightenment, while our Sahā world, particularly since the death of the Master, is not really so very good. Since there are infinite Buddha Fields, and therefore also infinite Pure Lands at this very moment throughout the ten directions, surely the overriding immediate task must be to visit these Pure Lands and eventually to be reborn there. Earlier Buddhism had taught that merit led to a heavenly rebirth after death, but all heavens are *saṃsāra*, impermanent and pervaded with final frustration and suffering. Now, therefore, one should practise the correct meditations (i.e. *buddhānusmṛti*) and direct the fruit of one's good deeds, merit, to be reborn in the chosen Pure Land. This is quite logical, and perfectly consistent with the development of Buddhist thought. The present world bereft of a Buddha is a difficult place in which to attain enlightenment. Nevertheless, in infinite universes there are still Buddhas, perhaps even Sākyamuni himself. It is possible to see them in meditation, and to hear their wonderful teachings. There is thus nothing to prevent one from being reborn in their presence. Consequently, the quest for *nirvāṇa*, or Perfect Buddhahood, requires in most cases the immediate goal of rebirth in a Pure Land in the presence of a Buddha.

But where does this leave poor Śākyamuni? His Buddha Field is impure, therefore Śākyamuni and his purifying activity as a Bodhisattva were obviously strikingly ineffective. To quote from Śāriputra in the *Vimalakīrtinirdeśa Sūtra*:

> If the buddha-field is pure only to the extent that the mind of the bodhisattva is pure, then, when Śākyamuni Buddha was engaged in the career of the bodhisattva, his mind must have been impure. Otherwise, how could this buddha-field appear to be so impure?
> (Trans. in Thurman 1976: 18)

Moreover Śākyamuni has now gone, while there are still many sentient beings here in this world to be saved. His compassion must therefore be defective.

There are a number of ways in which one can deal with these problems. First, one could simply say that all Buddhas are in fact identical. Śākyamuni appeared to help sentient beings at a particular time and place. Although he has died there are many other Buddhas, and also Pure Lands elsewhere. These Buddhas are continuing to help beings in this Sahā world. One could combine this with the scheme of the Buddha bodies. Śākyamuni was a Transformation Body, an emanation of another Buddha, who remains in a pure Buddha Field, still active in all ways for the benefit of sentient beings here on earth. In other words, the impure Buddha Field is not the primary Buddha Field, but is a skilful means of a Buddha who necessarily, as a Buddha, has a Pure Buddha Field. Alternatively this transmundane Buddha could himself be Śākyamuni (as in the *Lotus Sūtra*). Another strategy would be to see the Buddha Field as the range of a Buddha's activity, but not necessarily purified by his previous activity. He creates it as the most suitable Buddha Field for particular beings to be saved. This strategy was strikingly adopted by the *Karuṇāpuṇḍarīka Sūtra*, a *sūtra* which sought to restore Śākyamuni to pre-eminence in the face of Pure Land cults centred on Amitāyus and Akṣobhya. These other Buddhas teach sentient beings who can reach their Pure Lands. But the greatest Bodhisattvas, the real Bodhisattvas, vow to appear as Buddhas in *impure* realms, tainted Buddha Fields, out of their great compassion (Yamada 1968: I, 78). The very fact that Śākyamuni appeared in this Sahā realm, a ghastly place, indicates his remarkable compassion.

The most common solution to Śāriputra's dilemma, however, and of crucial importance in subsequent East Asian Buddhism, is that given by the *Vimalakīrtinirdeśa* itself. This impure Buddha Field is indeed the Pure Land. It only appears impure because of the minds of sentient beings dwelling in it. If there are mountains in this world, and all is flat in the Pure Land, that is because there are mountains in the mind! Śākyamuni is not a deficient Buddha. To him all is pure. The impurity is the result of impure awareness, and also the Buddha's compassion in creating a world within which impure beings can grow (Thurman 1976: 18–19; cf. Rowell 1937: 142 ff.). Thus the real way to attain a Pure Land is to purify one's own mind. Put another way, we are already in the Pure Land if we but knew it. This is very much like the Buddha-nature/*tathāgatagarbha* assertion that we are already fully enlightened Buddhas if we but recognize the fact, and it is only a short step from the Ch'an (Zen) notion that the Pure Land is the tranquil, clear, radiant, pure Mind. The Pure Land is truly, therefore, not a 'heavenly abode' but enlightenment itself.

SOME BODHISATTVAS

Maitreya

The truth that the Buddha discovered and taught was not unique to him. It is the true way of things, and 'whether Tathāgatas arise or do not arise the true way of things remains'. The idea that there were Buddhas previous to Śākyamuni must have originated fairly early, perhaps during the lifetime of the Buddha himself, and it is scarcely a dramatic inference to deduce from this that there will be further Buddhas in the future. Moreover if there are future Buddhas then the being who is to become the very next Buddha must already exist and be far advanced on his Bodhisattva path. That being is Maitreya (Pāli: Metteyya). Maitreya is the only present Bodhisattva with a 'celestial' status accepted by both the Mahāyāna and the non-Mahāyāna traditions.

A version of the story of Maitreya is contained in a Sanskrit work, the *Maitreyavyākaraṇa*, the *Prophecy of Maitreya*, which seems to have been an important text in establishing the Mahāyāna cult of Maitreya.[12] Life under the future Buddha Maitreya represents the Buddhist millennium, the second coming. Gods, men, and other beings will worship Maitreya and

> will lose their doubts, and the torrents of their cravings will be cut off: free from all misery they will manage to cross the ocean of becoming; and, as a result of Maitreya's teachings, they will lead a holy life. No longer will they regard anything as their own, they will have no possessions, no gold or silver, no home, no relatives! But they will lead the holy life of chastity under Maitreya's guidance. They will have torn the net of the passions, they will manage to enter into the trances, and theirs will be an abundance of joy and happiness; for they will lead a holy life under Maitreya's guidance.
>
> (Trans. in Conze 1959: 241)

Indeed, the story of Maitreya provided an impetus for messianic movements in China, associated sometimes with leaders who claimed to be prophets or incarnations of Maitreya. There were apparently nine such movements in China in the fifth and early sixth centuries alone (Zürcher in Berchert and Gombrich 1984: 202)! In Theravāda countries to the present day it is not uncommon to pray to be reborn on this earth at the time when Maitreya descends, there to become a monk and attain enlightenment under his tutelage.

Like Śākyamuni before his final birth, Maitreya now dwells in the Tuṣita heaven awaiting an opportune time to descend to the world. Since

Tuṣita is a heavenly realm and not a Pure Land, it is possible from the point of view of Mahāyāna and non-Mahāyāna traditions alike to visit there in meditation, and also to be reborn there. Not only this, but Maitreya is close to earth – literally, since Tuṣita is said to be much closer than a Pure Land. Maitreya visits this world in various forms to save and teach. Perhaps the best-known case is that of Asaṅga, where in the Tibetan version Maitreya takes Asaṅga to Tuṣita and delivers to him a series of texts containing details of the conduct of a Bodhisattva, and the Mind Only teachings. For this reason devotion to Maitreya was a particular concern of those who followed the Cittamātra. In China, for example, Hsüan-tsang vowed to be reborn in Tuṣita with Maitreya, and his translation and popularization of Mind Only works in China led to a revival of Maitreya worship.[13] One monk is said to have been carried to Tuṣita in meditation, and there granted the Bodhisattva ordination. According to Fa-hsien, in his account of his travels to India and Sri Lanka, through his powers an Arhat carried a sculptor to Tuṣita. The sculptor examined Maitreya and, on his return, created a colossal statue in a place north of Kashmir, which emitted light on fast days!

Maitreya's role as a visionary inspirer may be connected once more with the Kashmiri schools of meditation. Visions accompany meditation, and Kashmir was a centre of Mahāyāna and non-Manāyāna teaching, where a certain interfusion seems to have taken place. Maitreya was a Bodhisattva acceptable to both traditions, and it is not suprising therefore that Maitreya seems to have become a 'tutelary deity' of the Kashmiri meditators. It is quite possible also that Mind Only doctrines (Yogācāra) developed precisely in Kashmir, inspired by Maitreya, out of the contemplation of yogic experience (Demiéville 1954: 376 ff.).

Basham has pointed out, on the basis of inscriptions, that the whole phenomenon of celestial Bodhisattvas probably arose in North India. In Gandhāran art during the early centuries CE (which covers an area including Kashmir), Śākyamuni and Maitreya were apparently the most popular figures portrayed. From Kashmir, devotion to Maitreya spread to Central Asia and China. This spread began under the Kuṣāṇas, who held vast territories in Central Asia. We know that Maitreya was held in particular esteem in Central Asian Buddhism. At least one Maitreya *sūtra* may have been composed at the oasis site of Turfan. Maitreya also seems to have been a patron of missionaries. In Central Asia, Buddhism was in contact with various other cults, and several scholars have sought to connect the figure of Maitreya with Mithras, or posit the influence of Zoroastrianism. In spite of certain Central Asian iconographic features, however, I am inclined to agree with Basham that the figure of Maitreya and his role in Buddhism are perfectly comprehensible in terms of the development of Indian Buddhist ideas. This is not to say, however, that certain Central Asian or Zoroastrian ideas may not have influenced people's expectations – expectations of a heavenly helper, the need to opt positively for righteousness, the future millennium, and universal salvation – which were then focused on the figure of Maitreya, or other Mahāyāna Bodhisattvas and Buddhas (Basham 1981: 43). It is not surprising, moreover, that the figure of Maitreya was portrayed in Central Asian art in corresponding Central Asian guise.

In China the cult of Maitreya appears to have developed earlier than that of Amitāyus/Amitābha, and to have been for some time a rival to it. Hui-yüan's teacher, Tao-an (312–85), seems to have been pursued constantly by a fear of having distorted the Buddhist scriptures. Maitreya, as the Inspirer of Kashmir, had become the patron saint of exegetes, and Tao-an, together with a few of his disciples, is said to have prayed before an image of Maitreya in order to be reborn in Tuṣita and there receive final clarification of their doubts and uncertainties (Zürcher 1972: 194). Tsukamoto points out the significance of Maitreya as Śākyamuni's successor in a culture where family and unbroken lineage was of considerable importance (Tsukamoto 1985: 755). It seems likely that Tao-an and his disciples also practised some form of visualization and recollection centred on Maitreya. In 385 CE, Tao-an and his pupils are said to have received a vision of Tuṣita in this very life.

In art Maitreya is frequently portrayed not in the traditional lotus posture but rather seated on a throne in Western fashion. Depiction of Maitreya in his palace in the middle of Tuṣita may well have preceded historically the representation of the Pure Lands. In Central Asia there are many images and paintings of Maitreya surviving, placed particularly in the space above the door of a shrine, facing the main figure. Maitreya often carries a vase. Thus as the devotee turns to leave, having circumambulated the shrine, or prostrated to, say, Śākyamuni, he or she is confronted by the Buddha of the Future, awaiting his final birth on earth.[14] Gigantic statues of Maitreya were erected on the trade and pilgrimage routes through Afghanistan and Central Asia to China. It was apparently the custom to erect such a colossal statue on the border of each new country conquered by the faith – bound over to the millennium of Maitreya (Gaulier *et al.* 1976: 11). The custom of constructing such large statues may have given rise to the idea (or been influenced by the idea) that Maitreya is 80 cubits tall, a statement found in both Sanskrit and Pāli sources. This fact was witnessed, it seems, by the flying sculptor in Fahsien's travelogue.

In Asian art Bodhisattvas are generally portrayed as princes or princesses, with rich jewellery and robes, for they are indeed consecrated to succeed the Buddha as *dharmarāja*, Kings of the Doctrine. An exception to this is the fat, roly-poly 'Laughing Buddha' who is found in so many Western homes. He too is a Chinese form of Maitreya.[15] As in Central Asia, the Chinese cave sanctuaries also have a number of images of Maitreya. At Tun-huang, for example, there are large painted clay statues instantly identifiable by their 'Western' sitting posture.[16] There is also an impressive painting on silk from Tun-huang (ninth/tenth centuries) in the British Museum, depicting the delights of the world when Maitreya appears as a Buddha. The king and queen can be seen with shaved heads, renouncing the world to become enlightened under Maitreya's tutelage. Wedding feasts, ploughing, and reaping are old, pre-Buddhist devices for indicating a true age of plenty, the golden age of the past which is yet to come anew.[17]

Avalokiteśvara

In his (or her) different forms Avalokiteśvara is perhaps the most popular of all Mahāyāna Bodhisattvas. Like Maitreya, Mañjuśrī, and the others he is a Bodhisattva of the elevated tenth stage. We have already looked at one of the earliest sources for his cult, the Avalokiteśvara chapter of the *Lotus Sūtra*. This chapter frequently circulated as a separated *sūtra* in its own right. It describes how Avalokiteśvara will straightway heed those who call upon him, and save them from numerous sufferings – fire, rivers, storms on the ocean, murderers, demons and ghosts, prison (whether one be guilty or innocent), and also robbers. He will moreover remove lust, anger, and stupidity. He will grant sons or daughters to those who request him. Avalokiteśvara also appears in manifold different forms, whichever are most suitable for aiding, converting, and saving sentient beings. If a Buddha form is suitable, then he appears as a Buddha; if a Hearer form, as a Hearer; if a god, then as a god. We might add, if the form of a Jesus is suitable, then he appears in that form too. He appears as a householder, or as a monk; as a nun, boy, girl, or non-human. According to one Tibetan tale he appeared in the form of a cuckoo so that the birds too could hear the teaching of the Buddha. Tibetans also say that he appears among them in the form of His Holiness the Dalai Lama. Avalokiteśvara is the most wonderful compassionate saviour of the universe, constantly and tirelessly acting with all the powers of a tenth-level Bodhisattva for the benefit of all sentient beings without discrimination. As such, Avalokiteśvara is said to be the veritable incarnation of all the Buddhas' compassion, their essence, and very reason for being.[18] As compassion incarnate, Avalokiteśvara is concerned not only with enlightenment but with all the little sufferings of everyday life. Avalokiteśvara is a divine being to whom one can pray for aid and consolation.[19] Fa-hsien, on his long and dangerous journey to and from India, describes how he prayed earnestly to Avalokiteśvara to save him from shipwreck, and also to save him from his travelling companions, who would cast him adrift on a desert island as a bringer of bad luck!

The salvific powers of Avalokiteśvara are often depicted in Sino-Japanese art, frequently as block-print illustrations to popular tales concerning the Bodhisattva's miraculous interventions.[20] An ink and colour painting on silk from Tun-huang, dated 910 CE, portrays Avalokiteśvara with attendants, together with an inscription beseeching that the empire might be peaceful, that the Wheel of Doctrine perpetually turn in China, and that the donor's elder sister, teacher, and deceased parents may be reborn in the Pure Land (Zwalf 1985: 219). The Pure Land referred to here is Sukhāvatī, the Pure Land of Amitāyus, since Avalokiteśvara is also referred to in the various Amitāyus *sūtras* as one of the two Bodhisattvas who conduct the dead into the presence of Amitā yus. For this reason Avalokiteśvara is frequently portrayed in Buddhist art with a seated figure of Buddha Amitāyus(Amitābha) in his headdress, and is sometimes spoken of as an emanation of Amitāyus. Block-prints of Avalokiteśvara, together with a text in his honour, have been found in some quantity at Tun-huang, and it seems likely that these were used as protective talismans.

Apart from the *Lotus Sūtra*, the other principal Indian source for the Avalokiteśvara cult is the *Kāraṇḍavyūha Sūtra*. This text is entirely devoted to recounting and praising the miraculous deeds of the Bodhisattva. Avalokiteśvara descends into hell in order to save the suffering hell beings. The hot hells immediately become cool, lotuses appear, the torture cauldrons burst asunder. Hell is well and truly harrowed.[21] The Bodhisattva is praised as having one thousand arms and eleven heads, an important iconographic feature of one form of Avalokiteśvara. Quite extraordinarily, Avalokiteśvara is also said to have created the world, and all the Hindu gods with it:

> From his eyes arose the moon and sun, from his forehead Maheśvara (Śiva), from his shoulders Brahmā, from his heart Nārāyaṇa, from his teeth Sarasvatī, from his mouth the winds, from his feet the earth, and from his belly Varuṇa. When these gods were born from the body of Avalokiteśvara, then he said to the god Maheśvara, 'Thou shalt be Maheśvara in the Kali age, when the world of evil creatures arises. Thou shalt be called Adideva (the primal god), the creator, the maker....'
>
> (Trans. in Thomas 1952: 76–7)

Avalokiteśvara places the Hindu gods in their places, they rule by his permission. And yet he declares: 'I am no god, but a man, and have become a bodhisattva, having compassion on the abandoned and wretched, and a teacher of the way of enlightenment' (trans. in Thomas 1951: 191). Avalokiteśvara travels to Sri Lanka to save the demons who dwell there. In Benares (Varanasi) he hums the Doctrine in the form of a bee in order to save thousands of worms. Elsewhere he reveals his great *mantra*, the utterance which articulates and invokes his very being: *Oṃ maṇi padme hūṃ*.[22]

There is undoubtedly an iconographical connection of Avalokiteśvara with the Hindu god Śiva.[23] We have seen already that Avalokiteśvara bestows upon Śiva his place in the Hindu pantheon. Nevertheless, Avalokiteśvara himself is also called Maheśvara in the *Kāraṇḍavyūha* – Great Lord, a standard epithet of Śiva. He is described as 'a beautiful man ... wearing a diadem on his matted hair, his mind filled with the highest friendliness, and looking like a disc of gold' (Thomas 1952: 74). This could be a description of Śiva, for whom the matted hair is a symbol as Lord of the Yogins. In a lovely Kashmiri brass sculpture from *c.* 1000 CE, Avalokiteśvara is shown seated on Potalaka, his mountain home, with matted hair and deer. Behind is what initially looks very much like Śiva's trident. Śiva too dwells in the mountains as a yogin, and is associated with animals in his role of Lord of the Animals. Elsewhere Avalokiteśvara is described as 'blue-throated', a term for Śiva embedded in Śaivite mythology.[24]

Avalokiteśvara's mountain of Potalaka is frequently said to be somewhere in the south of India, but in China it was identified from at least the tenth century with P'ut-t'o Shan, a mountain island in the Bay of Hangchow. According to Chinese legend this is where Avalokiteśvara attained enlightenment. The temples and monasteries of P'u-t'o Shan form the centre of the Avalokiteśvara cult in East Asian Buddhism. As with other Chinese sacred mountains associated with Buddhist and Taoist divinities, crude block-printed tourist guides were produced, praising the relevant deity and indicating the best routes up the mountain and the principal temples and other sites.[25] Two statues in the monasteries at P'ut-t'o Shan were particularly famous and sacred. The first was a marble statue with an enormous head, swathed in a cape and hood, emphasizing the tranquil yet compassionate face of the Bodhisattva. The other was a breathtakingly beautiful bronze statue of 'White-Robed Avalokiteśvara', clothed, as is also frequently the custom with Tibetan statues. Avalokiteśvara is crowned, wears large earrings and a rosary, and in the elaborate halo are other small Bodhisattvas which emanate from him. Or her? According to Ernst Boerschmann, 'The face is very noble and kind, but without smiling', and 'She is a real Indian princess, proud and beautiful' (quoted in Oort 1986: II, 13; see also his illustrations).

In East Asia, Avalokiteśvara has changed sex! It is not clear why or how early this happened, although it may have had something to do with the absorption into the figure of Avalokiteśvara of other female deities.[26] D. T. Suzuki implies that the male version of Avalokiteśvara is the 'doctrinal' Bodhisattva, while the female is the 'popular' version (Suzuki 1935: 341). This is scarcely very helpful or convincing. A Sung dynasty (960–1126) painting shows Avalokiteśvara (known in China as Kuan-yin; Japanese: Kwannon or Kannon) with a moustache, and in this form he was also portrayed at Tun-huang. Nevertheless, we have seen that 'he' could manifest in female form, and the beginning of this transformation has been traced back as far as the fifth century (Tay 1976: 151). Which is the real form? Obviously neither male nor female. Each is taken according to needs and circumstances. Or, put another way, in 'his' true nature, as a Chinese poem has it, Avalokiteśvara is sexless:

> The Dharma-body of Kuan-yin
> Is neither male nor female.
> Even the body is not a body,
> What attributes can there be? …
> Let it be known to all Buddhists:
> Do not cling to form.
> The bodhisattva is *you*:
> Not the picture or the image.
>
> (Trans. in Tay 1976: 173)

Truly, the Bodhisattva is the Buddha-nature, which is equally in all sentient beings. In spite of this, the female form of Avalokiteśvara has provided some of the most attractive stories in Buddhist folk literature (see Blofeld 1977), and some of the most beautiful works in the world of religious art. Among the various forms of Kuan-yin, all female, we find the Kuan-yin 'Giver of Children' – the Chinese Madonna and Child – or the 'Lion's Roar' Kuan-yin, seated on the back of a playful Chinese lion, or the Kuan-yin 'Holder of the Lotus', reflecting the old versions of Avalokiteśvara Padmapāṇi found in India, most notably in the extraordinarily beautiful painting in Cave I at Ajantā (Gupta period, sixth century). In this painting Avalokiteśvara is at once male and female, with broad shoulders and a soft face, epitomizing compassion, gentleness, and yet inner strength, a willingness and ability to help. There is also Kuan-yin 'Holder of the Willow Branch', and many figures of Kuan-yin holding the slender-necked vase containing the elixir of immortality. But the East Asian Kuan-yin *par excellence* is probably the swirling porcelain White Robed Kuan-yin.[27] From Japan, where there are many places of pilgrimage sacred to Kwannon; there is a famous wooden statue carved from a single block of camphor wood; and also a striking wooden figure from the fourteenth century in which the wood itself is gilded, and then gilt bronze, crystal, and semi-precious stones are used for the detail and trappings, most notably an ornate 'spiky' headdress and halo. Both these figures appear to be male, although the female Kwannon is also popular. From the sublime to the ridiculous, perhaps, on a hill south-east of Tokyo was erected in the late 1950s an enormous Kwannon, more than 50 metres high, to serve as a war memorial. It is possible to ascend the statue and observe the view from a viewing platform in the crook of her protective arms![28]

Eleven-headed forms of Avalokiteśvara were popular in Central Asia and China during the seventh and eighth centuries, while eleven-headed, thousand-armed Avalokiteśvara, together with a four-armed version, are still the most popular forms in Tibetan Buddhism. In his four-armed version Avalokiteśvara (who in Tibetan Buddhism is always depicted as male) is shown seated in the lotus posture, a deer skin over his left shoulder, with two palms pressed together holding a wish-fulfilling jewel, his other right hand holding a rosary and his left a lotus. He is white in colour. He smiles, irradiating his devotee with compassion, a compassion the devotee seeks to generate in himself as he transcends the outer form and realizes his own nature as that of Avalokiteśvara.

One last point. Do all these Bodhisattvas really exist, or are they simply teaching devices of the Buddha, for the benefit of those who are at a particular level on the spiritual path? The answer is both – or neither!

From a Buddhist point of view these beings do not *really* exist, they are empty of inherent existence, or products of the mind. But then, so are we! The Bodhisattvas like Avalokiteśvara are as real as we are. On the level of their unreality there is enlightenment, and no one to be enlightened. But on the level of our unenlightened state they are real enough – and as unenlightened beings we need all the help we can get!

Tārā

All the forms of Avalokiteśvara found in Indo-Tibetan Buddhism are male. The feminine aspect of compassion is more than adequately fulfilled, however, by the lovely and playful form of Tārā, 'the most lovable of all the Buddhist deities' (Blofeld 1977: 54). In particular, devotion to Tārā is a hallmark of Buddhism in Tibet and those areas influenced by Tibet, a devotion which is also now widespread among Western centres of Tibetan Buddhism.

Tārā too dwells on the Potalaka mountain, for she is closely associated with the figure of Avalokiteśvara. Like Avalokiteśvara, Tārā appears to have Śiva elements in her tradition and iconography.[29] According to a popular Tibetan legend Avalokiteśvara despaired of saving so many sentient beings, even with a thousand arms and eleven heads. The task was so great that he wept, and from a teardrop of compassion Tārā was born to help him: 'So there is not a being, no matter how insignificant, whose suffering is not seen by Avalokiteśvara or by Tārā, and who cannot be touched by their compassion' (Hyde-Chambers and Hyde-Chambers 1981: 6; slightly modified). According to another, more 'literary' version, Tārā was born from a blue lotus which grew in his tears. Either way, her origin lies in her development of *bodhicitta* and her cultivation of the Bodhisattva path over many aeons. Particularly significant is her great vow in response to the suggestion that she should change sex in order to develop further along the path to enlightenment:

> There are many who desire Enlightenment in a man's body, but none who work for the benefit of sentient beings in the body of a woman. Therefore, until saṃsāra is empty. I shall work for the benefit of sentient beings in a woman's body.
>
> (Tāranātha, in Willson 1986: 34)

Tibetans are now quite happy to refer to Tārā as a fully enlightened female Buddha.

There are no major Tārā *sūtras*, although there is a *Tārā Tantra* which is relatively late. As far as we can tell, Tārā first appears in Indian art during the sixth century, together with Avalokiteśvara and representing his compassion. In the *Tārā Tantra* and elsewhere she is also said to be the 'Mother of all the Buddhas', in spite of the fact that she is held to be perpetually 16 years old – old but yet young. This suggests an absorption with the earlier image of the deity Prajñāpāramitā, also female, and therefore with emptiness itself. Praises of Tārā date from perhaps as early as the third century CE (see Willson 1986 for translations). Certainly, by the seventh century she is established as a deity in her own right, and is said in particular to save from eight great fears: lions, elephants, fires, snakes, bandits, captivity, shipwreck, and demons. Tārā has clearly taken over here some of the functions of Avalokiteśvara.

The great importance of Tārā in Tibetan Buddhism is due no doubt to the enthusiastic advocacy of her cause by Atiśa, the eleventh-century missionary to Tibet. Tārā was Atiśa's personal chosen deity, and she is said to have intervened at a number of crucial points in his life. Atiśa consulted her before going to Tibet. We are told that she predicted that if he went his life would be shorter, but he would benefit numerous beings. Atiśa wrote a brief praise of Tārā (Willson 1986: 293–4), but one of the most impressive praises of the Bodhisattva is the fervent prayer by the nineteenth-century Tibetan lama bLo bzang bstan pa'i rgyal mtshan (pronounced: Lo zang ten pay gyel tsen), in which he shows despair at the usual channels of religious activity and inspiration, and a deep, loving devotion to his chosen deity:

> I call the Jewels as witness – from not just my mouth, But the depth of my inmost heart and bones, I pray – Think of me somewhat! Show me your smiling face! Loving One, grant me the nectar of Your Speech!
>
> (Trans. in Willson 1986: p. 324)

Iconographically, Tārā has a number of forms. Tibetan iconography is very complex and strict, since the images are of crucial importance in Tantric meditation. Twenty-one forms of Tārā are common, and these are hymned in the most frequent of chants to Tārā.[30] In general, however, the most common forms are the Green and White Tārās. The Green is the principal form of Tārā, seated on a moon resting on a lotus, with left leg drawn up, and the foot of the right leg on a lotus 'footstool'. She is adorned with all the ornaments and trappings of a Bodhisattva, very beautiful, and her left hand in front of her heart holds the stem of a blue lotus, while the right arm and hand are extended, palm open, as if handing down blessings. Sometimes this hand too holds a blue lotus. Sūryagupta, a ninth-century Kashmiri scholar, cries out to her:

> Homage! Whose right hand grants boons to beings,
> Blue lotus in left; complete with all ornaments,
> Graceful, with shining blue-green complexion,
> Youthful, wide-eyed and full-breasted.'
>
> (Trans. in Willson 1986: 139)

The White Tārā is generally associated in Tibetan Buddhism with long-life practices. She is seated in the full lotus position, white in colour, with her left hand at her heart holding the stem of a white lotus. Her right arm and hand are again extended, bestowing blessings. She is easily recognized, since she has seven eyes, three on her face, and one in each palm and foot.

Mañjuśrī

Just as Avalokiteśvara is said to incarnate all the Buddhas' compassion, so Mañjuśrī manifests the other 'wing' of enlightenment – wisdom. Of course, both are tenth-stage Bodhisattvas and in reality have equal attainments. But just as Avalokiteśvara is met performing heroic deeds of compassion in the *Lotus Sūtra*, Mañjuśrī is particularly associated with the role of interlocutor on questions concerning ultimate truth in such *sūtras* as the *Vimalakīrti*. Like Tārā, on the other hand, Mañjuśrī is said to be ever young, a youth of 16, a 'crown prince' who is nevertheless ancient in wisdom. Mañjuśrī is not important in the earlier *Prajñāpāramitā*, but he does play a significant role in the *Saptaśatikā Prajñāpāramitā*,[31] and an important text for the cult of Mañjuśrī, the *Mañjuśrī buddhakṣetraguṇavyūha*, had already been translated into Chinese by the end of the third century. In Buddhist art Mañjusrī appears relatively late, and it is possible that the cult developed in Central Asia (Khotan?) or even China – where he is portrayed with Vimalakīrti, the lay Bodhisattva with whom he has a profound discussion in the *Vimalakīrtinirdeśa* – from the sixth century onwards.[32] The association of Mañjuśri with Mt Wu-t'ai in North-West China was known in classical times in India itself. There were pilgrimages from India and other Buddhist countries to Wu-t'ai Shan by the end of the seventh century.[33]

According to the *25,000 Verse Perfection of Wisdom*, a Bodhisattva who has reached the tenth stage is to be known, quite simply, as a Tathāgata – which is to say, a Buddha. Although he is not a Buddha, from our side he (or she) is so amazing that we could not distinguish him from a Buddha. In the *Mañjuśrībuddhakṣetraguṇavyūha* we are told how Mañjuśrī many, many aeons ago gave rise to the *bodhicitta* in the presence of a previous Buddha. In producing the *bodhicitta* he made a series of vows. He would always act for the benefit of sentient beings, without greed, miserliness, or resentfulness. He would always observe complete morality and be perfectly pure. Moreover, most significantly, Mañjuśrī would never wish to attain a rapid (self-seeking) enlightenment (*bodhi*), but rather would continue to benefit sentient beings 'until the end of future'.[34] He would purify an immense, inconceivable Buddha Field, and would cause his name to be known throughout the ten directions.

Mañjuśrī has now attained the tenth stage of a Bodhisattva. He is asked why he does not proceed straightway to full Buddhahood. The reply is that in fully understanding emptiness and acting accordingly there is nothing more to do. He has let go of the notion of full Buddhahood. He no longer seeks enlightenment; indeed, in the light of emptiness he cannot attain enlightenment (Chang 1983: 170 ff., 177–8, 183). In saying this, of course, Mañjuśrī indicates that he is already fully enlightened. According to the *Aṅgulimālīya Sūtra*, Mañjuśrī is now actually a Buddha, with a Buddha Field (Lamotte 1960: 29–30). We have seen that a tenth-stage Bodhisattva can manifest in whatever way he or she wishes for the benefit of beings. In an important section of the *Śūraṃgamasamādhi Sūtra*, a work first translated into Chinese perhaps towards the end of the second century, Mañjuśrī is said to have been in the past a Buddha, who manifested all the deeds of a Buddha and finally entered *parinirvāṇa* – or so it seemed. Nevertheless, in so doing the great Bodhisattvas do not give up their (compassionate) nature as Bodhisattvas, and in entering *parinirvāṇa* they have not in fact completely disappeared and abandoned sentient beings.[35] The same point is made in a short *sūtra* which may depend upon the *Śūraṃgamasamādhi*, known as the *Mañjuśrīparinirvāṇa Sūtra* (translated into Chinese at the end of third century). Mañjuśrī, through his meditative power, many times manifests entry into *parinirvāṇa* in different regions, and even leaves holy relics behind. All this is for the benefit of beings. He emanates as many Buddhas as are needed, but he can also manifest as a poor wretch, in order that beings can make merit through compassion and donations. Immense benefits arise from seeing even an image of Mañjuśrī, and also pronouncing his name. Through such practices beings will be freed from the lower realms (trans. in Lamotte 1960: 35–9). According to a Chinese tradition, Mañjuśrī vowed to take the same form as every pilgrim who visits his sacred mountain of Wu-t'ai. Thus he could appear even as a thief or gambler. An important abbot and Ch'an monk of modern times, Hsü-yün (1840?–1959), tells how he was helped on his arduous pilgrimage by a beggar whom he later realized to be Mañjuśrī himself (Welch 1967: 307). Various scholars in Buddhist history are said to have seen and received inspiration from Mañjuśrī, most notably, perhaps, Tsong kha pa, and Mañjuśrī is said in Tibet to be the inspirer of the profound wisdom teachings of the Madhyamaka.

According to one *sūtra*, Śākyamuni Buddha disclosed that in the past he was a disciple of Mañjuśrī, and his very status as a Buddha is now due to Mañjuśrī, who is both father and mother to innumerable Buddhas.[36] Mañjuśrī, is, of course, wisdom incarnate, and one remembers here both Prajñāpāramitā and Tārā as 'mother of all the Buddhas'. He is referred to by one scholar, appropriately named Mañjuśrīmitra, as 'the errorless comprehension of the character of *bodhicitta*, the birthplace of all the Buddhas' (trans. by Wayman, in *Mañjuśrīnāmasaṃgīti* 1985: 8). The supremacy of Mañjuśri is stated repeatedly in one of the most important texts on Mañjuśrī used for chanting in Tibetan Buddhism, the Tantric *Mañjuśrīnāmasaṃgīti*. Mañjuśrī 'holds the enlightenment of a fully enlightened Buddha' (8: 42). He is the fully awakened, supreme, omniscient one (9: 15). He is the progenitor of all the Buddhas, and at the same time their most excellent son (6: 19). Mañjuśrī is master (Indra) of the gods, and god of gods (10: 6), who dwells in the mind of all beings (9: 20).

At this sublime point, however, let us note that just as early Mahāyāna was apparently characterized by cults centred on certain *sūtras*, and certain meditative absorptions, so it was undoubtedly also marked by groups centred on different and often rival Buddhas and Bodhisattvas. In one lovely *sūtra*, Mañjuśrī is bettered in a discourse on wisdom by an 8-year-old girl.[37] She had been treading the Bodhisattva path for sixty aeons when Mañjuśrī made his vows, and her future Buddha Field will be much better than that of Mañjuśrī (Chang 1983: 93–4). Mañjuśrī's Buddha Field, on the other hand, is said elsewhere to be much better than Sukhāvatī (ibid., 183–4). So there!

The iconography of Mañjuśrī is a relatively late development. In Indo-Tibetan Buddhism he is usually represented as a young prince, seated on a lotus, with a sword in his right hand, held above his head, and a book in the left. Sometimes in the left hand he holds the stem of a lotus, and the book is placed on the lotus behind his left shoulder. The sword is said to be the sword of gnosis which cuts aside the bonds of ignorance. The book is the *Prajñāpāramitā*, usually held to be the *Aṣṭasāhasrikā* version.

In Sino-Japanese art in particular, and Central Asian art which is influenced by China, Mañjuśrī rides on a lion, and often parallels Samantabhadra, the Bodhisattva of the *Avataṃsaka Sūtra*, who rides a six-tusked elephant. Because of the importance of the *Avataṃsaka* in East Asian Buddhism, and also because of his role as guardian of the *Lotus Sūtra*, Samantabhadra has a significant place as a cult figure in Sino-Japanese Buddhism. In China he too is given a sacred mountain, this time Omei Shan is Szechwan province.

A block-print of Mañjuśrī and lion from Tun-huang (tenth century) makes clear the association of Mañjuśrī with Wu-t'ai Shan, where apparently the oldest wooden temple buildings in China (782–897) still stand (Zwalf 1985: 230). A lovely Chinese ink painting from the fourteenth century depicts a long-haired, relaxed Mañjuśrī reading a scroll (the *Perfection of Wisdom*?), seated on a sleepy but perhaps slightly peeved lion.[38] A statue of Mañjuśrī from Ta-tsu, in Szechwan (1154), also depicts him on his lion – a Chinese lion that looks facially more like a giant Pekingese dog, dogs which were bred precisely to look like Mañjuśrī's lion! In Mañjuśrī's left hand is the book. The sword seems more often than not to be missing in Sino-Japanese art. (van Oort 1986: 2, plate 23a).

Kṣitigarbha

The Bodhisattva Kṣitigarbha is little more than a name in Indo-Tibetan Buddhism. In East Asia, on the other hand, he is extremely important, and he too has a sacred mountain in China, Mt Chiu-hua, in Anhwei province of Eastern China. According to the *Daśacakrakṣitigarbha Sūtra*, a *sūtra* which was almost certainly composed in Central Asia, Kṣitigarbha was given the particular task of saving sentient beings during the period between the death of Śākyamuni and the coming of Maitreya. Iconographic evidence from Central Asia suggests that Kṣitigarbha may well have appeared originally in the retinue of Maitreya as one of his monk attendants.

The real reason for Kṣitigarbha's importance in East Asian Buddhism, however, is probably his central role in the *Ti-tsang p'u-sa pen-ying Ching* (*Kṣitigarbhabodhisattvapraṇidhāna Sūtra*?), a *sūtra* which seems to be of Chinese or just possibly Khotanese origin, and is not known in any Tibetan version. A principal theme of this work is filial piety, and particularly the deeds of Kṣitigarbha in saving the dead from even the lowest hells. Holmes Welch has pointed out that the notion of rebirth, and consequently of the hell realms, was introduced into Chinese thought during an age of turmoil, when many Chinese must have entertained a consideration that the political and social upheavals of the age might have something to do with their inadequate treatment of the ancestors (Welch 1967: 182). Inadequate indeed, for the poor Chinese has not realized that their nearest and dearest could be, in fact probably were, in hell. Hence the acute problem of how to save them. Charity begins at home; the universal compassion of the Bodhisattva starts with a little compassion for one's suffering family. Thus Kṣitigarbha in Chinese Buddhism became associated in particular with rituals that can be performed by those who remain behind for the welfare of their ancestors – rituals such as reciting the *Ti-tsang pen-ying sūtra* and bestowing the merit to the ancestors, or placing the name of an ancestor or an urn containing the ashes at regular intervals on a temple shrine to Kṣitigarbha, prostrating, burning incense, and perhaps holding a short service (Welch 1967: 188, 204).

In the *Ti-tsang pen-ying sūtra* Śākyamuni explains the immense power to save possessed by Kṣitigarbha.[39] To hear his powerful name, praise and worship him, make offerings to or an image of him, will lead to a heavenly rebirth and freedom from the lower realms (p. 72). The misdeeds of thirty aeons can be wiped out (p. 146). This is possible because of Kṣitigarbha's great power developed during his Bodhisattva path as a direct result of his compassionate vows. In two stories we are told that Kṣitigarbha was, in a previous life, a woman who vowed to save all sentient beings in the lower realms, in return or out of gratitude for the salvation of her mother who had been reborn in great suffering (pp. 88, 126). All sentient beings are in reality our mothers. Kṣitigarbha has vowed not to become a Buddha until he has saved all other creatures (pp. 72, 120). Reciting the *Sūtra* is said to save from illnesses, or it can be recited for the dead, or for ancestors who have become ghosts. They will straightway receive favourable rebirths, through the immense merit of the Bodhisattva Kṣitigarbha (pp. 157–9, 210–11). Many ways of helping the dead are indicated. Kṣitigarbha will pull even from the gates of hell those who can recite the name of a Buddha, or a Bodhisattva, or a verse from a *sūtra*.[40] Through reciting the *Ti-tsang pen-ying sūtra* itself one can also command the spirits and cause good fortune to those about to be born, the newly born, as well as the mother and family (pp. 161–2; cf. p. 183). Reciting the name of Kṣitigarbha and contemplating his image overcomes poverty and protects while on travel. Indeed, worshipping Kṣitigarbha can even increase intelligence and improve memory (pp. 211–13)! In other words, Kṣitigarbha is of value in everyday life and everyday death, as a good Bodhisattva should be. In particular, he is a Chinese Bodhisattva who offers practical spiritual solutions to the domestic problems of Chinese men and women. To the present day, in the seventh lunar month, the *Ti-tsang pen-ying Ching* is recited, and offerings are made, out of gratitude for Kṣitigarbha's saving of the ancestors. In Japan Kṣitigarbha has the same function as in China, but is also associated with the welfare of children, pregnant women, and travellers. This is for reasons obviously connected with the *sūtra* itself. In particular Kṣitigarbha (Japanese: Jizō) loves children. If a child dies, say by miscarriage or abortion, a small image of Jizō may be offered at a local temple (Levering 1987: 392–3).

In Buddhist art Kṣitigarbha is usually represented as a shaven-headed monk, an exception to the general depiction of Bodhisattvas as princes or princesses. In this form he appears as a guide of the dead from the lower realms to higher states. In a tenth-century wall painting from Bezeklik in Central Asia, Kṣitigarbha is depicted with a patched robe, and a staff with which to strike open the gates of hell.[41] He has almost exactly the same appearance – a dignified yet kindly monk, floating in the air with feet on a lotus, in robes, perhaps even rich robes, with a staff, a small medicine bowl, and halo – in numerous Japanese paintings, where the descent of Jizō to save beings is an important artistic theme. His staff is that of a beggar. The metal frame at the end, like an upside-down heart of wire, contains six rings which tinkle as he moves. He is surrounded by wispy vapour rising from the cauldrons of hell, as he compassionately descends to save those who suffer unspeakable torments.[42]

SOME BUDDHAS

Akṣobhya

The cult of Akṣobhya appears to be the earliest Buddha cult after Śākyamuni, quite possibly preceding that of Amitāyus. Our principal literary source for the cult and mythology of Akṣobhya is the *Akṣobhyavyūha Sūtra*. This *sūtra* exists in more than one recension, of which the earliest was translated into Chinese towards the end of the second century CE. In terms of antiquity of translation, therefore, this makes it one of the earliest datable Mahāyāna *sūtras*. The text was possibly written originally not in Sanksrit but in Gāndhārī, the local language of North-West India under the Kuṣāṇas.[43]

According to the *Akṣobhyavyūha Sūtra* there is in the east, far, far away, a Buddha Field named Abhirati. In that land, long ago, a monk vowed to follow the path to full Buddhahood. In so doing he made, as is the custom, a series of great vows which are very difficult to fulfil. In following the path he would never in any way bear malice, never retreat into the lower Vehicles, never engage in even the slightest immorality. As a monk he would always be the most perfect monk, austere, eloquent, dignified, mindful in the presence of women, not listening to non-Buddhist doctrines, and so on. This applies not just to the present life but to all lives, with body, speech, and mind. He would always save criminals about to be punished, even at the cost of his own life.[44] This account of the Bodhisattva's vows, particularly his perfect morality, is important. First, it indicates the scope of Akṣobhya's aspirations. Second, through adhering to mighty vows the Bodhisattva, and eventual Buddha, gains great, immeasurable merit, and as a direct consequence immense power to help others. Finally, as the text itself makes clear, the purity of the Bodhisattva's morality has a direct bearing on the purity of his eventual Buddha Field. Akṣobhya's realm of Abhirati is, after all, a fully qualified Pure Land.

As a consequence of his great aspiration and vows this Bodhisattva was predicted to full enlightenment, a prediction accompanied by suitably wonderful miracles. All has now come to pass, and he is indeed the Buddha Akṣobhya, who reigns over that land of Abhirati far, far distant in the east. At Akṣobhya's enlightenment Māra did not even bother to try and hinder him. The *sūtra* devotes some time to describing the delights of Akṣobhya's Buddha Field, for this indicates the greatness of Akṣobhya, tempts devotees, and serves as a basis for visualization and recollection of the Buddha Akṣobhya. In that land there is an enormous tree under which the Buddha sits on a raised platform:

> Around the bodhi-tree are rows of palm trees and jasmine trees, which in the gentle breeze, gave forth a harmonious and elegant sound surpassing all worldly music. Furthermore … that Buddha-land does not have the three miserable planes of existence.… All the sentient beings in that Buddha-land have accomplished the ten good deeds. The ground is as flat as a palm and the colour of gold, with no gullies, brambles, or gravel; it is as soft as cotton, sinking as soon as one's foot steps on it and returning to its original state as soon as the foot is lifted.[45]

In Abhirati there are no illnesses, no lying, no ugliness, or smelly things. There are no jails! No non-Buddhists. Trees are laden with flowers and fruit, and there are also trees which produce fragrant and beautiful garments. Food and drink appear as wished: 'There are also many gardens and pavilions, all pure and clean. The sentient beings there all live with joy in the Dharma' (Chang 1983: 322). There is no jealousy, women there are wonderfully beautiful, and they are freed from the curse of menstruation:[46]

> Furthermore, in that land, mother and child are safe and unsullied from conception to birth. How can this be? All this is due to the power of Tathāgata Akṣobhya's original vows.... in that Buddha-land there is such peace and bliss.... there is neither trade nor trader, neither farms nor farming; there is happiness at all times.... in that Buddha-land, singing and playing do not involve sexual desire. The sentient beings there derive their joy exclusively from the Dharma.
>
> (p. 323; cf. Dantinne 1983: 201–2)

According to the Tibetan version, in Abhirati there is no physical sexuality. As soon as a man approaches a woman with carnal thought and sees her, the carnal thought ceases and he enters a meditative absorption on detachment from impurity! She, on the other hand, by virtue of the mere glance, becomes pregnant. The pregnancy is apparently no problem (Dantinne 1983: 196)! The fact that there are women and child-bearing in Abhirati is a point worth noting, for these two features are specifically denied of Amitāyus' Sukhāvatī. Clearly, Abhirati is a wonderful world of happiness, free of all danger, a world which is the exact opposite of our dirty polluted world, where people toil with little reward but starvation and poverty, followed by a mean death. All these splendid things are the results, we are repeatedly told, of Akṣobhya's great vows and compassion. There is sun and moon in Abhirati, but they have no function, for they are completely eclipsed by the light of Akṣobhya (Chang 1983: 324).

One cannot be reborn in the Pure Land by greedily desiring it, for 'one with any passion or attachment cannot be born in that Buddha-land. Only those who have planted good roots and cultivated pure conduct can be born there' (p. 323; Dantinne 1983: 199). In fact, the principal purpose of being reborn in Abhirati is to follow the Buddhist path in the presence of Akṣobhya, under optimum facilities for spiritual growth. Not all in the Pure Land follow the Mahāyāna, however, for there are also Hearers and Arhats present. With these facilities enlightenement can be obtained very quickly. In Abhirati, 'They are said to be indolent because they fail to end all their defilements at one sitting' (p. 325)!

How is one to be reborn in this wonderful land? This is through strenuous moral and spiritual cultivation. First, one should follow the Bodhisattva path, and vow to be reborn in that land of Abhirati. Second, all merit obtained through good works should be dedicated to one's future rebirth there. Nevertheless, one should not be selfish. The motive power for this rebirth is in order to attain enlightenment and then 'illuminate the whole world' (p. 332). One should learn meditation and frequent holy people. It is also important to visualize the Buddhas in their Buddha Fields expounding the Doctrine, and vow to be like them. By such means one can be reborn in the Pure Land of Buddha Akṣobhya in the future, yet immediately fall under his divine protection (pp. 332–5).

One noteworthy feature of Akṣobhya and his Pure Land is that this Buddha will eventually enter *parinirvāṇa*, having arranged for his successor, in the same way that Śākyamuni arranged for Maitreya. Akṣobhya's final act will be self-cremation, apparently through internal combustion, a phenomenon which has Tibetan parallels and which may reflect in some way actual practices of the Akṣobhya cult.[47] The Doctrine preached by Akṣobhya will endure for many aeons after his passing, but will eventually decline. All this will happen because of the declining merit of people in Abhirati: 'It is because people of that time will lack interest in learning the Dharma that those who can expound the Dharma will go away from them' (p. 332). People will hear little of the teaching, and will cease to practise. The learned monks will therefore withdraw into seclusion, and eventually the Dharma will be no more.

It is clear throughout this discussion that the land of Abhirati and the Tathāgata Akṣobhya are modelled on Śākyamuni and this world – but raised in all respects to a higher plane of loveliness and spirituality. It is our world *as it ought to be*, the world of dreams. This very fact suggests the antiquity of the cult of Akṣobhya, although we have no idea now what concrete form the cult took. The Akṣobhya cult was clearly important in certain circles during the early centuries CE, although it seems not to have survived, or to have been transmitted in any identifiable form as a separate cult to other Buddhist countries. This may be because it was eclipsed early on by other forms of Buddhism in India, and the Sukhāvatī cult of Amitāyus in Central and East Asia. Nevertheless, Akṣobhya does become an important Buddha in a rather different context, the Tantric traditions of late Indian Buddhism (ninth to twelfth centuries), and through these traditions he is also important in Nepalese and Tibetan Buddhism. It is from this late period that most of the Indian figures of Akṣobhya come, where he is usually represented as a Buddha, sometimes crowned, in a lotus posture with his left hand on his lap and right hand outstretched to touch the earth. As a Tantric Buddha, Akṣobhya is often the principal Buddha of the *maṇḍala*, the cosmogram which is so important in Tantric ritual and meditation. In such a context he is coloured blue, and associated with four other Buddhas: Vairocana, Ratnasambhava, Amitābha, and Amoghasiddhi.

Bhaiṣajyaguru

Bhaiṣajyaguru is the Medicine Buddha. We have seen that other Buddhas and Bodhisattvas include among their functions the preventing and curing of illness, but Bhaiṣajyaguru represents an incarnation of the dimension of healing in all its aspects – from the curing of a cold through that of mental disease to enlightenment itself, a healing of the human condition. In Tibet, Bhaiṣajyaguru serves as the patron saint of medicine, most of which is carried out by monk-physicians. Meditative generation of Bhaiṣajyaguru, together with the recitation of his *mantra*, can be used to empower and enrich the medicines themselves.

There are two *sūtras* particularly devoted to the topic of Bhaiṣajyaguru – the *Bhaiṣajyaguru Sūtra*, and a *sūtra* which is best known by the short title of *Saptabuddha Sūtra*. The latter text incorporates much of the *Bhaiṣajyaguru Sūtra*, but adds a further six Buddhas to Bhaiṣajyaguru, giving a set of seven. Both *sūtras* are available in Tibetan, and the Sanskrit *Bhaiṣajyaguru Sūtra* was discovered at Gilgit. In spite of this we should not assume that the presence of a Sanskrit and a Tibetan version means that the *sūtra* was necessarily composed in India. Raoul Birnbaum has noted that there are no images of Bhaiṣajyaguru in India predating the transmission of the *Bhaiṣajyaguru Sūtra* to China, and none of the Chinese pilgrims to India mentions a cult of Bhaiṣajyaguru. The oldest Chinese translation of the *sūtra* (fourth century) is contained in a composite *sūtra* the authencity of which has been doubted from early times.[48] By the fourth century, on the other hand, Bhaiṣajyaguru had already become an important figure in other *sūtras* translated into Chinese, and appears to have been significant in Central Asia. There is some evidence to suggest that the *Bhaiṣajyaguru Sūtra* was composed in Central Asia, and then introduced into India, where it became sufficiently popular to be quoted extensively by Śāntideva in the seventh or the eighth century (Birnbaum 1980: 52 ff.). The most popular version in East Asia is that translated by Hsüan-tsang in the seventh-century, and this corresponds closely with the Sanskrit and Tibetan versions.

The *Bhaiṣajyaguru Sūtra* is much like other *sūtras* of its type. It describes the great vows of Bhaiṣajyaguru as a Bodhisattva, devotes a brief note to his Buddha Field, which, suffice to say, is just wonderful, and describes at length, with details for ritual, the benefits which flow from worshipping Bhaiṣajyaguru and in particular invoking his name. In setting out on the Bodhisattva path, Bhaiṣajyaguru is said to have made twelve great vows, namely that when he becomes a Buddha, according to Birnbaum's version from the Chinese: (i) he will have an extensive radiance, the 112 marks of a superior being, and will cause all sentient beings to resemble himself; (ii) his body will be like flawless lapis lazuli, surpassing the sun and moon in radiance, (iii) he will enable all beings to have whatever is needed; (iv) he will cause non-Buddhists to enter the path of enlightenment, and those who follow the lower Vehicles to adopt the Mahāyāna; (v) he will enable his followers to have perfect morality and aspirations, and through the salvific power of his name he will purify those who transgress and prevent them from falling into the lower realms; (vi) he will cure those with deformities, 'leprous, convulsive, insane', again through the power of his name; (vii)

> when I attain enlightenment ... if there are any sentient beings who are ill and oppressed, who have nowhere to go and nothing to return to, who have neither doctor nor medicine, neither relatives nor immediate family, who are destitute and whose sufferings are acute – as soon as my name passes through their ears, they will be cured of all their diseases and they will be peaceful and joyous in body and mind. They will have plentiful families and property, and they will personally experience the supreme enlightenment; (pp 153–4)

(viii) women who are weary of their female state (in primitive conditions a state of constant pregnancy with poor medical facilities) can be reborn as males through his name (the *Saptabuddha Sūtra* states this this can occur in the *present* life!); (ix) all will escape the net of Māra, abandon false views, and progress on the Bodhisattva path; (x) all who are confronted by fears and pains, particularly due to royal punishment, may be relieved through hearing his name; (xi) those who transgress through hunger or thirst will attain excellent food and drink, then afterwards the Doctrine, once more through the name of Bhaiṣajyaguru; and finally, (xii) those who are too poor to afford clothes, and are tormented by cold, heat, flies, and mosquitoes, will obtain through the power of recollecting the Buddha's name not just clothing but ornaments, garlands, incense, music, and entertainment (pp. 152–5). How can all this happen simply through hearing the name of Bhaiṣajyaguru? The *Saptabuddha Sūtra* implies that it is due to the great vows of these Buddhas, and their consequential immense power.

The Buddha Field of Bhaiṣajyaguru is, like that of Akṣobhya, in the east. Its description is very brief, for it is said to be just like Sukhāvatī, with the ground of lapis lazuli and roads marked with gold. There are no women in that land, for all women are reborn there in the superior state of men. The tradition of the spiritual superiority of men is an old one in Buddhism. The social reality was that men had much greater facilities for spiritual advancement. It was taken for granted in most descriptions of a Pure Land that since they involve by their very nature superior facilities so all beings there must be male. Akṣobhya's Abhirati is an interesting exception, closer, perhaps, to a heavenly realm, and correspondingly more archaic. In his own Pure Land Bhaiṣajyaguru is accompanied by two Bodhisattvas, as is Amitābha, known as Sūryaprabha and Candraprabha. These Bodhisattvas lead the dead into the presence of Bhaiṣajyaguru. There appear to be no non-Mahāyāna practitioners in this Pure Land.

The benefits of worshipping Bhaiṣajyaguru, or the *sūtra*, are strikingly 'this-worldly'. First, Bhaiṣajyaguru saves those who would otherwise go straight to the lower realms – even the most wicked. He can also save those who have already reached the lower realms but who, as with a distant echo, remember for some reason his name. Through his power they then attain favourable rebirths, including, under certain conditions, rebirth in Sukhāvatī itself – although strangely no mention is made in this context of his own Pure Land. The best method of worshipping Bhaiṣajyaguru is to set up an image of the Buddha on a throne, scatter flowers, burn incense, and adorn the area with banners and pennants:

> For seven days and seven nights they should accept and hold to the eight-fold vows, eat pure food, bathe in fragrant and pure water, and wear new and clean clothing. They should give birth to the unstained, single-minded state, with no thought of anger or harm. Towards all sentient beings there should arise the thoughts of blessings and benefits, peace, loving kindness, sympathetic joy, and equanimity. They should play musical instruments and sing praises while circumambulating to the right of the Buddha image. Furthermore, they should recall the merits of that Tathāgata's fundamental vows and study and recite this *sūtra*. They should think only of its principles and lecture on the *sūtra*, elucidating its main points. (p. 162)

Such encapsulates rather well, I think, a Buddhist cult of the Buddha. Through practices like these one can attain longevity, wealth, an official position, sons, daughters, freedom from nightmares, or whatever is required (ibid.). Concentration on the name of the Buddha and worshipping him is of value at the time of death, and also for women in childbirth. It can bring back beings who have been presumed dead, and who have already travelled beyond this world to the court of Yama, the King and Judge of the Dead.[49] Such a person will have witnessed the fruits of good and bad deeds 'like a dream', and will become a reformed person for ever more (p. 165). Naturally the sick too can be saved by worshipping Bhaiṣajyaguru (details are given for a special ritual). A king can overcome epidemics, invasions, rebellion, meteorological, astronomical, and astrological calamities. The state can be made tranquil. The *Saptabuddha Sūtra* adds a *mantra* or *dhāraṇī* which can be used at times of illness, for longevity, and so on. It can also be recited over medicine to increase its efficacy. According to Tibetan sources it is beneficial to recite this *mantra* and also the name of Bhaiṣajyaguru in the ear of a dying person, and even to recite the *mantra* and then blow upon meat or old bones, for this can lead to a lessening of the sufferings of the dead creature, and possibly a favourable rebirth. To those who uphold the worship of Bhaiṣajyaguru and his *sūtra* twelve *yakṣa* generals (a sort of demigod) and their armies will offer protection. Longevity, health, prosperity, protection of the state – these were the messages that Chinese and Japanese emperors wanted to hear, this was what they wanted from a worthwhile religion!

In Japan in particular the worship of Bhaiṣajyaguru has been especially important. We have seen already that recitation of *sūtras* to ward off pestilence and disasters and to protect the state was an integral part of Japanese Buddhism from the beginning. In 720 the empress commanded that the *Bhaiṣajyaguru Sūtra* be read in forty-eight temples for one day and one night in order to save the life of her minister. He died the very next day![50] Nevertheless, a general amnesty was declared, one of the meritorious deeds recommended by the *sūtra*. In the ninth century Bhaiṣajyaguru rites were performed to counter droughts and pestilence. Ceremonies centred on the seven Buddhas were used to repel the Mongol invasions in the thirteenth century, and the worship of Bhaiṣajyaguru was often performed when the emperor or one of his family was ill.

In Buddhist iconography Bhaiṣajyaguru is usually represented seated as a Buddha in full lotus posture. He is blue, the colour of lapis lazuli, or gold with a halo of blue rays. In his left hand on his lap he holds a bowl containing medicine, although sometimes in Japanese versions Bhaiṣajyaguru holds a small medicine bowl in the palm of his left hand, which rests on his left knee. The Buddha's right hand is characteristically open and resting on his right knee with the palm facing outwards. He holds the stem of a medicinal myrobalan plant.[51] In artistic representation Bhaiṣajyaguru may be flanked by his two Bodhisattvas, Sūryaprabha and Candraprabha, and perhaps also the twelve *yakṣa* generals. Some of these features can be seen in a large and complex painting on silk from Tun-huang (ninth century) in the British Museum, which also contains side-scenes of the nine forms of violent death from which, according to the *sūtra*, one can be protected by Bhaiṣajyaguru – illness aggravated by lack of proper treatment or through recourse to spirit-mediums, execution, death due to over-indulgence, burning, drowning, wild beasts, falling off a mountain, poisonous herbs, spells or magic, and finally starvation or dehydration. On the other side are depicted the twelve vows of Bhaiṣajyaguru.[52] The Pure Land itself is modelled closely on Amitāyus' Sukhāvatī as one might expect.

Amitābha/Amitāyus

The Amitābha *sūtras*

The most widespread of the cults devoted to Buddhas is that of Amitābha or Amitāyus. In contemporary Japanese Buddhism it accounts for more practitioners than any other Buddhist tradition, and in these forms in practice it most nearly approaches a devotional monotheism, no matter how inadequate such terms may ultimately turn out to be. For centuries the Amitābha *sūtras* and their exegesis by Chinese and Japanese devotees have formed the vision and the hope of millions of East Asian Buddhists, and their influence on East Asian culture has been correspondingly immense.

The Indic textual basis for the Amitābha cult, often known simply as 'Pure Land Buddhism', lies in three *sūtras* – the Larger and Smaller *Sukhāvatīvyūha Sūtras*, and a *sūtra* of particularly obscure origin which has been given the Sanskrit title *Amitāyurdhyāna Sūtra* (Chinese: *Kuan-wu-liang-shou-fo Ching*), but is probably more accurately referred to as the *Amitāyurbuddhānusmṛti Sūtra*.

It is unclear which of the two *Sukhāvatīvyūha Sūtras* is the earliest. The Larger *Sukhāvatīvyūha Sūtra* is said to have been translated first into Chinese during the second century CE, although the version most frequently used today by the Pure Land traditions is that attributed to Saṅghavarman and said to have been translated in 252. This attribution now looks unlikely. Either way, however, there seems little doubt that the Larger *Sukhāvatīvyūha Sūtra* is an old *sūtra*, dating from before the end of the second century. Japanese scholars suggest that it may have originated among monks of the Mahīśāsaka school in Gandhāra during the Kuṣāṇa period, possibly influenced by the Lokottaravāda tradition, and like the stylistically similar *Akṣobhyavyūha* it was probably originally in the Gāndhārī language or a language very similar to it (Nakamura 1980: 205). The Smaller *Sukhāvatīvyūha Sūtra* was first translated into Chinese by Kumārajīva in about 402 CE, and this version has become the accepted text of the Smaller *Sukhāvatīvyūha* among East Asian Buddhists. Western scholars generally accept the Larger *Sukhāvatīvyūha* as the older of the two *sūtras*, although a case can be made for the greater antiquity of the Smaller *Sukhāvatīvyūha*. In Japan it is indeed held that the Smaller *Sukhāvatīvyūha* is the older of the two *sūtras*, and it has even been suggested that the original form of this *sūtra* may be as old as the first century BCE. This would identify some form of Pure Land teaching with one of the earliest recognizable streams of Mahāyāna Buddhism. Such, it seems to me, is quite possible. We have seen the development of the importance of *buddhānusmṛti*, and we have also seen that early Mahāyāna was characterized by a number of cults which may well have been rival and mutually incompatible. That some of these cults were centred on particular Buddhas is an obvious inference, and therefore Buddha – and consequently Pure Land – cults like that of Amitābha were part of the very fabric of Mahāyāna Buddhism from its inception. Both the *Sukhāvatīvyūha Sūtras* also survive in Tibetan and Sanskrit, although there are a number of interesting differences between the versions, particularly in the number of vows listed in the different texts of the Larger *Sukhāvatīvyūha Sūtra*. Indeed it is not impossible that some passages were interpolated into this *sūtra* in China.

The *Sukhāvatīvyūha Sūtras* speak of the Buddha Amitābha or Amitāyus (Japanese: Amida). Generally, and for the Pure land traditions these are two names of the same Buddha, although in Tibet the two are treated separately. According to the Larger *Sukhāvatīvyūha*, he is called 'Amitābha' – Infinite Light – because his light is immeasurable, illuminating myriads of Buddha Fields in every direction with its radiance. Later Pure Land exegetes state that this Infinite Light of Amitābha is in fact a reference to his infinite wisdom, his all-illuminating and infinite omniscience. He is called 'Amitāyus' – Infinite Life – because his life is immeasurable, lasting for innumerable aeons. He remains for the benefit of sentient beings, constantly helping them in many different ways. Thus, corresponding to his infinite light as wisdom, Pure Land scholars refer to Amitābha's infinite life as an expression of his boundless compassion (Eracle 1973: 33–4).

The Larger *Sukhāvatīvyūha Sūtra* tells of the Bodhisattva Dharmākara who, in the presence of a previous Buddha, conceived and set his mind on a most marvellous Buddha Field, embodying all the virtues of myriads of other Buddha Fields, and exceeding them all. He then made a series of vows, as Bodhisattvas are wont to do in such circumstances. The number of these vows differs from version to version, with forty-six in the Sanskrit, and forty-eight in the 'Saṅghavarman' translation, which forms the basis of the Pure Land schools. Common to all of these vows, however, is the condition – 'if this vow is not fulfilled, then may I not become a Fully Enlightened Buddha'. Since the Bodhisattva Dharmākara is now none other than the Buddha Amitābha, reigning in his Pure Land of Sukhāvatī in the west, we know that these conditions must indeed have been fulfilled. Thus Dharmākara vows that all who are born in his land will never return to the lower realms.[53] They will all remember their past lives, and have other miraculous abilities (vows 5 ff.). They will be firmly established in a state set on enlightenment.[54] Those in his land will have, if they wish, an unlimited lifespan (vow 15). Innumerable Buddhas will glorify the name of Amitābha and praise him (vow 17). Those who believe in Amitābha and sincerely wish to be reborn in his Pure Land need repeat the name of Amitābha, or think of him, only ten times and they will be reborn there – provided they have not committed any of the five great crimes of murdering father or mother, or an Arhat, harming a Buddha, or causing schism in the Saṅgha, or have slandered the Dharma.[55] At the time of death Amitābha will appear, together with a heavenly host, to conduct his followers, who have awakened *bodhicitta* and practised merit, wishing to be reborn in the Pure Land, to Sukhāvatī (vow 19).[56] All those who hear the name of Amitābha and sincerely wish to be reborn in the Pure Land, directing their merits towards such a birth, will indeed be reborn there (vow 20). Moreover if Bodhisattvas elsewhere wish to be reborn in Sukhāvatī they thus enter the state of 'one more birth', which is to say that they require only one more rebirth, apparently the birth into Sukhāvatī, before attaining enlightenment. In other words, they will attain enlightenment in that Pure Land – always supposing, the *sūtra* adds, that such is what they want. If they desire, out of compassion, to be continually reborn in order to help in such a manner other sentient beings, then they can continue to do so (22; 20 in Sanskrit).

All has come about as Dharmākara wished. There is indeed a most wonderful Pure Land, and both versions of the *Sukhāvatīvyūha Sūtra* give extensive details of the appearance of Sukhāvatī, probably as a basis for the recollection of the Buddha Amitābha within his Pure Land. If someone wishes to be reborn in that Pure Land, in order to attain enlightenment, he or she should produce *bodhicitta*, hear the name of Amitābha, meditate on him and think of him, pray to be reborn in Sukhāvatī, and attain merit as a basis for such a birth. Even those who are not very keen on Amitābha will be led to Sukhāvatī at death – not by Amitābha personally but by a magically produced Buddha. Within such a framework rebirth in Sukhāvatī and eventual enlightenment is not difficult. It is much easier than trying to attain enlightenment under adverse conditions in this decadent world! At death generally Amitābha will himself conduct someone to his Pure Land, and this descent of Amitābha is the subject of innumerable Japanese paintings. In one example Amitābha, together with his heavenly host, drums, and music, descends rapidly across the mountain tops, trees bursting into spring blossoms at his approach. He crosses the canvas diagonally towards the monk who awaits the coming of the Lord, peacefully invoking Amitābha's holy name from his hermitage.[57] In the Pure Land the being (one hesitates in a Buddhist context to say the soul) is reborn non-sexually, for there are no women in Sukhāvatī. The blessed appear, seated on lotus blossoms, in the presence of Amitābha. A Central Asian wall painting from eighth-century (Qočo depicts the reborn beings as swarms of naked children seated on lotuses or playing in the beautiful garden of Sukhāvatī. One lotus is still closed, however, in a tight bud with the naked being still within (Gaulier *et al.* 1976: plate 49). According to the Larger *Sukhāvatīvyūha Sūtra* those who still harbour some doubt concerning Amitābha and his Pure Land are reborn within closed lotuses, where they dwell comfortably for 500 years, seeing the inside of the lotus as a palace with gardens. Nevertheless, being apart from the Buddha and his doctrine, relatively this is not a terribly good or happy rebirth. Eventually overcoming these doubts, such beings are grateful to emerge from this purifying purgatory, wherein they have been deprived of the celestial vision.

The principal concern of the Smaller *Sukhāvatīvyūha Sūtra* is to describe the Pure Land of Sukhāvatī (a description which does not tally completely with that of the Larger *Sūtra*) and give further elucidation of the means to attain such a favourable rebirth. In that Pure Land all is contingent upon the need for spiritual growth. It is clearly not intended merely as a sensual paradise, a place of unrestricted pleasure, alongside the various heavenly realms accepted as occupied by the gods and generally viewed with a certain disdain in the Buddhist traditions. The birds of Sukhāvatī, the result of Amitābha's great power, all proclaim the Dharma, as do the trees when gently stirred in the soft breeze. The particular instrument of rebirth in Sukhāvatī is said by this *sūtra* to be holding in mind the name of Amitābha with undistracted thought for a day, or up to seven days. Thereupon Amitābha will appear at the time of death, and the practitioner will attain to Sukhāvatī.[58] One is reminded here of the *Pratyutpanna Sūtra*, although the recollection of the Buddha in the *Sukhāvatī Sūtra* is much less elaborate, and the *pratyutpanna samādhi* is said to lead in this very life to a vision of Amitābha. It is possible that there was yet another controversy in India in classical times between advocates of a vision of Amitābha in this life, and those who sought the vision at the time of death.[59]

The *Amitāyurbuddhānusmṛti Sūtra* (if it is correct to give it a Sanskrit title) is a rather different type of *sūtra*. It was supposedly translated into Chinese by Kālayaśas in the earlier part of the fifth century. It is one of a series of *sūtras* concerned with the visualization of Buddhas and Bodhisattvas which were translated into Chinese at about the same time, and were probably composed during the preceding century (Pas 1977: 200 ff.). Scholars are now inclined to see the *Amitāyurbuddhānusmṛti Sūtra* as a text from either Central Asia or from China itself. Julian Pas, on the other hand, has pointed out that almost all the translators of these visualization *sūtras* have some connection with the area around Kashmir, and it is possible that the *sūtras* themselves were composed in that area, or nearby regions of Central Asia. His own view is that the *Amitāyurbuddhānusmṛti Sūtra* as it stands contains a series of interpolations, some quite lengthy and some of which are undoubtedly Chinese. Among these interpolations are sections important to subsequent Pure Land thought in East Asia (Pas 1977: 210).

As a text the *Amitāyurbuddhānusmṛti Sūtra* concentrates less on rebirth in the Pure Land than on *buddhānusmṛti* practices for seeing Amitābha in this present life. It purports to be a teaching given by Śākyamuni Buddha to Queen Vaidehī, who had been imprisoned by her wicked son Ajātaśatru. The dramatic situation arises out of the sufferings of Queen Vaidehī: 'Please tell me of a place free from troubles and afflictions, where I can be reborn because I do not like this impure earth....'[60] The Buddha, full of compassion, explained that Amitābha is not very far away, and taught her a series of thirteen visualization meditations: (i) on the setting sun in the west; (ii) on pure, still, limpid water, then visualized as ice, then as crystal, and then gradually visualized as the Pure Land itself; (iii) this visualization of the ground is fixed in the mind unwaveringly; and then are added (iv) the trees; (v) the lakes; (vi) the palaces; (vii) the lotus throne of Amitābha; (viii) with Amitābha upon it, and to the left of the Buddha Avalokiteśvara, while to the right is Bodhisattva Mahāsthāmaprāpta; (xi) then one contemplates the form of Amitābha; (x) then the form of Avalokiteśvara; (xi) and then the form of Mahāsthāmaprāpta; (xii) one prays for rebirth in Sukhāvatī, and visualizes completely, in detail with a fixed mind, oneself born on a lotus in the Pure Land; and finally (xiii) one visualizes before one Amitābha and the two Bodhisattvas in front.

These thirteen meditations clearly require some time and ability. They are also placed by the *sūtra* on a firm moral foundation. The text now continues with a further three meditations, each of which refers to three types of birth in the Pure Land, graded according to superiority. There are thus nine grades of rebirth in Sukhāvatī.[61] Even the lowest person can attain rebirth in Amitābha's Pure Land. Even someone who has committed the five worst deeds (see p. 253 above) may just before death meet a 'good friend' who will teach of the Buddha. Even if the miscreant cannot think of Amitābha he (or she) may call on his name ten times. This will eradicate immense misdeeds, and he will be reborn inside a lotus in Sukhāvatī, staying there for twelve aeons. The lotus will then open, our reformed miscreant will behold Avalokiteśvara and Mahāsthāmaprāpta who will preach the Doctrine. He will consequently develop *bodhicitta*. Only hearing the names of Amitābha and his two Bodhisattvas eradicates many misdeeds, let alone remembering and reciting their names.[62]

On this *sūtra* in particular, which teaches help for even the wickedest sinners who are incapable of the complex visualization practices even if they wished to do them, lie the hopes of the Pure Land tradition. If the hopes of those who feel themselves to be helpless sinners, or who cannot practise the more complex teachings, rest on a Chinese interpolation – well then, the interpolation is no doubt inspired by the compassion of the Buddha who neglects no one, no matter how wicked, inferior, or obscure!

Amitābha's Pure Land in China

According to the Chinese Pure Land tradition, the founder of their tradition in China was Hui-yüan. In Japan, however, Hui-yüan is excluded from the list of patriarchs because his practice was not a mass-movement aimed at the salvation of the common people, but rather a restricted and elitist activity based not on the three Amitābha *sūtras* but on the *Pratyutpanna Sūtra*. Hui-yüan sought to attain Sukhāvatī through his own power, not through the compassion of Amitābha and his vows to save those who called upon him. The honour of being the first Chinese patriarch, therefore, falls to T'an-luan.

Whether one accepts Hui-yüan as a patriarch or not, however, it is necessary in fact to go beyond the Chinese masters in order to trace the lineage, the patriarchate, back to respected Indian teachers. For the Pure Land traditions of both China and Japan the Indian patriarchs, their link with the fountainhead of all Buddhist doctrine, are Nāgārjuna and Vasubandhu. The Pure Land teachings are thus given a respectable ancestry embedded within the Indian schools of Madhyamaka and Cittamātra.

The basis for considering Nāgārjuna a patriarch of the Pure Land school lies primarily in a particular section of a work attributed to Nāgārjuna and known in Sanskrit reconstruction as the *Daśabhūmikavibhāṣā Śāstra*. This is a commentary on the *Daśabhūmika Sūtra*. There is considerable doubt about its attribution to Nāgārjuna, and it survives only in a Chinese version. It does not appear to be known elsewhere in Sanskrit or Tibetan sources. In the *Śāstra* 'Nāgārjuna', in the context of discussing the activity of the Bodhisattva, distinguishes between the easy and the difficult ways of practising the Dharma:

> To discipline oneself in deeds of austerity is difficult; whereas to proceed by means of faith is easy.... Those who wish to reach the stage of non-retrogression quickly should have a mind filled with reverence and pronounce the Buddha-Name, always keeping it in mind.[63]

Our author mentions all the Buddhas of the ten directions, but he particularly singles out Amitābha for praise, and tells us that he thinks of Amitābha constantly.

The relevant work attributed to Vasubandhu is known, again in Sanskrit reconstruction from the Chinese, as the *Sukhāvatīvyūhopadeśa*. Once more, this text may be by Vasubandhu or it may not. It is even possible that it was written in China itself, for it is not known as a work of Vasubandhu in any Indian or Tibetan source. According to the Pure Land masters, both Nāgārjuna and Vasubandhu turned to the Pure Land teachings in old age, although there is no independent evidence for this. Nevertheless, in China, where the *Sukhāvatīvyūhopadeśa* has been very significant, it served as a basis for T'an-luan's development of Pure Land doctrine. Particularly important is 'Vasubandhu's' clarification of the concept of 'faith' as worshipping Amitābha, praising his name, vowing constantly to be reborn in the Pure Land, meditating on Sukhāvatī, and transferring the merit thus attained to perfecting the state of great compassion in order to benefit all sentient beings (trans. in Kiyota 1978a: 278). Our author, whoever he was, makes it quite clear that the purpose of rebirth in the Pure Land is to attain enlightenment, and then out of great compassion to manifest in various ways in *saṃsāra* for the benefit of others and ultimately for their enlightenment.

During the third and fourth centuries in China as far as we can tell there was very little specific devotion to Amitābha, although there is an almost isolated reference to Chih-tun (314–66) worshipping an icon of Amitābha and seeking rebirth in Sukhāvatī where, he assures us, 'in this country there is no arrangement of royal regulations, ranks and titles. The Buddha is the ruler, and the three Vehicles are the (state) doctrine' (Zürcher 1972: 128)! The first dated image of Amitābha at Lung-men in North China is 519, although we know of further images in the south from the preceding century. Even then, the study of images produced during the sixth century indicates only 9 of Amitābha compared with 50 of Śākyamuni and 35 of Maitreya (Weinstein 1987: 69). A dramatic change occurs during the seventh century, however. From 650 to 704 only 20 images of Śākyamuni and Maitreya were erected, compared with 144 of Amitābha and Avalokiteśvara.[64] These changes occur during the collective lifetimes of the three great Chinese patriarchs of Pure Land: T'an-luan, Tao-ch'o (562–645), and Shan-tao (613–81).

T'an-luan's principal work was a commentary to the *Sukhāvatīvyūhopadeśa*. He appears to have been overcome by a certain depression concerning the possibilities of spiritual growth in the age in which he lived – things were different in the golden ages of the past, when there were sages like the Buddha. Nowadays how could one make any spiritual progress? T'an-luan adopted from 'Nāgārjuna' the distinction between difficult and easy paths, and used this distinction in order to create a religion of 'Other Power' with broad popular mass appeal, a religion for those who delve and spin, who cannot make religious progress through their own feeble actions. It is now very difficult to advance to enlightenment through relying on one's Own Power, through the results of one's own practices of spiritual discipline and study. Through relying on the power of Amitābha and his great vows, on the other hand, one can be reborn in Sukhāvatī and there most certainly attain enlightenment.

Reliance on Other Power has the advantage of being easy, but it also overcomes the philosophical and religious problem of how it is possible through one's own finite and ultimately feeble deeds to attain a state of unconditioned enlightenment, of Buddhahood (Bloom 1965: 10–11). In the light of the form of Buddha-nature thought becoming prevalent in East Asian Buddhism, a great gap was opening up between the ultimate state of Buddhahood and the conventional realm of *saṃsāra*. To seek to move from one to the other is logically impossible. Religiously, it is a basis for spiritual pride.

T'an-luan adopted the five forms of practice mentioned by 'Vasubandhu', but he placed particular emphasis on the virtues of reciting or praising the name of the Buddha Amitābha. The name, for T'an-luan, is the essence of Amitābha, and to invoke the name is to articulate the reality itself. The reference in the *sūtra* to reciting the name of Amitābha ten times means reciting it perfectly, not literally ten times and no more. Numbers are not important. To repeat constantly the name of Amitābha with a unified mind is to purify the mind of all its sins, and ensure rebirth in the Pure Land, which is ultimately enlightenment itself. Once one abandons recourse to one's own resources all activities can be seen as Other Power, the salvific activity of Amitābha working through us. But reciting the name in accordance with the *sūtra* exemplifies Amitābha's power to save most fully. Through the power of Amitābha even the worst sinner, even one who has committed the five worst acts, can attain to the Pure Land – providing the miscreant has not reviled the Doctrine.[65] This is a religion for everyone. According to a later writer, Tao-hsuan: 'T'an-luan not only practiced the teachings of Amida Buddha but also preached on them to all kinds of people, monks and nuns, laymen and laywomen, and even to non-Buddhists' (trans. in Matsumoto 1986: 38). Once in the Pure Land, once having attained enlightenment, T'an-luan follows 'Vasubandhu' in asserting that the purpose is to descend, to return for the benefit of others (Bary *et al.* 1960: 380).

The spiritual son of T'an-luan was Tao-ch'o, whose main contributions to Pure Land thought were contained in a work in which he responded to critics of the Pure Land faith. Tao-ch'o experienced a persecution of Buddhism in China, and perhaps for this reason he concluded that we are approaching the Last Days. In our age the most effective of spiritual practices is 'to repent of our sins, to cultivate virtues, and to utter the Buddha's name' (trans. in Suzuki 1950: 146). The era in which we now live is not suitable for the old practices of spiritual development, which were only really possible in previous ages. To follow the 'holy path' of study, meditation, and other traditional practices in order to attain enlightenment in this world of ours is no longer realistic. The age has passed. It is best now, therefore, to enter by the 'Gate of the Pure Land'. By this gate it is not necessary to still the passions, but only single-mindedly to reject this world and aim for rebirth in the Pure Land through the power of Amitābha and his wonderful vows.[66]

In his replies to critics, Tao-ch'o stressed that the Pure Land is indeed a relative, conventional realm with definite characteristics, that is, appropriate marvellous features. Not all Mahāyāna, however, is a search for the unconditioned. In the Mahāyāna we are repeatedly urged not to neglect the conventional truth. The Pure Land is a conventional truth, a skilful means, for the benefit of sentient beings who otherwise have no possibility of spiritual development. It is true, moreover, that the Pure Land is said in the *sūtras* to equal in reality a fully purified mind (cf. *Vimalakīrtinirdeśa*), but for those who cannot aspire to such heights there is also the conventional Pure Land in the west into which one can indeed be reborn after death. Again, it is all very well advocating rebirth in our own contaminated world rather than in the Pure Land, out of compassion for others. But who is sufficiently strong to do this without being tainted by it? Who is going to claim to be a great Bodhisattva beyond all impurities? It is better therefore to aim for enlightenment in the Pure Land of Sukhāvatī, and then act to help sentient beings. It should be clear, however, that the Pure Land is not a sensuous paradise, it is not a realm of desire and attachment, for otherwise it would not be a *pure* land. One last point. How can reciting Amitābha's name have such dramatic results? This, says Tao-ch'o, is because the name of the Buddha Amitābha is a very powerful name, the result of the Buddha's own immense merits (Bary *et al.* 1960: 381 ff.).

Tao-ch'o was the teacher of Shan-tao, who is held by the Japanese Pure Land tradition to have been an incarnation of Amitābha. He lived in the Chinese capital of Ch'ang-an, and was a contemporary of Hsüan-tsang and Fa-tsang. Unlike these masters, however, Shan-tao made little or no impact upon the imperial court. He rather concentrated on spreading the message of Amitābha and his Pure Land among ordinary people. Shan-tao is said to have attracted countless followers, some of whom were sufficiently enthusiastic for Sukhāvatī, and disparaging of what the Tibetans call this 'precious human body', to commit suicide in order to hasten their rebirth and consequent enlightenment for the benefit of sentient beings. There is even a legend that Shan-tao himself eventually committed suicide.[67] Shan-tao is said also to have made and distributed thousands of copies of the *Sukhāvatīvyūha Sūtra*, and painted some 300 paintings of the Pure Land itself (Ch'en 1964: 347). Thus he embraced in his propaganda those who could read, and also those who were illiterate but could immediately grasp the message when confronted by a painting of the attractions of Sukhāvatī contrasted with the drudgery and real misery of everyday peasant life.

Shan-tao's Pure Land teaching is contained in literary form principally in his four-volume commentary to the *Amitāyurbuddhānusmṛti Sūtra*. According to Shan-tao, Queen Vaidehī in the *sūtra* is intended as a symbol of the ordinary mortal, imprisoned in suffering and seeking a way to a better world. Thus the teaching of the *Amitāyurbuddhānusmṛti Sūtra* is a teaching for all beings.[68] Shan-tao's own starting point is yet again the spiritual decay of the age, and his own incapability for spiritual growth: 'I am actually an ordinary sinful being who has been, from time immemorial, sunken in and carried down by the current of birth-and-death. Any hope to be helped out of this current has been wholly denied to me' (trans. in Kaneko 1965: 52). This is then universalized. All people, or almost all people, in this present age are in reality in the same situation as Shan-tao himself. Buddhas have been teaching for infinite aeons, and yet we are still not enlightened. Now there is no Buddha on the earth. What chance do any of us have? We are all embedded in unskilful acts – in sin. Because of this, confession and repentence becomes an integral and important part of Shan-tao's vision of the religious life. Since we have all committed even the five great sins, if not in this life then in previous ones, the only recourse is to Amitābha, who vowed in the *sūtra* to save all beings, and who is capable of saving even the lowest sinners, as is stated in the *Amitāyurbuddhānusmṛti Sūtra*.

What shall we do to be saved? First, we must have faith in Amitābha and his vows. This faith is said to have three features. It must be sincere, that is, it must be a real faith. Also it should be a deep faith. Lastly, it should be accompanied by an overriding desire for rebirth in Amitābha's Pure Land of Sukhāvatī. Merit should be transferred accordingly. These three aspects of faith apply to all beings. If one is missing, then there will be no rebirth in the Pure Land (Bloom 1965: 14).

Supposing one has this deep and sincere faith in Amitābha. Then what? It is necessary for the devotee to engage in five forms of religious activity directed towards Amitābha. The principal practice is reciting the name of the Buddha, constantly and in all situations. This is said to be the act that truly determines entrance into the Pure Land, and can obviously be practised by those in all walks of life.[69] Auxiliary practices are chanting or reciting the *sūtras* of Amitābha, meditating on Amitābha, worshipping Amitābha and his images, and praising and making offerings to the Buddha Amitābha. Although these practices are soteriologically auxiliary, they were seen nevertheless by Shan-tao as very important. In particular, Shan-tao was concerned with the use of the *Amitāyurbuddhānusmṛti Sūtra* in meditation and visualization practice, and he enriched his commentary to the *sūtra* with his own experiences of *buddhānusmṛti* (see Pas 1974).

From Shan-tao springs the parable of the white path, an important teaching aid and oft-repeated image in subsequent Pure Land thought. A man is travelling to the west when before him stretch two rivers. On the left is a river of fire. On the right, water. Between the two is a white path 'barely four or five inches wide'. From east to west is a hundred steps. The fire scorches one side of the path, the waves ceaselessly wash the other. As if this is not enough, in the east where our traveller stands is a band of hooligans and wild animals, seeking to kill him. The poor man is seized with terror, but resolves to try to follow the path. At that very moment he hears a voice behind him from his own bank: 'Friend, just follow this path resolutely and there will be no danger of death. To stay here is to die.' And on the west bank there is someone calling out: 'Come straight ahead, single-mindedly and with fixed purpose. I can protect you. Never fear falling into the fire or water!' As our traveller sets off, however, the hooligans call to him: 'Come back – we won't hurt you!' Nevertheless, he goes resolutely forward, reaches the west bank safely, 'he is greeted by his good friend and there is no end of joy'.[70]

In brief, the hither shore in the parable stands for the world of *saṃsāra*; the further shore in the west that of Sukhāvatī. The hooligans and animals, seeming friends, are our senses, consciousnesses, and so on. Fire is anger and hatred; water, greed and affection. The white path is the aspiration for rebirth in the Pure Land, which actually arises amidst the passions themselves. The voice from the hither shore is that of Śākyamuni, who has disappeared from sight but continues to point the true way. From the west bank comes the voice of Amitābha, his vow to save all beings. In such an image, easily understood and remembered by the lowest peasant, is encapsulated the message of Pure Land thought.

I have spoken of the three Chinese Pure Land patriarchs accepted by Japanese Pure Land Buddhism. There were, however, other great Pure Land teachers in China. After the traumas of the An Lu-shan rebellion the increasing popularity of Pure Land among the masses, together with, perhaps, a growing pessimism concerning this world, meant that Pure

Land Buddhism eventually came to the notice of the imperial court. Fa-chao (second half of the eighth century) was instrumental in this growing awareness, and was posthumously granted by the emperor the title of 'Master of Great Enlightenment'. He is said to have been the reincarnation of Shan-tao, and to have had a number of visions of Amitābha. In one vision, Fa-chao was taught a method of reciting the name of the Buddha using five different rhythms, a method described as a 'priceless and rare treasure'.[71] Fa-chao was also responsible for the standardization of the name to be recited as 'A [or O]-mit-t'o Fo', the Chinese transliteration of the name 'Amitābha Buddha'. The oft-repeated utterance thus becomes 'Na-mo A-mi-to Fo' – 'Adoration [or prostration] to Amitābha Buddha'. In Japanese pronunciation this becomes 'Namu Amida Butsu'. Paintings of the period were fond of such pedagogic devices as depictions of the hells on one side and the Pure Land on the other – as was common in many medieval church wall paintings in the West.

Tz'u-min (otherwise known as Hui-jih; 680–748) was a Pure Land master who visited India and also contributed to the growing rapprochement between Ch'an and Pure Land practice. His attack on the Ch'an of his day bears notable similarities with the criticisms of Ho-shang Mahāyāna's Ch'an half a century or so later in Tibet. These Ch'an practitioners argue that there is no need to recite the *sūtras*, or the name of Amitābha, or erect statues, serve teachers and elders, or indeed do any other virtuous deeds. All these belong to the conditioned and not the unconditioned. The same can be said of all the perfections except for practising Ch'an (which here must mean the perfection of wisdom). This is wrong, says Tz'u-min, for the *sūtras*, the word of the Buddha, teach otherwise. In practice these Ch'an 'adepts' do a little meditation in the evening, and the rest of the day they neglect discipline and sleep or run riot (trans. in Suzuki 1935: 357–8). Actually, Tz'u-min notes, to attain enlightenment through Ch'an is very difficult, but we know that recourse to Amitābha is easy, and thence one can attain enlightenment and help sentient beings. Nevertheless, within the context of the Amitābha practice it may also be possible and indeed beneficial to practise Ch'an. The Ch'an master Yen-shou (904–75) from his side made a positive attempt to unite the practice of Ch'an with Pure Land on the basis that everything is after all but mind – as the *Vimalakīrtinirdeśa* teaches, the Pure Land is in fact a pure mind, and many texts state that the Buddha is in reality none other than one's own mind. Moreover both Ch'an and Pure Land aim to cut egoistic grasping and to purify the mind of the practitioner. When the Pure Land practitioner speaks of abandoning Own Power and having recourse to Other Power, when he speaks of the impossibility of enlightening himself by his own efforts, what is this but another statement of the basic Buddhist teaching of no-Self (Ch'en 1964: 404–5)? This blending of Ch'an and Pure Land practice became further established in the Ming and Manchu dynasties, particularly in the thought of Chu-hung (1535–1615), and in Chinese Buddhism to the present day it is common to combine Ch'an and Pure Land practice in Ch'an monasteries.

Holmes Welch describes the graded practice he encountered in China, whereby beginners would recite the name of Amitābha while fixing their eyes on his image. When they had become more experienced they would mentally visualize the form of the Buddha. The most advanced practice is to have no Buddha to visualize, and no self to do the visualization – pure non-dual awareness (Welch 1967: 399). Moreover constant repetition of the name of the Buddha is a technique which could be useful in engendering meditative absorption and purifying the mind. There is thus no difference between Pure Land and Ch'an. Needless to say, however, this use of reciting the name of Buddha Amitābha as a mere technique, even if a meritorious technique, in order to calm and purify the mind exemplifies Own Power, and makes no reference to the crucial roles of Other Power, Amitābha and his salvific vows. Such a Ch'an use of recitation is therefore rather remote from that envisaged by Pure Land masters like Shan-tao – and much further still from a Japanese like Shinran.

Hōnen Shōnin (1133–1212)

The civil warfare, famine, disease, economic collapse, and general misery in Japan which accompanied the end of the Heian era and the ushering in of the Kamakura age gave an immense impetus to the growth of Pure Land Buddhism, for all could vividly appreciate the wish of Queen Vaidehī for another world of happiness far from the present troubles. We have already seen that these ghastly sufferings and the accompanying 'other worldliness' gave a strong impetus to the development of the theory of the Last Days (*mappō*). The problem was how to live and practise religion when the end is nigh? The reply, broadly speaking, was to simplify and embrace further the laity – whether in Dōgen's austere Sōtō Zen or in Nichiren's combative advocacy of the *Lotus Sūtra* as alone sufficient, exemplified in the chanting of its title. Pure Land Buddhism was ideally suited to respond to the situation, for in China it had already presented itself as a response to the declining spiritual age. The Japanese sufferings gave it a new urgency, and it responded with further simplification, a complete abandonment to the Buddha's compassion, and an ever-widening popular and non-monastic basis.

Hōnen became a Tendai monk on Mt Hiei at the age of 9, and appears to have graduated a distinguished scholar. Yet, he felt that this had not brought him anywhere nearer to enlightenment. Like other Tendai monks of the age, but with an honesty they perhaps lacked, Hōnen felt

> that I am one whose eyes are blind to the truth and whose feet, paralyzed, are unable to walk the Holy Path ... I bitterly regret that day and night my thoughts turn in the direction of prestige and money.
>
> (Quoted in Yui-en 1961: vii)

He began to study the principal work of Genshin (942–1017), an earlier Japanese advocate of Pure Land practice within the framework of the Tendai tradition. This work had a profound effect on Hōnen, although he came to reject Genshin's emphasis on visualization practice as too difficult – and, quite frankly, Hōnen could not see the point:

> Even if spiritual novices are successful in creating a vision of Amida, in beauty it will never rival the carvings of the great masters, nor could a vision of the Pure Land be as lovely as the real flowers of the cherry, plum, peach or pear.
>
> (Trans. Matsunaga and Matsunaga 1974/6: II, 59)

What are visions seen through visualization meditation but second-hand images floating before the eyes? In his search Hōnen is said to have read the entire Buddhist Canon five times, and yet he still felt as far away from enlightenment as ever. Eventually, however, according to tradition at the age of 42 or 43, Hōnen was inspired by a reading of Shan-tao to let go entirely, to have recourse totally to reciting the name of Amitābha as the only practice suitable for the present age. In the ghastly era in which we live, only Other Power, the power of Amitābha's infinite compassion, can save us. Recitation of the name of Amitābha is alone sufficient for that salvation.

Hōnen's principal work is known as the *Senjakushu*, but his view is simply stated in a 'One Page Document' which he composed at the request of a disciple in order to stress the basic simplicity of his teaching. By reciting the Buddha's name, Hōnen states, I do not mean meditation, or reciting it as a result of studying and understanding its deep meaning. No – all I mean is simply reciting the Buddha's name (Japanese: *nembutsu*) with no doubt that this will lead to rebirth in the Pure Land. The spirit in which this recitation is done is, as Hōnen states elsewhere, one of 'joy ... as high as the heavens above and as deep as the earth beneath ... always ... returning thanks for the great blessedness of having in this life come in contact with the Original Vow of the Amida Buddha'.[72] Nothing else is necessary – all is contained in this. Indeed it is positively wrong to imagine that there is more to it than this. No matter how learned one is, one should be like a simple person and simply recite the *nembutsu*.[73] Again, in his letters Hōnen states that no matter how great a sinner one is, one should not give way to doubts, for Amitābha does not hate anyone. Although in reciting the *nembutsu* one should have, as Shan-tao taught, the three factors of sincerity, deep faith, and desire for rebirth in the Pure Land, still, if one has complete trust in Amitābha's vow and recites the *nembutsu* one already has these three factors (Burtt 1955: 213–16).

All that is necessary is to recite the name of the Buddha with complete trust in Amitābha's vows. Even the worst sinner will most certainly be saved. There remains a Japanese folk song from about the same period in which the singer laments.

> I'm shunned
> By the ten thousand Buddhas,
> For having hunted and fished,
> To live this sentient life –
> What must I do for salvation?
>
> (in Tetsurō 1971: 102)

Hōnen himself is said to have met some poor and elderly fisherfolk who were terrified and depressed because of the consequences of their occupation. He preached to them the salvific power of Amitābha's name. Overjoyed, they went on their way, catching fish by day and reciting the *nembutsu* by night (Eliot 1935: 265). What are we to say? Compassion transforms those who can be transformed, but helps those who cannot?

Hōnen impressed all who met him with his humility and attractive personality – although Nichiren, who did not meet Hōnen but hated him for his emphasis on Amitābha and corresponding neglect of Śākyamuni, asserted that after death Hōnen became an evil spirit! Sir Charles Eliot has commented that Hōnen's

> great personal influence was due to his singularly amiable character, which made him beloved of all his friends and acquaintances. ... He offered in the gentlest and most persuasive form a simple and attractive teaching ... which offered salvation to those who could justify themselves neither by learning nor by good works....
>
> (Eliot 1935: 266–7)

As a monk, Hōnen was austere and consumed neither meat nor alcohol. As an austere Tendai monk, Hōnen himself continued to take part in Tendai ordination rites, and even ordained laity for the cure of illness (through the merit they gained by joining the order). The extent to which Hōnen differed from his Tendai predecessors is thus a matter of some dispute. Nevertheless, Hōnen's teaching that the *nembutsu* is sufficient for salvation, and Amitābha saves even the lowest sinner, was open to charges of antinomianism. Why not do evil, or at least behave as one likes, since Amitābha will save us anyway? There is no notion that we are saved through our inadequate moral deeds, but only through the Other Power of Amitābha. This argument provided Hōnen with a real problem, familiar also, of course, in Western theology. In a nine-point attack upon his teaching, Hōnen's opponents accused him, among other things, of rejecting the Vinaya, and claiming that 'those who are worried about such sins as gambling or meat eating failed to place total reliance upon the power of Amida' (Matsunaga and Matsunaga 1974/6: II, 66). It is known that certain of Hōnen's disciples publicly broke the Vinaya code as presented for monks, eating meat and declaring that one should not respect any Buddhas other than Amitābha.[74] A highly respected scholar of the Kegon school, on the other hand, Myōe Shōnin (1173–1232), accused Hōnen of neglecting the *bodhicitta*. The concern is not with saving sentient beings, not with developing compassion, but simply with rebirth in the Pure Land. As such, Hōnen's teaching is not Mahāyāna – in fact it is not Buddhism, but is just the non-Buddhist search for heaven in another guise (Shōjun 1971: 72 ff.). Such a criticism is cutting. Hōnen would probably have answered with 'Vasubandhu' and T'an-luan that in the present age only by attaining enlightenment in the Pure Land can one actually fulfil the requirements of *bodhicitta*. Far from neglecting *bodhicitta*, he is embracing it in the only realistic way.

Eventually, as a result of a scandal involving Hōnen's disciples, the Master was defrocked and exiled. He accepted this humbly, ever grateful to Amitābha for his compassion. After Hōnen's death the blocks used to print his *Senjakushu* were destroyed, and there was even an attempt to destroy his tomb and throw his body into the river. Hōnen himself responded to his critics with a seven-point pledge which he drew up for the adherence of his followers, pledging in particular not to criticize other traditions, encourage or engage in immorality, or advocate one's own views as those of the Master (Matsunaga and Matsunaga 1974/6: II, 63–4). Hōnen asserted in his letters that one should on no account despise the excellent *sūtras*, or any part of the teaching of Śākyamuni. Nowhere in the *sūtras* does the Buddha encourage one to sin. And

> while believing that even a man guilty of the ten evil deeds and the five deadly sins may be born into the Pure Land, let us, as far as we are concerned, not commit even the smallest sins. If this is true of the wicked, how much more of the good.[75]

Yet, to state that his followers should adhere to the moral code is not to say why it is necessary, given Hōnen's teachings. What effect does morality have on salvation? Is not recourse to morality recourse to Own Power? Another point: how many times is it necessary to recite the name of Amitābha Buddha in order to be saved? Whatever the answer, one or many, surely this is also recourse to Own Power? Hōnen was a great spiritual figure, a saint, but one feels that he was not a systematic or abstract thinker. He seems to have held that chanting the name of Amitābha removes the effects of sin, and consequently the more it is chanted the better it will be. Hōnen appears anyway to have felt that constant repetition is useful for disciplinary reasons (Bloom 1965: 21). He himself is said to have recited the *nembutsu* some 60,000 times a day. If there is time left after repeating the name of the Buddha, then one should engage in good works! Nevertheless, Hōnen argued that frequent repetition does not equal Own Power, from which it should follow that the amount of repetition does not in itself earn salvation. Even one utterance of the *nembutsu* could be Own Power if done in the wrong spirit, while many utterances are not Own Power if chanted with complete faith in Amitābha and his great vow (in Burtt 1955: 215). Paradoxically, however, Hōnen also seems to have held that if at the time of death the mind is in a state of evil then, no matter how much someone has repeated the *nembutsu*, that person will loose the Pure Land. For this reason too it is necessary to repeat constantly the name of Amitābha – to 'watch and wait' (Bloom 1965: 21–2). It may be wrong anyway even to try and portray Hōnen as a systematic thinker. Rather, perhaps, his utterances should be seen as individual responses to the specific problems of his followers, and his age.

It was traditional in Japan for a devotee of Amitābha, at the time of death, to lie facing a picture or image of Amitābha and his Bodhisattvas, placed in the west of his or her room. A five-coloured cord would be used to connect the dying person with the image. Many of the Japanese paintings of the Amitābha trinity were no doubt used for this purpose. At Hōnen's death, however, we are told that he said no cord or image was necessary. For the last ten years or so he had constantly before his eyes a vision of the Pure Land, Amitābha, and his attendant Bodhisattvas. Whatever Hōnen thought of visions, they pursued him to his grave!

Shinran Shōnin (1173–1262)

Hōnen's tradition, which in the generations after his death split into two main schools, is known as the Jōdo Shū, the Pure Land Sect. Shinran, as a disciple of Hōnen, always considered that he was simply transmitting his Master's teaching in all its purity, and for this reason, perhaps, Shinran is not included as a patriarch even in his own school, known in modern times as the Jōdo Shin Shū – the True Pure Land Sect.

It is very difficult to disentangle legend from fact in the story of Shinran's life, and until relatively recently there was even a doubt expressed in some quarters as to whether Shinran ever really existed. These doubts have now been dispelled, largely due to the discovery in 1921 of letters written by Shinran's wife after his death. The fact that Shinran married (possibly more than once) and had children is itself of enormous importance for, like Hōnen, Shinran trained as a monk on Mt Hiei. He became a close disciple of Hōnen, and was defrocked and sent into exile at the same time as his Master. During the time of his exile Shinran came into close contact with the common peasantry and their everyday problems and fears. Initially he began to see his mission as to save the ordinary people of the remote area of Japan to which he had been sent, and eventually to minister to all people, but particularly the lowest peasantry throughout Japan (see Bloom 1968: 16 ff.).

Shinran appears to have married after going into exile. He was a defrocked priest unused to lay life. In his own words he was neither priest nor layman; he was legally no longer a monk, but he could not and would not assume the worldly attitudes and aspirations of a layman. Eventually pardoned, as was Hōnen, Shinran remained a married layman. He established no temples, but rather his followers met in private houses – even though such private groups were actually illegal at that time.[76]

Shinran's married state was a visible symbol of a teaching which denied the validity of the lay/monk distinction, since Own Power is in no way possible as a means to liberation. In the eyes of Amitābha there is no distinction between monk and laity; all can become enlightened, enlightenment is not the concern of the monastic orders alone. It is possible that Shinran thought of marriage as a state in which the partners help to develop each other in following the spiritual path. The existence of children (one of which, Zenran, gave Shinran so much trouble that he was eventually disowned by his father), on the other hand, eventually led to the development of a blood-lineage within the Jōdo Shin Shū which has continued down to the present day. With the growth of great and powerful land-owning Shin Shū temples in the centuries after the death of Shinran, eventually complete with private armies, the Jōdo Shin Shū hierarchs at times looked more like feudal barons than simple devotees of Amitābha.

But then – Amitābha's vow (the eighteenth vow, which is of crucial importance to Jōdo Shin Shū) is precisely for those enmeshed in worldly passions, the greedy, the angry, the ignorant, the wicked, those who otherwise have no hope. Shinran's principal work is known as the *Kyōgyōshinshō*, a series of extracts, with his own commentary, from the scriptures and the writings of the Shin Shū patriarchs. His teaching is found in its most accessible form, however, in the *Tannisho* (Yui-en 1961), a short work written by Yui-en, one of Shinran's disciples (or 'friends'). It is in two parts. In the first part Yui-en gives Shinran's oral teachings as he remembered them from the Master himself. In part two, Yui-en clarified Shinran's teaching on a number of issues on which disputes or misinterpretations had arisen since Shinran's death.

Amitābha, Shinran says, accepts us all with our cravings. It is for this very reason that his compassionate vow has been declared for all beings (Yui-en 1961: 16–17). 'If we could root out all tormenting cravings we could become a Buddha through our own efforts.' But if that were possible then Amitābha's great vow would have been in vain (ibid., 33–4). Amitābha's vow is for those lowest beings who cannot save themselves through their Own Power. Yui-en comments that one should not dispute with or defame the advocates of Own Power. But as for us, we are simply incapable of that difficult path (ibid., 25–6). Shinran described himself as 'drowned in a broad sea of lust' and wandering 'confusedly in the great mountain of fame'. 'O how shameful, pitiful' (Bloom 1965: 29)! He is not the kind of person who can become a Buddha through the Own Power path of strenuous religious practices. He is definitely a sinner, definitely destined for hell. Therefore what can he do – he is going to hell anyway, so there is nothing to be lost in taking a gamble and following what

Hōnen taught: 'Just call the name and you will be saved by Amida' (Yui-en 1961: 3–4). It was on Amitābha's vow that Shinran based his entire hope: 'When I reflect deeply on the Grand Vow . . . I am convinced that it was made utterly and solely for my sake. Bound up as I am with deep and heavy karma, I feel profoundly grateful it was vowed to save the like of me' (ibid., 52–3). Shinran is also clear that none of this is a matter of reasoning. He simply follows his teacher (ibid., 3; cf. 19). In his disparaging of reasoning Shinran shares a common ground with much of East Asian Buddhism (with its Taoist influences), particularly those forms which, through their simplicity, increased their appeal during the Last Days from the Kamakura period onwards.

Like Hōnen, Shinran abstracted from his own sense of sin and powerlessness to the general human condition itself. Not only is he riddled with sin, but we are all like this. We cannot perform a non-egoistic act, and for this reason we cannot perform a truly good act.[77] We are self-centred and therefore, compared with the Buddha, we as unenlightened beings are evil by our very nature. Acts, consequently, cannot lead to Buddhahood, and attaining Buddhahood has nothing to do with earning it through merit or good deeds (Yui-en 1961: 22–3; Bloom 1965: 32 ff.).

The only meaning that can be given to the notion of egolessness, no-Self, is to 'let go', leaving good and evil 'to the natural working of karmic law and surrendering wholeheartedly to the Grand Vow' (Yui-en's words). Amitābha saves despite sins (Yui-en 1961: 33). If Buddhism is based on the doctrine of no-Self, then Shinran claims that Other Power alone is completely letting go, complete abandonment of all notions of self. But Shinran does not want us to think that his teaching enables us to behave as we like. He does not deny the karmic law – if we do evil we still suffer – and, as Shinran said in a letter, 'One should not relish taking poison simply because an antidote is at hand' (ibid., 31). Shinran seems to have thought that the real devotee would cease to do good deeds in a contrived egoistic way, as a means to a desired end. Rather, good deeds, like the *nembutsu*, would flow naturally from his or her inner nature.[78] Nevertheless, when his teaching on the power of Amitābha to save is combined with his strict denial of free will, it seems to me that there remains a certain worry over the coherence of Shinran's basis for ethical acts.[79]

We cannot be saved by Own Power (Japanese: *jiriki*), but only through Other Power (Japanese: *tariki*). Put another way, we can be saved only through faith in Amitābha and his vow. When this faith arises the ego dies; when the ego dies 'tormenting cravings and evil hindrances are converted into enlightenment' (Yui-en 1961: 36). But Shinran does not mean by 'faith' an intentional volition on our part, for if salvation came from faith and *we* produced the faith then salvation would be the result of Own Power. The faith (Japanese: *shinjin*) which Shinran refers to is a complete letting go, and therefore cannot come from the egoistic sin-ridden individual. In that sense the faith of Jōdo Shin Shū is very difficult. The ego is always egoistic – it is difficult to let go completely, 'most difficult among the difficult' (quoted in Bloom 1965: 41). In another sense, however, it is not difficult, for one does not have to do anything. Faith can save because it is Other Power. That is, faith must be the action of Amitābha himself, shining from within.

Shinran adopted a version of Shan-tao's characterization of faith, as sincerity, trustfulness, and a desire for rebirth in the Pure Land – stressing not the acts these entailed but rather the attitudes (ibid., 38). Chief among these is the attitude of sincerity, and all three are gifts from Amitābha, Other Power working in us. Put a different way, faith is not a volitional belief in something, but an articulation of our Buddha-nature.[80] This is crucial, and places Shinran's thought squarely within the development of East Asian Buddhist theory. We can become enlightened because we are already enlightened – as Dōgen said, only Buddhas become Buddhas. We cannot enlighten ourselves, for the ego cannot bring about egolessness. Only Other Power can help us. This is because within us all, at our very core, is Other Power itself, or the Buddha-nature which is Amitābha. It is Other Power beyond the ego of Own Power. In other words, we can become enlightened through faith. This is not possible if faith is Own Power. Therefore faith is Other Power. Only Other Power can save us. We can only have faith because faith is a shining forth of our innate Buddha-nature, which is Amitābha himself. All can be saved through faith, for all have the Buddha-nature, and all that is required is to stop striving and allow the Buddha-nature to radiate faith. The Buddha-nature is the Buddha, which is to say Amitābha himself, and we are saved solely through his shining forth – that is, his compassion. Faith, therefore, is in this sense the result of Amitābha's grace, for in no way can it be earned. For Shinran all transference of merit is from Amitābha to man, and not from man to a rebirth in the Pure Land. Sentient beings themselves have no merit, they have nothing to transfer; if it was left to our Own Power then there would be no rebirth in the Pure Land, and no enlightenment at all (Bloom 1965: 49).

When faith arises, and the Buddha-nature shines, one is instantly assured of rebirth in the Pure Land. That is, one is already saved (Bloom 1965: 50–1, 59). The teaching of the Pure Land is one of 'sudden enlightenment'. In this very life the moment faith arises we are definitely assured of enlightenment. Shinran states:

> We say that we abide in the rank of the company of the truly assured when we encounter the profound Vow of the gift of Amida's Other Power and our minds which rejoice at being given true faith are assured, and when, because we are accepted by him, we have the adamantine mind. (ibid., 61–2)

As a result of the arising of faith one fervently recites the name of Amitābha. Nevertheless this recitation does not earn one's salvation in any sense. In particular, there is no question of recitation at the time of death being crucial in attaining the Pure Land. The moment faith truly arises our rebirth is assured (Yui-en 1961: 37–8). No act we do brings about our salvation. Rather, faith manifests itself in the recitation of the name of Amitābha Buddha. Thus the appearance of Amitābha's grace within issues naturally in the flow of the *nembutsu*. It is 'a sign of praise and gratitude in which the devotee acknowledged his great debt to Amida Buddha'. Gratitude, for Jōdo Shin Shū, becomes a way of life (Bloom 1965: 73–4). As Yui-en puts it:

> for rebirth in the Pure Land cleverness is not necessary – just complete and unceasing absorption in gratitude to Amida. Only then does the Nembutsu come forth effortlessly. This is what is meant by naturalness. Naturalness, therefore, is that state in which there is no self-contrivance, just the grace and strength of Amida.
>
> (Yui-en 1961: 45)

If faith is the result of Amitābha's grace, if Amitābha has universal compassion, and only one moment of faith is necessary in order to be saved, and if also Amitābha has been exerting his salvific influence now for some aeons, and we have all been reborn many times, then why is it that we have not been saved already? It is not clear to me how this can be answered without recourse to some form of Other Power. One possible avenue, however, is to refer to a comment made in a modern Shin Shū manual. No Buddhist tradition, as far as I know, maintains that the Buddha is literally omnipotent. Among the things that even a Buddha cannot do is exhaust the infinite sentient beings needing to be saved, and save a person against his or her will (in Lloyd 1910: 152). Assuming that it takes an infinite time to complete an infinite task, perhaps the Buddha has to date been too busy elsewhere to save us! I do not find this a very satisfactory answer, however – one reason being that it is not clear to me that it should take an infinite time to save infinite beings. We might adopt the other tack. An impetus must logically come from the person who is to be saved, for the Buddha-nature that shines forth in faith, while not ego, is nevertheless *his* Buddha-nature. Otherwise *he* (or she) would not produce faith, and *he* would not be saved. Alternatively, it seems that if one person is saved then all should be saved – which is in one obvious sense patently false. I am not, alas, a Buddha in act, even if I am one in potential – and I assume I am not the only one lacking the supreme vision. If anything at all is needed from my side, however, this surely sails very close to Own Power. Perhaps one could argue nevertheless that it is not Own Power precisely because it lies in the letting go of all Own Power? But surely it is *I* who have to let go! Is this possible, however, or should it be for Shinran another contradiction?

At death, says Yui-en:

> We are enlightened the moment we become one with the all-illuminating, all-pervading light of the bright moon of truth shining forth as the dark clouds of tormenting cravings are dispersed when we reach the shore of the Pure Land of Fulfilment. For having crossed over the turbulent sea of suffering that is life-and-death on the vessel of Amida's Grand Compassion, we are enabled to save every sentient being.
>
> (Yui-en 1961: 40–1)

It seems, therefore, that the Pure Land is effectively not some place where we go, eventually to become enlightened. Rather, we are immediately enlightened at death – we become what we always were. From this position of enlightenment we are able to act for the benefit of others. Whereas in the other Pure Land schools one attains the Pure Land at death, and thereupon definite assurance of enlightenment, for Shinran definite assurance occurs in life at the arising of faith. When death occurs it appears that one attains enlightenment there and then. Thus the Pure Land as understood by Shinran is in the very last resort not a beautiful Buddha Field with trees, terraces, and pools, although it may be presented like that in order to help those who find such images more accessible. Rather, the Pure Land is Buddhahood itself, the *dharmakāya*, or the pure mind of the *Vimalakīrtinirdeśa*.[81] Through the complete letting go, the egolessness of the arising of faith, therefore, one can attain perfect Buddhahood for the benefit of all living beings. Of course, such a teaching, whether true or false, suited very well a social situation where the ancestors could now be portrayed as Perfect Buddhas, no longer subject to rebirth, and remaining full of compassion to look after their descendants, among other sentient beings. The notion that the dead could and should be referred to as Buddhas developed relatively early in Japanese Buddhist history (Matsunaga and Matsunaga 1974/6: I, 253 ff.). It shows in a new guise the occasional discomfort felt in China and Japan when the pan-Indian doctrine of rebirth confronted indigenous cults of respect for ancestors.

Shinran's system is all very well, but is it Buddhism? Shinran makes it clear in his *Kyōgyōshinshō* that the motivation for seeking rebirth in the Pure Land is *bodhicitta*, the desire to help sentient beings, and not pleasure, one's own happiness (Shinran 1973: 193). Since *bodhicitta* is crucial to, and characteristic of, any notion of Mahāyāna this should be sufficient to class Jōdo Shin Shū as Mahāyāna in one of its many skilful guises. In addition, it is argued that faith is the result of complete egolessness, emptiness, and the Pure Land is in its highest expression another name for Buddhahood, the *dharmakāya* itself. Perhaps most of all the Pure Land tradition should be judged by its effectiveness as a mind training, a means of cutting greed, hatred, and delusion and generating their opposites, a means of 'ceasing to do evil and learning to do good'. Although the expression of Shinran's system in this context is certainly rather different from, say, Theravāda or the dGe lugs traditions, nevertheless in practice, as is borne out by the stories of the Pure Land saints (the *myōkōnin*), the Pure Land tradition has often been strikingly effective.[82] True, Shinran's Pure Land teaching disparages Own Power, although it sees a clash between Own Power and the no-Self doctrine and can thus on its own terms claim to be truer to the Buddhist wisdom teachings than other traditions. In fact, in the light of Buddhist doctrinal history any conception of Buddhism which would see exclusive use of Own Power as essential to Buddhism would have to rule out also most of Mahāyāna from Buddhism as well! Moreover in its broad appeal to all classes of people Pure Land Buddhism can claim to be closer to the spirit of the Mahāyāna teaching of universal liberation and compassion than most other more exclusive forms of Buddhism.

In the last analysis, of course, to define Buddhism in a way which would rule out Shinran's Jōdo Shin Shū would be to beg the question. Shinran's system is *de facto* Buddhism, for it calls itself Buddhism and can be traced back through a linear series of shifting ideas and influences to China and thence to India, and through the series to the Buddha himself. There is probably no clear-cut, unchanging core to Buddhist doctrine. Buddhism as a religion in history has no essence, although the truth – whatever it is – remains for ever. And that, I think, is where we came in!

Notes

CHAPTER 1 INTRODUCTION

1 The notion of the *svabhāva* (Pāli: *sabhāva*), inherent or essential existence, appears to be missing from the earliest Theravāda Abhidhamma literature, which may well have had far less concern with ontology than was later the case and is most familiar from the Sarvāstivāda.

2 Dating of *sūtras* is always fiendishly difficult. The *Lokānuvartuna Sūtra* was translated into Chinese during the second century CE, which places it among the very earliest Buddhist *sūtras* to be translated into Chinese. There is no particular reason to think that it was directly influenced by Mahāyāna.

3 Lance Cousins has suggested to me in a private note an alternative view that the Sthaviravādins may have been the innovators, in introducing new and stricter rules.

4 Richard Gombrich has suggested to me the importance of the fact that the Canon was first committed to writing at the end of the first century BCE (Pāli). This is the very period of the growth of the Mahāyāna. Without writing, the scriptures could not be worshipped. Thus the writing of the scriptures may have had some impact on the origins of the Mahāyāna.

5 I am influenced here by Schopen's concept of 'generalization' (Schopen 1983: 133–4).

6 On the ambivalent position of Theravāda monks as renunciates *and* society's leaders in Sri Lanka, see Gombrich (1988). In Brahmanic political theory the principal function of the king is precisely to protect.

7 I believe I am right in saying that the Gilgit manuscripts are the only classical Mahāyāna scriptures found on Indian soil. This may again suggest the

relative unpopularity of Mahāyāna. Given the number of Mahāyāna *sūtras* important to East Asian Buddhism which were probably composed in Central Asia and China, it is just possible that the popularization of Mahāyā na was a phenomenon which took place outside the Indian subcontinent, for reasons connected, perhaps with the transmission of Buddhism to other cultures.

8 The notion of the Buddha still being available, while important in the rise of Mahais not so remote from non-Mahāyāna practice (as opposed to doctrine) as it may appear. Gregory Schopen has recently shown evidence for the widespread belief from the early centuries of Buddhism that the Buddha was somehow still present in his *stūpa* relics (Schopen 1987).

CHAPTER 2 THE *PERFECTION OF WISDOM (PRAJÑĀPĀRAMITĀ) SŪTRAS*

1 Conze (1960: 10) has 'West' for 'East', but perhaps this is a slip. The Sanskrit reads *vartanyāṃ*. See also Bareau (1955: 296–305).

2 In particular Conze betrays his own bias in the expression 'concessions to the Buddhism of Faith', a bias which has perhaps affected his discussions on relative chronological priority of sections within, particularly, the *Aṣṭasāhasrikā* (Conze 1967a: 168 ff.).

3 See the Fifth Dalai Lama in Hopkins (1974: 3), for example.

4 Lance Cousins points out to me the possible connection of Subhūti in the pre-Mahāyāna traditions with *mettā*, loving kindness. Hence the choice of Subhūti in the Mahāyāna would reflect the correspondingly great emphasis on compassion.

5 Pratyekabuddhas are a category of enlightened beings superior to the Arhats but still deficient from the Mahāyāna point of view in compassion. They are classed with the Arhats as non-Mahāyāna saints, and there is said to be a Pratyekabuddhayāna along with the Śrāvaka (Hearer) and Mahā-yānas. The whole notion of the Pratyekabuddha requires further research.

6 This whole topic is extensively discussed by Tsong kha pa in his sub-commentary to the *Madhyamakāvatāra*; see the translation in Hopkins (1980: 150–81).

7 For an account of the Bodhisattva's analysis through *dharmas* and beyond see the *Vimalakīrtinirdeśa Sūtra*, translation in Lamotte (1962: 228 ff.). This is not a *Prajñāpāramitā sūtra*, but it is a very early *sūtra* of the *Prajñāpāramitā* type. For Tsong kha pa's criticisms of the 'blank mind', see Wayman (1978: 395; cf. Thurman 1982: 176 ff.).

CHAPTER 3 MADHYAMAKA

1 This is true in particular of the Svātantrika school. See now Iida (1980),

Lopez (1987), and Eckel (1986). For the Madhyamaka in general, see Ruegg (1981).

2 For Tsong kha pa's arguments see his *Lam rim chen mo*, trans. in Wayman (1978: 279–83). Cf. also Hopkins (1983: 441–53).

3 See Ruegg (1983) and Williams (1985). For a translation by Bhattacharya of the *Vigrahavyāvartanī*, see Nāgārjuna (1978).

4 For arguments in Tibet against the Self, and the way it should be seen conventionally, see Hopkins (1983: 47–51) and Wilson (1980: esp. 46).

5 Lai (1979: 47–8); cf. Hurvitz (1975).

6 See the German translation by Walleser (1912: 88). For Chi-tsang see his *San-lun hsüan-i*, trans. in Chan (1963: 365–8).

7 See Fung Yu-lan (1948: 246) and Chan (1963: 361). For Indian Madhyamaka discussions of language, silence, and non-conceptuality, see Williams (1980: esp. 23 ff.).

CHAPTER 4 CITTAMĀTRA (MIND ONLY)

1 Frauwallner (1951a) has argued that there were in fact two Vasubandhus. The author of the *Abhidharmakośa* was not the same Vasubandhu as Asaṅga's brother. Against this, Jaini (1958) has pointed out on the basis of the *Abhidharmadīpa* that the author of the *Abhidharmakośa* may well have subsequently converted to the Mahāyāna. There is not necessarily a contradiction here. Schmithausen has argued that the *Viṃśatikā* and *Triṃṃśikā* differ from other works attributed to Vasubandhu, and show the Sautrāntika origins of their author. The author of the *Abhidharmakośa* was also probably a Sautrāntika. It is therefore reasonable to suggest that the author of the *Abhidharmakośa* became a Mahāyānist, while at the same time holding with Frauwallner that this is a different Vasubandhu from the brother of Asaṅga, who also converted to Mahāyāna (see Schmithausen 1967).

2 This point is well made by a contemporary Tibetan lama, Khenpo Tsultrim Gyamtso (1986: 39–40), and we shall return to it in Chapter 6.

3 Sanskrit: *trisvabhāva*. The word '*svabhāva*' here does not mean inherent existence, as it does for the Madhyamaka, although that is not to say that the word is never used for inherent existence in Cittamātra.

4 See here the translation of the *Yogācārabhūmi* chapter on Reality by Willis (1979: 160 ff.); cf. Thurman (1984: 210 ff.) for Tsong kha pa and the Sanskrit texts.

5 *Mahāyānasaṃgraha* 2: 18 plus commentaries; dKon mchog 'jigs med dbang po, in Sopa and Hopkins (1976: 113).

6 There is sometimes a suggestion among contemporary scholars that Cittamātra should not be seen as an ontology but rather as an epistemology. For this reason it is not an idealism. I disagree. It seems to me that the distinction

between epistemology and ontology would have made little or no sense in Ancient India. They are two sides of the same coin. Certainly the Cittamātra tradition is concerned with experiences and perceptions. It does maintain that all we know of is a flow of perceptions. Nevertheless, this flow of experiences *exists*. Were it not to do so then, as we have seen, for Cittamātra there would be nothing at all.

7 The point that without an object mind does not exist is also made at length in the *Mahāyānasūtrālaṃkāra* 6: 6–10 and repeated in the *Mahāyānasaṃgraha* 3: 18.

8 See Rahula (1978a); Willis (1979: 20–36).

9 Those who maintain that for Cittamātra mind has no greater reality than anything else sometimes combine this with the suggestion that there is at bottom no real difference between Madhyamaka and Cittamātra. The assertion that finally mind has no greater reality than anything else is, of course, an assertion of Śāntarakṣita, the Yogācāra-Svātantrika Māādhyamika. If *this* is the Cittamātra position then indeed there is no final difference between Cittamātra and Madhyamaka. But Śāntarakṣita thought there was, for he criticizes Cittamātra in his *Madhyamakālaṃkāra*. So did Bhāvaviveka and Candrakīrti, for they both criticize Cittamātra stridently and at length. Cittamātra sources, too, criticize a position which looks suspiciously like that of the Madhyamaka. All Tibetan schools are united (a rare occurrence in doctrine) on the fact that Cittamātra teaches the real existence of mind as substratum, and differs in this respect from Madhyamaka. The notion that there is no fundamental difference between Madhyamaka and Cittamātra appears to have taken nearly two millennia to be realized!

10 *Triṃśikā* v.5; the Tibetan, however, has 'reverses'. Cf. Wayman and Wayman in *Śrīmālādevīsiṃhanāda Sūtra* (1974: 53); and Wayman (1984: 330).

11 For Paramārtha see Paul (1984). Cf. Demiéville (1973: 38 ff.); Ruegg (1969: Ch. 5); and Frauwallner (1951b: 637 ff.).

12 There are parallels here within Indian Buddhism. See, for example, Ratnākaraśānti (*c.* eleventh century), otherwise known as the Tantric yogin Śānti pa, who combines this with a 'without form' viewpoint; Kajiyama (1965: 34 ff.).

13 See Frauwallner (1956: 396); May (1971: 299).

CHAPTER 5 THE *TATHĀGATAGARBHA* (BUDDHA-ESSENCE/BUDDHA-NATURE)

1 See Frauwallner (1956: 255); for a century later see Takasaki (1966: 61).

2 *Laṅkāvatāra Sūtra*, section 82; see Takasaki (1966: 57–61). On the Cittamātra connections see also Keenan (1982: 14–16).

3 The Chinese version may differ rather from the Tibetan. See Ruegg (1973: 49 ff. and 71).

4 This is in the *Tathāgatotpattisaṃbhavanirdeśa*, a *sūtra* now included in the *Avataṃska* collection. See Takasaki (1958: 52; 1966 35–6).

5 Ch'en (1964: 115–6); on the *icchāntikas*, see Liu (1984).

6 Lhasa edn, Nya, f.147b. 'Buddha-element' here is Tibetan *sangs rgyas kyi khams*, i.e. *buddhadhātu*. Cf. the translation from the Chinese version by Yamamoto *Mahāyāna Mahāparinirvāna-sūtra* 1973: I, 181).

7 Translated from the quote in the *mDzes rgyan* of the Tibetan Bu ston (1290–1364) (Bu ston 1971: 43–5); cf. Ruegg (1973: 113–4); Yamamoto translation (op. cit., III, 660); and Liu (1982: 87–8).

8 Translated by Wayman and Wayman, 1974. See 1–4. Cf. also the translation in Chang (1983: 363 ff.), and Paul (1980a). All citations are from the former translation.

9 The exact meaning of *dharmakāya* depends on tradition. See Chapter 8.

10 Takasaki (1966: 186–7). All references are to this translation.

11 Note, however, that David Seyfort Ruegg, in his important work on the Tathāgatagarbha theory, has interpreted the *Ratnagotravibhāga* as a Madhyamaka work, arguing that the *tathāgatagarbha* is in fact nothing more than the Madhyamaka emptiness (Ruegg 1969: esp. 313 ff; cf. the dGe lugs view discussed in the next section). Ruegg's thesis has been criticized at length in a review article by Schmithausen (1973b: 123 ff.). Schmithausen has argued that reference to the *tathāgatagarbha* as emptiness must be understood in terms of the particular meaning of emptiness for this tradition – that emptiness is a particular aspect of the *tathāgatagarbha*, i.e. that the *tathāgatagarbha* is empty of defilements, not that it is identical with the Madhyamaka emptiness (133 ff.). I agree.

12 See Takasaki (1966: 210–11); cf. Schmithausen (1973b: 135–6).

13 For this topic, and the dGe lugs tradition in particular, see Chapter 8. See here also Tsong kha pa's pupil, mKhas grub rje (1968: 51 ff.); also Hopkins (1983: 382). mKhas grub rje lived from 1385–1438.

14 Ruegg (1963: 73 ff.) and Williams (1982: 72 ff.). Michael Broido argues, in a forthcoming paper, that the thinker most associated with this Jo nang pa ontology, Dol po pa Shes rab rgyal mtshan (pronounced: Shay rap gyel tsen – 1292–1361), did not in fact hold such a theory. The matter requires considerable further research.

15 *dBu ma chen po*; see Ruegg (1973: 4) and Kuijp (1983: 43 ff.).

16 On the *Fo-hsing lun* see Takasaki (1966: 47–9) and King (1984: 255–67); on Paramārtha and the *Ta-ch'eng ch'i-hsin lun*, see Demiéville (1973). For a recent and cautious statement see also Grosnick (1983: esp. 44–5).

17 Translation Hakeda (1967: 28). All references are to this translation.

18 Chinese text in Eliot (1935: 160). Cf. Eliot's translation. The Chinese word translated as 'Essence' is *hsing*, the same word used in *fo-hsing*, Buddha-essence.

CHAPTER 6 HUA-YEN – THE FLOWER GARLAND TRADITION

1 Trans. in Cook (1977: 107–8). Cf. Cook's Chapter 7.
2 See the *Avataṃsaka Sūtra*, Bk 20 (trans. in Cleary 1984/6: I, 451–2); Cleary (1983: 188); Gomez (1967: 30).
3 Of course, we are close here to the philosophical teaching of the *tathāgatagarbha*, one of the sources for which is a section of the *Avataṃsaka Sūtra* (see above, Chapter 5, note 4) and which, in its *Awakening of Faith* version, profoundly influenced Fa-tsang.
4 For summaries of the *sūtra* see Suzuki (1968: 147 ff.); Cleary (1983: 3 ff.); Sangharakshita (1985: 221 ff.). A complete translation from the Chinese is expected in the final volume of Cleary's multi-volume translation of the *Avataṃsaka Sūtra* (Cleary 1984/6).
5 See Gregory (1983a: 284–6). On Tu-shun see also Chang (1971).
6 On Empress Wu, see Paul (1980b: 191 ff.), and Weinstein (1987: 37–47).
7 For translations see Chan (1963: 409–14); Chang (1971: 224–30); Bary *et al.* 1972: 168–72.
8 From the biography of Fa-tsang in Chang (1971: 224).
9 See Cook (1977: 29–30). Cf. here Dōgen's views on the Buddha-nature. For Dōgen, I suspect, Fa-tsang's teaching would still be tinged with duality, inasmuch as Fa-tsang made any distinction at all between *li* and *shih*, noumenon and phenomena.
10 Cook (1977; 1978).
11 See Cook (1977: 44 ff.), and Fa-tsang in Cleary (1983: 152 ff.).
12 This is the text known as the *Hua-yen wu-chiao chih kuan*. See Cleary (1983: 56).
13 Translated in Cleary (1983: 152).
14 See here Chang (1971: 136–71).
15 Gimello (1983: 335, 337 – italics in original). For Fa-tsang see Cook (1977: 112 ff.; see also Gregory (1983b: esp. 33–9) for Fa-tsang on the Sudden Teaching. On faith in Buddhism see below, Chapter 10.
16 For illustrations and discussion see Hikata (1960: 1–50).
17 For comments and illustrations see Gaulier *et al.* (1976, Part I).
18 See Sickman and Soper (1956: 71–2, and ill. 55A).
19 Figures from the Agency for Cultural Affairs (1972).

CHAPTER 7 THE *SADDHARMAPUṆḌARĪKA (LOTUS) SŪTRA* AND ITS INFLUENCES

1 For the Chinese reciters, see Tay (1976: 161–2); for the Japanese reciters, see Dykstra (1983: 85, 91). In Hurvitz's (1976) English translation the whole *sūtra* is 337 pages long!

2 All references will be to Hurvitz's (1976) translation from Kumārajīva. The only complete English translation from the Sanskrit, that by Kern in the *Sacred Books of the East*, is now dated and inadequate.
3 See Nakamura (1980: 186–7); Pye (1978: 179); and Fujita (1980: 118–19).
4 On the whole issue of skilful means see the book by Pye (1978).
5 See Welch (1972: 280 ff., esp. 284–7); cf. Demiéville (1973: 261 ff.).
6 Always supposing, of course, that historical events can be traced in the *sūtra* – at least a debatable point.
7 On all of these parables see Pye (1978: 37 ff.).
8 Note also that the *Lotus Sūtra* speaks of many Buddhas, not just Śākyamuni. A further point to remember when considering the issue of 'deification' in the *Lotus Sūtra* is that the *sūtra* seems to accept the Madhyamaka teaching that all, including the Buddha himself, is empty of inherent existence. The Buddha of the *Lotus Sūtra* is no more an ultimate reality, or the final source of things, than anything else.
9 There are many wonderful stories recounted in the *Hokkegenki*. The *sūtra* protects from injury or death in battle (Dykstra 1983: 132); a blind devotee regains her sight (ibid., 138)!
10 Cf. another *sūtra*, known as the *Buddhabalādhānaprātihāryavikurvāṇanirdeśa*, found at Gilgit and belonging with the *Lotus Sūtra* (Schopen 1978: 334–5).
11 See here Fujita (1980); on Pure Land Buddhism see below, Chapter 10.
12 Dykstra (1983: 116–7); a story like this is a useful antidote to a 'holier than thou' attitude!
13 On Avalokiteśvara see Chapter 10; cf. also in the last chapter of the *Lotus* the additional protection given by Samantabhadra.
14 Lamotte (1962: Ch. 6); cf. Paul (1979: 224 ff.).
15 Note also the case of self-immolation by a Chinese monk in 1948 as a protest against the Chinese Communist suppression of Buddhism (Welch 1967: 327).
16 The Buddha is indeed the universe. The tenth-century Korean T'ient-t'ai monk Chegwan quotes the *Avataṃsaka Sūtra*: 'The mind, the Buddha, and all beings, these three have no essential difference' (Chegwan 1983: 147). T'ient-t'ai also strongly asserted the Buddha-nature in all things, including plants and even rocks.
17 Note, however, that meditation as well as *sūtra* recitation was an integral part of T'ient-t'ai practice in both China and Japan. For an illustration of the diagram, see Zwalf (1985: 275). The comment on p. 282 relates this to the *Avataṃsaka Sūtra* and not the *Lotus*, but it must be a mistake.
18 One handsome monk, Dōkyō, almost succeeded in becoming emperor through his influence on ex-Empress Kōken (Sansom 1958: p. 90)!
19 Eliot (1935: 246–7); cf. Sansom (1958: 222–3, 270 ff.).
20 Welch (1972: 281); cf. Demiéville (1973: 293).
21 Note, however, that Dōgen, to take just one example, protested against this

pessimism of *mappō* (LaFleur 1983: 3–4).

22 See the Emmerick trans. in *Suvarṇabhāsottama Sūtra* (1970: 23 ff.); also Lloyd (1911: 310–12).

23 Petzold (1977: 92 ff.); Welch (1972: 281, 284, and notes 73–4); Demiéville (1973: 292).

CHAPTER 8 ON THE BODIES OF THE BUDDHA

1 *Susthitamatiparipṛcchā Sūtra*, in Chang (1983: 65 ff.).

2 *Atthasālinī*, pp. 171–2; cf. *Pāli-English Dictionary* (1921–5). We have the same in English, of course, when we refer to 'a great body of people'.

3 For a list of these strange 'marks of a superman' see Thomas (1949: 220–1).

4 See Dutt (1976: 150–3); Poussin 1928/48: III, 767–8). This discussion comes from the *Abhidharmakośa*, the great fifth century CE (?) compendium of Vaibhāṣika and Sautrāntika doctrine.

5 Note that the use of the word *dhammakāya* in the Theravāda is a matter of dispute among scholars. It occurs only once in the Pāli canon (*Dīgha* iii 84), and appears to be glossed by Buddhaghosa to refer to the word of the Buddha contained in the canon, that is, the teachings themselves. This interpretation is opposed, however, by Lance Cousins (private note) who would argue that the Theravāda does not differ in this respect from the Vaibhāṣika. However, this interpretation of the *dharmakāya* as the teachings is found here in the Mahāyāna, and it is by no means impossible that it has a pre-Mahāyāna or non-Mahāyāna origin.

6 Verse 17, from the Sanskrit and Tibetan texts in Tucci (1932: 318).

7 Trans. according to the Tibetan. Sanskrit – 'made of the Dharma' v.22.

8 Poussin (1928/48: III, 783–4); cf. Venkata Ramanan (1976: 313 ff.).

9 *Prapañcopaśamaḥ śivaḥ*; *MadhyamakahMeṛtondaya* 3: 276 ff. in Gokhale (1962: 273).

10 See Gokhale and Bahulkar (1985: 81–2); cf. Poussin (1932–3: 136–7).

11 *Paramārthatattva*; *Bodhicaryāvatārapañjikā* (Vaidya 1960: 168, 200).

12 See *M.Saṃg*. and comms. 10: 1; *M. sūtr. āl.* comm. on 21: 60–1.

13 That is, ultimate awareness (*anuttarajñāna*); comm. on *M.Saṃg*. 7: 11. Cf., however, the Tibetan sGam po pa's point that since it is beyond language so 'ultimate awareness' is only a word of fools (Guenther's translation in sGam po pa 1970: 261).

14 Revolution of the basis = *āśrayaparāvMeṛtontti*: *M.Saṃg*. 10: 3 and comms.

15 *Dharmas: M.sūtra.āl.* comm. 9: 4; cf. *M.Saṃg* and comm. 10: 3.

16 *M.sūtr.āl.* and comm. 9: 26/62/77; cf. *M.Saṃg* 10: 3/8.

17 *M.Saṃg* 10: 37 and comm. This is interpreted by some traditions to mean that it remains but is constantly changing in response to the needs of sentient beings.

18 *Ch'eng-wei-shih lun*, p. 793; cf. Nagao (1973: 32–3).

19 Perhaps as one's teacher. Great teachers are thought of as Buddha's Transformation Bodies, and Tibetans will sometimes speak of their lama as a Transformation Body Buddha.

20 On all of this see Hopkins (1983: 119–21); cf. Dalai Lama (1985: 99–100).

21 In the *Akaniṣṭha* realm known as *Ghanavyūhakṣetra*.

22 Hopkins (1983: 121–2); Dalai Lama (1985: 101); mKhas grub rje (1968: 21–3).

23 Dalai Lama (1985: 102 ff.); Dhargyey (1976: 208); cf. Hopkins (1983: 122–3).

24 Of course, what is said concerning the Buddha here will apply to any one of the myriads of Buddhas in the Mahāyāna.

CHAPTER 9 THE PATH OF THE BODHISATTVA

1 Cf. Gomez (1977: 232–3). See also the story well-known in Tibet of the Mādhyamika Candrakīrti supplying milk for the monastery by milking the picture of a cow!

2 This is not to say, however, that it *originated* within Mahāyāna, or indeed any other form of mainstream Buddhism. The origins of Tantric religion are very obscure indeed.

3 See here T. Gyatso (1975: 21–2). On the whole topic of Highest Yoga Tantra, as it is presented by the dGe lugs tradition, following Indian commentaries, see Cozort (1986).

4 Kvaerne (1984: 256). Cf. Tucci, (1980: 2).

5 Kvaerne (1984: 268 ff.; 1985: 3 ff.). Cf. Snellgrove (1980: 20–1).

6 It should be noted, however, that contrary to what is often stated the Dalai Lamas are not as such heads of the dGe lugs tradition. This honour is held by whoever is chief abbot of dGa' ldan monastery, the Holder of the Throne of Tsong kha pa.

7 *Bhūmi* – Bodhisattva stage. Trans. in Houston (1980: 93) from the account by Bu ston.

8 Houston (1980: 93–5); Gomez (1983: 70–1). Note that in spite of this there is a basis for Mahāyāna's view in Indian Buddhism. See the commentary to Aryadeva's *Pai-lun* (*Śataśāstra2*) in Tucci (1929: 19). This work appears to be unknown as such in Indo-Tibetan Buddhism, but was very influential in China.

9 From the third *Bhāvanākrama*, in Demiéville (1952: 349).

10 Text in Tucci (1958: 229); cf. translation by Beyer (1974: 100).

11 See the translation, together with Atiśa's own commentary, in Sherburne (1983).

12 See here Rahula (1978b: 76–7) for examples of people in Theravāda lands who appear to have some form of Bodhisattva aspiration.

13 Verses 10 and 26; trans. from the Tibetan version by Batchelor (1979). Unless otherwise stated, quotations are from this translation. Cf. the detailed commentary in English by Geshe Kelsang Gyatso (1980: 8 ff.).
14 See Tsong kha pa's *Three Principal Aspects of the Path* in Wangyal (1978: 127 ff.), and Thurman (1982: 57–8).
15 There are now many books on these meditations. See Rabten (1974; 1980); Dhargyey (1976: 98 ff.); S. Gyatso (1982); and also the eighth chapter of the *Bodhicaryāvatāra*.
16 Of course, one could do this practice with any other relative, and it would be more appropriate if, for instance, one had a bad relationship with one's mother. Is the fact that it was developed by monks, often taken at an early age from their parents, in particular their mothers, of any significance?
17 *Bodhicaryāvatāra* 8: 94–5. Any answer to Śāntideva's question must be given in egoistic terms, and the ego is the cause of my suffering. Thus the development of *bodhicitta* requires and is a corollary of the teaching of emptiness.
18 The Eighth Karma pa (1507–54) died of leprosy after clearing an area of the disease!
19 Atiśa (1983: 42 ff.). Cf. Kamalaśīla, trans. in Beyer, (1974: 103). For greater details see Gyaltsen (1982: 26 ff.).
20 Trans. by Guenther, from the quote in sGam po pa (1970: 114).
21 Beyer (1974: 103); cf. Tsong kha pa in Dargyay (1981: 97).
22 I am sure, however, that this combination did not originate with Atiśa and Kamalaśīla.
23 See Dhargyey (1976: 188–93); T. Gyatsho (1968: 83).
24 Except, one assumes, out of compassion. Certain Bodhisattvas are said, for example, to visit the hells in order to help suffering hell beings.
25 Dhargyey (1976: 193–5); T. Gyatsho (1968: 83–4). Cf. sGam po pa (1970: 233).
26 The *Daśabhūmika* is now part of the *Avataṃsaka Sūtra*, which, as we have seen, expands the achievements of Bodhisattvas and Buddhas to immense magnitudes.
27 Dayal (1932: 66). Cf. the translation of the *Daśabhūmika Sūtra* from the Sanskrit by Honda (1968: 130 ff.), and the translation from the Chinese by Cleary in his *Avataṃsaka* translation (1986: II, 161 ff.).
28 See Dayal (1932: 172 ff.) and sGam po pa (1970: 156).
29 For one of the best-known tales see the story of the Bodhisattva giving his body to a starving tigress, in the *Suvarṇabhāsottama Sūtra* (1970: 85–97). For the giving of wife and children see the Pāli version in the *Vessantara Jātaka*, Cone and Gombrich (1977).
30 Schopen (1985: 31 ff.).
31 Note that there is a view, however, that a Bodhisattva after the first *bhūmi* no longer feels pain as such.
32 Although in our integrated schema this should have happened already,

before entering the Path of Insight, or should wait, surely, for the sixth *bhūmi* and the perfection of wisdom. One feels at a number of points like this that the system, the need to fit everything into an impressive graded path, is beginning to break down.

33 See the *Daśabhūmika*, trans. in Honda (1968: 175) and Cleary (1984/1986: II, 48).

34 Cf. sGam po pa: it is detachment of the senses from agitation and the mind from artificial categorization!

35 Honda (1968: 179–80); Cleary (1984/1986: II, 51). A number of these were forbidden to monks under the Vinaya, at least as professions. This is an example where the rules could be flexible in the light of compassion. The *sūtra* makes no mention of these secular arts for the laity alone. Nevertheless, how many people could claim to be on the fifth *bhūmi*?

36 It is a view held in China by Fa-tsang, for example. See Cook (1977: 110).

37 See *Daśabhūmika*, trans. in Honda (1968: 206). Cleary's Chinese seems to be different (1984/1986: II, 70).

CHAPTER 10 FAITH AND DEVOTION: THE CULTS OF BUDDHAS AND BODHISATTVAS

1 *Ratnāvalī* 1: 5, trans. by Hopkins (Nāgārjuna 1975). Cf. the *Ta-chih-tu lun* in Park (1983: 11).

2 See, for example, the *Visuddhimagga* 3: 75, trans. in Conze (1962: 49).

3 Trans. by Saddhatissa, 1985, vv. 1133, 1136. Cf. the translation by Norman, 1984 (*Sutta Nipāta* 1984).

4 *Visuddhimagga* 7: 2, trans. by Ñāṇamoli in Buddhaghosa (1975), quoting from the standard formula found in the canon.

5 Trans. in Chang (1983: 110). From the Chinese. Cf. the translation by Conze (1973a: 101).

6 See Demiéville (1954: 360 ff.).

7 Notice the Buddhas are plural; Amitāyus is given only as an example. Trans. in Harrison (1978: 45).

8 Zürcher (1972: 220); cf. text of Hui-yüan's biography (ibid., 244–5); Tsukamoto (1985: 844 ff.).

9 See the *Ta-chih-tu lun* in Lamotte (1980a: 2272–4); Lamotte's notes (ibid., vii, 2263 ff.); Tsukamoto (1985: 851–4); Zürcher (1972: 226 ff.).

10 Purity, incidentally, was and is an important cultural notion in India, pervading Indian society and underlying, for example, caste divisions.

11 *Saṃdhinirmocana Sūtra*, in Lamotte (1962: 397). Note, however, that in Akṣobhya's Pure Land of Abhirati there are also found non-Mahāyāna practitioners.

12 The origins of the Metteyya cult in Theravāda can be traced to the *Cakkavattisīhanāda Sutta* (*Dīgha* 3: 26).

13 On the rivalry in China with the Amitāyus cult, a rivalry which Maitreya lost, see Demiéville (1954: 389 ff.).

14 For illustrations see Gaulier *et al.* (1976: picture 46; cf. pictures 55–7, 58 (all wall paintings), and the embroidery from ninth/tenth centuries).

15 See Suzuki (1935: 328 ff.); Ch'en (1964: 405–8).

16 See van Oort (1986: I, plates 5ab, 6, 15, and 18).

17 For an illustration see Zwalf (1985: 216).

18 For this reason, perhaps, in the *Kāraṇḍavyūha* he appears to be lauded as higher than the Buddha himself.

19 All of this is, of course, perfectly understandable in terms of the development of Mahāyāna Buddhism. It does not require reference to external influences.

20 For examples: Bechert and Gombrich (1984: 210); Zwalf (1985: 234); van Oort (1986: II, plate 34b). For some modern tales see the wonderful book by Blofeld (1977).

21 See the translation in Thomas (1952: 73). See also Thomas (1951: 190); Mallmann (1948: 39–40).

22 Which, incidentally, assuming it is in correct grammatical form, cannot possibly mean 'Oh, the jewel in the lotus, *hūṃ*' as it is usually translated. See Thomas (1951: 187–8).

23 See Mallmann (1948: 111 ff.); she also speaks of possible Iranian influences.

24 Zwalf (1985: 80, 103).

25 For a P'u-t'o example, see Zwalf (1985: 231); cf. Jan (1981: 142).

26 See Ch'en (1964: 341–2); Blofeld (1977: Ch. 3); cf. Paul (1979: Ch. 7).

27 For illustrations see van Oort (1986: II, plates 3, 45 and 48), and Zwalf (1985: 209).

28 Illustrated in Zwalf (1985: 245, 7). For the war memorial, see Bechert and Gombrich (1984: 179).

29. See Willson (1986: 96), who refers to a study by Ghosh (1980).

30 Translated in Willson (1986: 21–2, and Part 2).

31 700 verse; trans. in Chang (1983) and Conze (1973a).

32 See Lamotte (1960: 4 ff.); Gaulier *et al.* (1976: 15).

33 Lamotte (1960: 80); for a description of a visit to Wu-'T'ai in the 1930s see Blofeld (1959: Ch. 6).

34 Chang (1983: 175); cf. Lamotte (1960: 20–3).

35 *Śūraṃgamasamādhisūtra* (1975: 263–4); Lamotte (1960: 30–1). English translation by Kalsang and Pasadika (1975: 44).

36 The *AjātaśatrukaukMeṛtontyavinodana Sūtra*, quoted in Lamotte (1960: 93–4).

37 The *VimaladattāparipMeṛtoncchā*, in Chang (1983: 84).

38 Illustrated in van Oort (1986: II, plate 13); I confess that I do not find the lion looking sick and unhappy, as van Oort does.

39 Trans. in Hua (1974b: 66 ff.).

40 See pp. 219–20. Hence the benefit of reading the *sūtras* in the presence of the corpse, and therefore the 'spirit', in the days after death.

41 Gaulier *et al.* (1976: plate 69; cf. plates 67–8).
42 See the illustrations in Okazaki (1977: 160–3).
43 See Dantine (1983: 1). Of course, there were also early cults directed towards previous Buddhas.
44 Trans. in Chang (1983: 316–8); cf. the French translation by Dantinne (1983: 79 ff.). Principal citations are to Chang.
45 Chang (1983: 322); cf. Dantinne (1983: 189–90).
46 See pp. 323, 319; cf. Dantinne (1983: 97, 194 ff.).
47 See p. 331; cf. Yamada (1968: I, 242 ff.).
48 Birnbaum (1980: 56–7). The quotations from the *Bhaiṣajyaguru Sūtras* are taken from this translation; cf. Nakamura (1980: 181).
49 Cf. Western accounts of near-death states. There is also a considerable Tibetan literature on people who have returned from the dead and describe their experiences – the *'das log* (pronounced: day lok).
50 *Encylopaedia of Buddhism* (1966: 664–5).
51 See Birnbaum (1987: 129). The plant appears to be missing in Japanese examples, where the Buddha holds his right hand palm facing outwards in the posture of banishing fear.
52 Zwalf (1985: 217).
53 Vow 2 in the Chinese version (Chang 1983: 341 ff.). Cf. the Sanskrit, trans. by Max Müller in Cowell *et al.* (1969: 12 ff.).
54 Vow 11 – the interpretation of this vow is important in subsequent Japanese Buddhism.
55 Vow 18 – this is the crucial vow, and is taken from the 'Saṅghavarman' version trans. in Cowell *et al.* (1969: 73). The Sanskrit version differs, and so does the Bodhiruci version translated in Chang, where the directing of merit to the Pure Land is required (Chang 1983: 342).
56 Vow 19, or 18 in the Sanskrit. The order and some details of vows 18–21 are different in the Sanskrit. Cf. also Max Müller's translation from the Sanskrit (Cowell *et al.* 1969: 45), and Chang (1983: 352–3).
57 Late Kamakura painting, in Okazaki (1977: 130; cf. 131).
58 According to Max Müller's translation of the Sanskrit version, rebirth in Sukhāvatī is *not* the result of meritorious deeds (Cowell *et al.* 1969: 98). This contradicts the Larger *sūtra*, and appears to be a mistranslation. The Chinese of Kumārajīva states that it is not the result of *inferior* roots of virtue (Hua 1974a: 134; Eracle 1973: 76), which corresponds with the Tibetan (*dge ba'i rtsa ba ngan ngon tsam gyis*; Lhasa edition Ja f. 311a) and the straightforward meaning of the Sanskrit (*avaramātrakeṇa* ... *kuśalamūlena*; Vaidya edn, *Sukhāralīvyūha Sūtra* (Smaller) 1961).
59 Cf. here Kṛṣṇa in the *Bhagavad Gītā* 8: 5–6.
60 Trans. in Luk (1969: 87); cf. the Takakusu trans. in Cowell *et al.* (1969: 165).
61 This appears certainly to be a Chinese interpolation; see Pas (1977: 210).
62 Luk (1969: 105–6); Takakusu (1969: 198, 200–1); cf. Beyer (1974: 124).
63 From Shinran's quotation in the *Kyōgyōshinshō*, trans. by Suzuki (Shinran

1973: 25).

64 Chappell (1977: 24). Both Weinstein and Chappell refer to work by Tsukamoto.

65 Kiyota (1978a: 274); Bary *et al.* (1960: 379).

66 Bloom (1965: 11–13); Weinstein (1987: 70–1).

67 Weinstein (1987: 72); Matsunaga and Matsunaga (1974/6: II, 27).

68 Matsunaga and Matsunaga (1974/6: II, 27); Bloom (1965: 13).

69 Weinstein (1987: 72). Cf. Ch'en (1964: 346).

70 Translation in Bary *et al.* (1972: 205–6); cf. the Japanese paintings of the parable in Okazaki (1977: 148–9).

71 Weinstein (1987: 73–4); Ch'en (1964: 348–50).

72 From a letter, trans. by Coates and Ishizuka, quoted in Burtt (1955: 214).

73 Translation of the One Page Document in Eliot (1935: 267); Suzuki (1950: 289–90).

74 In strictly controlled circumstances meat eating is permitted by the non-Mahāyāna Vinayas. Both Theravāda monks and Tibetan monks and nuns eat meat. However, the influence of Mahāyāna texts which condemn meat eating, particularly the *Fan-wang ching* (*Brahmajāla Sūtra*), in China has given East Asian Buddhism a strong vegetarian tendency. The *Fan-wang ching* is probably a Chinese composition. See Ruegg (1980) and the interesting comments in Welch (1967: 112–13).

75 In Burtt (1955: 214–5); Matsunaga and Matsunaga (1974/6: II, 69).

76 Shinran denied that he had any disciples – they were his fellow believers, his friends. See the *Tannisho*, Yui-en (1961: 12–13).

77 Shinran appears to think of this as a logical impossibility, but he also seems to have denied free will, holding a rigidly deterministic view of *karma*: Yui-en (1961: 29 ff.).

78 This is another notion in common with Zen, again with a decidedly Taoist flavour.

79 Cf. the later attempts by Rennyo (1415–99) to construct a Jōdo Shin Shū ethics (Ingram 1976).

80 Shinran (1973: 108 ff.); Bloom (1965: 39 ff.).

81 Cf. Yui-en (1961: 48); Bloom (1965: 67, 77, and 79–80).

82 The characters of Hōnen and Shinran themselves testify to this. On the *myōkōnin* see Kawamura (1981a: 223 ff.).

References

Agency for Cultural Affairs (1972) *Japanese Religion*, Tokyo: Kodansha.

Anacker, S. (1984) *Seven Works of Vasubandhu*, Delhi: Motilal Banarsidass.

Asaṅga (1938) *La Somme du Grand Véhicule d'Asaṅga (Mahāyānasaṃgraha)*, trans. Etienne Lamotte, 2 vols, Louvain: Bureaux du Muséon. Also contains Tibetan and Chinese texts.

Asaṅga (1971) *Le Compendium de la Super-Doctrine (Philosophie) (Abhidharmasamuccaya) d'Asaṅga*, trans. Walpola Rahula, Paris: Ecole Française d'Extrême-Orient.

Atiśa (1981) *Satyadvayāvatāra*, Tibetan text and translation in Chr. Lindtner, 'Atiśa's introduction to the two truths, and its sources', *Journal of Indian Philosophy* 9: 161–214.

Atiśa (1983) *A Lamp for the Path and Commentary*, trans. Richard Sherburne, SJ, London: George Allen & Unwin.

Bailey, H. W. (1974) 'The Pradakṣiṇā-Sūtra of Chang Tsiang-kuin' in L. Cousins, A. Kunst, and K. R. Norman (eds) *Buddhist Studies in Honour of I. B. Horner*, Dordrecht: D. Reidel.

Bareau, A. (1955) *Les Sectes bouddhiques du Petit Véhicule*, Saigon: Ecole Française d'Extrême-Orient.

Bareau, A. (1962) 'La Construction et le culte des stūpa d'après les Vinayapiṭaka', *Bulletin de l'Ecole Française d'Extrême-Orient* L, fasc. 2: 229–74.

de Bary, Wm Theodore (1960) *Sources of Chinese Tradition*, compiled by Wm. T. de Bary, W. Chan, B. Watson, with contributions by Y. Mei, L. Hurvitz, T. Chu, C. Tan, and J. Meskill, New York: Columbia University Press.

de Bary, Wm. Theodore (1972) *The Buddhist Tradition*, with the collaboration of Y. Hakeda and P. Yampolsky, and with contributions by A. L. Basham, L. Hurvitz, and R. Tsunoda, New York: Vintage Books.

Basham, A. L. (1967) *The Wonder that was India*, 3rd edn, London: Sidgwick & Jackson.

Basham, A. L. (1981) 'The evolution of the concept of the bodhisattva' in Kawamura (1981b: 19–59).

Basham, A. L. (1982) 'Asoka and Buddhism: a reexamination', *Journal of the International Association of Buddhist Studies* 5 (1): 131–43.

Bechert, H. (1982a) 'The importance of Aśoka's so-called schism edict' in Hercus *et al.* (1982: 61–8).

Bechert, H. (1982b) 'The date of the Buddha reconsidered', *Indologica Taurinensia* X: 29–36.

Bechert, H. and Gombrich, R. (eds) (1984) *The World of Buddhism*, London: Thames & Hudson.

Beyer, S. (1974) *The Buddhist Experience: Sources and Interpretations*, Encino and Belmont, CA: Dickenson

Beyer, S. (1977) 'Notes on the vision quest in early Mahāyāna' in Lancaster (1977: 329–40).

Birch, C. (ed.) (1967) *Anthology of Chinese Literature*, London: Penguin.

Birnbaum, R. (1980) *The Healing Buddha*, London: Rider.

Birnbaum, R. (1987) 'Bhaiṣajyaguru' in Eliade (1987: II).

Blofeld, J. (1959) *The Wheel of Life*, London: Rider.

Blofeld, J. (1977) *Compassion Yoga*, London: George Allen & Unwin.

Bloom, A. (1965) *Shinran's Gospel of Pure Grace*, Tucson: University of Arizona Press.

Bloom, A. (1968), 'The life of Shinran Shonin: the journey to self-acceptance', *Numen* 15 (1): 1–62.

Broido, M. (forthcoming) 'The Jo-nang-pas on Madhyamaka: a sketch', *Tibet Journal*.

Buddhaghosa (1920/1) *The Expositor (Atthasālinī)*, trans. Maung Tin, London: Pali Text Society.

Buddhaghosa (1975) *The Path of Purification* (*Visuddhimagga*), trans. Bhikkhu Ñāṇamoli, Kandy: Buddhist Publication Society.

van Buitenen, J. A. B. (1981) *The Bhagavadgītā in the Mahābhārata*, Chicago: University of Chicago Press.

Burtt, E. A. (1955) *The Teachings of the Compassionate Buddha*, New York: Mentor.

Buston (1971) *Shin tu zab cing brtag par dka' ba de bzhin gshegs pa'i snying po gsal zhing mdzes par byed pa'i rgyan* (*mDzes rgyan*), in *The Collected Works of Bu-ston*, part 20 (Va), ed. Lokesh Chandra, folio sides 1–78. Trans. in Ruegg (1973).

Candrakīrti (1960) *Prasannapadā* in Vaidya (1960).

Candrakīrti (1970) (reprint) *Madhyamakāvatāra par Candrakīrti*, ed. Louis de la Vallée Poussin, Osnabruck: Biblio Verlag. Also the Cone edition, mDo xxiii, ff. 217a–349b.

Chan, Wing-tsit (1963) *A Sourcebook in Chinese Philosophy*, Princeton, NJ: Princeton University Press.

Chang, Garma, C. C. (1971) *The Buddhist Teaching of Totality*, Pennsylvania:

Pennsylvania State University Press.
Chang, Garma, C. C. (ed.) (1983) *A Treasury of Mahāyāna Sūtras*, trans. Buddhist Association of the United States, Pennsylvania: Pennsylvania State University Press.
Chappell, D. W. (1977) 'Chinese Buddhist interpretations of the Pure Lands' in Saso and Chappell (1971: 23–53).
Chegwan (1983) *T'ien-t'ai Buddhism*, Tokyo: Daiichi-Shobō.
Ch'en, K. (1964) *Buddhism in China*, Princeton, NJ: Princeton University Press.
Cleary, T. (1983) *Entry into the Inconceivable*, Honolulu: University of Hawaii Press.
Cleary, T. (1984/6) *The Flower Ornament Scripture*, 2 vols, translation continuing, Boulder, Colo.: Shambhala.
Collins, S. (1982) *Selfless Persons*, Cambridge: Cambridge University Press.
Cone, M. and Gombrich, R. (1977) *The Perfect Generosity of Prince Vessantara*, Oxford: Oxford University Press.
Conze, E. (1958) *Buddhist Wisdom Books*, London, George Allen & Unwin.
Conze, E. (1959) *Buddhist Scriptures*, London, Penguin.
Conze, E. (1960) *The Prajñāpāramitā Literature*, 's-Gravenhage: Mouton.
Conze, E. (1962) *Buddhist Thought in India*, London: George Allen & Unwin.
Conze, E., Horner, I. B., Snellgrove, D. and Waley, A. (1964) *Buddhist Texts through the Ages*, New York: Harper & Row.
Conze, E. (1967a) 'The composition of the Aṣṭasāhasrikā Prajñāpāramitā', reprinted in E. Conze, *Thirty Years of Buddhist Studies*, Oxford: Bruno Cassirer.
Conze, E. (1967b) 'The development of Prajñāpāramitā thought', reprinted in E. Conze, *Thirty Years of Buddhist Studies*, Oxford: Bruno Cassirer.
Conze, E. (1968) *Selected Sayings from the Perfection of Wisdom*, London: Buddhist Society.
Conze, E. (1973a) *The Short Prajñaparamita Texts*, London: Luzac.
Conze, E. (1973b) *The Perfection of Wisdom in Eight Thousand Lines and its Verse Summary*, Bolinas: Four Seasons Foundation.
Conze, E. (1979) *The Large Sūtra of Perfect Wisdom*, Delhi: Motilal Banarsidass.
Cook, F. H. (1977) *Hua-yen Buddhism: The Jewel Net of Indra*, Pennsylvania: Pennsylvania State University Press.
Cook, F. H. (1978) 'Fa-tsang's brief commentary on the Prajñāpāramitā-hṛdaya-sūtra' in Kiyota (1978b: 167–206).
Cook, F. H. (1983), 'Enlightenment in Dōgen's Zen', *Journal of the International Association of Buddhist Studies* 6 (1): 7–30.
Cowell, E. B. *et al.* (1969) *Buddhist Mahāyāna Texts*, New York: Dover Publications.
Cozort, D. (1986) *Highest Yoga Tantra*, New York: Snow Lion.
Dalai Lama (1985) *Opening the Eye of New Awareness*, trans. D. S. Lopez, Jr. London: Wisdom. For another translation, see Gyatsho (1968).
Dantinne, J. (1983) *La Splendeur de l'Inébranlable* (*Akṣobhyavyūha*), I, Louvain-la-Neuve: Institut Orientaliste.
Dargyay, L. (1981) 'The view of bodhicitta in Tibetan Buddhism' in Kawamura

(1981b: 95–109).

Dásabhūmikasūtra, in Cleary (1984/6: II), and also Honda (1968).

Dayal, H. (1932) *The Bodhisattva Doctrine in Buddhist Sanskrit Literature*, London: Kegan Paul, Trench, Trubner.

Demiéville, P. (1952) *Le Concile de Lhasa*, Paris: Presses Universitaires de France.

Demiéville, P. (1954) 'La Yogācārabhūmi de Saṅgharakṣa', *Bulletin de l'Ecole Française d'Extrême-Orient* XLIV, fasc. 2: 339–436.

Demiéville, P. (1973) (reprint) *Choix d'études bouddhiques (1929–1970)*, Leiden: E. J. Brill. Includes reprints of 'Sur l'authenticité du Ta tcheng k'i sin louen' (1929), and 'Le bouddhisme et la guerre' (1957).

Dhargyey, N. (1976) *Tibetan Tradition of Mental Development*, 2nd edn, Dharamsala: Library of Tibetan Works and Archives.

Dōgen Zenji (1983) *Shōbogenzō* IV, trans. Kōsen Nishiyama, Tokyo: Nakayama Shobo.

Dumoulin, H. (ed.) (1976) *Buddhism in the Modern World*, New York: Collier Macmillan.

Dutt, N. (1970) *Buddhist Sects in India*, Calcutta: Firma K. L. Mukhopadhyay.

Dutt, N. (1976) *Mahayana Buddhism*, Calcutta: Firma KLM Private.

Dutt, N., D. M. Bhattacharya, and V. Shiv Nath Sharma (eds) (1939), *Gilgit Manuscripts* I, Srinagar: Calcutta Oriental Press.

Dykstra, Y. K. (1983) *Miraculous Tales of the Lotus Sūtra from Ancient Japan*, Hirakata City: Kansai University of Foreign Studies.

Eckel, M. D. (1986) *Jñānagarbha's Commentary on the Distinction Between the Two Truths*, Albany, NY: State University of New York Press.

Eliade, M. (ed.) (1987) *The Encyclopedia of Religion*, 16 vols, New York: Macmillan.

Eliot, C. (1935) *Japanese Buddhism*, London: Edwin Arnold. 4th impression, 1969, Routledge & Kegan Paul.

Encyclopedia of Buddhism (1966), II, fasc. I, Colombo: Government of Ceylon. Article on 'Bhaiṣajyaguru'.

Eracle, J. (1973) *La Doctrine bouddhique de la Terre Pure*, Paris: Dervy-Livres.

Frauwallner, E. (1951a) *On the Date of the Buddhist Master of the Law Vasubandhu*, Rome: Instituto Italiano per il Medio ed Estremo Oriente.

Frauwallner, E. (1951b), 'Amalavijñānam und Ālayavijñānam', reprinted in Erich Frauwallner (1982) *Kleine Schriften*, Wiesbaden: Franz Steiner Verlag Gmbh, 637–48.

Frauwallner, E. (1956) *Die Philosophie des Buddhismus*, Berlin: Akademie-Verlag.

Fujita, K. (1980) 'Pure Land Buddhism and the Lotus Sūtra', in Lamotte (1980b: 117–30).

Fung Yu-lan (1948) *A Short History of Chinese Philosophy*, New York: Free Press.

sGam po pa (1970) *The Jewel Ornament of Liberation*, trans. H. V. Guenther, London: Rider.

Gaulier, S., Jera-Bazard, R., and Maillard, M. (1976) *Buddhism in Afghanistan and Central Asia*, two parts, Leiden: E.J. Brill.

Ghosh, M. (1980) *Development of Buddhist Iconography in Eastern India*, Delhi:

Munshiram Manoharlal.

Gimello, R. M. (1983) 'Li T'ung-hsüan and the practical dimensions of Hua-yen' in Gimello and Gregory (1983: 321–89).

Gimello, R. M. and Gregory, P. N. (eds) (1983) *Studies in Ch'an and Hua-yen*, Honolulu: University of Hawaii Press.

Gokhale, V. V. (1962) 'Masters of Buddhism adore the Brahman through non-adoration', *Indo-Iranian Journal* 5: 271–5.

Gokhale, V. V. and Bahulkar, S. S. (1985) 'Madhyamakahṛdayakārikā Tarkajvālā, Chapter 1' in Chr. Lindtner (ed.) *Miscellanea Buddhica*, Copenhagen: Akademisk, Forlag.

Gombrich, R. (1988) *Theravāda Buddhism: A Social History from Ancient Benares to Modern Colombo*, London: Routledge.

Gomez, L. O. (1967) 'Selected verses from the Gaṇḍavyūha', unpublished doctoral thesis, Yale.

Gomez, L. O. (1976) 'Proto Mādhyamika in the Pāli canon', *Philosophy East and West* 26 (2): 137–65.

Gomez, L. O. (1977) 'The bodhisattva as wonder-worker' in Lancaster (1977: 221–61).

Gomez, L. O. (1983) 'The direct and gradual approaches of Zen master Mahāyā na', in Gimello and Gregory (1983: 69–167).

Gregory, P. N. (1983a) 'The teaching of men and gods: the doctrinal and social basis of lay Buddhist practice in the Hua-yen tradition' in Gimello and Gregory (1983: 253–319).

Gregory, P. N. (1983b) 'The place of the sudden teaching within the Hua-yen tradition: an investigation of the process of doctrinal change', *Journal of the International Association of Buddhist Studies* 6 (1): 31–60.

Griffiths, P. J. (1986) *On Being Mindless*, La Salle, Ill.: Open Court.

Grosnick, W. (1983) 'Cittaprakṛti and ayoniśomanaskāra in the Ratnagotravibhā ga', *Journal of the International Association of Buddhist Studies* 6 (2): 35–47.

Guenther, H. V. (1972) *Buddhist Philosophy in Theory and Practice*, London: Penguin.

Gyaltsen, Sakya Dragpa (1982) *Candragomin's Twenty Verses on the Bodhisattva Vow and its Commentary*, trans. Mark Tatz, Dharamsala: Library of Tibetan Works and Archives.

Gyamtso, Tsultrim (1986) *Progressive Stages of Meditation on Emptiness*, trans. S. Hookham, Oxford: Longchen Foundation.

Gyatsho, T. (1968) Fourteenth Dalai Lama, *The Opening of the Wisdom Eye*, trans. various, Bangkok: Social Science Association Press of Thailand. For aother translation see Dalai Lama (1985).

Gyatso, K. (1980) *Meaningful to Behold*, trans. Tenzin Norbu, Ulverston: Wisdom.

Gyatso, S. (1982) Third Dalai Lama, *Essence of Refined Gold*, trans. Glen Mullin, New York: Gabriel/Snow Lion.

Gyatso, T. (1975) Fourteenth Dalai Lama, *The Buddhism of Tibet and The Key to the Middle Way*, trans. Jeffrey Hopkins, London: George Allen & Unwin.

Gyatso, T. (1979) Fourteenth Dalai Lama, *Aryashūra's Aspiration and A Meditation on Compassion*, trans. Brian Beresford and others, Dharamsala: Library of Tibetan Works and Archives.

Hakeda, Y. S. (1967) *The Awakening of Faith*, New York: Columbia University Press.

Hall, B. C. (1986) 'The Meaning of vijñapti in Vasubandhu's concept of mind', *Journal of the International Association of Buddhist Studies* 9 (1): 7–23.

Harrison, P. M. (1978) 'Buddhānusmṛti in the Pratyutpanna-buddha-saṃmukhā vasthita-samādhi-sūtra', *Journal of Indian Philosophy* 9: 35–57.

Harrison, P. M. (1979) 'The Pratyutpanna-buddha-saṃmukhāvasthita-samādhi-sūtra', unpublished doctoral thesis, Australian National University.

Harrison, P. M. (1982) 'Sanskrit fragments of a Lokottaravādin tradition' in Hercus *et al.* (1982: 211–34).

Hercus, L. A. *et al.* (1982) *Indological and Buddhist Studies*, Canberra: Australian National University, Faculty of Asian Studies.

Hesse, H. (1951) *Siddhartha*, trans. Hilda Rosner, New York: New Directions.

Hikata, R. (1958) *Suvikrāntivikrāmi-paripṛcchā-prajñāpāramitā-sūtra*, Fukuoka: Kyushu University.

Hikata, R. (1960) 'Gaṇḍavyūha and the reliefs of Barabuḍur-galleries', *Studies in Indology and Buddhology*, Wakayama: Koyasan University.

Hirakawa, A. (1963) 'The rise of Mahāyāna Buddhism and its relationship to the worship of stūpas', *Memoirs of the Research Department of the Toyo Bunko*, Tokyo: Toyo Bunko.

Hoffman, H. (1975) *Tibet: A Handbook*, Bloomington, Ind.: Indiana University.

Honda, M. (1968) 'Annotated translation of the Daśabhūmikasūtra', in Denis Sinor (ed.) *Studies in South, East and Central Asia*, Delhi: Śata-Pitaka Series 74.

Hopkins, J. (1974) *Practice of Emptiness*, Dharamsala: Library of Tibetan Works and Archives.

Hopkins, J. (1980) *Compassion in Tibetan Buddhism*, London: Rider.

Hopkins, J. (1983) *Meditation on Emptiness*, London: Wisdom.

Hopkins, J. (1984) *The Tantric Distinction*, London: Wisdom.

Houston, G. W. (1980) *Sources for a History of the bSam yas Debate*, Sankt Augustin: V.G.H. Wissenschaftsverlag.

Hsüan-tsang (1973) *Ch'eng wei-shih lun*, trans. Wei Tat, Hong Kong: Ch'eng wei-shih lun Publication Committee. For another translation see Poussin (1928/48).

Hua, H. (1974a) *A General Explanation of The Buddha Speaks of Amitābha Sūtra*, San Francisco: Buddhist Text Translation Society.

Hua, H. (1974b) *Sūtra of the Past Vows of Earth Store Bodhisattva*, New York: Institute for Advanced Studies of World Religions.

Hurvitz, L. (1963) 'Chih-i (538–597): an introduction to the life and ideas of a Chinese Buddhist monk', *Mélanges chinois et bouddhiques* 12: 1–372.

Hurvitz, L. (1975) 'The first systematizations of Buddhist thought in China',

Journal of Chinese Philosophy 2: 361–88.

Hurvitz, L. (1976) *Scripture of the Lotus Blossom of the Fine Dharma*, New York: Columbia University Press.

Hyde-Chambers, F. and Hyde-Chambers, A. (1981) *Tibetan Folk Tales*, Boulder, Colo.: Shambhala.

Iida, S. (1980) *Reason and Emptiness*, Tokyo: Hokuseido Press.

Ingram, P. O. (1976) 'The teachings of Rennyo Shōnin: the life of faith', *Numen*, 23 (1): 1–22.

Jaini, P. S. (1958) 'On the theory of two Vasubandhus', *Bulletin of the School of Oriental and African Studies* 21 (1): 48–53.

Jaini, P. S. (1977) 'Prajñā and dṛṣti in the Vaibhāṣika Abhidharma' in Lancaster (1977: 103–15).

Jan, Yün-hua (1981) 'The bodhisattva idea in Chinese literature: typology and significance' in Kawamura (1981b: 125–52).

Joshi, L. M. (1967) *Studies in the Buddhistic Culture of India*, Delhi: Motilal Banarsidass.

Kajiyama, Y. (1965) 'Controversy between the sākāra and nirākāra-vādins of the Yogācāra school – some materials', *Journal of Indian and Buddist Studies* (Tokyo) 14 (1): 26–37.

Kajiyama, Y. (1985) 'Stūpas, the Mother of Buddhas, and Dharma-body' in Warder (1985: 9–16).

Kaneko, D. (1965) 'The meaning of salvation in the doctrine of Pure Land Buddhism', *Eastern Buddhist* (new series) 1 (1): 48–63.

Kawamura, L. (1981a) 'The myōkōnin: Japan's representation of the bodhisattva' in Kawamura (1981b: 223–37).

Kawamura, L. (ed.) (1981b) *The Bodhisattva Doctrine in Buddhism*, Waterloo, Ontario: Wilfred Laurier University Press.

Keenan, J. P. (1982) 'Original purity and the focus of early Yogācāra', *Journal of the International Association of Buddhist Studies* 5 (1): 7–18.

mKhas grub rje (1968) *Fundamentals of the Buddhist Tantras*, trans. Ferdinand Lessing and Alex Wayman, The Hague: Mouton.

King, S. B. (1984) 'The Buddha nature: true self as action', *Religious Studies* 20: 255–67.

Kiyota, M. (1962) 'The three modes of encompassing in the Vijñāptimātratā system', *Journal of Indian and Buddhist Studies* (Tokyo) 10 (1): 19–24.

Kiyota, M. (1978a) 'Buddhist devotional meditation: a study of the Sukhāvatīvyūhopadeśa' in Kiyota (1978b: 249–96).

Kiyota, M. (ed.) (1978b) *Mahāyāna Buddhist Meditation: Theory and Practice*, Honolulu: University Press of Hawaii.

Kochumuttom, T. A. (1982) *A Buddhist Doctrine of Experience*, Delhi: Motilal Barnarsidass.

van der Kuijp, L. W. J. (1983) *Contributions to the Development of Tibetan Buddhist Epistemology*, Wiesbaden: Franz Steiner Verlag GmbH.

Kvaerne, P. (1984) 'Tibet: the rise and fall of a monastic tradition', in Bechert and

Gombrich (1984: 253–70).

Kvaerne, P. (1985) *Tibet: Bon Religion*, Leiden: E. J. Brill.

LaFleur, W. (1983) *The Karma of Words*, Berkeley and Los Angeles: University of California Press.

Lai, W. (1977) 'The meaning of "mind-only" (wei-hsin): an analysis of a sinitic Mahāyāna phenomenon', *Philosophy East and West* 27 (1): 65–83.

Lai, W. (1979) 'Non-duality of the two truths in sinitic Mādhyamika: origins of the "third truth"', *Journal of the International Association of Buddhist Studies* 2 (2): 45–65.

Lai, W. (1985) 'Wŏnhyo (Yüan Hsiao) on the Nirvāṇa school: summation under the "one mind" doctrine', *Journal of the International Association of Buddhist Studies* 8 (2): 75–83.

Lamotte, E. (1935) *Saṃdhinirmocana Sūtra*, Louvain: Université de Louvain.

Lamotte, E. (1954) 'Sur la formation du Mahāyāna', *Asiatica: Festschrift F. Weller*, Leipzig: 377–96.

Lamotte, E. (1958) *Histoire du Bouddhisme indien*, Louvain: Université de Louvain.

Lamotte, E. (1960) 'Mañjuśrī', *T'oung Pao* 48: 1–96.

Lamotte, E. (1962) *L'Enseignement de Vimalakīrti* (*Vimalakīrtinirdeśa*), Louvain: Université de Louvain. For another translation, see Thurman (1976).

Lamotte, E. (1980a) *Le Traité de la grande vertu de sagesse de Nāgārjuna* V, Louvain: Université de Louvain.

Lamotte, E. (1980b) *Indianisme et Bouddhisme*; *mélanges offert à Mgr. Etienne Lamotte*, Louvain: Université Catholique de Louvain.

Lamotte, E. (1983/4) 'The assessment of textual authenticity in Buddhism', trans. S. Boin-Webb, *Buddhist Studies Review* 1 (1): 4–15. Originally published in 1947 as 'La Critique d'authenticité dans le bouddhisme' in *India Antiqua*, Leiden: E. J. Brill, 213–22.

Lancaster, L. (1975) 'The oldest Mahāyāna sūtra: its significance for the study of Buddhist development', *Eastern Buddhist* (new series) 8 (1): 30–41.

Lancaster, L. (ed.) (1977) *Prajñāpāramitā and Related Systems*, Berkeley, Calif.: University of California.

Lankavatara Sutra (1973) trans. D. T. Suzuki, London: Routledge & Kegan Paul. Originally published in 1932.

Leclerc, J. (1961) *The Love of Learning and the Desire for God*, New York: Mentor Omega.

Lethcoe, N. R. (1977) 'The bodhisattva ideal in the Aṣṭa and Pañca. Prajñāpā ramitā sūtras' in Lancaster (1977: 263–80).

Levering, M. (1987) 'Kṣitigarbha' in Eliade (1987: VIII).

Liebenthal, W. (1955) 'Chinese Buddhism during the 4th and 5th centuries', *Monumenta Nipponica* II (1): 44–81.

Liebenthal, W. (1959) 'New Light on the Mahāyāna-śraddhotpāda Śāstra', *T'oung Pao* 46 (3–5): 155–216.

Liebenthal, W. (1961) 'One-mind-dharma', *Essays on the History of Buddhism*

Presented to Professor Zenryu Tsukamoto, Kyoto: Kyoto University, 41–6.

Lindtner, Chr. (1982) *Nāgārjuniana*, Copenhagen: Akademisk Forlag.

Liu, Ming-wood (1982) 'The doctrine of the Buddha-Nature in the Mahāyāna Mahāparinirvāṇa Sūtra', *Journal of the International Association of Buddhist Studies* 5 (2): 63–94.

Liu, Ming-Wood (1984) 'The problem of the icchāntika in the Mahāyāna Mahāparinirvāṇa Sūtra', *Journal of the International Association of Buddhist Studies* 7 (1): 57–81.

Lloyd, A. (1910) *Shinran and his Work*, Tokyo: Kyobunkwan.

Lloyd, A. (1911) *The Creed of Half Japan*, London: Smith, Elder, & Co.

Lopez, D. S., Jr (1987) *A Study of Svātantrika*, New York: Snow Lion.

Luk, C. (Lu K'uan-yü) (1969) *The Secrets of Chinese Meditation*, London: Rider.

MacQueen, G. (1981) 'Inspired speech in early Mahāyāna Buddhism I', *Religion* 11: 303–19.

MacQueen, G. (1982) 'Inspired speech in early Mahāyāna Buddhism II', *Religion* 12: 49–65.

Mahāparinirvāṇa Sūtra (n.d.) Tibetan text in the Lhasa bKa' 'gyur, mDo mnga, vol. 54, Nya, ff. 1–222b.

Mahāvastu (1949–56) trans. J. J. Jones, 3 vols, London: Luzac.

Mahāyāna Mahāparinirvāṇa-sūtra (1973–5) trans. K. Yamamoto, 3 vols, Ube City: Karinbunko.

Maitreyanātha (?) (1937) *Madhyāntavibhāga*, trans. Friedmann, see Sthiramati (1937). For Sanskrit, see Vasubandhu (1964).

Maitreyanātha (?) (1970) *Mahāyānasūtrālaṅkāra*, ed. S. Bagchi, Darbhanga: Mithila Institute. Also contains the commentary attributed to Asaṅdga or Vasubandhu. For a translation see S. Lévi (1907–11) *Asaṅga, Mahāyāna-Sūstrālaṃkāra*, 2 vols, Paris: Librarie Honoré Champion.

Mallmann, M.-T. de (1948) *Introduction à l'Etude d'Avalokiteçvara*, Paris: Civilisations du Sud.

Mañjuśrīnāmasaṃgīti (1985), in A. Wayman, *Chanting the Names of Mañjuśrī*, Boston, Mass.: Shambhala.

Masao, A. (1971) 'Dōsgen on Buddha Nature', *eastern Buddhist* (new series) 4 (1): 28–71.

Matsumoto, S. (1986) 'The modern relevance of Donran's Pure Land Buddhist thought', *Pacific World* (new series) 2: 36–41.

Matsunaga, D. and Matsunaga, A. (1974/6) *Foundations of Japanese Buddhism*, 2 vols, Los Angeles and Tokyo: Buddhist Books International.

May, J. (1971) 'La Philosophie bouddhique idéaliste', *Etudes Asiatiques* 25: 265–323.

Nagao, G. (1973) 'On the theory of Buddha-Body (Buddha-kāya)', *Eastern Buddhist* (new series) 6 (1): 25–53.

Nagao, G. (1981) 'The bodhisattva returns to this world' in Kawamura (1981b: 61–79).

Nāgārjuna (1975) *Ratnāvalī*, trans. J. Hopkins in *The Precious Garland and The*

Song of the Four Mindfulnesses, London, George Allen & Unwin. For Sanskrit fragments see Vaidya (1960).

Nāgārjuna (1977) *Mūlamadhyamakakārikāḥ*, ed. J. W. de Jong, Madras: Adyar Library and Research Centre. Also contained in Candrakirti's (1960) *Prasannapadā*. For a partial translation see P. Williams (1977) 'Nāgārjuna: selections from the Madhyamakākarikā', *Middle Way*, 52 (1–3): 15–18, 72–6, 119–23.

Nāgārjuna (1978) *Vigrahavyāvartanī*, trans. in K. Bhattacharya, *The Dialectical Method of Nāgārjuna*, Delhi: Motilal Banarsidass. Also contains the Johnston and Kunst edition of the Sanskrit text. For another edition see Vaidya (1960).

Nakamura, H. (1964) *Ways of Thinking of Eastern Peoples*, ed. P. P. Wiener, Honolulu: University Press of Hawaii.

Nakamura, H. (1980) *Indian Buddhism*, Hirakata City: Kansai University of Foreign Studies.

Niwano, N. (1981) *A Guide to the Threefold Lotus Sutra*, trans. E. Langston, Tokyo: Kosei Publishing Co.

Okazaki, J. (1977) *Pure Land Buddhist Painting*, trans. E. ten Grotenhuis, Tokyo: Kodansha.

van Oort, H. A. (1986) *The Iconography of Chinese Buddhism in Traditional China*, 2 vols, Leiden: E. J. Brill.

Pali-English Dictionary (1921–5) ed. T. W. Rhys Davids and W. Stede, London: Pali Text Society.

Park, S. B. (1983) *Buddhist Faith and Sudden Enlightenment*, Albany: State University of New York Press.

Pas, J. F. (1974) 'Shan-tao's interpretation of the meditative vision of Buddha Amitāyus', *History of Religions* 14: 96–116.

Pas, J. F. (1977) 'The Kuan-wu-liang-shou Fo-ching: its origin and literary criticism', in L. S. Kawamura and K. Scott (eds) *Buddhist Thought and Asian Civilization*, Emeryville, CA: Dharma Publishing: 144–218.

Paul, D. M. (1980a) *The Buddhist Feminine Ideal*, Missoula, Mont.: Scholars Press.

Paul, D. M. (1980b) 'Empress Wu and the historians: a tyrant and saint of Classical China', in N. A. Falk and R. M. Cross (eds) *Unspoken Worlds*, San Francisco, Harper & Row: 190–206.

Paul, D. Y. (1979) *Women in Buddhism*, Berkeley, CA: Asian Humanities Press.

Paul, D. Y. (1984) *Philosophy of Mind in Sixth-Century China*, Stanford, Calif: Stanford University Press.

Petzold, B. (1977) *Buddhist Prophet Nichiren – A Lotus in the Sun*, ed. S. Iida and W. Simmonds; published in Japan, no place or publisher mentioned in Roman script.

Poussin, L. de la Vallée (1928–48) *Vijñaptimātratāsiddhi. La Siddhi de Himan-tsang*, 3 vols, Paris: Guethner.

Poussin, L. de la Vallée (1932–3) 'Le joyau dans la main', *Mélanges Chinois et Bouddhiques* 2: 68–138.

Prajñākaramati (1960) *Bodhicaryāvatārapañjikā*, ed. P. L. Vaidya, Darbhanga: Mithila Institute. Also contains the *Bodhicaryāvatāra* of Śāntideva.

Pye, M. (1978) *Skilful Means*, London: Duckworth.

Ratben, Geshe (1974) *The Preliminary Practices*, Dharamsala: Library of Tibetan Works and Archives.

Rabten, Geshe (1980) *The Life and Teaching of Geshe Rabten*, trans. B. A. Wallace, London: George Allen & Unwin.

Rahula, W. (1978a), 'Vijñaptimātratā philosophy in the Yogācāra system – some wrong notions' in Rahula (1978b: 79–85).

Rahula, W. (1978b) *Zen and the Taming of the Bull*, London: Gordon Fraser.

Rowell, T. (1935) 'The background and early use of the Buddha-Kṣetra concept, chs. 2–3', *Eastern Buddhist* 6 (4): 379–431.

Rowell, T. (1937) 'The background and early use of the Buddha-Kṣetra concept, ch. 4, plus appendices and bibliography', *Eastern Buddhist* 7 (2): 132–76.

Ruegg, D. S. (1963) 'The Jo-nang-pas: a school of Buddhist ontologists according to the Grub-mtha' shel-gyi me-long', *Journal of the American Oriental Society* 83: 73–91.

Ruegg, D. S. (1969) *La Théorie du Tathāgatagarbha et du Gotra*, Paris: Ecole Française d'Extrême Orient.

Ruegg, D. S. (1973) *La Traité du Tathāgatagarbha de Bu ston Rin chen grub*, Paris: Ecole Française d'Extrême Orient.

Ruegg, D. S. (1980) 'Ahiṃsā and vegetarianism in the history of Buddhism', in S. Balasooriya, A. Bareau, R. Gombrich, S. Gunasingha, U. Mallawarachchi, and E. Perry (eds) *Buddhist Studies in Honour of Walpola Rahula*, London: Gordon Fraser.

Ruegg, D. S. (1981) *The Literature of the Madhyamaka School of Philosophy in India*, Wiesbaden: Otto Harrassowitz.

Ruegg, D. S. (1983) 'On the thesis and assertion in the Madhyamaka/dBu ma' in E. Steinkellner and H. Tauscher (eds) *Contributions on Tibetan and Buddhist Religion and Philosophy*, Vienna: Arbeitskreis für Tibetische und Buddhistische Studien Universität Wien, 205–41.

Sangharakshita (1985) *The Eternal Legacy*, London: Tharpa Publications.

Sansom, G. B. (1931) *Japan: A Short Cultural History*, London: Cresset Press.

Sansom, G. (1958) *A History of Japan to 1334*, London: Cresset Press.

Śāntideva (1960) *Bodhicaryāvatāra*; see Prajñākaramati (1960). For a translation from the Tibetan version see Stephen Batchelor, trans. (1979) *A Guide to the Bodhisattva's Way of Life*, Dharamsala: Library of Tibetan Works and Archives.

Śāntideva (1961) *Śikṣāsamuccaya*, ed. P. L. Vaidya, Darbhanga: Mithila Institute.

Saso, M. and Chappell, D. W. (1977) *Buddhist and Taoist Studies I*, Honolulu: University Press of Hawaii.

Schmithausen, L. (1967) 'Sautrāntika-voraussetzungen in Viṃśatikā und Triṃśikā', *Wiener Zeitschrift für die Kunde Süd- und Ostasiens* 11: 109–36.

Schmithausen, L. (1973a) 'Spirituelle praxis und philosophische theorie im

Buddhismus', *Zeitschrift für Missionswissenschaft und Religionswissenschaft*: 57, no. 3, 161–86.

Schmithausen, L. (1973b) 'Zu D. Seyfort Ruegg's buch "La théorie du tathā gatagarbha et du gotra"', *Wiener Zeitschrift für die Kunde Südasiens und Archiv für Indische Philosophie* 17: 123–60.

Schopen, G. (1975) 'The phrase "sa pṛthivīpradeśaś caityabhūto bhavet" in the Vajracchedikā: notes on the cult of the book in Mahāyāna', *Indo-Iranian Journal* 17: 147–81.

Schopen, G. (1978) 'The five leaves of the Buddhabalādhānaprātihāryavikurvāṇanirdeśa-sūtra found at Gilgit', *Journal of Indian Philosophy* 5: 319–36.

Schopen, G. (1979) 'Mahāyāna in Indian inscriptions', *Indo-Iranian Journal* 21: 1–19.

Schopen, G. (1983) 'The generalization of an old yogic attainment in medieval Mahāyāna sūtra literature: some notes on jatismara', *Journal of the International Association of Buddhist Studies* 6 (1): 109–47.

Schopen, G. (1985) 'Two problems in the history of Indian Buddism: the layman/monk distinction and the doctrines of the transference of merit', *Studien zur Indologie und Iranistik*, 10: 9–47.

Schopen, G. (1987) 'Burial "ad sanctos" and the physical presence of the Buddha in early Indian Buddhism', *Religion* 17: 193–225.

Schopen, G. (forthcoming) 'The inscription on the Kuṣān image of Amitābha and the character of the early Mahāyāna in India', *Journal of the International Association of Buddhist Studies* 10 (2).

Shakabpa, W. D. (1984) (reprint) *Tibet: A Political History*, New York: Potala Publications.

Shaw, M. (1985) 'Nature in Dōgen's philosophy and poetry', *Journal of the International Association of Buddhist Studies*, 8 (2): 111–32.

Shinran (1973) *The Kyōgyōshinshō*, trans. D. T. Suzuki, Kyoto: Shinshū Ōtaniha.

Shōjun, B. (1971) 'Shinran's indebtedness to T'an-luan', *Eastern Buddhist* (new series) 4 (1): 72–87.

Sickman, L. and Soper, A. (1956) *The Art and Architecture of China*, London: Penguin.

Snellgrove, D. L. (1973) 'Śākyamuni's final nirvāṇa', *Bulletin of the School of Oriental and African Studies* (University of London) 36 (2): 399–411.

Snellgrove, D. L. (ed.) (1978) *The Image of the Buddha*, London: Serindia Publications/Unesco.

Snellgrove, D. L. (1980) (reprint) *The Nine Ways of Bon*, Boulder, Colo.: Prajñā Press. Originally published in 1967 by Oxford University Press.

Sopa, Geshe Lhundup and Hopkins, J. (1976) *Practice and Theory of Tibetan Buddhism*, London: Rider.

Śrīmālādevīsiṃhanāda Sūtra (1974), trans. in Wayman, A. and Wayman, H. (1974) *The Lion's Roar of Queen Śrīmālā*, New York: Columbia University Press. For other translations see Chang (1983) and Paul (1980a).

Sthiramati (1937) *Madhyāntavibhāgaṭikā*, trans. D. L. Friedmann, Utrecht:

University of Utrecht.
Sukhāvatīvyūha Sūtra (Larger) (1961) in Vaidya (1961: 221–53). Translated from the Sanskrit by F. Max Müller in Cowell *et al.* (1969). Originally in the *Sacred Books of the East* 49. Originally published in 1894, Clarendon Press, Oxford, ed. F. Max Müller. Translated from the Chinese of Bodhiruci in Chang (1983: 339–60).
Sukhāvatīvyūha Sūtra (Smaller) (1961) in Vaidya (1961: 254–7). Tibetan in Lhasa bKa' 'gyur, mDo mnga, vol. 53, Ja, ff. 307b–314b. Translated from the Sanskrit by F. Max Müller in Cowell *et al.* (1969: 89–103). Translated from the Chinese of Kumārajīva in Hua (1974a).
Śūraṃgamasamādhisūtra (1975) (reprint) trans. E. Lamotte in *La Concentration de la marche héroique*, Brussels: Institut Belge des Hautes Etudes Chinoises. Originally vol. 13 of *Mélanges Chinois et Bouddhiques*, 1965. For a partial English translation see T. Kalsang and Bhikkhu Pasadika (1975) *Excerpts from the Surangama Samadhi Sutra*, Dharamsala: Library of Tibetan Works and Archives.
Sutta Nipāta (1984) trans. K. R. Norman in *The Group of Discourses (Sutta Nipāta)* I, London: Pali Text Society. Also trans. H. Saddhatissa (1985) *The Sutta Nipāta*, London: Curzon Press.
Suvarṇabhāsottama Sūtra (1970) trans. R. E. Emmerick in *The Sūtra of the Golden Light*, London: Luzac.
Suzuki, D. T. (1935) 'Impressions of Chinese Buddhism', *Eastern Buddhist* 6 (4): 327–78.
Suzuki, D. T. (1950) *Essays in Zen Buddhism* (2nd series), London: Rider.
Suzuki, D. T. (1963) *Outlines of Mahāyāna Buddhism*, New York: Schocken.
Suzuki, D. T. (1968) *On Indian Mahāyāna Buddhism*, ed. E. Conze, New York: Harper Torchbook.
Takakusu, J., trans. (1969) 'The Amitāyur-dhyāna-sūtra', reprinted in E. B. Cowell *et al.* (1969). Originally in the *Sacred Books of the East* (1894) 59, Oxford: Clarendon Press.
Takasaki, J. (1958) 'The Tathāgatotpattisaṃbhava-nirdeśa of the Avataṃsaka and the Ratnagotravibhāga', *Journal of Indian and Buddhist Studies* (Tokyo) 7 (1): 48–53.
Takasaki, J. (1966) *A Study on the Ratnagotravibhāga (Uttaratantra)*, Rome: Instituto Italiano per il Medio ed Estremo Oriente.
Tay, C. N. (1976) 'Kuan-yin: the cult of half Asia', *History of Religions* 16 (2): 147–77.
Tetsurō, W. (1971) 'Japanese literary arts and Buddhist philosophy', trans. H. Umeyo, *Eastern Buddhist* (new series) 4 (1): 88–115.
Thomas, E. J. (1949) *The Life of Buddha*, 3rd rev. edn, London: Routledge & Kegan Paul.
Thomas, E. J. (1951) *The History of Buddhist Thought*, 2nd edn, London, Routledge & Kegan Paul.
Thomas, E. J. (1952) *The Perfection of Wisdom*, London: John Murray.

Thurman, R. A. F. (1976) *The Holy Teaching of Vimalakīrti*, Pennsylvania: Pennsylvania State University Press.

Thurman, R. A. F. (ed.) (1982) *Life and Teachings of Tsong Khapa*, Dharamsala: Library of Tibetan Works and Archives.

Thurman, R. A. F. (1984) *Tsong Khapa's Speech of Gold in the Essence of True Eloquence*, Princeton, NJ: Princeton University Press.

Tsong kha pa (1966) *dBu ma rtsa ba'i tshig le'ur byas pa shes rab ces bya ba'i rnam bshad Rigs pa'i rgya mtsho*. Modern blockprint of Tsong kha pa's commentary to the *Madhyamakakārikā*. 282 folios, India.

Tsukamoto, Z. (1985) *A History of Early Chinese Buddhism*, trans. L. Hurvitz, 2 vols, Tokyo: Kodansha.

Tucci, G. (1929) *Pre-Diṅnāga Buddhist Texts on Logic*, Baroda: Gaekwad Oriental Series 49.

Tucci, G. (1932) 'Two hymns of the Catuḥ-stava of Nāgārjuna', *Journal of the Royal Asiatic Society*: 309–25.

Tucci, G. (1958) *Minor Buddhist Texts*, part II, Rome: Instituto Italiano per il Medio ed Estremo Oriente.

Tucci, G. (1980) *The Religions of Tibet*, trans. G. Samuel, London: Routledge & Kegan Paul.

Vaidya, P. L. (ed.) (1960) *Madhyamakáśātra of Nāgārjuna*, Darbhanga: Mithila Institute. Contains *Prasannapadā*, *Madhyamakakārikā*, *Vigrahavyāvartanī*, and *Ratnāvalī* fragments.

Vaidya, P. L. (ed.) (1961) *Mahāyānasūtrasaṃgraha*, part I, Darbhanga: Mithila Institute.

Vasubandhu (1932–3) *Trisvabhāvanirdeśa*, in Louis de la Vallée Poussin, 'Le petit traité de Vasubandhu-Nāgārjuna sur les trois natures', *Mélanges Chinois et Bouddhiques* 2: 147–61. Sanskrit text and translation also in Anacker (1984).

Vasubandhu (1964) *Madhyāntavibhāga-Bhāṣya*, ed. G. M. Nagao, Tokyo: Suzuki Research Foundation. Also contains the Sanskrit text of the *Madhyāntavibhā ga*. For translation, see Friedmann, in Sthiramati (1937) and Anacker (1984).

Vasubandhu (1970) *Mahāyānasūtrālaṃkāra Bhāṣya*, see Maitreyanātha (1970).

Vasubandhu (1970–73) *Abhidharmakośa and Bhāṣya*, ed. Swami Dwarikadas Shastri, Varanasi: Bauddha Bharati. Also contains the *Sphuṭārtha* commentary by Yaśomitra. The *Abhidharmakośa* and *Bhāṣya* have been translated by Louis de la Vallée Poussin (1971–80) (reprint) *L'Abhidharmakośa de Vasubandhu*, 6 vols, Brussels, Institut Belge des Hautes Etudes Chinoises.

Vasubandhu (1984) *Viṃśatikā* and *Triṃśikā*; Sanskrit texts and translation Anacker (1984). See also Kochumuttom. For Tibetan text of *Triṃśikā*: Cone bsTan 'gyur, vol. 57, Shi, ff 1–3a.

Venkata Ramanan, K. (1976) (reprint) *Nāgārjuna's Philosophy as Presented in the Mahā-Prajñāpāramitā-Śāstra*, Delhi: Motilal Banarsidass. Originally printed in 1966.

Walleser, M. (1912) *Die Mittlere Lehre des Nāgārjuna, nach der chinesischen Version übertragen*, Heidelberg: C. Winter.

Wangyal, Geshe (1978) *The Door of Liberation*, New York: Lotsawa.

Warder, A. K. (1970) *Indian Buddhism*, Delhi: Motilal Barnarsidass.

Warder, A. K. (ed.) (1985) *New Paths in Buddhist Research*, Durham, NC: Acorn Press.

Wayman, A. (1978) *Calming the Mind and Discerning the Real*, New York: Columbia University Press.

Wayman, A. (1984) *Buddhist Insight*, ed. G. Elder, Delhi: Motilal Banarsidass.

Weinstein, S. (1987) *Buddhism under the T'ang*, Cambridge: Cambridge University Press.

Welch, H. (1967) *The Practice of Chinese Buddhism, 1900–*1950, Cambridge, Mass.: Harvard University Press.

Welch, H. (1972) *Buddhism Under Mao*, Cambridge, Mass.: Harvard University Press.

Wilhelm, R. (1986) *Lao Tzu: Tao Te Ching*, trans. into English by H. G. Ostwald, London: Routledge & Kegan Paul.

Williams, P. (1977) 'Nāgārjuna: selections from the Madhyamakākarikā', *Middle Way*, 52 (1–3): 15–18, 72–6, 119–23.

Williams, P. M. (1980) 'Some aspects of language and construction in the Madhyamaka', *Journal of Indian Philosophy* 8: 1–45.

Williams, P. M. (1981) 'On the Abhidharma ontology', *Journal of Indian Philosophy* 9: 227–57.

Williams, P. M. (1982) 'Silence and truth: some aspects of the Madhyamaka philosophy in Tibet', *Tibet Journal* 7 (1–2): 67–80.

Williams, P. (1983) 'A note on some aspects of Mi bskyod rdo rje's critique of dGe lugs pa Madhyamaka', *Journal of Indian Philosophy* 11: 125–45.

Williams, P. (1985) 'rMa bya pa Byang chub brtson 'grus on Madhyamaka Method', *Journal of Indian Philosophy* 13: 205–25.

Willis, J. D. (1979) *On Knowing Reality*, New York: Columbia University Press.

Willson, M. (1986) *In Praise of Tārā: Songs to the Saviouress*, London: Wisdom.

Wilson, J. (1980) *Chandrakīrti's Sevenfold Reasoning: Meditation on the Selflessness of Persons*, Dharamsala: Library of Tibetan Works and Archives.

Yamada, I. (1968) *Karuṇāpuṇḍarīka*, 2 vols, London: School of Oriental and African Studies, University of London.

Yui-en (1961) *Tannisho*, Kyoto: Higashi Honganji.

Zürcher, E. (1972) *The Buddhist Conquest of China*, 2 vols, Leiden: E. J. Brill. First Published in 1959.

Zwalf, W. (ed.) (1985) *Buddhism: Art and Faith*, London: British Museum.

Index

A

E

F

G

H

T

U

V